Christ Church

T0494

D1587274

WITHDRAWN FROM
CHURCH LIBRARY
OXFORD

A History of
Anglican Liturgy

A History of
Anglican Liturgy

G. J. CUMING

MACMILLAN

ST MARTIN'S PRESS

© G. J. Cuming 1969

First edition 1969
Published by
MACMILLAN AND CO LTD
Little Essex Street London WC2
and also at Bombay Calcutta and Madras
Macmillan South Africa (Publishers) Pty Ltd Johannesburg
The Macmillan Company of Australia Pty Ltd Melbourne
The Macmillan Company of Canada Ltd Toronto
St Martin's Press Inc New York

Library of Congress catalog card no. 69–15582

Printed in Great Britain by
ROBERT MACLEHOSE AND CO LTD
The University Press Glasgow

DEDICATED TO THE MEMORY OF

E. C. RATCLIFF

Contents

	List of Plates	7
	Preface	9
1	The End of the Middle Ages	15
2	Reformation	32
3	First Stages in England	49
4	The First Prayer Book of Edward VI	66
5	The Second Prayer Book of Edward VI	96
6	Rome, Canterbury, and Geneva	117
7	The Grand Debate	136
8	Branching off the *Via Media*	168
9	Battle Rejoined	191
10	The Royal Letters of Business	213
11	New Paths	245

DOCUMENTS

Mass of the First Sunday in Advent	269
Office of the First Sunday in Advent	292
Luther's *Taufbüchlein*, 1526	318
Luther's *Trau-Ordnung*, 1534	321
The Lord's Supper at Strasbourg, 1524	324
Mass at Nuremberg, 1532	326
Church Order for Brandenburg-Nürnberg, 1533	327
Church Order for Pfalz-Neuburg, 1543	333
Church Order for Cologne, 1545	334

A Litany with Suffrages, 1544   358
Cranmer's projected Processional   362
The Order of the Communion, 1548   364
Liber Precum Publicarum, 1560   367
An Admonition to the Parliament, 1572   370
A Second Admonition to the Parliament, 1572   374
Proposals for Revision, 1689   375
Form of Consecrating Churches, etc., 1714   380
Thanksgiving for Harvest, 1862   386
The 'Shortened Services' Act, 1872   389
Rubrics on Reservation, 1911–28   391
Proposals for an Alternative Canon, 1920–8   396
Prayer Book Measure, 1965   399

BIBLIOGRAPHY

Abbreviations   401
Texts   401
Books   420
Articles   426

Notes   431
Index   443

List of Plates

The beginning of Vespers, from a Book of Hours,
 1407 96
 Bodleian Library

The beginning of Evensong, from the Book of
 Common Prayer, 1549 97
 Lambeth Palace Library

Henry VIII, by Holbein 112
 Thyssen Collection

Thomas Cranmer in 1546, aged 57, by G. Flicke 113
 National Portrait Gallery

Elizabeth I in her coronation robes, by Nicholas
 Hilliard 160
 His Grace the Duke of Portland

John Cosin (1594–1672): a portrait published
 shortly after his death 161
 British Museum

Prayers from the Proposals of 1689, attributed to
 Archbishop Sancroft 176
 Lambeth Palace Library

Walter Howard Frere, 1863–1938 177
 Illustrated London News

Preface

I N 1900 W. H. Frere began the preface of *A New History of the Book of Common Prayer* with the words :

> Nearly half a century has passed since the first edition of Mr Procter's *History of the Book of Common Prayer* was published: it has been a period full of an enthusiasm for liturgical studies which is almost, if not quite, without parallel. While these facts speak eloquently of the solidity and value of Mr Procter's work, they also explain amply why it was necessary that it should undergo considerable change.

Much the same can now be said of Frere's work. There can be few textbooks which have had a life of over a century, and it was felt that 'Procter and Frere' was beginning to show its age. It seemed best, not to attempt such a rejuvenation as Frere administered to Procter's *History*, but to produce an entirely new work.

My object has been to arouse interest in the history of the Prayer Book and to provide a basis for further study. Reading about liturgies is no substitute for reading the liturgics themselves. I have assumed a certain familiarity with Church history and doctrine, though constantly tempted to turn aside into each of these fields. It has been equally necessary to remember that this is a history, not a commentary. Here a further passage from Frere's preface remains apposite :

> It is inevitable in a book of this scale that much should be stated very briefly and dogmatically which would demand, if space allowed, a much fuller discussion or a much more balanced and reserved kind of statement. Such brevity and dogmatism is all the more deplorable in a study such as that of liturgical history, in which again and again evidence is painfully deficient, even upon points of first-class importance, and where deductions have to be drawn and theories constructed from data which are only too lamentably insufficient.

A2

The present work does not follow the layout of 'Procter and Frere', which is divided into three sections: General Literary History, Documents, and Sources and Rationale. Instead, each successive edition of the Prayer Book is discussed at the appropriate chronological point in the historical narrative, and the documents are placed at the end of the main body of the work, followed by a full bibliography. No attempt has been made to trace separately the evolution of each individual service, a procedure which must involve much repetition, and has been rendered superfluous since 1915 by the existence of F. E. Brightman's *The English Rite*. The choice of documents may appear arbitrary and unbalanced; it was made chiefly to fill gaps. A complete coverage of relevant texts would run to perhaps twenty volumes, and would duplicate many modern reprints. The collection printed here is made up of material that is not to be found in the most commonly used works of reference, and of excerpts designed to illustrate a single point. All translations are mine, unless otherwise stated.

A textbook does not have to claim originality, and the chief sources on which I have drawn will be obvious to liturgical scholars, apart from such acknowledgment as is made in the Notes. I am grateful to their authors for permission to reprint Professor W. D. Maxwell's translation of a passage from Bucer's *Grund und Ursach*, and Dr R. C. D. Jasper's summary of the 1871 Lectionary. Much of chapter 7 appeared in *The English Prayer Book 1549–1662*, and I am indebted to the S.P.C.K. for allowing me to incorporate it into this book. Many friends have helped me, wittingly or unwittingly, by answering my questions: first and foremost, the late Professor E. C. Ratcliff, at whose suggestion this book was written; the members of the Ecclesiastical History Society; and, not least, the members of the Liturgical Commission, whose deliberations have taught me a great deal about the process of Prayer Book revision. 'The captain of the Hampshire Grenadiers has not been useless to the historian of the Roman Empire.'

In conclusion, I borrow some words of Bishop George Horne, from the preface to his commentary on the Psalms :

Could the author flatter himself that anyone would take half the pleasure in reading the following exposition, which he hath taken in writing it, he would not fear the loss of his labour. The employment detached him from the bustle and hurry of life. . . . Vanity and vexation flew away for a season, care and disquietude came not near his dwelling. . . . Happier hours than those which have been spent on these meditations on the Songs of Sion, he never expects to see in this world.

G. J. CUMING

Humberstone, Leicester
6 October 1967

The purpose of reascending to origins is that we should be able to return, with greater spiritual knowledge, to our own situation.

T. S. ELIOT, *The Idea of a Christian Society*

I hope you will never hear from me any such phrase as our 'excellent or incomparable Liturgy' ... I do not think we are to praise the Liturgy, but to use it.

F. D. MAURICE, *The Prayer-Book*, Sermon I

1 The End of the Middle Ages

> Everyone sees and hears Mass every day; they say numbers of
> *Paternosters* in public; the women carry long rosaries in their hands;
> those who can read take the Office of Our Lady with them and say it
> in church with a companion, verse by verse, in a low voice, just as
> monks do; yet they always hear Mass on Sunday in their parish
> church . . . neither do they neglect any practice that betokens a good
> Christian.
>
> ANON., *A Relation of the Island of England*[1]

THIS impression of the religious life of the English, as
reported by a member of the Venetian Embassy about the
year 1500, may seem over-optimistic, but it is supported by
other evidence.[2] Certainly it is right in regarding the Mass as
central; whether it was High Mass on Sunday, celebrated in
Salisbury Cathedral with full ceremonial, or weekday Low
Mass in a remote country hamlet, whether at a wedding or a
funeral, the Mass was the most important of the services of
the Church. Other services were attended by the very devout,
but everyone went to Mass. It is important, therefore, to
consider not only the structure and language of the service,
but also the meaning that was read out of it and into it, and
the circumstances in which it was celebrated.

The reader can still trace in the pages of the medieval rite
as celebrated in this country the chief constituent parts of the
service described by Justin Martyr in the first century A.D.:
the reading of the Epistle and Gospel, the sermon, the
intercession, the kiss of peace, the offertory, the thanksgiving,
and the communion.[3] But the order has been altered, the
bare bones have been clothed with a good deal of flesh, the
emphasis has been placed on different aspects, and the whole
atmosphere of the service has been changed. Two complete
sections have been added at the beginning: first, the priest's

preparation, which consisted of the hymn *Veni, creator Spiritus*, the Collect for Purity, Psalm 43,[4] the Lord's Prayer, and 'Hail, Mary', said in the vestry; and at the altar step, during the singing of an introit psalm by the choir, the mutual confession and absolution of the celebrant and his assistants, and a prayer said privately by the celebrant, the first of a number inserted throughout the service.

The service proper begins with the second new section : a ninefold *Kyrie* (all that is left of a litany), *Gloria in excelsis* (a fourth-century hymn), the Salutation, and the Collect of the day (often followed by others). The service now reaches the beginning of Justin's outline with the Epistle and Gospel, separated by another choral interjection consisting of a psalm-verse, an *Alleluia*, and a Sequence, or prose-poem with a non-biblical text. Immediately after the Gospel comes another new section : the Nicene Creed and the Offertory, when the elements are placed on the altar. This action is accompanied by more psalmody and a series of private prayers for the acceptance of 'this sacrifice of praise'. After the Bidding of the Bedes (a lengthy intercession in the vernacular) the service picks up Justin again with the Sermon, but this is followed, not by the Kiss of Peace, but by the Thanksgiving.

The Thanksgiving, already in Justin the most substantial part of the service, has now acquired the name of 'Canon', and is divided into several parts. The first of these, the Preface, consists of the ancient dialogue already attested by Hippolytus in A.D. 215: 'The Lord be with you . . .', 'Lift up your hearts . . .', 'Let us give thanks unto the Lord our God . . .', followed by a giving of thanks which varies according to season (the Proper Preface) and leads into *Sanctus*, the angelic hymn of Isaiah 6: 3. The eucharistic prayer itself is really a series of six prayers, with the Lord's Prayer said after the fifth. The first of them is a prayer for the Church, the pope, the king, and all true believers, especially those present, in association with the memory of the Blessed Virgin Mary, the Apostles, the earliest popes, and all the saints; the second is similar in theme to the offertory prayers. The third asks God to bless the 'oblation', and rehearses the gospel accounts of the Last Supper; then, after making mention of the Resurrection and Ascension of Christ, the celebrant offers to God 'the holy bread of eternal life and the cup of everlasting salvation', and asks him to accept it on his heavenly altar, that all who partake may be filled with grace. The next two prayers are for the dead and the living; and the last picks up the last phrase of the Lord's Prayer, asking for deliverance from evil and for the gift of peace.

The prayers of the Canon are followed by the breaking of the bread (or Fraction) and the hymn 'O Lamb of God' (*Agnus Dei*); two private prayers for worthy reception; and the Kiss of Peace (now given by kissing a wooden implement which is passed round). The celebrant says four more private prayers before receiving the Body, another before receiving the Blood, and a sixth after reception. After the Communion the vessels are cleansed, to the accompaniment of further private prayers; a post-communion prayer is said; and the people are dismissed. On his way out the priest recites John 1: 1–14, and further vestry prayers are said as he disrobes.

Such is the Mass as it meets us in the pages of the service-books. To those who had the knowledge of Latin and the theological insight to enter fully into its meaning, it offered a rich and deep commentary on the nature and purpose of the action that was being performed. The Scripture lessons were chosen with great care and considerable acumen, giving the biblical background for the successive celebrations of the Church Year, and the feasts of the saints, thus rooting the Mass firmly in history; while in the months from Pentecost to Advent, and on Wednesdays and Fridays throughout the year, they provided a selected reading, sometimes continuous, which it is easier to criticize than to improve upon. The chants, which also varied according to season, threw further light on the lections, either by picking out crucial sentences from them, or by drawing on other passages of Scripture for confirmation and elucidation, notably from the Psalms and the Old Testament prophets. The whole system is a model of devotional use of the Bible.

But the great accession of new material has altered the theological emphasis of the service. In the priest's prayers the predominant thought is that the communicant will be cleansed from all his sins by receiving the sacrament, a medieval departure from the primitive conception of the eucharist as a thanksgiving for benefits already received. The Canon, however, still retained the far-ranging intercession, and the commemoration of the historical events by reciting the Words of Institution, which were, at least since the time of St Thomas Aquinas, regarded as effecting consecration. It still enshrined the concept of the service as an offering of Christ's sacrifice: we offer God's gifts of bread and wine, which are made by God to 'be unto us the body and blood' of Christ; we offer a 'pure, holy, undefiled victim', an offering comparable to the sacrifices of Abraham and Melchizedek, carried up by an angel to the high altar in the presence of God. Finally, the Canon stresses the hope of fellowship with the saints.

But those who were able to benefit from the actual words of the rite were in a minority. The use of Latin and the practice of saying the service in a low murmur meant that the effect of the words was restricted to the ministers who were conducting the service; the laity could occupy themselves only with their own devotions. Expositions of the Mass in English were in circulation among the more prosperous of the laity. One such, the *Lay-Folk's Mass-Book*, includes directions for standing and kneeling, and prayers to pray simultaneously with the priest. English translations of *Gloria in excelsis* and the Apostles' Creed are to be said while the choir is singing the Latin text (which, of course, would be the *Nicene* Creed). Here and there, gaps are to be filled by saying the Lord's Prayer, 'Hail, Mary', and the Creed. When the priest says the Lord's Prayer,

> Answer at '*temptacionem*',
> '*sed libera nos a malo, amen*'.
> It were no need thee this to ken,
> for who con not this are lewèd men.[5]

The worshipper is then to say the whole of the Lord's Prayer privately, first in Latin, then in English. Not a word is said about communicating. Until the invention of printing, even this degree of participation in the actual words of the service was confined to owners of manuscript copies.

These devotional writers usually lay their greatest stress on the memorial aspect of the Mass. Dom Gregory Dix[6] has drawn attention to the *Meditations in the time of Mass* of B. Langforde, a fifteenth-century author of whom nothing is known. For him the Mass is a 'daily meditation, to stir you to the diligent and compendious remembrance of the Passion of Christ' ; and he proceeds to give detailed instructions on the subject-matter of the meditations which are to occupy the worshipper's mind during the different parts of the Mass, each being related to an episode in the Passion. Brother Gararde, a Minorite friar from the Low Countries, whose treatise appeared in English in 1532 as *The Interpretation and Signification of the Mass*, lists twelve virtues that arise from remembering the Passion of our Lord during Mass. He also quotes 'the doctors' as ruling that 'it is sufficient if the man be present at the Mass, whether he hear and understand the words or no'.

A link between the worshipper and the words of the service could, of course, be made in the sermon. A good example of popular eucharistic teaching is to be found in a sermon for Corpus Christi by John Mirk,[7] prior of Lilleshall in the early fifteenth century. His *Festial* was a very popular book, widely circulated in manuscript, first printed in 1483, and reprinted eighteen times in the next fifty years. Mirk speaks of 'Christ's Body, the which is each day offered up in Holy Church in the altar to the Father of Heaven in remission of sin to all that live here in perfect charity'. Christ 'ordained a perpetual memory of his passion for to abide with his people' by giving to his disciples and 'to all other priests, power and dignity for to make his body of bread and wine in the altar'; and so the sacrament is made 'by virtue of the holy words that the priest says there, and by working of the Holy Ghost'. Christ left 'this sacrament for four skills to all God's People: for man's great helping, for Christ's Passion minding, for great love showing, and for great meed (merit) getting'. In short, the Mass is an offering of Christ's Body as a memorial of his Passion, with the object of obtaining forgiveness of sins.

The setting of the service provided a further obstacle to congregational participation. The typical medieval English church had a long chancel, to accommodate the numerous clerics. At its west end it was divided from the nave by the rood-screen, whose loft housed the choir and organ. The laity in the nave could see the high altar only with difficulty; of all the ceremonial of the Mass, only the elevation of the host would be plainly visible. This was therefore the great moment of the service for them: they were actually seeing their Maker present among them.[8] The most conspicuous object in the church, as far as they were concerned, was the great rood (crucifix), with the Last Judgment above it filling up the chancel arch; the two together provided a visual reminder of the purpose of the rite which was being performed in the distance at the high altar.[9] Preaching and practice combined to lay great emphasis on the Day of Judgment, and the Cross and Passion of our Lord as the means of deliverance from it. The purpose of hearing Mass was the propitiation of a stern Deity. Repetition of the sacrifice of Calvary effected forgiveness of the worshipper's sins. This doctrine led to a belief in the distinct propitiatory value of each single Mass: to mitigate the pains of purgatory, ten masses were ten times as effective as one. Hence the multiplication of masses for the dead and of votive masses, said to secure a particular end. These were just as effective when said by a priest on his own; there was no need for the presence of a congregation.

Communion was administered only after the discipline of Penance, which plays a very prominent part in medieval manuals of instruction for the clergy. It was so thorough that it was normally undergone only once a year, in preparation for communion at Easter, which accordingly became the solitary occasion in the year on which laymen would receive the sacrament. Thus the primitive aspect of the service as the expression of fellowship with the rest of the faithful was almost entirely lost.

If the layout of the building militated against the laity's joining in the service, the other externals helped to create an impression of other-worldly beauty. The norm of performance was set by High Mass, which required the co-operation of, at least, a priest, a deacon, a sub-deacon, several acolytes, and a choir.[10] Low Mass needed only a priest and a server, and the ceremonial was reduced accordingly. The Mass had its own vestments, each appropriate to one of the ministers. The celebrant wore alb and chasuble, with amice, stole, and maniple; the deacon wore a dalmatic, the sub-deacon a tunicle, and the choir surplices. In cathedrals and town churches the vestments and furnishings were often of great richness and splendour. The music of the Mass would be, for the most part, Gregorian chant, a single melodic line of great beauty and subtlety; but in cathedrals and colleges, and from about 1450 in the more prosperous parish churches, polyphonic settings of the text were sung, especially at festivals. These helped to provide the element of thanksgiving, which at Low Mass had almost disappeared, but they also rendered the service even less congregational than before.

As far as the clergy were concerned, the Mass was the

foundation on which rested an elaborate superstructure of services known as the Office, or Hours. This scheme of communal prayer at regular intervals originated in the monasteries, and had spread to the secular clergy. There were eight services in all : Mattins, also known as Nocturns, at midnight, followed without a break by Lauds ; Prime, before the daily meeting of the Chapter ; Terce (at 9 a.m.) ; Sext (midday) ; None (3 p.m.) ; Vespers, in the evening ; and Compline, at bedtime. In structure they fall into four classes :

1. Mattins
2. Lauds and Vespers
3. Terce, Sext, and None (the 'Little Hours')
4. Prime and Compline

Mattins, in size a considerable service, is unique in including a course of bible-reading, which is indeed its chief feature, based on a unit of psalms and lessons known as a Nocturn. On high days the service includes three Nocturns, ordinarily only one. Each Nocturn consists of three psalms or groups of psalms, followed by a versicle and response and three lessons, each answered by a choral Responsory. The Psalms are worked through 'in course' as far as Psalm 110 every week, and the Lessons are appointed on a serial basis, those in the Second and Third Nocturns often being taken from a homily by one of the Fathers. As an introduction to this central block, after the priest's private prayers (the Lord's Prayer and 'Hail, Mary') and the dialogue beginning 'O Lord, open thou my lips', the choir sings *Venite*, with a seasonal refrain (Invitatory) interpolated at intervals, and a seasonal hymn. After the central block, *Te Deum* is sung on festivals, and the conclusion is a variable versicle and response.

Lauds and Vespers differ at the start, in that Lauds, being said immediately after Mattins, does not have the private prayers that begin all the other Hours. In these two services the main business is the recital of a group of five psalms, invariable at Lauds (and including *Benedicite*), working through from Psalm 111 to Psalm 150 at Vespers, thus complementing the Mattins recitation. The psalms are preceded by the usual dialogue, beginning at 'O God make speed to my help', and followed by a *capitulum* (a text from Scripture, usually from the Epistle of the day), a variable hymn, and a canticle: *Benedictus* at Lauds, *Magnificat* at Vespers, each with a variable Antiphon (a choral text sung before and after a psalm or canticle). On weekdays the canticle is followed by a section of suffrages, consisting of threefold *Kyrie*, Lord's Prayer, and *preces* (versicles and responses). The services end with the Collect of the day, and a Memorial, i.e. an antiphon and collect of special relevance to the season, or in honour of the Blessed Virgin Mary.

The Little Hours are principally devoted to the daily recitation of Psalm 119, verse 33 to the end, in portions of forty-eight verses at each service, preceded by the usual prefatory matter and an invariable hymn, and followed by *capitulum*, responsory, versicle, and collect, all variable. Prime and Compline both have invariable psalms (those at Prime including the first thirty-two verses of Psalm 119), preceded by the standard introduction, and invariable canticles (*Quicunque vult* at Prime, *Nunc dimittis* at Compline); but there is a slight divergence of form. At Prime the order is hymn, psalms, canticle, *capitulum* and responsory; at Compline psalms, *capitulum* and responsory, hymn, canticle. Both end with suffrages and a collect; the suffrages include a confession and absolution, and in the case of Prime run to considerable length, no less than twenty-five pairs of versicle and response.

In the later Middle Ages further Offices, of the Blessed Virgin Mary and of the Dead, had been added to the obligation, together with various groups of psalms to be said at particular times. Under Franciscan influence the celebration of festivals was prolonged for eight days (the Octave), which displaced the proper readings of the days concerned, so that the system of serial reading was virtually lost to sight. In practice the secular clergy tended to group the Office into two main services, Mattins and Evensong. Mattins was said immediately before Mass, and so was attended by laymen to some extent, at any rate on Sundays ; Evensong rather less so.

It was these services, especially the later accretions, which provided the laity with their chief help to devotion, the Primer, or Book of Hours, the book to which the Venetian observer refers. Primers abounded in the later Middle Ages, first in manuscript, then in print, in which form they ran into many editions. There was no standardized content: some were in Latin, some in English, some in both languages. The Primer printed by William Maskell in his *Monumenta Ritualia Ecclesiae Anglicanae* may be taken as a fair specimen of the type. The manuscript was written about 1410, entirely in English ; it contains The Hours of Our Lady (a complete set of invariable Hours), the seven Penitential Psalms (6, 32, 38, 51, 102, 130, 143), the fifteen Gradual Psalms (120–34), the Litany, the *Placebo* and *Dirige* (Vespers and Mattins, respectively, from the Office of the Dead), the Commendations (Psalms 119 and 139), the Lord's Prayer, 'Hail, Mary', the Apostles' Creed, the Ten Commandments, and the Seven Deadly Sins. The first printed Primer, which appeared about 1494, contains all these devotions in Latin, and adds others, including the Psalms of the Passion (22–31), a selection of psalm-verses known as 'St Jerome's Psalter', and a set of prayers on the Passion entitled 'The XV Oes of St Bridget' in both Latin and English. In the last century before the Reformation this was the sort of book that laymen took with them to Mass, read to themselves during the service, and read by themselves on weekdays. The great attraction of the Primer was the invariability of the services, which thus became extremely familiar to the laity, as the canonical Hours were to the clergy.

The other occasions for which services would normally be held in an ordinary parish church were baptisms, weddings, and funerals. The baptismal service was still set out in the service-books in three parts : the making of a catechumen, the blessing of the font, and baptism. Though virtually confined to children, it still bore these traces of its direct descent from the primitive rite for the baptism of adults. The first part is held at the door of the church, and consists chiefly of exorcism. The priest first signs the child three times with the sign of the cross ; places salt in its mouth, with appropriate prayers ; and then adjures the devil to depart from it, with further signings. The gospel of Jesus' welcome to the children (Matthew 19 : 13–15) is read, and the *Ephphatha* story is re-enacted. After a charge in English to the godparents, they join with the priest in repeating the Lord's Prayer, 'Hail, Mary', and the Apostles' Creed. After a final signing, the child is taken into the church. The Blessing of the Font consists of a litany, a collect, and a lengthy Preface, exactly similar in form to that in the Mass, after which the priest pours holy oil into the water. The Baptism begins with the godparents' renunciation of Satan and his works and 'pomps', after which the priest anoints the child with the 'oil of salvation'. The godparents then make their profession of faith, and the child is immediately baptized by threefold immersion. It is then anointed with oil (chrism), clothed in a white robe (chrisom), and given a lighted candle. The parents are then charged by the priest (in his own words) to preserve the child from fire, water, and all other dangers ; the godparents are to teach it the Lord's Prayer, 'Hail, Mary', and the Apostles' Creed, to return the chrisom, and to bring the child to confirmation as soon as the bishop comes within seven miles of the church. The service ends with two Gospel lessons, Mark 9 : 17–29 (the epileptic boy) and John 1 : 1–14. Compared with this lengthy service and its elaborate ceremonial, Confirmation was both rare and brief, consisting merely of an anointing between two prayers.

Of all the medieval services, Matrimony would seem most familiar to a twentieth-century worshipper. The first half of the service was wholly in English, and has been little changed to the present day. The priest requires, first the congregation, then the couple, to reveal any impediment known to them ; the couple declare their desire to marry, and plight their troth ; and the bridegroom produces gold, silver, and a ring, which latter is blessed by the priest, and placed by the bridegroom on the bride's thumb and next three fingers in turn. The rest of the service is in Latin, and continues with a blessing, Psalm 68 : 28–30, *Kyrie*, Lord's Prayer, and another blessing. Priest and couple then proceed to the altar during the singing of Psalm 128, and after another *Kyrie* and Lord's Prayer, a series of six collects and blessings leads into the nuptial Mass, which has its own proper. When the couple finally reach the marriage bed, the priest blesses it and them.

Visitation of the Sick was regarded as of the greatest importance, and the host was reserved for the purpose of administering communion to those visited. On the way to the house the priest says the seven Penitential Psalms ; on arrival he places a crucifix before the sick man, and sprinkles him with holy water. After a series of nine prayers, the priest enunciates the fourteen articles of the faith, in which the sick man then affirms his belief. The priest exhorts him to the love of God and of his neighbour, and to Christian hope, and hears his confession. By way of penance, he recommends him to almsgiving, and pronounces absolution. If Extreme Unction is to be administered, a psalm and collect are said, and then eight more psalms between which seven different parts of the body are anointed. A further prayer is followed by communion, another collect and psalm, and finally a long prayer and a series of short blessings. When the sick man is at death's door, the Nicene Creed, the seven Penitential Psalms, and a litany are said.

Funerals, compared with modern times, were much more elaborate liturgically, and with frequent and early mortality must have played a much more prominent part in everyday

life. They are divided into four parts : Commendation of
Souls, Office of the Dead, Mass for the Dead, and Burial of
the Dead.[11] They begin in the house of the departed with a
responsory, Psalms 114 and 116–19 (hence the name
'Commendations'), and a number of collects. While the body
is being laid out, Vespers of the Dead are said, followed by
six more psalms and further prayers. A procession is made to
the church, during which two more psalms are sung. On
entering church, the Office (Mattins and Lauds) of the Dead
and Mass for the Dead (*Requiem*) are sung. Then the body is
taken in procession to the grave, and the grave is opened, to
the singing of three psalms. Three more accompany the
burial, and a further three introduce a section of thanksgiving
and intercession, which also includes *Benedictus* and Psalm 51.
Finally, the procession returns to church with at least one of
the Penitential Psalms. In all, during these rites, twenty-six
psalms and twenty-nine collects were said, and the Lord's
Prayer was repeated seven times, apart from the service in
church which included another twenty-one psalms. When
the numerous antiphons and responsories are taken into
account, the exequies must have been both impressive and
long-drawn-out.

Besides the regular worship of Sundays and holy days, and
the services marking the great moments of human life, there
were also extra services at times of special liturgical importance, such as the lighting of candles at the Purification,
the blessing of the ashes on Ash Wednesday, the procession
of palms on Palm Sunday, veneration of the cross on Good
Friday, beating the bounds of the parish at Rogationtide,
and the Greater Excommunication. The Candlemas and Ash
Wednesday ceremonies followed Sext and led into High
Mass. The Blessing of Light on Candlemas consisted chiefly
of a Preface like that in the Mass, and *Nunc dimittis*, with
appropriate prayers ; its effect was mainly visual, with candles
being lit all over the church. The Blessing of the Ashes was
introduced by the seven Penitential Psalms and seven collects

about forgiveness of sins; during the singing of antiphons and psalm-verses the sign of the cross was made in ashes on the foreheads of the congregation. Palm Sunday had two lessons before the exorcism, blessing, and sprinkling of the palms, which were then carried round the church in procession, led by a priest carrying the reserved sacrament, to the accompaniment of antiphons, responsories, and hymns. A first station was made in the north-eastern corner of the building; the second on the south side, where the hymn *Gloria, laus, et honor* was sung (at Salisbury by seven boys 'in a more lofty place'). The procession then went out of church and returned by the west door, where the third station was made; the fourth and last was made at the rood. On return to the chancel, Mass began.

On Good Friday, Mass was said after None (i.e. about 3 p.m.) and included the singing of the Passion of our Lord according to St John. In the middle of the service, after fifteen 'solemn prayers' of intercession for a wide range of people, a cross was set up behind the high altar, and the choir sang the 'Reproaches' and Psalm 67. The cross was then placed on a step in front of the altar, and the clergy and congregation came to kneel before it. When the ceremony was ended the rest of Mass was said, followed by Vespers. At Rogationtide a procession perambulated the boundaries of the parish, singing the Litany. The Greater Excommunication was held either twice or four times a year. A very lengthy list of sins which involved excommunication was read out, and penitents were absolved from previous excommunication. These various ceremonies perhaps stood out for the ordinary worshipper more vividly than the weekly Sunday Mass. Beautiful and edifying on paper, in practice they were often debased.[12]

The performance of all these services involved the use of a number of separate books, the most important of which were the Missal, the Breviary, the Manual, the Pontifical, and the Processional. The main contents of the Missal were the

Ordinary and Canon of the Mass, that is, the invariable framework; the *Temporale*, or portions proper to Sundays, Wednesdays, and Fridays, and certain special days; and the *Sanctorale*, or portions proper to saints' days. Beyond this there was no uniformity of content: manuscript copies would contain additions and omissions which reflected the particular needs of the monastery for which they were written, or the special devotion of a private owner. Even the printed editions are not identical in content, though a tendency towards standardization becomes apparent. Other important elements in the Missal were the Kalendar, votive masses in great diversity, the Requiem Mass, the Easter Vigil, and a large number of prayers. Sometimes services from the Manual might be included. Different parts of the Mass were also available in separate books for particular persons. All the liturgical Epistles were collected in an Epistle-book for the convenience of the reader of the Epistles, and the Gospels in a Gospel-book. A sub-species of these contains only the lessons for the more important occasions. The Gradual (or Grail) contained the scriptural parts of the Mass which were to be sung, while the non-scriptural parts were collected in the Troper and the Sequencer, though these distinctions tended to disappear, so that the later Graduals contain tropes, and the Tropers sequences.

The Breviary contained the Divine Office. Though of considerable length and bulk, it was often issued in pocket editions (quarto or smaller), which went by the name of *Portiforium* or Portuis, to distinguish them from the large 'Couchers', which could not easily be moved from the desk. The text collected the contents of a number of smaller compilations, such as the Homiliary and the Hymnal, and set out the Daily Office in an arrangement like that of the Missal. The volume usually consisted of the Kalendar, the *Temporale*, the Psalter (including the Ordinary of the Hours), the Offices of the Dead and of the Blessed Virgin, the Ordinary and Canon of the Mass, and the *Sanctorale*. It also was available in its component parts, the Antiphoner (for the choir), the Psalter (with the antiphons), the Hymnal, the Collectar, the *Legenda* (the Lessons, biblical and otherwise), and the Martyrology (the calendar), besides others of less importance.

The Manual contained the priest's services, and is hence sometimes known as the Sacerdotal. Other names are Ritual and *Agenda* (the continental term). It comprises Baptism, Matrimony, Churching, Visitation of the Sick, and the Office of the Dead. Other items such as Confirmation or the Canon of the Mass may be added for practical convenience. The Pontifical (or Benedictional) similarly contained the services at which a bishop was the celebrant, such as Ordination, Confirmation, the Installation of an Abbot, the Consecration of a Church, the Degradation of a Heretic, and the bishop's special blessings, which often also existed on their own. The Processional contains the music for processions on Sundays, Rogation Days, and the like. The books described above contained the text of the rites, but originally lacked any rubrics, which were to be found in the Consuetudinary and the Ordinal (or *Directorium*, or Pie, so-called because it was printed in black and white, not in red). The former gave directions for the actions and movements to be performed; the Ordinal gave rules for regulating clashes between feasts. In the later Middle Ages both these books were incorporated into the Missal and the Breviary.

The contents of all these books varied according to local usage, except for Pontificals, which belonged to an individual bishop rather than to a diocese. By the sixteenth century at least five 'uses' were still extant in England : Sarum (Salisbury), York, Hereford, Bangor, and Lincoln. Of these, the last two have virtually disappeared, while the relative importance of the first three may be assessed from the numbers of printed editions of each that appeared between 1475 and 1549 :[13]

	Sarum	York	Hereford
Missal	51	5	1
Breviary	42	5	1
Manual	13	2	—
Processional	11	1	—
Ordinal	4	1	—
Primer	184	5	—

The differences between the Sarum and York books are of interest only to specialists, being largely confined to the antiphons and responsories of the Breviary, and the sequences in the Missal, of which York contains 172 against 94 in Sarum. The overwhelming predominance of Sarum shows that, well before the Reformation, 'all the whole realm' was very close to having 'but one use'.

2 Reformation

> Next comes all that abomination known as the Offertory, to which all the foregoing part of the Mass is compelled to be subservient. From this point onwards practically everything speaks and smells of oblation. In the midst of it all are placed the words of life and salvation, just like the ark of the Lord of old in the idols' temple, next to Dagon. . . .
>
> So then, let us repudiate all those things that speak of oblation, together with the whole of the Canon, and keep what is pure and holy; and thus let us order our Mass.
>
> LUTHER, *Formula Missae et Communionis*, 1523

DISCONTENT with the medieval services was widespread, if not universal. The renewal of scholarship in the Renaissance and the rediscovery of the Bible produced the attitude of mind which went by the name of 'the New Learning', a title slightly misleading to modern ears, for which 'the New Teaching' would more accurately convey the sense. A contemporary summed up the differences between the Old and the New Learnings at the crucial point of eucharistic doctrine as follows. According to the Old, the Mass is a sacrifice for the living and the dead, and 'oblation is made in the person of the whole Church'. For the New, the Supper is a memorial only of Christ's death, 'and not a sacrifice, but a remembrance of the sacrifice that was once offered upon the cross'; and 'all oblations except that of our Lord are vain and void'.[1] Luther's first application of this teaching to the Mass was made in his sermons,[2] in which he directed his fire against the denial of the chalice to the laity, the doctrine of transubstantiation, and, above all, the whole concept of offering and sacrifice, whether expressed in actions or words, which flatly contradicted the doctrine of justification by faith alone. Most of the offensive passages occurred in the Canon, and this was the main point of attack. All private masses were sinful, and especially votive and requiem masses. Luther also desired the curtailment or abolition of the Daily Office, and the removal of a multitude of 'dumb' ceremonies. Wittenberg led the way, but there was a simultaneous stirring in Strasbourg and Zurich, where similar principles produced similar results. Martin Bucer at Strasbourg was in constant touch with both Luther and Zwingli, and each of the three leaders was well informed about the others' progress in liturgical reform.

In changing the actual words of the service, Luther was anticipated by such lesser men as Andreas Carlstadt, Kaspar Kantz, Thomas Müntzer, and Johann Oecolampadius ;[3] but he was not left far behind. His first forms of service, for the two Gospel sacraments, appeared in 1523.[4] In the *Formula Missae et Communionis* he retains the Latin language, the mass-vestments, and the elevation of the host, and makes little alteration in the traditional form until the sermon, which, in Germany as in England, followed the Creed. The only omissions are the *Confiteor* and the Sequence. The private prayers at the Offertory were naturally full of references to offering, and Luther sweeps them away entirely. The Canon is likewise reduced to the Words of Institution, which are ingeniously inserted after *Sursum corda* in the place of the Proper Preface, and followed by *Sanctus* and *Benedictus*, the Lord's Prayer, and *Pax Domini*. All inter-cession disappears, and consecration is effected by the Words of Institution. The priest's prayers at the Communion are reduced to one, that said during the ablutions ; communion is given in both kinds, while the choir sing *Agnus Dei* and the variable communion chant. Notice is to be given beforehand by intending communicants, so that they may be examined at least once a year, and they are to sit by themselves, so that others may observe whether their lives conform to their profession. Private confession is recommended, but not made compulsory. Evil livers are to be excluded. Hymns in the vernacular are much to be desired. Mattins, the Hours, Vespers, and Compline are to be continued, with their

B

lessons read in German, and the number of psalms and responsories reduced. *Das Taufbüchlein verdeutscht* only translates the medieval baptismal rite in the form in which it was familiar to Luther.

These conservative alterations were only a first step, and in 1526 Luther issued a drastic revision of each service. The *Deutsche Messe* still follows the traditional order in broad outline; mass-vestments, altars, and candles are still permitted; and the host is still elevated. But the whole service is now to be sung in German; the westward position is suggested (though it was never adopted); Introit, Gradual, Creed, *Sanctus*, and *Agnus Dei* are replaced by Luther's own metrical translations; and *Gloria in excelsis* is omitted altogether. After the sermon comes a paraphrase of the Lord's Prayer and an exhortation to the communicants. The latter, which may have been suggested to Luther by Bucer's example, is designed to lead up to the Words of Administration, which are still read at the altar. Luther would prefer that the bread should be consecrated and administered before the wine is consecrated, but there is no evidence that he ever actually did so. During communion *Sanctus* is sung (in German), and the service ends with a prayer of thanksgiving, which helps to restore an element noticeably lacking in the medieval Low Mass, and with the Aaronic blessing. Men and women are to sit apart. The Daily Office is reduced to two services on Sundays, with a modified version for schools on weekdays. The Sunday morning service consists of psalms, sermon, *Te Deum* or *Benedictus*, Lord's Prayer, collect, and 'Let us bless the Lord'; in the evening Vespers is said, with a sermon. The form for weekdays comprises psalms, a chapter from the Bible, in both Latin and German, an exposition in the morning or *Magnificat* in the evening, a German hymn, and the same ending as on Sundays.

The Baptism service is less drastically treated than the Mass or the Office, but even so the lengthy exorcism is reduced to a single adjuration, and six of the ceremonies are discarded, leaving only signing with the cross and baptism. During the next few years various other forms followed. The first was a Litany, which appeared in 1529 in both Latin and German: Luther omits all invocation of the saints, and considerably amplifies the petitions. Matrimony (1534) was again a conservative adaptation of the traditional form, which in Germany already tended to be much briefer than in the Sarum rite; Luther's chief contribution was a homily with scriptural quotations. Ordination completed the series in 1537: it is a simple rite, including examination of the candidates, the singing of *Veni, sancte Spiritus*, and the laying-on of hands with prayer for the gift of the Holy Spirit; the whole to take place at Mass after the sermon. Two Catechisms, based on the Ten Commandments, the Creed, the Lord's Prayer, and the Sacraments, had appeared in 1529; to Luther may be ascribed the choice of these four topics as fundamental, and also the actual name 'Catechism'. No provision was made for Burial.

Luther's liturgical ideas were hastily conceived and sometimes contradictory. Even in 1526 he was still reluctant to provide a German Mass, and hoped that Latin would continue to be used. His fear of retaining any traces of the medieval doctrine of sacrifice led him into an excessively violent treatment of the Canon; but his sense of the numinous element in the Mass enabled him to preserve some of the medieval devotional feeling. The great importance which he attached to the concept of fellowship ensured the continuance of the weekly celebration of the Lord's Supper as the central feature of Lutheran worship.

At Zurich, Huldreich Zwingli also produced a conservative revision of the Latin Mass in 1523, as part of the tract *De Canone Missae Epicheiresis*.[5] It has much in common with Luther's *Formula Missae* of the same year. Zwingli also keeps the Latin language (except for the lessons, which are to be read in German) and the mass-vestments. He also keeps the outline of the first part of the service, while cutting out the

Sequence and the Offertory. The sermon comes after the Gospel, and the Nicene Creed is followed by the Preface (without *Sursum corda*) and *Sanctus*. Zwingli does not 'remove the Canon, but puts another in its place', consisting of four prayers in elegant Renaissance Latin. The first tells the story of our redemption and ends with the Lord's Prayer; the second prays God to feed the hungry with the bread of heaven (interpreted by Zwingli as 'the Word'); the third speaks of Christ's sacrifice, and prays that those who partake may be one in him; and the fourth is a prayer for worthy reception. Communion follows the Words of Institution with only two texts of Scripture in between: the delay at this point in the medieval Mass 'was more displeasing than anything else'. The second of the texts is 'Come unto me, all that travail', which is also the motto on the title-page. The service ends with a very brief thanksgiving and *Nunc dimittis*.

As with Luther, this was only a provisional rite, and was replaced in 1525 by a radically reformed vernacular service, *Action oder Brauch des Nachtmahls*. This is to be used only four times in the year, at Christmas, Easter, Pentecost, and in the autumn. After a sermon and a collect, the lessons, which are always 1 Corinthians 11: 20–29 and John 6: 47–63, are followed by *Gloria in excelsis* and the Apostles' Creed respectively, said antiphonally by men and women. A short exhortation, the Lord's Prayer, and a prayer for worthy reception lead to the Words of Institution. Communion (received sitting) follows at once, and the service ends with Psalm 113, a thanksgiving, and a blessing. *Sanctus* has disappeared, and so has the entire principle of elements varying from Sunday to Sunday. As with Luther again, there is neither intercession nor prayer of consecration. Zwingli's Baptism Service consisted of a single prayer and the Gospel from Mark 10; and his Marriage Service was not much longer.

The course of events in Strasbourg was rather different. Here revision was more or less continuous for some years, with versions differing only slightly from each other in simultaneous use.[6] The Mass was first said in German in a revision by Theobald Schwarz in 1524. This begins with a confession of sins which included the phrase 'I have done much that I ought to have left, and left much that I ought to have done', and is followed as Absolution by 'This is a true saying ...' (1 Timothy 1 : 15), which became a constant feature of Strasbourg liturgies. Instead of the Offertory prayers, a short bidding is said, based on Romans 12, in which God is asked to send the Holy Spirit to make our bodies 'a living, holy, acceptable sacrifice'. The rest departs but little from the traditional order, though sacrificial language is excised, and communion is in both kinds. *Sursum corda* is translated '*Erhebt eure Herzen*' ('Lift up your hearts') ; and proper prefaces are reduced to five in number. Five editions appeared during 1524, the last of which provides an intercessory Canon (still called by that name, and including the words 'write thy law in our hearts'), and ends with the same post-communion collect (*Quod ore sumpsimus*) as Luther, the Aaronic blessing, and *Nunc dimittis*, one of several points of contact with Zwingli. Schwarz's rite keeps most of the traditional ceremonial, but is to be said audibly throughout. 'Evangelical in spirit, but Catholic in form', it is the direct progenitor of all the Strasbourg services, and through them a distant ancestor of the Book of Common Prayer.

During the same year, Martin Bucer printed a programme of reform, *Grund und Ursach ... der Neuerungen an dem Nachtmahl des Herren* ('Grounds and Motives for the Innovations in the Lord's Supper'), which foreshadowed further changes, some of which are already found in the editions of 1525. The service is now entitled 'The Lord's Supper', and more alternatives are permitted. 'If any man sin ...' (1 John 2 : 1, 2) appears as an absolution ; the Epistle and Gospel are chosen by the minister, and are to consist of an entire chapter apiece. The Apostles' Creed, already admitted as an alternative to the Nicene, becomes, first, the preferred alternative, and then the only choice. By the end of the year the 'altar' has become the 'table', and the minister faces west. All ceremonial has been dropped, and the minister may stand for the confession. The Words of Institution have been taken out of the 'Canon', and placed closer to the communion. More congregational singing has been introduced.

The year 1526, which was also marked by the definitive revisions of Luther and Zwingli, saw a pause in the development of the Strasbourg rite which lasted for some ten years. Bucer was by now the leading light in the religious life of the city, and a fresh edition of 1537 reveals a further step away from the traditional form in the direction of Zwingli. There is now a choice of three confessions, including one which ultimately found its way into the Prayer Book, and another based on the Ten Commandments. 'This is a true saying' is now described as a *'Trostspruch'*, or 'comfortable word', and is followed by four more texts, among them 'So God loved the world', as well as 'If any man sin'. The Introit is replaced by a metrical psalm (the 1539 service-book is actually entitled *Psalter*), while *Kyrie* and *Gloria in excelsis* are optional. The Collect has become an extemporary prayer, and the Epistle is replaced by another psalm. The Gospel (chosen on the principle of continuous reading) is followed by the sermon, which should end with an explanation of the Lord's Supper, for which four points are provided; then comes the Creed in a metrical version. After the short bidding follows an adaptation of Schwartz's 'Canon', with two alternative intercessory prayers, each ending with the Lord's Prayer. After further exhortation, the Words of Institution are said, communion is administered to the singing of a psalm, and the service ends with more extemporary prayer, a choice of three thanksgivings, and the Aaronic blessing. *Sursum corda* and *Sanctus* have now disappeared; all saints' days have been abolished; and communion was in practice celebrated only once a month in parish churches. When there was no communion, the relevant parts of the service were omitted. In their structure the Strasbourg masses are finally closer to Zwingli than to Luther, as also in their abandonment of the Church Year; unlike Luther or Zwingli, they still find a place for intercession.

Besides the Lord's Supper, there were three other services on Sundays, two early in the morning, one in the afternoon. They consisted of confession, reading, sermon, and prayer. The 1525 Baptism Service includes the traditional recitation of the Lord's Prayer and Creed, and the Gospel about the children (this time from Matthew 19); but the godparents are asked only one question, about the upbringing of the child, and even this has been dropped in the 1539 *Psalter*. All the ceremonies are discarded from the start. Unlike Luther and Zwingli, Bucer keeps Confirmation; and the Marriage Service is much more traditional in character, retaining Psalm 128 and some prayers from the Manual, as well as the vernacular section.

These first-generation liturgies gave rise to a host of descendants. The process of reformation in Lutheran Germany resulted in the issue of a *Kirchenordnung*, or Church Order, for each individual princedom, and for individual cities and towns within the princedom, of which over a hundred are extant. They bear a strong family resemblance to each other, but are by no means identical in content. Each normally contains doctrinal statements, rules of discipline, and forms of service. Generally speaking, in the more northerly parts a larger proportion of the medieval service is kept, while in the south the influence of Zwingli is more strongly marked. Bucer also has his following, particularly in the Rhineland.

One of the liveliest centres of experiment was Nuremberg, where several versions of the Mass appeared in 1524 and 1525, notably one by Andreas Döber, who obviously knew the early Strasbourg services. These were superseded by the issue in 1533 of the Order for the Principality of Brandenburg and the Free City of Nuremberg, compiled by Johann Brenz and Andreas Osiander, two prominent minor figures in the history of the Reformation.[7] This Order had a very widespread influence in Germany, and is the most interesting of all from the point of view of the Book of Common Prayer. In 1532 the English ambassador to the Emperor Charles V, Sir Thomas Elyot, visited Nuremberg in company with his appointed successor, a young Cambridge don named Thomas Cranmer, who during his stay in Nuremberg married Osiander's niece Margaret. Elyot has left a description of the Mass as it was then being said, clearly recognizable as an intermediate stage in the production of the form as we have it.[8]

The first half of the printed service ('Order for the celebration of Mass') follows the medieval order, the said parts in German, the sung parts in Latin or German according to local conditions. The traditional collects are replaced by a series of twenty-five printed in the main body of the service. Fifteen of these are of general application, the remainder consist of proper collects for Christmas, Passiontide, Easter, Ascension Day, Pentecost, and Trinity Sunday, the collects for Trinity IV and IX, and the two memorials for peace from Lauds and Vespers of the Blessed Virgin (familiar to Anglicans as the second collects of Mattins and Evensong). Several were taken from Luther's Litany, others from the Catechism of Andreas Althamer (1528). One of these relating to spiritual things must always be said, and one for temporal goods may be added. As Cranmer was informed during his visit, the traditional Epistle and Gospel has been discarded, and a chapter is read in order every day, as at Strasbourg. The Sequence is dropped, as always, but the other chants are retained. The second part is headed 'Order for the Lord's Supper', and is clearly influenced by Luther's *Deutsche Messe*. After the sermon follows an exhortation (described by the critical Elyot as 'a long process'); it was written by Osiander, and originally appeared in a Parish

Mass of 1524; after being taken over into the Cologne Order, it served as a model for the exhortations in the Prayer Book.[9] As with Luther, it leads up to the Words of Institution. Next, however, follows *Sanctus*, the Lord's Prayer with its bidding, and *Pax Domini*. During the administration (to the characteristic Lutheran formula, 'Take and eat, this is the body of Christ, which is given for thee') *Agnus Dei* is sung, followed, if there is a large number of communicants, by a communion chant and the responsory *Discubuit Jesus* (a favourite Lutheran chant). The service ends with two alternative prayers of thanksgiving, the second from the *Deutsche Messe*, and a choice of four blessings.

If there are no communicants, the minister wears a surplice instead of vestments, psalms are sung before the Epistle and a hymn before the Gospel; after the sermon come *Te Deum* and three collects. This service is described as 'Common Prayer'. Vespers is modified on Luther's lines. Baptism and Matrimony follow Luther's orders quite closely, with a single addition from a baptism service which Osiander had published in 1524. Forms are provided for the Visitation of the Sick and for Burial; the latter includes *Benedictus* or Psalm 90, with an antiphon ('In the midst of life' or 'I am the resurrection and the life'), and an exhortation based on 1 Thessalonians 4 : 13–18. All the minor ceremonies are abolished, but enough holy days are retained to justify the printing of a table, a feature found in most Lutheran Orders.

Other Orders of the same family which have left their mark on our Prayer Book include that of Albertine Saxony.[10] This was largely the work of Justus Jonas, and first appeared in 1539, then in a revised form in 1540. The main points of contact are in the baptismal services. Public Baptism is based on Luther's form, but adds three exhortations, which later provided portions of our service. Private Baptism is allotted a separate form, instead of being covered by a rubric, as is more usual in the Orders; and to this the Prayer Book is heavily indebted. The Saxon Order also retains some of the

Proper Prefaces, namely the five found in the Prayer Book, and also The Epiphany.

The Order for Electoral Brandenburg of 1540[11] (which is not to be confused with the Brandenburg-Nürnberg Order described above) arose out of circumstances not unlike those obtaining in England. The Elector Joachim II desired reform, but was 'not bound by Wittenberg any more than by Rome'. In this he had the full support of his archbishop, Matthias von Jagow. As a result the Order (compiled by Georg Witzel, Melanchthon, and others) is extremely conservative, even keeping all the baptismal ceremonies. Luther was in agreement with this procedure, so long as the doctrine taught was pure. Confirmation appears for the first time in a Lutheran service-book, and includes examination in the Catechism by the bishop. The Mass sticks closely to the traditional form, except that the Canon is replaced by four prayers taken from the Brandenburg-Nürnberg series of collects, for the Emperor, for the clergy, for peace, and for forgiveness. The Words of Institution are then read accompanied by elevation of the host. The Brandenburg-Nürnberg exhortation is inserted immediately before communion, and the prayer of thanksgiving from the same Order takes the place of the Postcommunion chant. Matrimony likewise follows Brandenburg-Nürnberg, but restores two of the traditional collects; Burial shows a similar mixture of Lutheran and medieval elements. The most striking feature of the Order is the copious directions for Communion of the Sick, which may well have influenced the phrasing of the Prayer Book rubrics.

The Order for Pfalz-Neuburg, compiled by Osiander in 1543, is unusual in providing a prayer to replace the Canon, which is inserted between the Brandenburg-Nürnberg exhortation and the Words of Institution, and contains the phrase 'we bring before thy divine majesty these thy gifts of bread and wine'.[12] Osiander was always something of a deviationist. The Order for Calenberg and Göttingen (1542,

Anton Rabe) has a form of Mattins very similar to that of 1549, consisting of the introduction, 'O Lord, open thou my lips', *Venite*, three psalms, a lesson from the Old or New Testament, *Te Deum*, a New Testament lesson with exposition, *Benedictus*, and two collects, the second being 'O God, the author of peace'.[13] In view of the interdependence of the Orders, it is often impossible to say on internal evidence from which Order Cranmer took a prayer that occurs in several; but it is clear that he knew more than one, and was always ready to pick and choose between them. It will be noticed that all the Orders mentioned to a greater or less extent restore traditional elements which Luther had discarded, and it is therefore these Orders which Cranmer found most useful in preparing the reformed English services. In June 1549 Richard Hilles, an English merchant, wrote to Zurich that 'we have a uniform celebration of the Eucharist throughout the whole kingdom, but after the manner of the Nuremberg Churches and some of those in Saxony'; if this is not 'inside information', it is very acute analysis.[14]

Bucer's service-forms also spread beyond the place of their origin. In 1539 he himself produced an adaptation for the city of Cassel in Hesse.[15] The previous year Jean Calvin, exiled from Geneva, arrived in Strasbourg, and took charge of the French-speaking congregation. In 1540 he adopted a French translation of Bucer's *Psalter* of 1539, adding to the service the Ten Commandments in metre, with *Kyrie eleison* at the end of each verse, in the place of the first psalm. On his return to Geneva in 1541 he introduced this service there with minor modifications forced upon him by the inhabitants.[16] The normal service, 'Common Prayers', consisted of confession, prayer for pardon, psalm, another prayer, sermon, reading, and intercession ending with a paraphrase of the Lord's Prayer. When the Lord's Supper was to be celebrated, the intercession had a special ending, and was followed by the Creed, an exhortation on the Supper, communion (during which psalms were to be sung or a relevant passage of Scripture read), thanksgiving, and blessing. The Baptism Service was simple and far removed from the medieval rite. Matrimony is largely derived from the Strasbourg service through Guillaume Farel, who had been minister there, and had published a French translation in 1533. These forms of service had little direct influence on the text of the Prayer Book, but they play an important part in the history of the Church of England. Translated into English by William Huycke and published in 1550, they formed the liturgical ideal of many Englishmen during the next hundred years.

The Strasbourg services had a further offshoot in a very different direction. In 1536 Hermann von Wied, prince-archbishop of Cologne, called a provincial council which passed a number of canons, many designed to remove abuses in the liturgy. They were published in 1538, together with a doctrinal *Encheiridion* (handbook) by Johann Gropper, a learned canon of Cologne with leanings towards conservative reform.[17] The canons were warmly welcomed by progressive elements in the Church, but nothing was done to implement them. Bucer and Gropper met at the Diet of Regensburg, and established friendly relations, while Hermann was drawn more and more strongly to Lutheranism. Finally in 1542 Hermann invited Bucer to come to Cologne and draw up a Church Order. He also invited Melanchthon, who contributed the section *De Doctrina*, Bucer having already prepared the section *De Administratione Religionis*. By Hermann's express desire, the Brandenburg-Nürnberg Order was taken as the basis, but Bucer interpreted this instruction with some freedom. He also incorporated parts of the kindred Order for Albertine Saxony, and large portions of his own services as adapted for Cassel, which lay in the territory of Hermann's chief supporter, Philip of Hesse. Thus there was a confluence of two rather disparate streams. The result was printed in 1543 for private distribution, and in 1544 for public purchase, under the title *Einfältiges*

Bedenken. It was then thoroughly revised, and translated into Latin (by Albert Hardenberg), appearing in 1545 as *Simplex ac Pia Deliberatio*. The proposals aroused furious opposition, led by Gropper, and expressed in his *Antididagma* (1544), a restatement of traditional Catholic doctrine which was sufficiently liberal in tone to be placed on the *Index Librorum Prohibitorum*. Bucer replied in his *Constans Defensio* (1545), but the reform was never put into effect, and Hermann was deposed. All, however, was not lost. The controversy had been followed with interest in England, and an English translation of the Latin version appeared in 1547 as *A Simple and Religious Consultation*, and was reissued with minor alterations in 1548.[18] Cranmer certainly owned copies of the *Encheiridion*, the *Antididagma*, and the *Deliberatio*, and studied them with great care. Each of them has left some mark on the Prayer Book.

Hermann's Service of the Lord's Supper is divided into two parts, the first a preparation to be held on Saturday evening after Vespers. It consists of a hymn, a lesson (the Institution Narrative from one of the gospels, or a passage from 1 Corinthians 10 or 11, or John 6), a choice of two exhortations (the first based on Strasbourg, the second from Brandenburg-Nürnberg), and prayers for worthy reception. It is followed by individual confession, which is still compulsory. The Sunday morning service begins with the second Confession from the Strasbourg *Psalter* (the same that Calvin chose), the Comfortable Words from the same source, and a new Absolution, then follows traditional lines as far as the Gospel, which is followed by the sermon. The chants are sung in Latin by the choir, by the people in German. Before the Creed comes a prayer for all estates of men in two versions, a longer and a shorter, ending with a paraphrase of the Lord's Prayer. Both these are taken from the Cassel version of Strasbourg. The communicants then put their offerings in some prominent place, and gather near the altar, men and women separately. *Sursum corda* has an invariable preface which recalls primitive examples by mentioning the Creation and the Fall. The Words of Institution are then sung in German, with the people answering Amen. The Lord's Prayer and *Pax Domini* are followed by communion in both kinds, the men receiving before the women. *Agnus Dei* is sung, with two Lutheran hymns in German. The service ends exactly as in Brandenburg-Nürnberg. In spite of the strong Strasbourg influence, the overall impression made by the service is of a rite as conservative as that of Electoral Brandenburg, an impression which must be attributed to Hermann himself. Luther criticized the eucharistic doctrine of the service as Zwinglian, and indeed Bucer's position had become steadily closer to that of Zwingli, though he never abandoned his belief in a Real Presence. The restraining hand of the archbishop preserved much of the traditional structure, such as the Absolution, which Bucer had long since discarded at Strasbourg.

Baptism is similarly divided into two. The first part, entitled Catechism, also takes place on Saturday evening. It begins with a very long address, combining those of Saxony and Brandenburg-Nürnberg, after which the pastor puts the interrogations to the parents and godparents, and exhorts them to bring the child up properly. Next follows the Exorcism, which is extremely brief, with no ceremonies except signing with the cross. Two prayers from Luther's service and the Gospel (from Mark) with a short exposition complete the section. Then the pastor lays his hands on the child's head, and the Lord's Prayer and the Creed are said. After a choice of psalms, a prayer ends the service. The rest takes place the next day at the Communion Service, after the Creed; an exhortation, proper Epistle and Gospel, and a long prayer (from the Cassel Order) are followed by baptism, a prayer from Luther, and a hymn. As in Electoral Brandenburg, Confirmation is included, here preceded by a lengthy catechism from Strasbourg sources. Laying-on of hands with prayer and a hymn constitute the actual service.

Private Baptism and Visitation of the Sick are based on the Saxon Order, Matrimony on Brandenburg-Nürnberg, Burial on the Order for Schwäbisch-Hall, by Johann Brenz, which had only appeared the same year. Mattins and Vespers are to be sung in the usual Lutheran form on holy days, and the Litany on Wednesday or Friday, again a common Lutheran procedure. The book is thus highly eclectic, but Bucer seldom leaves any borrowed passage in exactly its original form without some expansion, while his own contributions are subjected to continual rewriting, always in the direction of greater length.

Even among Catholics there was considerable dissatisfaction with the Daily Office. In 1529 Pope Clement VII commissioned from Cardinal Francesco de Quiñones, General of the Franciscans, a revision of the Breviary, which he produced in 1535.[19] Since Quiñones had in mind the solitary recitation of the Office, a great deal of dialogue was removed, including all antiphons, responsories, and *preces*. Repetition was also greatly reduced. Each office had three psalms, and continuous reading of the Scriptures was restored throughout the year. To take a single example, the old Breviary read Genesis, chapters 1, 2, 5, 6, 7, 8, 12, 13, and 14 (not all complete), between Septuagesima and the beginning of Lent, and then no more of the book ; Quiñones goes right through to chapter 50, which he reaches on the Octave of Corpus Christi. Mattins had always only one Nocturn, its lessons taken from the Old Testament, the gospels, and the epistles, respectively. There was to be only one proper lesson on holy days. *Te Deum* is used daily, except in Advent and Lent ; and the Apostles' Creed replaces *Quicunque vult*, except on Sundays. The Office of the Blessed Virgin was restricted to Saturdays, provided they were not otherwise occupied. A new feature for Catholic service-books was the inclusion of a preface, after the example of Luther in his two Masses, setting out Quiñones' reasons for change, and his *modus operandi*.

This revision met with severe criticism from the theologians of the Sorbonne, and a 'second recension' appeared the following year, in which the author stressed his faithfulness to antiquity. Antiphons were restored to the psalms; the third lesson at Mattins was often taken from a patristic homily; and the Office of the Dead, which had been omitted altogether, was restored on All Souls' Day. In this modified form the book achieved a wide distribution, running into more than a hundred editions, but without establishing itself securely. It was finally suppressed in 1568, in preparation for the issue of an official revision in 1570.

The Reformers were as varied in their attitude to externals as they were in their treatment of the text of the services. Luther kept the vestments and the altar; Zwingli and Calvin introduced the gown and the table, in full view of the congregation; Bucer personally advocated the latter usage, but was prepared to tolerate the old ways under certain circumstances. In all their services music plays a prominent part, but now it has become the congregation's chief means of participation; no longer is it the exclusive preserve of the choir. Fragments of the Gregorian chant survive in the Lutheran books, sometimes adapted to German words; but the bulk of Lutheran hymnody is newly composed, both words and music. At Strasbourg they began the custom of putting the Psalms into metre, a custom which Calvin took with him to Geneva, where the musician Louis Bourgeois and others gave the melodies the form and the harmonies which remain to this day. Their grave and austere beauty forms the perfect counterpart to the dignified simplicity of the Calvinist services.

3 First Stages in England

> You know, my brother, the custom of the Roman Church, in which you remember you were brought up. But my advice is that you should make a careful selection of anything that you have found either in the Roman, or the Gallic, or any other Church, which may be more acceptable to Almighty God, and diligently teach the Church of the English. . . .
>
> Choose therefore, from each Church those things that are pious, religious, and seemly; and when you have, as it were, incorporated them, let the minds of the English be accustomed thereto.
>
> GREGORY THE GREAT to Augustine, A.D. 601

NEWS of the Reformation soon crossed the Channel, and Luther's books were already known in both universities by 1520. Henry VIII was soon engaged in controversy with Luther, but many of his subjects felt differently, and towards the end of the decade Luther's writings figure prominently in lists of prohibited heretical books. In the liturgical field the first impact of the Reformation was made in 1530 by the publication of a Psalter translated by George Joye from Bucer's Latin version of 1529, followed the same year by Joye's *Hortulus Animae*. The title of the latter work was one often given to primer-type books of devotions, and Joye's book included, conventionally enough, the Hours in English, the Penitential Psalms, and the Commendations; but these were preceded by the story of the Passion translated from a harmonization of the four gospel narratives by Bucer, and a number of prayers taken from Luther's newly published *Short Catechism* (1529) and from the *Precationes Biblicae* of Otto Brunfels, an ardent Lutheran.[1] Both works were promptly banned, in the case of the *Hortulus* so effectively that it disappeared completely until a single copy turned up in 1949, which is now in the British Museum.

When Henry determined on a break with Rome, and brought it about in the years 1532–4, a thaw set in, and

Lutheranism was winked at, if not actively encouraged. The first result was the appearance in 1534 of *A Goodly Primer in English*, edited by William Marshall.[2] He reprinted the whole of the *Hortulus Animae* except the Kalendar, which he replaced by one of his own, and added an almost equal amount of new matter, consisting of expositions of the Creed, the Lord's Prayer, 'Hail, Mary', and the Ten Commandments, again probably taken from Luther's *Short Catechism*, though they had already appeared in his *Encheiridion Piarum Precationum* of 1520, one of the forbidden books mentioned above. Two sermons of Luther's are also included, both dating from 1519, and also Savonarola's exposition of Psalm 51. As in the *Hortulus*, the Litany and the Office of the Dead are omitted, because of the Reformers' objection to invocation of saints and prayers for the departed. In response to criticism, a second edition in the following year restored these omissions ; but the Litany printed was a translation of Luther's Litany of 1529, disguised by the addition of a large number of saints. This was the first Reformed liturgical form to appear in English.

In Marshall's Primer the canticles and responses of Morning and Evening Prayer can already be seen beginning to take the form familiar from the Prayer Book, and translation into English was indeed the keynote of the decade. In 1537 Edward Lee, the archbishop of York, ordered the liturgical Epistles and Gospels to be read in English, and editions of the Sarum Primer appeared which included them in Tyndale's translation. The latter, completed from Coverdale's version, was licensed in 1537 as 'Matthew's Bible', and reissued in 1539 in a revision by Coverdale, known as the 'Great Bible'.[3] In 1538 Henry, feeling a momentary need to show his zeal for reform, issued a set of Injunctions which directed that a Bible should be placed in every church ; that the Creed, the Lord's Prayer and the Ten Commandments should be recited in English in turn ; and that no-one should be admitted to communion until he could recite them. No candles were to be allowed before any image or picture ; and in singing the Litany, the invocations of some of the saints should be omitted so that 'the good suffrages following, as *Parce nobis, Domine* and *Libera nos, Domine*' should be sung, and not *vice versa.* [4]

A new primer, *The Manual of Prayers*, compiled by John Hilsey, bishop of Rochester, appeared in 1539 with the approval of Cranmer and of Henry's minister, Crumwell, who had strong leanings to reform.[5] It was a selection in English from the Sarum Primer, including the '15 Oes'; Marshall's translation of the Canticles is used, but the Litany reverts to the traditional form. The choice of psalms was altered, and their number reduced. In the *Dirige* some of the lessons from Job were replaced by passages of a more Christian content, such as 1 Corinthians 15. The biblical readings were all printed from Coverdale's Bible.

During the 1530s Henry was inclined to look sympathetically at the Lutherans for reasons of foreign policy and, with the encouragement of Crumwell, made more than one attempt to form an alliance with them. Since his motives were entirely political, and the Lutherans insisted on purity of doctrine and practice, no agreement was ever reached, but the negotiations gave some incentive to reform of the liturgy, one effect being the issue of the Injunctions mentioned above. As has been said, Cranmer himself had his first experience of Lutheran worship in Lent 1532 at Nuremberg. Whether he began to make plans for an English service-book forthwith is not known, but it is highly probable that an undated manuscript scheme for the revision of the Breviary was prepared with an eye to the negotiations in progress during 1538. Evidence for this dating is found in a letter from Cranmer to Crumwell dated 11 April 1538, which refers to 'the affairs of our church service', on which Crumwell's chaplain has been occupied ; 'the writing up of so much as he had to do' ; and the 'further furtherance and final finishing of that we have begun'.[6] There are also points of similarity with the morning service in Johann Bugenhagen's *Ordinatio Ecclesiastica* for Denmark (1537), a copy of which was presented by the author to Henry VIII.[7] Finally, in a Preface, which is largely derived from Quiñones' Breviary, and therefore cannot be earlier than 1535, Cranmer alludes not only to the Uses of Sarum, Hereford, Bangor, and York, but also to the multiplicity of monastic rites; when he printed this Preface in the 1549 Book, he omitted this phrase as being no longer topical. It cannot have been written long after the Dissolution. All these considerations point to a date in the vicinity of 1538. The scheme (the first of two in the manuscript[8]) is no rough draft, but a fully elaborated form, written out with great care in red and black inks. It has a decidedly Lutheran flavour: Prime, Compline, and the 'Little Hours' are dropped, because they entail too much repetition, and in any case the Hours are customarily grouped into two services. There are three psalms at each service, the longer ones being divided, and the three lessons go straight through the Bible chapter by chapter, starting with Genesis, Isaiah, and Matthew at Mattins, and Genesis and Romans at Evensong. A fourth lesson may be added on suitable occasions. All are to be read from the pulpit, not in the chancel. The hymns are copied from the scholarly edition by Clichtoveus, of which Cranmer possessed the 1516 edition; and collects are appointed for whole seasons (as in the Brandenburg-Nürnberg Order), not for single weeks. The Lord's Prayer and the lessons are in English, the rest in Latin. In order to make room for preaching, *Te Deum* and *Quicunque vult* may be omitted. Cranmer was already well on the way to the Daily Office of 1549.

In parallel with these developments, from 1536 onwards a series of attempts was made 'to stablish Christian quietness and unity . . . and to avoid contentious opinions'. The first of these took the form of *Ten Articles* passed by Convocation, which depend heavily upon the *Apology* written by Melanchthon in defence of the Augsburg Confession, the foundation document of Lutheranism. The next year the bishops issued a handbook of teaching under the title *The Institution of a Christian Man*, and commonly known as *The Bishops' Book*.[9] This includes expositions of the Creed, the Sacraments, the Ten Commandments, and the Lord's Prayer, making free use of the Lutheran material in Marshall's Primer. But Henry's fitful interest in the Lutherans came to an abrupt and final end in 1540; Crumwell fell, and Cranmer's breviary scheme was presumably shelved. There was a marked swing back to Catholic doctrine and practice, which necessitated the revision of *The Bishops' Book*. A revised version, purged of Lutheranism, appeared in 1543. Though also compiled by a commission of bishops, it is known as *The King's Book*, its actual title being *A Necessary Doctrine and Erudition for any Christian man*.[10] Though it is purely a doctrinal treatise, its language subsequently suggested many a phrase in the Book of Common Prayer. Another commission of bishops was set to work simultaneously, and produced a work which remained unpublished for 150 years, entitled *Ceremonies to be used in the Church*, but known as *A Rationale of Ceremonies*.[11] It is a conservative exposition of the various ceremonies then in use, chiefly interesting for the fact that it draws freely on the Cologne *Encheiridion*, which shows that Cranmer was aware of Hermann's reforming efforts, and was looking to him for inspiration for an attempt at reform within the traditional framework.

Simultaneously with these official doctrinal statements, the first tentative steps were taken towards reform of the service-books. In 1541 an emended edition of the Sarum Breviary appeared, omitting any mention of the Pope or of St Thomas à Becket, whose service was widely criticized, even by traditional Catholics. This edition apparently did not command much sale, as Cranmer had to draw attention to these omissions in Convocation in 1542 ; a further edition followed in 1544.[12] Cranmer also spoke of the need for the people to learn and recite the Creed, the Lord's Prayer, and the Ten Commandments in the vernacular; they had heard them read since 1538. By 1543 Cranmer felt able to resume his discreet introduction of reformed practice. 'The Great Bible' was put to liturgical use when Convocation ordered that 'every Sunday and holy day throughout the year, the curate of every parish church, after the *Te Deum* and *Magnificat*, should openly read unto the people one chapter of the New Testament in English, without exposition; and when the New Testament was read over, then to begin the Old'. At the same time Cranmer announced that it was the King's will 'that all mass-books, antiphoners, [and] portuises in the Church of England should be newly examined, corrected, reformed, and castigated from all manner of mention of the bishop of Rome's name, from all apocryphas, feigned legends, superstitious orations, collects, versicles, and responses; and that the names and memories of all saints which be not mentioned in the Scripture, or authentical doctors, should be abolished'.13 A committee was appointed for the purpose, consisting of the bishops of Salisbury and Ely and six of the Lower House, but the Lower House refused to nominate any representatives. This may have been the occasion of Cranmer's other scheme for a reformed breviary,14 which displays a more conservative approach than that of 1538. All the Hours are kept, apparently to be said in three groups; the layout is closely based on that of Quiñones, though Cranmer introduces a lesson at Vespers which is not found in his model. Although there are still three lessons at Mattins (four on high days), the first and second are now taken from the same book, which is a step towards the eventual reduction to two. Unlike Quiñones, Cranmer keeps the *preces*, though he uses a set from the Bidding of the Bedes (which he carried on into the 1549 Book) rather than the traditional series. This manuscript scheme also remained in obscurity.

In 1544 the King, about to invade France, ordered

processions to be said and sung throughout the province of Canterbury, a quite normal procedure in times of emergency. On this occasion, however, Cranmer took the opportunity to issue an adaptation of the traditional Litany, translated into English and prefaced by an Exhortation which is full of phrases that reappear in the Prayer Book.[15] In the Sarum rite, a procession *causa necessitatis* followed the form for Rogation-tide with few variations, and consisted, on the outward journey, of antiphons proper to the occasion, the Penitential Psalms (if time allowed), the Litany, the Lord's Prayer, *preces*, and seven collects. A station (halt for prayer) was made with *Kyrie*, Lord's Prayer, and collect, leading into Mass. On the return journey the Litany was repeated, with a final collect. Cranmer limited his new form to the outward procession, and reduced that to the Litany, the Lord's Prayer, *preces*, and collects, with a few additions from other sources. He did not follow slavishly the text of the Litany as given in the Processional, but shortened it materially, while drawing freely upon the similar, but not identical, litany included in the office for the Visitation of the Sick in the Manual under the title *Commendatio animae*. He also used Luther's Litany, which was already known from Marshall's Primer.[16] Behind both Luther and Cranmer may also be discerned the Solemn Prayers of Good Friday. Many of the chief features of Cranmer's liturgical work are already discernible in his version of the Litany : bold handling of traditional forms, notably by abbreviation and conflation ; borrowing from different portions of the Sarum rite ; insertion of Reformed elements into the traditional frame-work ; and occasional recourse to a totally unexpected source.

The opening phrases at once provide an excellent illustration of Cranmer's methods as applied to small details. He follows the *Commendatio* in beginning at once with the threefold invocation, but uses the actual words of the Processional. The Latin runs :

Pater de coelis Deus: *miserere nobis.*
Fili redemptor mundi Deus: *miserere nobis.*
Spiritus Sancte Deus: *miserere nobis.*
Sancta Trinitas, unus Deus: *miserere nobis.*

Each phrase is said by the officiant and repeated by the choir, and Cranmer keeps this arrangement. The response *miserere nobis* is translated literally, 'have mercy upon us'; but Cranmer has also before him the more expressive response of the *Commendatio, miserere animae famuli tui* ('have mercy upon the soul of thy servant'), and this may have led him to add the words 'miserable sinners', which in any case recall the sound of the Latin. The choice of the word 'sinners' may have been suggested by the later petition, *Peccatores te rogamus* ('We sinners do beseech thee'). Similarly with the addresses to the Persons of the Trinity: he begins by translating literally; then, observing that the Holy Spirit is not given any attribute, he borrows a phrase from the Athanasian Creed, *a Patre et Filio . . . procedens.* The address to the Trinity is expanded on the lines of the next phrase but one in the *Commendatio: Qui es trinus et unus Deus* ('Who art God, threefold and one'). But the word 'persons' again recalls the Athanasian Creed, and the words 'blessed and glorious' come from the antiphon sung with that creed in Trinity week, *O beata et benedicta et gloriosa Trinitas.* An analysis of almost any part of Cranmer's liturgical work will yield results similar to these.

In the medieval Litany each petition was followed immediately by its response; Cranmer achieves a striking increase in dignity and rhetorical effect by gathering the petitions into groups of two, three, or four to each response. This had been begun by Luther, but Cranmer takes it further. At this stage he still retains petitions to the Blessed Virgin Mary, the saints, and the angels, but he omits some fifty invocations of individual saints by name, in accordance with the Injunctions of 1538. Before proceeding to the detailed petitions, Cranmer inserts the antiphon sung with the Penitential Psalms, which preceded the Litany in processions. Marshall had slightly shortened it in his Primer, and kept it at the start of the Litany; Cranmer adopts Marshall's version, but inserts this 'good suffrage' in the place of the invocations, again following the Injunctions. The petitions are thirty in number, partly translated from the Processional and the *Commendatio*, partly translated from Luther, and partly added by Cranmer himself. One instance will suffice :

From all evil	*Ab omni malo*
and mischief,	(Processional & *Commendatio*),
from sin,	*ab omni peccato* (Luther),
from the crafts and	*ab insidiis et laqueis diaboli*,
assaults of the	*ab incursu malignorum spirituum*,
devil,	(*Commendatio*) ;
	ab insidiis diaboli, ab infestati-
	onibus daemonum (Processional),
from thy wrath,	*ab ira tua* (*Commendatio*),
and from everlast-	*a damnatione perpetua*
ing damnation ;	(Processional & *Commendatio*),
Good Lord,	*Libera nos, Domine* (Processional);
deliver us.	*lieber Herre Gott* (Luther).

Luther's influence appears chiefly in the later petitions, and is responsible for many particularized intercessions. The words in the concluding petition, 'sins, negligences, and ignorances' are found in St Bernard, and in a Primer of 1530; Cranmer uses them to sum up in one phrase the *cuncta ejus peccata . . . delicta juventutis ejus et ignorantias* ('all his sins . . . the offences and ignorances of his youth') of the *Commendatio*. No parallel to the rest of the petition has been traced nearer home than the diocesan Use of Brixen, in the South Tyrol.

Cranmer makes minor changes in the *Agnus Dei* which follows, and after the Lord's Prayer he follows Luther in reducing the ten versicles and responses to a single pair. Instead of the seven collects of the medieval Litany, Cranmer borrows the single collect that Luther has at this point, to be said before the rood, and then inserts an antiphon and a set of versicles *in tempore belli* from the ordinary Rogation procession, to be sung during the entry into the choir. Six more collects follow, to be sung at the east end of the choir, thus making up the total of seven in the end, but taking them from various sources. The first was the final collect of the return procession ; then come three of the medieval series of seven ; the collect of Rogation Monday ; and a prayer from the *Liturgy of St John Chrysostom*, translated from a Latin version published in Venice in 1528, which may also have suggested a phrase or two in the petitions.

The Litany, issued with plainsong and also in a five-part setting which has not survived, was kept in print ; and Cranmer followed it up by translating and adapting other processions 'to be used upon festival days', and submitted the result to the king's judgment.[17] This was apparently unfavourable, as no trace has survived of the proposed forms, even after the 'due correction and amendment' suggested by Cranmer. Instead, the new Litany was ordered by a royal Injunction of October 1545 to be sung 'every Sunday and festival day, and none other'; and this injunction was renewed by Edward VI in August 1547. Hitherto the Litany had been used only on Wednesdays and Fridays in Lent, and in Rogationtide. It was now to replace all other processions, and the entire Processional thus became obsolete.

Although Henry's policy of enforcing strict Catholic doctrine and practice made official progress towards liturgical reform necessarily slow, unofficial pressure continued to build up, and Cranmer felt that some degree of uniformity should be pursued which would at any rate quieten the advocates of reform for a time. This end was to be achieved by the issue in 1545 of *The Primer set forth by the King's Majesty and his Clergy*, 'for the avoiding of the diversity of primer books that are now abroad, whereof are almost innumerable sorts . . . and to have one uniform order of all such books throughout all our dominions'. So runs the prefatory Injunction, adding that all other primers are to be withdrawn from sale. *The King's Primer* was published in English, in Latin, and in both languages combined.[18] The contents are traditional, except for the new Litany. The translations of the Canticles were revised, and have virtually reached the form in which they were to appear in the Prayer Book, while the renderings of the Creed, the Lord's Prayer, and the Ten Commandments are those officially and exclusively authorized in 1541. The choice of psalms was again vigorously revised : 30 out of 58 in the medieval Hours were omitted, and eight new ones introduced. Some of the antiphons were remade from the Beatitudes, Marian devotions were omitted, and the *Dirige* was much shortened. Prayers by Erasmus and Lodovicus Vives here make their first appearance in the vernacular ; they were soon to become the staple of English devotional manuals. Another Reformer, Wolfgang Capito of Strasbourg, is represented by prayers translated by Richard Taverner. From here to 1549 is but a short step.

In 1546 Henry took two tentative steps in the direction of reform. One was the abolition of certain ceremonies such as ringing bells all night at Hallowe'en, kneeling to the rood on Palm Sunday, and the veneration of the cross on Good Friday. The other was 'to change the Mass into a Communion', in concert with Francis I of France and the Emperor Charles V ; Cranmer was to 'pen a form thereof to be sent to the French King'. The first step was cancelled for fear of upsetting the negotiations involving the second, which in turn was prevented by the deaths of Francis and Henry.[19] The passing-bell for the old king sounded the death-knell of the old services. The story of his successor's reign is very different.

Edward VI came to the throne in January 1547 ; brought

up in the New Learning, his own religious inclinations were supported by the Protector, Somerset, and the rest of the Council. On 31 July of that year a *Book of Homilies* was issued by the king's appointment, and in August a set of Injunctions appeared for a general visitation of the whole country. Among them are directions to read the Epistle and Gospel 'in English and not in Latin'; to read the Litany kneeling in the midst of the church, and not in procession; to read one of the Homilies every Sunday; to omit three lessons at Mattins and the responds and memorials at Evensong, to make room for a chapter of the Bible in English, the New Testament at Mattins and the Old at Evensong; to omit Prime and the Little Hours when there was a sermon; and when there was no sermon, to recite the Creed, the Lord's Prayer, and the Ten Commandments in English after the Gospel.[20] The visitors were also required to take down images before which candles were burnt, including pictures and stained-glass windows, but in fact 'they pulled down all indifferently'. Only two lights might be left on the high altar. In January 1548 the use of candles, ashes, and palms at Candlemas, Ash Wednesday, and Palm Sunday was forbidden, together with the veneration of the cross on Good Friday; by implication the forms of service associated with these ceremonies were discarded also.

Experiment in English services began at once. At Easter Compline was said in English in the Chapel Royal, presumably from *The King's Primer*. During May 1548 Mattins, Mass, and Evensong were being said in English at St Paul's, and the mass for the anniversary of Henry VII's death was sung in Westminster Abbey in English.[21] Somerset sent the services of Mattins, Mass, and Evensong to Oxford in June and to Cambridge in September, to be used until the appearance of an official order; and in October a marriage was solemnized in English. English Psalters were being bought by churchwardens throughout the country, and parish churches were having the Mass translated into

English. A four-part setting of the Mass in English dating from this period uses the translation of the Apostles' Creed from *The King's Primer*, no official translation of the Nicene Creed being available; this may be the setting which was sung at the opening of Parliament in November 1547.[22] During that month an edition of the new Litany appeared from which the invocations of the saints had been omitted.

Whether or not Cranmer had begun to 'pen a form' before Henry VIII's death, a commission of 'grave and well-learned prelates and other learned men in the Scripture' had meanwhile, 'after long conference', agreed upon an order for the receiving of the communion in both kinds. This was enjoined in an Act of Parliament of December 1547, and the order was printed in March 1548 as *The Order of the Communion*,[23] a title reminiscent of Luther's *Formula . . . Communionis*. It is prefaced by a royal proclamation which promises 'the reformation and setting forth of such godly orders as may be most to God's glory', and urges men 'in the meantime to stay and quiet themselves with our direction . . . not enterprising to run afore, and so by their rashness become the greatest hinderers of such things . . .' 'God be praised', it concludes, 'we know both what by his word is meet to be redressed, and have an earnest mind, by the advice of our most dear Uncle, and other of our Privy Council, with all diligence and convenient speed to set forth the same'. The Act had laid stress on worthy receiving, and so the object of the *Order* is twofold: to provide for the communion of the laity, and to encourage them to prepare themselves before communicating. This approach was justified by events, as the inclusion of a general confession was at once taken to mean that private confession was no longer compulsory, a point which Elyot had criticized at Nuremberg in 1532.

The *Order* begins with an exhortation to be read the previous Sunday; the remainder is to be said after the priest's communion, and consists of the following:

another exhortation,
a warning against impenitent reception,
an invitation to confession,
a general confession,
an absolution,
four sentences of Scripture,
a prayer for worthy reception,
the words of administration, and
a final blessing.

It is possible that vernacular devotions of this kind may have been in common use, but there is very little evidence for the practice. Their position may well have been suggested by Lutheran practice, which Cranmer had heard for himself at Nuremberg, and was still directed, for example in the Order for Electoral Brandenburg, where the exhortation immediately precedes the administration. The *Order* remains firmly within the framework of the Mass, and impenitently sacerdotal in outlook : the confession and the prayer for worthy reception are both to be said by the priest, 'or else by one of the ministers, in the name of all them that shall receive the Communion' ; the congregation is allowed only to say 'Amen' to the blessing.

The whole form is closely modelled upon the services put forth by Hermann for Cologne, following the Latin version of 1545, Cranmer's copy of which is now in the Cathedral Library at Chichester. In accordance with the normal layout of the *Kirchenordnungen*, Hermann prefixes to his services a long doctrinal chapter (actually written by Bucer) *De Coena Domini*, and then gives the texts of the preparation service and the Lord's Supper itself (also prepared by Bucer). The Preparation includes two alternative exhortations, *Brevis Institutio* (from the Cassel Order) and *Exhortatio alia* (from Brandenburg-Nürnberg), which Cranmer took as the starting-points of his two exhortations. In each case he borrows Hermann's opening words, and then strikes out on his own, but using language which shows that his mind was full of both Hermann's exhortations and the chapter *De Coena Domini*. While it is obviously impossible to write an exhortation about the Holy Communion without using such words as 'body', 'blood', 'cup', or 'table', the cumulative effect of all the coincidences of language is conclusive. Brightman gives a list of parallels for the second exhortation,[24] and an equally impressive series can be provided for the first, in which Cranmer also used Hermann's chapter *De conversione a peccatis et vera poenitentia*. At the same time, Cranmer never feels himself tied down to the content or phraseology of his models. He only needs the external stimulus of an existing form to release the creative impulse.

The first exhortation urges the duty of self-examination before communion. It echoes such teaching as that of Mirk by offering 'the most comfortable Sacrament of the body and blood of Christ to be taken ... in the remembrance of his most fruitful and glorious Passion'. The communicants are to come with 'hearty repentance ... steadfast faith ... and most hearty thanks'. Auricular confession is recommended for scrupulous consciences, and is recognized as of equal validity with private confession to God, and general confession to the Church. The second exhortation covers much the same ground, but without specific instructions; once again the emphasis is on remembering 'the exceeding love of our Master and only Saviour Jesus Christ thus dying for us'. There follows a warning to open and impenitent sinners not to communicate, after which the priest is to 'pause a while, to see if any man will withdraw himself', and if anyone does, he is to commune with him at leisure. After the pause, the priest invites the communicants to make their confession; this appears to be a new composition of Cranmer's, though there is an invitation to communion in the Strasbourg services which has points of contact with it. In the General Confession Cranmer follows Hermann's form (a rewriting of the Strasbourg confession) more closely than in the exhortations;

he abbreviates it considerably, and introduces a phrase from Sarum ('thought, word, and deed'), and some of his own making, such as 'the remembrance of them is grievous unto us'. For the Absolution he uses the Sarum form, to which he prefixes Hermann's opening, a strong statement of the power of the Church to absolve penitent sinners.

Of the four 'comfortable words' (another feature originating in Strasbourg), three are taken directly from Hermann's set of five, which, however, were to *precede* the Absolution, and were only to be used one at a time. Cranmer's first text ('Come unto me . . .') is quoted by Hermann in the doctrinal chapter, but it is more likely that Cranmer took it from Zwingli's Latin Mass, where it is read immediately before communion. If Cranmer already thought of it in this position, it would account for his appending Hermann's sentences to it, rather than keeping them where Hermann put them. What is now called the Prayer of Humble Access is in no way dependent on Hermann, who has no prayer at all at this point, but is an excellent example of Cranmer's method of composition. It was clearly intended to provide a prayer for worthy reception for the laity on the analogy of the priest's private prayers before communicating, as Luther did in the *Formula Missae*. Indeed, it begins with a phrase from a priest's private prayer found in two missals printed before 1548.[25] The rest of the prayer reflects the range of Cranmer's reading: possible sources of its language include the Liturgies of St Basil and St James, the Book of Daniel, the Gospels of St Mark and St John, the Hereford Missal, the Litany, St Thomas Aquinas, Florus of Lyons, and Paschasius Radbert. With the exception of the gospel references, none is so literally reproduced as to be definitely identifiable as a source; but each, filtered through Cranmer's retentive memory, may have contributed something to the general sense, and a word or two of the actual phrasing.

No words of administration to the laity are recorded in the Missals, but there must have been some; probably those in the Communion of the Sick were generally used, and Cranmer has adopted these with the characteristically Lutheran addition of 'given for thee' and 'shed for thee'. The words as printed in the *Order* continue the thought expressed in the previous prayer, that the Body preserves the body and the Blood the soul. Each of the wafers is to be broken into two pieces at least, and directions are given for reconsecrating wine, a wise precaution in view of the small size of medieval chalices, and the general lack of experience of communion in both kinds. Finally the people are dismissed with a scriptural text about the peace of God.

As a result of Charles V's temporary ascendancy during this period, a number of notable continental divines came to England as a refuge from persecution at home. Among them were Peter Martyr (December 1547), Francis Dryander (January 1548), John à Lasco and Valérand Poullain (September 1548), and Martin Bucer (April 1549). Many exiles also returned, including Miles Coverdale from Germany in 1548, and John Hooper from Zurich in May 1549. Both refugees and returned exiles kept in close touch with their friends on the Continent, and their letters provide a chief source of information for the period. It was Zurich, and to a less extent Geneva, that was the oracle ; Wittenberg turned a deaf ear to all appeals. Cranmer deliberately encouraged this influx in order 'to have the assistance of learned men who, having compared their opinions together with us, may do away with all doctrinal controversies, and build up an entire system of true doctrine'.[26] Even if this hope was not to be realized, both groups, though too late to have much influence on the impending production of an English Prayer Book, were to make their contribution when the book came to be revised.

c

4 The First Prayer Book of Edward VI

In some processions I have altered divers words; in some I have added part; in some, taken away; some I have left out whole, either for bycause the matter appeared to me to be of little purpose, or bycause the days be not with us festival days; and some processions I have added whole, because I thought I had better matter for the purpose than was the procession in Latin.

CRANMER to Henry VIII, 7 October 1544

THE Church of England had not long to wait for the 'godly orders' promised in March 1548.[1] Some of the preparatory discussions have survived in the form of a set of questions put to the bishops, probably in connection with the meeting of Convocation in November 1547, and relating to different aspects of the Mass.[2] Prayer Book revision was certainly under discussion at this session, for the Lower House asked to see 'certain books' made by 'certain prelates and other learned men' in the previous reign, so that they might be 'perused by them for a better expedition of Divine Service to be set forth accordingly'.[3] This request no doubt referred to Cranmer's reformed Breviary. Meanwhile 'divers and sundry forms and fashions' were being introduced all over the country.

The next step was the appointment of a committee consisting of 'the archbishop of Canterbury and certain of the most learned and discreet bishops, and other learned men of this realm to consider and ponder the premises' of 'a uniform, quiet, and godly order'.[4] It had assembled at Chertsey Abbey by 9 September 1548.[5] The bishops appointed were Thomas Goodrich (Ely), Nicholas Ridley (Rochester), Henry Holbeach (Lincoln), Thomas Thirlby (Westminster), John Skip (Hereford), and George Day (Chichester); the learned men, Doctors William May (Dean of St Paul's), Richard Cox (Dean of Christ Church, Oxford), John Taylor (Dean of Lincoln), Simon Haynes (Dean of Exeter), Thomas Robertson (Archdeacon of Leicester), and John Redman (Master of Trinity College, Cambridge). The 'Old Learning' was represented by Day, Skip, Robertson, and Redman, while Goodrich and Thirlby were moderates ; all the others favoured the 'New Learning'. According to Somerset, they were chosen as men who 'had most opinion of learning in the Scriptures of God, and were likeliest to give least to affection'.[6] The discussions seem to have lasted only three weeks, after which the new Order was delivered to the king at Windsor.

The committee's terms of reference were to 'draw and make one convenient and meet order, rite, and fashion of common and open prayer and administration of the sacraments . . . having as well eye and respect to the most sincere and pure Christian religion taught by the Scripture, as to the usages in the primitive Church'.[7] Although the book was ostensibly 'concluded with one uniform agreement', the subsequent debate in the House of Lords on the Act of Uniformity on 15, 17, and 18 December revealed that the committee had not been in fact unanimous. According to Thirlby, Day had refused to subscribe the book ; he himself had subscribed because it was in accordance with Scripture, but in the belief that it had only been agreed to as a basis of discussion, and on the understanding that certain omissions should be dealt with afterwards, notably 'adoration'. 'Oblation', on the other hand, had been in the draft when he saw it, but was now left out. He also wanted 'the verity of the body and blood . . . spoken plainly in the sacrament'.[8] When the vote was eventually taken, on 15 January, eight bishops voted against the bill, including Day, Skip, and Thirlby. According to Peter Martyr, transubstantiation was now 'exploded, and the difficulty respecting the presence is at this time the most prominent point of dispute'.[9]

It is clear from the speed with which the committee

produced the book that a draft must have been prepared
beforehand. Cranmer had had a good deal of experience in
drawing up schemes for the Daily Office, and practically
every word of Mattins and Evensong was already in print in
English. So were the traditional Epistles and Gospels, while
the Litany and *The Order of the Communion* needed little
revision. There is some evidence that Cranmer had been
working on Baptism and Matrimony years before (see p.
84); and the revisions of the *Dirige* in the various primers
pointed the way for the Burial Service. Several German
Orders had been available for some years, including
Hermann's, which was shortly to appear in English.
The Canon of the Mass was by far the most controversial
portion of the book, and both external and internal evidence,
as well as *a priori* probability, suggest that it must have
formed the subject of by far the greatest part of the committee's discussions. About the preparation of the book little
else is known or can be inferred.

*The Book of Common Prayer and Administration of the
Sacraments and other Rites and Ceremonies of the Church, after
the Use of the Church of England* finally passed through
Parliament on 21 January, and copies were on sale on
7 March. 'Paul's quire, with divers parishes in London and
other places' began to use it at the beginning of Lent[10] (the
First Sunday in Lent was 10 March), and it was to come into
general use on Whit Sunday, 9 June. It was available as a
paperback at 2s and in hard covers at 3s 4d, though by June
the prices had risen to 2s 2d and 4s respectively. The title-
page indicates that it was meant to cover the services
previously contained in the Breviary, the Missal, the
Processional, and the Manual; the Pontificals remained in
force for the time being. The contents form the Use of the
whole Church of England, and all diocesan Uses are
superseded. As the Preface points out, the only other book
needed for the conduct of services was the Bible, though a
separate Psalter would be a convenience. An edition of the

Great Bible with Mattins, Evensong, the Collects, and the Tables of Psalms and Lessons included actually appeared in 1552, making it possible to say the Daily Office from one volume. A Psalter with all the services reduced to the parts said by the parish clerk had already appeared in August 1549. None of these editions contained any music, but in 1550 this gap was filled by *The Book of Common Prayer Noted*, containing 'so much of the Order of Common Prayer as is to be sung in churches', set to music by John Merbecke, a minor canon of Windsor. Merbecke's setting is for unison voices unaccompanied ; he uses one or two simple Gregorian tones, and his idiom is derived from plainchant, but for the most part it is newly composed. His book covers Mattins, Evensong, Communion, Burial of the Dead, and Communion 'when there is a burial'.

The Book of Common Prayer begins with a Preface, translated from Cranmer's first breviary scheme, and slightly revised. Its original is heavily dependent upon Quiñones, and in consequence it deals almost entirely with the Daily Office, which it refers to as 'common prayers . . . commonly called divine service'. It declares the aim of the book to be the provision of a regular reading of Holy Scripture in order, without interruption or needless elaboration. The method is set out in a Table of Psalms 'to be said at Mattins and Evensong' and a Table of Lessons. Here Cranmer parts company with Quiñones, first by spreading the Psalter over a whole month, and secondly by not adhering rigidly to the figure of three psalms at each service. Quiñones could only maintain this figure by departing from the numerical order ; Cranmer keeps the order and varies the figure. Even so, out of sixty portions, twenty-six consist of three psalms. The numbering of the Great Bible is naturally adopted. The Table of Lessons is also based on the civil calendar, and, as in Quiñones, the biblical references for the lessons are incorporated in the Kalendar. Two lessons are provided for both Mattins and Evensong, a break with the traditional scheme of groups of three at Mattins and a *capitulum* at each of the other offices. The layout is based on that of the first manuscript breviary scheme: the Old Testament begins with Genesis at Mattins and Evensong, the New with Matthew at Mattins and Romans at Evensong (another following of Quiñones). A whole chapter is read at each service. The Apocrypha follows on after the Old Testament is finished, with Isaiah beginning out of order, in deference to tradition, on 28 November. Acts follows the Fourth Gospel, and the whole New Testament is read thrice over, except the Apocalypse, of which only two chapters are heard. Proper Lessons are provided on saints' days and holy days when appropriate passages are available.

The framework for these Psalms and Lessons is formed by putting the medieval Mattins, Lauds, and Prime together, and fusing Vespers with Compline. The consequent duplications are removed, and the 'little hours' of Terce, Sext, and None are discarded altogether. The table (p. 71) makes the relationship clear; those elements which were retained by Cranmer are printed in capitals. Mattins begins traditionally with the Lord's Prayer, but said aloud; the translation, as of the versicles which follow, is an improved version of that in the Primers. The promise of the Preface to 'cut off' all 'suchlike things as did break the continual course of the reading of Scripture' is put into effect at once by removing the invitatory of *Venite*, which latter is sung straight through in the translation of the Great Bible. The Psalms and Lessons follow in accordance with the Tables, without any antiphons or responds; and each of the lessons is followed by a canticle. This pattern had already been adopted in the Calenberg-Göttingen *Frühmesse* (1542),[11] but Cranmer had been feeling his way towards it, in his first scheme by inserting a lesson between *Te Deum* and *Benedictus* on high days, and in the second by making the first two of the three lessons continuous. In any case, if the *capitulum* at Lauds is regarded as a lesson, the traditional service afforded ample precedent. The

THE DAILY OFFICE

Mattins

LORD'S PRAYER
Hail, Mary
Creed
O LORD, OPEN THOU, etc.
VENITE
Hymn
PSALMS
Lord's Prayer
LESSONS
TE DEUM (on high days)

Lauds

O God, make speed, etc.
Psalms (including BENEDICITE)
CAPITULUM
Hymn
BENEDICTUS
Kyrie ⎫ only
Lord's Prayer ⎬ on
Preces ⎭ weekdays
COLLECT OF THE DAY
Memorial COLLECTs
Let us bless the Lord

Prime

Lord's Prayer
O God, make speed, etc.
Hymn
Psalms
QUICUNQUE VULT
Capitulum
KYRIE
LORD'S PRAYER
CREED
PRECES
Confession
Absolution
COLLECT
Let us bless the Lord

Vespers

LORD'S PRAYER
O GOD, MAKE SPEED, etc.
PSALMS
CAPITULUM
Hymn
MAGNIFICAT
KYRIE
LORD'S PRAYER
PRECES
COLLECT OF THE DAY
Memorial COLLECTs

Compline

Lord's Prayer
O God, make speed, etc.
Psalms
CAPITULUM
Hymn
NUNC DIMITTIS
Kyrie
Lord's Prayer
CREED
Confession
Absolution
Preces
COLLECT
Let us bless the Lord

translation of *Te Deum* and *Benedictus* is taken over from *The King's Primer*, that of *Benedicite* from the Great Bible. The latter is alternative to *Te Deum* in Lent, as in the Mozarabic rite; but the idea of a Lenten alternative is already found in Quiñones, as is the daily use of *Te Deum*. *Quicunque vult* (in Hilsey's translation) is only to be said on six days in the year, instead of daily. *Kyrie eleison*, the Creed, and the Lord's Prayer are then said by the minister. The first four pairs of *preces* which follow are taken from the Bidding of the Bedes, which would be more familiar to the laity than the versions of the Breviary. Instead of '*Domine, fiat pax in virtute tua*', the fifth pair is made from the antiphon to a collect for peace, which follows soon after. These five are already found in Cranmer's second scheme; now he adds a sixth, from the long series at Prime. The service ends with the Salutation and 'Let us pray', leading to three collects: one of the day, one for peace (from the memorials of Lauds of the Blessed Virgin), and the third, for grace to live well, the invariable collect at Prime. The number of three was perhaps suggested by the Order for Brandenburg-Nürnberg.

It seems probable that Cranmer's first intention was to combine only Mattins and Lauds, following *Benedictus* with *Kyrie*, Lord's Prayer, and *preces* (as on weekdays in Sarum), the Collect of the day, and a collect from the memorials, and rounding it off with the collect of Prime, as in the draft schemes. Then he decided to include *Quicunque vult*, at any rate occasionally, and the Apostles' Creed daily (both of which were said in Prime), and inserted each of them at a quite unprecedented place. *Quicunque vult* was certainly an afterthought: it is not mentioned in the rubrics of Mattins, and is printed after Evensong. The Apostles' Creed should not separate *Kyrie* from the Lord's Prayer, and it is hard to see why it does, unless through haste. Evensong was designed on the same lines as Mattins, though it lacks the characteristic Mattins features of 'O Lord, open thou my lips' and *Venite*. The *capitulum*, *Nunc dimittis*, Creed, and invariable collect from Compline were inserted into Vespers at such points as to render the structure of the two services identical. The belated addition of *Quicunque vult* concludes the Breviary section of the book. The drastic simplification of the services has enormously reduced the bulk of this section, and a further reduction has been achieved by not printing the lessons in full. Besides the antiphons, responds, and invitatories specified in the Preface, all the metrical hymns have been discarded, although Cranmer had taken considerable trouble over these in his draft schemes. Presumably the dearth of adequate translators was the reason. Cranmer was aware that his own 'English verses lack the grace and facility' that he desired, a description which certainly applies to the versions in *The King's Primer*. Besides innumerable versicles and responses, the other notable omission is that of the Confession and Absolution said at Prime and Compline; Cranmer was probably thinking of Mattins as followed immediately by Communion, which was well provided in this respect. Cranmer's prolonged labours on the Breviary have produced a form without exact parallel elsewhere. He has gone far beyond Quiñones in simplifying and abridging the medieval services; and while his form is close to the Lutheran Orders in spirit, it differs from them in many points of detail. The sequence Psalms – Lesson – Canticle – Lesson – Canticle, which became the pattern of the classical Anglican service, is found only in one or two minor Lutheran Orders; the typical Lutheran service is based on a group of Psalms, one Lesson, and one Canticle, both in the morning and in the evening.

The next section of the book corresponds to the Missal. This too is greatly diminished in size by reason of the reduction in the number of saints' days and of the rubrics and prayers of the ordinary service. The *Temporale* is little altered from the medieval series, except for the suppression of eves and octaves and of weekdays in Lent, Ember Days, and Rogation Days. The *Sanctorale* consists of all the

Apostles and Evangelists (including Paul and Barnabas), two feasts of the Blessed Virgin Mary, John the Baptist, Mary Magdalen, Stephen, the Innocents, Michael and all Angels, and All Saints. The normal proper consists of an Introit Psalm, Collect, Epistle, and Gospel. Occasionally no psalm or collect is appointed (as on Monday to Thursday before Easter); Easter Even has no proper collect, the Purification no epistle. Although the feast-days are not classified in importance as in pre-Reformation usage, a small number are distinguished by having proper Prefaces in the Communion Service, proper psalms at Mattins and Evensong, and by the recitation of *Quicunque vult*. These feasts are Christmas Day, Easter Day, Ascension Day, Whit-Sunday, and Trinity Sunday. Christmas and Easter are further distinguished by having two sets of Epistles and Gospels; and Easter Day, alone of all the feasts, has a short Procession, to be said or sung before Mattins while the reserved sacrament and the cross were brought from the Easter Sepulchre to their respective altars. It consists of two antiphons from Romans and 1 Corinthians with alleluias appended, a versicle and response, and a collect.[12] Ash Wednesday also has a peculiar service, which is considered later (p. 91).

The Introit Psalms are chosen for their appropriateness, when possible; and the remaining days have suitably brief psalms in their numerical order. With the Collects, Cranmer sticks very closely to the Sarum rite: all but eight of the sixty-three in the *Temporale* are translations from the Latin, including all the Sundays after Trinity without exception; in the *Sanctorale*, however, there are twelve new compositions to seven translations. The discarded collects were unacceptable in asking for the prayers of the saints. The Epistles and Gospels are also taken over from Sarum with few changes, and those of no great import; their text is that of the 'Great Bible'.

'The Supper of the Lord and the Holy Communion,

commonly called the Mass' neatly suggests in its title the main sources from which it is compounded. 'The Supper of the Lord' is Hermann's name for the service; 'the Mass' is both the medieval and the Lutheran name; 'the Holy Communion' is a vernacular name, now for the first time applied to the whole service. As the table on page 76 shows, the structure of the service is very closely based on the medieval form. Common material is printed in capitals.

When the three groups of private prayers and the Gradual-Alleluia-Sequence series of chants have been removed, what remains is virtually identical in order of events with the new service. The only changes are the opening of the service with the Lord's Prayer, by analogy with the Offices, and the placing of the Sermon before the Offertory, as the Lutherans did, instead of after it. The additions to the framework are almost confined to *The Order of the Communion*, whose two exhortations are printed between the Sermon and the Offertory, while the remainder is now placed *before* the priest's communion. The only completely new item is a short catena of biblical passages after the end of the Canon ('Christ, our paschal Lamb'). Two prayers are new in content, if not in form or position : a collect for the king is now the only memorial, and the Post-Communion collect is invariably what we now call the Prayer of Thanksgiving. The proportion of seasonal material is further diminished, first by the provision of new texts for the Offertory and Communion (the latter confusingly described as 'the Post-Communion') : a choice is offered, but there is no variation according to occasion ; and likewise, by the reduction of the Proper Prefaces from ten to five in number, and those five to be used on many fewer days. The Introit, on the other hand, is always a complete psalm, or portion of Psalm 119, as Luther had desired. A sermon or homily is to be delivered every Sunday, in contrast to the quarterly discourse encouraged by medieval archbishops.

Of the new material, the two collects for the king are

THE HOLY COMMUNION

Hymn : Come, Holy Ghost
COLLECT FOR PURITY
Psalm 43
Kyrie
LORD'S PRAYER
Hail, Mary
Confession
Absolution
INTROIT
KYRIE
GLORIA IN EXCELSIS
SALUTATION
COLLECT OF THE DAY
MEMORIALS
EPISTLE
Gradual
Alleluia
Sequence
GOSPEL
CREED
OFFERTORY SENTENCE AND ACTIONS
Bidding of the Bedes
SERMON
Private prayers
SURSUM CORDA
SANCTUS
CANON, ending with
LORD'S PRAYER, PAX DOMINI, and AGNUS DEI
Private prayers
COMMUNION
POST-COMMUNION
Dismissal

completely original, both in conception and in phrasing. They read like alternative drafts, with a good deal of overlapping. The Prayer of Thanksgiving seems to belong stylistically with *The Order of the Communion*, in view of its opening, taken from Hermann or Brandenburg-Nürnberg, its rubric 'in the name of all them that have communicated', and its wide range of origins. The latter may include William Bond's *The Pilgrimage of Perfection*, an orthodox devotional manual published in 1526 ('to be incorporate in him as one of the members of his mystical body'), and Hermann's sermon before the service of Exorcism (*'beatam sanctorum omnium societatem'*). A small but significant alteration is made in the Absolution: instead of Hermann's phrase, 'Our blessed Lord, who hath left power to his Church to absolve penitent sinners from their sins, and to restore to the grace of the heavenly Father such as truly believe in Christ', the prayer now begins 'Almighty God, our heavenly Father, who of his great mercy hath promised forgiveness of sins to all them which with hearty repentance and true faith turn unto him'. On closer inspection it turns out that Cranmer has put the new phrase together from the original and adjacent sentences: 'heavenly Father', 'repentance', 'sins', and 'true faith' are in the earlier version; 'turn to him' comes from 'Hear what comfortable words . . .'; and 'hearty' is in the Invitation and the Confession.

The Canon (so entitled in 'The Communion of the Sick') needs more detailed consideration. Its most remarkable feature is its mere existence. The abolition of the Canon was an article of faith with all the continental Reformers. It is normally replaced by the Words of Institution, read as a lesson. Sometimes they are to be read facing the altar, as a prayer; and occasionally, as in the earliest Strasbourg rite or in Osiander's form for Pfalz-Neuburg,[13] the place of the Canon is taken by a short collect. Even the conservative Electoral Brandenburg Order has only a group of intercessory prayers following the Offertory. Only in Zwingli's Latin

Mass is a Canon to be found, and there it is not an adaptation, but a new composition ('*Canonem loco non movimus, sed in eius locum . . . alium ponimus*'). Cranmer follows the subject-matter of the medieval Canon fairly closely, with enough literal translation to show that he took it as his starting-point; but he diverges freely from the actual language, and finally uses very little of it.

After the Preface and *Sanctus*, the main body of the Sarum Canon consisted of six prayers marked off by Amens, with the Lord's Prayer said after the fifth. Cranmer's Canon is divided into three main sections, indicated by new para-graphs, corresponding to the three prayers into which it was later divided. (There is also a new paragraph at 'Likewise after supper', but this is inseparable from what precedes it, and is printed continuously in Merbecke's edition.) The first section is introduced by a bidding 'Let us pray for the whole state of Christ's Church', which applies to this section, but not to the others.

The first section corresponds to the first two prayers of the medieval Canon (*Te igitur – Memento Domine – Communicantes* and *Hanc igitur oblationem*), with the fourth prayer (*Memento etiam*) inserted between them. Frere[14] prints *Hanc igitur* as a parallel to Cranmer's next section, to which it bears no resemblance, while its last words 'numbered with the flock of thine elect' surely correspond to 'be set on his right hand' in the first section of 1549. Brightman lists a number of resemblances to Hermann's prayer *pro omnibus hominum statibus et necessitatibus Ecclesiae.*[15] Once again as in the Exhortations of 1548, taken together they suggest a diffused memory rather than deliberate copying, but Hermann has clearly influenced Cranmer's expansion of his original in such matters as the inclusion of the King's Council, all pastors and curates, and those in adversity. Another source is 1 Timothy 2 : 1, to which Cranmer had already appealed in the Exhortation before the 1544 Litany, a passage which shows marked affinities with the present one. The Blessed

Virgin Mary, the Patriarchs, Prophets, Apostles, and Martyrs, recently expelled from the Litany, find a temporary resting-place in the thanksgiving for the departed. The section ends with the allusion to Matthew 25 : 34 already quoted, which is based on a Passion prayer in *Hilsey's Primer*.

The second section begins with an entirely new exordium, 'O God, heavenly Father, which of thy tender mercy didst give thine only Son Jesu Christ . . . until his coming again', based on passages from *The King's Book*, and possibly also from the Cologne *Antididagma*. It corresponds in position to the section *Quam oblationem*, and possibly replaces the passage dealing with oblation which Thirlby said was left out after the Chertsey conference. After an epiclesis, or invocation of the Holy Spirit upon the elements, one of the 'usages of the primitive Church' referred to in the Act of Uniformity, it ends with the Words of Institution, in a version harmonized from the Synoptic Gospels and 1 Corinthians 11. At this point it is only half-way through the long third prayer (*Quam oblationem*) of the medieval Canon.

The third section, marked by a rubric as well as a new paragraph, continues with an anamnesis, or commemoration of Christ's Passion, Resurrection, and Ascension, just as *Quam oblationem* does, then diverges to an offering of 'our self, our souls and bodies' (apparently a reminiscence of the German version of Hermann), rejoining the Sarum Canon with a prayer for blessings on all worthy partakers. Here again there are echoes of Hermann's *Brevis Institutio*, which had already influenced the Exhortations : '*instituto eius . . . haec dona coelestia . . . memoriam . . . celebremus . . . his tantis beneficiis . . . meritum suum . . . remissionem peccatorum*'.

As Brightman[16] points out, the doctrinal basis of Cranmer's Canon is the threefold sacrifice, of our Lord on the cross, of praise and thanksgiving, and of ourselves ; and only with reference to these offerings is any sacrificial language employed. At the beginning of the Canon, God is asked to receive 'our prayers' instead of 'these gifts'; and when the gifts do make an appearance, in the third section, they are for celebrating the memorial which Jesus commanded us to make, not for offering. The word 'oblation' is used only of Christ's 'one oblation once offered'; and even the scriptural offerings of Abel, Abraham, and Melchizedek are censored. It remains uncertain how far this Canon expressed Cranmer's own eucharistic doctrine. He himself strongly maintained at his trial that he had held only two opinions in the whole course of his life, having been persuaded by Ridley to abandon a belief in the 'Real' Presence, probably in 1546, when Ridley was his chaplain. One of the two opinions was obviously the Catholic, but what was the other? Many scholars would say, Zwingli's. If so, the 1549 Canon certainly does not express Cranmer's own opinion. His prosecutors alleged that he had held three successive positions, the second of which would be the Lutheran, though Cranmer was not professedly a Lutheran at any time. In fact his attitude to contemporary schools of thought is best summed up in his own remark to Joachim Vadianus: 'I have seen almost everything that has been written and published either by Oecolampadius or Zwingli, and I have come to the conclusion that the writings of every man must be read with discrimination'.[17]

It is most probable that Cranmer did not intend the 1549 Canon to express exclusively any one doctrinal position. It was a first step, following the precedent of the older Reformers, who all began with a conservative revision, and gave full liturgical expression to their opinions only when they felt the time to be ripe. Cranmer likewise began planning a second edition as soon as the first was off the presses. The three sections of the Canon may well have been intended from the start to occupy the positions which they were given in 1552, and other modifications may also have been already in Cranmer's mind. It is true that Cranmer, in controversy with Stephen Gardiner, wrote a lengthy defence of the 1549 service which sets out an essentially Zwinglian position, but the service itself is still deliberately ambiguous.[18] Even a moderate like Dryander thought that 'the book speaks very obscurely, and however you may try to explain it with candour, you cannot avoid great absurdity'.[19] It must not be forgotten that Cranmer, unlike most of the Reformers, was an archbishop. He had seen Hermann's attempt at reformation brought to nothing by the resistance of the clergy and the intervention of the Emperor. A substantial proportion of the bishops were against any change, and an obviously Zwinglian service might very well have aroused enough opposition to ensure its rejection.

In the book of 1549 Cranmer was trying to edge a nation notorious for its conservatism into accepting a reformed service, though, for all its comprehensiveness, the book turned out to have gone almost too far. He hoped to satisfy the reforming zealots by suppressing all mention of oblation, to pacify the conservatives by keeping the time-hallowed framework, and to supply a positive, reformist-Catholic statement of what all had in common. This would provide the basis for further advance. For the moment, the more doctrinal positions that could be read out of it, the better. Perhaps there was also a conflict of heart and head, and Brilioth's comment on Luther may fit Cranmer as aptly : 'throughout his life he retained a deep religious impression from the old Latin service, which his controversial writings indeed might seem to belie, but which never allowed him to lose hold of the element of Mystery in the Eucharist, nor to break altogether with the traditional forms of the Church's worship'.[20]

Compared with those of the Sarum Missal, the ceremonial directions of 1549 are scanty. The celebrant is to wear a white alb 'plain' (i.e. without an apparel) and 'a vestment or cope', and the assistants albs with tunicles. In keeping with the general intention of comprehension, 'kneeling, holding-up of hands, knocking upon the breast, and other gestures' are neither enjoined nor forbidden : 'they may be used or left as every man's devotion serveth'. The elements are to be prepared after the Offertory; crossing is indicated at the epiclesis, and the priest is to take the bread and the cup into his hands at the Words of Institution; but elevation is specifically forbidden; and the fraction and commixture are tacitly ignored, though fraction is implied by the retention of the rubric which says that every wafer 'shall be divided in two pieces at the least'. Wafers are to be 'without all manner of print', and are to be placed in the people's mouths. Otherwise, the only rubrical directions for the priest are to turn towards the altar or towards the people. Hermann's procedure for the Offertory is adopted, with intending communicants remaining in the chancel, and all others departing.[21] Medieval practice in the matter of attendance is continued : all must attend weekly, but need communicate only once a year; during divine service the congregation are to occupy themselves 'with devout prayer or godly silence and meditation'. On weekdays the first part of the service may be shortened by the omission of *Gloria*, Creed, Homily, and Exhortation; and on Wednesdays and Fridays the Litany is to be said, followed (if there are no communicants) by Ante-Communion. For this service a series of eight collects is provided to be used before the Blessing; as with the similar series in the Brandenburg-Nürnberg Order, some are translated from Sarum, the majority newly composed. Notice of intention to communicate must be given overnight or at Mattins, and 'open and notorious evil-livers' may be repelled from communion; both these practices are recommended by Luther.

The service is conceived as essentially choral : the 'clerks' are directed to stay throughout the service, even if not intending to communicate. The choral portions include the Introit Psalm, *Kyrie, Gloria in excelsis*, Creed, Offertory Sentence or Sentences, *Sanctus, Agnus Dei*, and the 'Post-Communion' Sentence. The Epistle and Gospel (like the

Lessons at Mattins and Evensong) are to be 'sung in a plain tune'; and Merbecke has the priest intone the Canon (including the Preface) and the Prayer of Thanksgiving. He gives the Lord's Prayer a melodic line for the priest to sing, taken up by the clerks at 'But deliver us from evil'.

The Litany comes next, rather surprisingly, as it would naturally belong between Mattins and Communion; in some copies it is even placed at the end of the book. Together with the tiny Procession on Easter Day and the Ash Wednesday service, it represents the medieval Processional. Cranmer had apparently not yet given up hope of producing some English processions, in spite of Henry's rejection of his first attempt, as he announces in 'Certain Notes' that parts of holy Scripture 'hereafter to be certainly limited and appointed' may be used on Christmas Day, Easter Day, Ascension Day, Whit-Sunday, and Trinity Sunday, 'in the stead of the Litany'. These do not seem to have materialized, unless they are to be found in the *Psalmi, Lectiones, et Preces Selectae* for those feasts, with the addition of Good Friday, in the *Preces Privatae* of 1564.[22] For the present Cranmer contented himself with reprinting the 1544 Litany as revised in 1547, when the invocation of the saints had been removed, and the last six collects were reduced to two by omitting three and amalgamating two of the remainder. As it was not to be sung in procession, two were ample.

The rest of the Prayer Book consists of services from the Manual: Baptism, Confirmation, Matrimony, Visitation of the Sick, Burial, Churching, and Commination. For 'The Administration of Public Baptism' Cranmer follows the main outline of Sarum, with its two parts, Exorcism at the church door and Baptism at the font. The service was of considerable length, and included several 'dark and dumb ceremonies', with attendant prayers. Of these ceremonies, exorcism of salt, *Ephphatha*, signing of the hand, anointing of the breast, and giving of a candle were discarded, and with them a number of prayers; signing of the forehead, exorcism of the devil, anointing of the head, and giving of a white robe were retained. One out of each pair is kept and one dropped. The two final gospels are omitted, and there are two minor changes of order. As in his treatment of the Mass, Cranmer has kept the essentials and preserved the structure, while reducing the number of ceremonies and prayers, and filling up the gaps with exhortations from Lutheran sources (see p. 85).

An interesting point is that in translating a prayer composed by Luther and reproduced with slight alterations by Hermann, Cranmer has kept to Luther's original text.[23] In this service he draws freely on Hermann, and could easily have taken this prayer from the *Deliberatio*, for the differences are quite insignificant. The inference is that Cranmer had already made his translation before the *Deliberatio* came into his hands; similar instances can be found in Matrimony. Possibly Cranmer drafted other services besides the Breviary during the Lutheran negotiations of the late 1530s. If all traces of Hermann be removed from the 1549 Baptism, the remainder is very similar to Luther's form, which was also adopted by Brandenburg-Nürnberg. Another possibility is that the main source for the service was Justus Jonas's Order for Albertine Saxony (1540), which also takes over Luther's service *verbatim*, and adds three exhortations, each of which have contributed to the English service.[24] Jonas was personally known to Cranmer and visited England in 1539, and his son was living with Cranmer in 1548. In Private Baptism Cranmer made full and literal use of the rubrics in Jonas's service.[25] Hermann also borrowed from Jonas in both Public and Private Baptism, and it is not always possible to say which of the two Cranmer is using, but he undoubtedly used both. Hermann certainly contributed the opening words of Public Baptism, the formula of signing with the cross, parts of the exposition of the Gospel, the whole prayer which follows it, and the charges to the godparents.[26]

In Private Baptism signing and exorcism, which precede

BAPTISM

Sarum	1549
At the church door	*At the church door*
Questions: Male or female?	
BAPTIZED OR NO?	THE PRIEST SHALL ASK
NAME?	
Almighty and everlasting God	
We beseech thee Lord	
SIGNATION OF THE FOREHEAD	Dear beloved
O GOD, WHO DIDST CREATE	('THAT THING . . . CANNOT HAVE')
I exorcize thee (salt)	
O GOD OF OUR FATHERS	ALMIGHTY AND EVERLASTING GOD
	NAME?
	SIGNATION OF THE FOREHEAD
God of Abraham	
Therefore, accursed devil	
O GOD, THE IMMORTAL DEFENCE	ALMIGHTY AND IMMORTAL GOD
Hearken, accursed Satan	
I EXORCIZE THEE ⎫	I COMMAND THEE
THEREFORE, ACCURSED DEVIL ⎭	
I beseech thine eternal	
Be not deceived	
SALUTATION	SALUTATION
GOSPEL (Matthew)	GOSPEL (Mark)
	Friends, you hear
Effeta	
LORD'S PRAYER	LORD'S PRAYER
Hail, Mary	
CREED	CREED
	Almighty and everlasting God
Signation of hand	
At the font	*At the font*
	The Lord vouchsafe
	Well-beloved friends
RENUNCIATIONS	N. DOST THOU FORSAKE . . .?
Anointing of breast	
AFFIRMATIONS	DOST THOU BELIEVE . . .?
BAPTISM	BAPTISM
ANOINTING OF HEAD	
RECEIVE A WHITE ROBE	TAKE THIS WHITE VESTURE
Receive a lamp	
	ALMIGHTY GOD (ANOINTING)
CHARGE TO GODPARENTS	FORASMUCH AS THESE CHILDREN
Gospel (Mark 9)	
Gospel (John 1)	
	Benedictus or *Nunc dimittis*

baptism, are naturally omitted; and so is anointing, for no obvious reason, its place being taken by the thanksgiving and prayer for the Spirit which ends the section of exorcism. At the end of the service is appended a short form for blessing the water in the font, almost entirely translated from the Mozarabic Missal. This is a much more dramatic composition, with its series of short prayers, than the Sarum form, which consisted of all the invocations of the Litany, followed by an enormously long Preface.

All the Reformers laid great stress on education, and particularly on religious instruction. Catechisms are found in many Lutheran Orders, and Cranmer himself translated Jonas's Latin version of the Brandenburg-Nürnberg Catechism. He did not, however, make use of it in the Prayer Book, but published it separately in 1548, having presumably decided not to include it. Nor did he make use of the lengthy Catechism in Hermann, but prepared a new one himself, which is exceptional in not containing a section on the sacraments. Reformed Catechisms were not usually connected with Confirmation, but were intended to cover the whole field of doctrine. This was not Cranmer's aim. He confined himself to the syllabus laid down in the charge to the godparents at the end of the Baptism Service, namely, the Creed, the Lord's Prayer, and the Ten Commandments. It was the duty of godparents to teach their godchildren these formulas, and by ancient tradition the children could not be confirmed until they could repeat them.[27] Cranmer's Catechism is designed to meet this requirement. The first four answers relate the Catechism to the Baptism Service, the third paraphrasing the charge to the godparents before the renunciations, while the fourth quotes from the prayer of signing. The Ten Commandments are shortened, as in *The King's Book*, and their expositions are clearly from the same source, while the exposition of the Lord's Prayer goes back to the Exhortation before the 1544 Litany.

Confirmation is literally translated from the Sarum rite,

with the one alteration that anointing is replaced by laying-on of hands, with a reference to 'the inward unction of the Holy Ghost'; signing with the cross is kept. The service ends with a greatly shortened version of the prayer in Hermann's *Deliberatio*, one of the very few Orders to have a confirmation service at all. Cranmer is obviously copying Hermann's arrangement of the whole section, beginning with an introduction headed 'Confirmation, wherein is contained a Catechism for children', in which Hermann's influence is clearly apparent, then printing the Catechism, and finally the actual service of Confirmation. He also agrees with Hermann in giving up the use of oil and introducing the laying-on of hands.

'The Form of Solemnization of Matrimony' follows the Sarum service with only minor rearrangements and altera-tions. The introductory exhortation is much lengthened, on lines which appear to be traditional, for references to Paradise, Cana, and the causes of matrimony are to be found in the Parson's Tale in Chaucer's *Canterbury Pilgrims*; and similar parallels occur in the Cologne *Encheiridion* and in Hermann.[28] Much of the actual wording is already present in *The King's Book*. Thereafter the service proceeds with literal translation of the Latin, touched up with a phrase or two from Luther's service, possibly by way of Brandenburg-Nürnberg. Hermann also made use of this service, but once again, where there are differences between Hermann and Luther, Cranmer follows Luther.[29] The plighting of troth and giving of the ring were said in English before the Reformation, and Cranmer has simply retained the familiar words. The ring is no longer blessed, but the two prayers of blessing are made into a single blessing of the couple. This is followed by the text 'Those whom God hath joined' and the declaration of marriage, both from Luther, taking the place of a psalm and the Lord's Prayer. The rest of the service follows the medieval order, and leads on to the Communion, only moving two prayers said before *Pax Domini* into the

Marriage Service proper, and providing a homily to be read in the absence of a sermon.

The Sarum forms for Visitation of the Sick and Extreme Unction were printed as two separate services, the latter including Communion. They might be, and no doubt often were, said continuously. Cranmer includes Unction in the Visitation, and has a fresh heading for Communion of the Sick, with directions for combining it with Visitation and Unction. In general his service is a straightforward abbreviation of Sarum. The seven Penitential Psalms, said on the way to the house are reduced to the last, 143, said in the house; it still retains its antiphon, which is actually described as such; the nine collects are reduced to two; the charge about charitable giving is turned into a rubric; and whereas in Sarum the sick person is anointed on seven different parts of the body, each with a complete psalm, Cranmer confines the unction to 'the forehead or breast only', with its psalm (13), and puts together a short address out of fragments of the various prayers. The opening address is an amalgam of Sarum and the *Homily against the Fear of Death*, which also contributed the answer to the second question in the Catechism. The Absolution is constructed in the same way as that in *The Order of the Communion*, by prefacing Hermann's opening words to the Latin form; here Hermann's phrase is slightly compressed, but not altogether rewritten as in the Communion Service. The section devoted to Unction begins with Psalm 71, which also retains its antiphon.

In Sarum, communion follows immediately after unction, from the reserved sacrament. Cranmer envisages communion being administered to sick persons who are not at the point of death, and so directs the priest to reserve 'at the open communion' as much as necessary, and to go to the sick person's house, repeating the General Confession, Absolution, and Comfortable Words before communion, and the Prayer of Thanksgiving afterwards. On days when there is no celebration in church the whole service is said in the house, in the shortened weekday form (omitting *Gloria*, Creed, Homily, and Exhortation), with proper Introit Psalm, Collect, Epistle, and Gospel. When it is combined with Visitation and Unction, the latter are slightly shortened, but not the Communion. The rubrics, though not the service, seem to be based on the directions in the Order for Electoral Brandenburg, which are unusually full.

The enormously lengthy Sarum Burial Service contained six sections : in the house (Vespers), procession to church, service in church (Mattins and Mass), procession to the grave, committal, and procession back to church. Cranmer's service begins 'at the church stile', and consists of three sections : procession, committal, and service in church. Alternatively, the service in church may precede committal ; no provision is made in either case for the procession between the second and third sections. Vespers and Mattins of the Sarum service had long been familiar from the Primers, and an authorized translation was still available in *The King's Primer*, which could be used in the house to take the place of the first section of the Sarum rite. Cranmer's Procession consists of three sentences of Scripture, the first two from different parts of Sarum, and found on successive pages of *The King's Primer*, the third newly chosen. In Merbecke's setting each sentence is headed 'Response' ; he treats the first sentence as a Responsory, with Verse and repetition of the first part. The second, which was so treated in Sarum, is set without repetition, but the third is set like the first.

The Committal begins with a sentence from the fifth lesson at Mattins, and continues with the Sequence *Media vita*, appointed in Sarum as an antiphon to *Nunc dimittis* in Compline during the third and fourth weeks in Lent ; its use in the Burial Service is a constant feature of Lutheran Orders, and Cranmer's translation owes much to Coverdale's rendering of Luther's German paraphrase.[30] Merbecke again provides a setting in responsory form. The words of committal consist of the Sarum formula, augmented by Philippians

3 : 21, one of the passages suggested by Hermann as a lesson at the graveside. The sentence which follows comes from one of the alternative Epistles at the daily Requiem Mass. The first collect starts with an opening from Sarum and ends with a passage very similar to the prayer for the departed in the Canon ; the second is based on a prayer from Hermann, who also contributed the phrase 'his body we commit to the earth' in the first collect.

The service in church consists of Psalms 116, 139, and 146, all three occurring in the first section of Sarum ; 139 was added out of order, and the other two are closely associated in the *Dirige* of *The King's Primer*. The lesson from 1 Corinthians was already used in part in *Hilsey's Primer*, and taken on by *The King's Primer* ; it was also the other Epistle at the Requiem. The suffrages are literally translated from Sarum ; the collect is again assembled from fragments of four Sarum prayers, and ends with yet another quotation of 'Come, ye blessed of my Father'. The Communion is set out as for Communion of the Sick, with proper Introit, Collect, Epistle and Gospel. Merbecke's setting is confined to Introit, *Kyrie*, *Sanctus*, and *Agnus* : clearly the *Gloria* and Creed were omitted, and the Offertory, Preface, Lord's Prayer, and Post-Communion said. The Psalm (42) comes from the Sarum Committal ; the Collect is another cento, including a phrase from the Primers. The Epistle is that of Sarum, also chosen by several German Orders (including Hermann) and *The King's Primer*, while the Gospel appears to be a new choice. Cranmer's service shows again his extraordinary skill in picking out small portions of a lengthy whole and welding them into a convincing unity ; he also foreshadows the characteristic Anglican approach in finding the mean between the excessive elaboration of Sarum and the unceremonious brevity of the continental Reformers.

'The Order of the Purification of Women' is simply translated from Sarum, with the omission of one psalm and the sprinkling with water. Also, the woman is allowed to enter the church at the start of the service, instead of remaining at the door until the end.

Ash Wednesday shares with Easter Day the distinction of having a form of service peculiar to itself (described in the table of contents, though not in the body of the book, as 'A declaration of Scripture'). On 'the first day of Lent', after Mattins, the people are to be summoned by a bell; and, in accordance with the Injunctions of 1547, the Litany is to be said, after which the priest goes to the pulpit and begins the special service. In Sarum[31] this followed after Sext, and began with a sermon, here replaced by 'sentences of God's cursing against impenitent sinners, gathered out of the twenty-seventh chapter of Deuteronomy and other places of Scripture'. Each sentence is answered by *Amen*, as in the biblical text; and an exhortation follows, in which a large number of texts are ingeniously woven into a continuous discourse. Thereafter the service receives the usual treatment: the seven Penitential Psalms are again reduced to one (51), said kneeling, without antiphon; the suffrages are again retained; and the collects are reduced from seven to two, the second being a cento from four different prayers. The service is linked to the Introit Psalm of the Communion which follows by an antiphon partly translated from Sarum, partly based on the Epistle shortly to be heard. The Introit, incidentally, is another Penitential Psalm (6), and two more (32 and 130) are appointed for the next two Sundays; only 38 and 102 are not found a special place. Although the main body of the service, in occasion and language, is so closely based on the Sarum Blessing of the Ashes, the introductory portion has affinities with the quarterly Greater Excommunication. In 1538 Nicholas Shaxton, Bishop of Salisbury, ordered Deuteronomy 28 to be read instead of the traditional form of service,[32] and this may have influenced Cranmer's choice.

These last two services, compendiously described on the title-page as 'other Rites and Ceremonies', would naturally follow Baptism and the Litany respectively. Their position at the end of the book suggests that they may have been added in deference to conservative susceptibilities.

There remain two appendixes with self-explanatory titles, 'Of Ceremonies, why some be abolished and some retained', and 'Certain Notes for the more plain explication and decent ministration of things contained in this book'. The essay 'Of Ceremonies' is an expansion of two of the *Thirteen Articles* of 1538, which were drawn up in discussion with Lutheran envoys, and shows Cranmer under pressure from extremists on both wings. His defence is the first tentative statement of the Anglican *via media*. Excess of ceremonies is wrong; meaningful ceremonies are profitable ; so, 'some be abolished and some retained'. The argument leads in a direct line to Hooker. 'Certain Notes' fills up one or two gaps in the rubrics : for Mattins, Evensong, Baptism, and Burial the minister is to wear a surplice. This still leaves the Litany, Matrimony, Churching, and 'Ash Wednesday' undetermined, but as each of these is normally followed by the Communion, it may be assumed that the mass-vestments will be worn for them also. The bishop always wears a rochet, and carries his pastoral staff, unless it is held by his chaplain ; but no mitre is mentioned. Lastly, on Sundays when there is a sermon, the Communion may be shortened as on weekdays, and in addition the Litany may be omitted.

All the seven 'commonly called' sacraments were included in the Book of Common Prayer with the exception of Orders, and this defect was soon remedied. A year after the issue of the book, it was completed by the appearance of 'The Form and Manner of Making and Consecrating Archbishops, Bishops, Priests, and Deacons', compiled by a committee of twelve appointed under an Act of Parliament, and set forth under the Great Seal. There is some evidence that Cranmer had already completed and used the form before the end of 1549.[33] The Act had included 'other ministers of the Church', presumably sub-deacons, acolytes, exorcists, readers, and doorkeepers, but the new form quietly suppresses them. As usual, the main outlines of the medieval service are still retained, in the form followed at Canterbury and preserved in a Pontifical now at Magdalen College, Oxford. This is modified in accordance with a treatise *De Ordinatione Legitima* by Bucer, who had arrived in England in April 1549 and stayed with Cranmer until he took up the post of Regius Professor at Cambridge. He may have written the treatise to assist Cranmer in preparing the new form, or it may have originated in Cologne, since Hermann only treats of ordination in the most sketchy fashion. Bucer proposes a single form of service (*Ratio Ordinandi*) for all three orders, suggesting that some distinction should be made between them, but not providing any details.

Like the Daily Office, Baptism, and Confirmation, the services are preceded by a Preface setting out and defending the principles underlying their construction. Each service is designed to be inserted into the Communion, in such a way that all three orders could be conferred at the same service, the deacons being 'ordered' after the Epistle, the priests after the Gospel, and the bishop after the Creed. As far as deacons and priests are concerned, this is in accordance with tradition, as is the placing of the Sermon at the very beginning of the service. If deacons are being ordered, the candidates are presented immediately, and the Litany is said, with a proper final collect; this previously took the place of *Gloria in excelsis*. The Communion Service then takes its normal course to the end of the Epistle. If priests are being ordered, there is a choice of three proper Introit Psalms, selected by Bucer. The collect is that of the day, but a choice of proper Epistles is provided, for the first time. Those for priests are again chosen by Bucer; one of them is 1 Timothy 3, the last nine verses of which are also appointed for deacons. A peculiarly Anglican feature follows in the Oath of the King's Supremacy, which leads to the Examination of the Candidates for the diaconate, based on Bucer, though not as closely as in the Examination for the priesthood, which Bucer no doubt regarded as the essential order. Laying-on of hands and tradition, or handing-over, of the New Testament complete the ordering, the tradition of stole and dalmatic being omitted.

The Gospel is read by a deacon, if any have been made; if priests are being ordered, there is a choice of proper Gospels from Bucer; otherwise that of the day is read. Following Canterbury usage, the hymn *Veni, creator Spiritus* is then sung in a translation which certainly lacks Cranmer's requisites of 'grace and facility'. The candidates for the priesthood are now presented, and the Litany follows, if it has not already been said, then the Oath of the King's Supremacy. The bishop delivers a long exhortation on the duties of the ministry, after which he examines the candidates, and, after a short period of silent prayer, utters a thanksgiving. All this section follows Bucer very closely with slight omissions, one of them a prayer for the gift of the Holy Spirit. The laying-on of hands is done by bishop and priests together: here Sarum, Bucer, and Cranmer are unanimous; but the bishop's words, 'Receive the Holy Ghost', are the traditional formula, not Bucer's (hence the omission noted above). Omitting the tradition of stole and chasuble, and the blessing and unction of the priests' hands, the bishop delivers to the priests the traditional chalice 'with the bread', and also a Bible, concentrating the Anglican interpretation of the Reformation in a single gesture. The congregation then sing the Creed, and the rest of the Communion Service follows as usual, except that between the Prayer of Thanksgiving and the Blessing two collects are inserted, one for each order. That for deacons is based on the Sarum prayer at the laying-on of hands; that for priests is Cranmer's own.

'The Form of Consecrating of an Archbishop or Bishop' begins with the same choice of Introit Psalms, one of the same Epistles, and one of the same Gospels as for the Ordering of Priests; the alternative Gospel, though peculiar to this service, was among those chosen by Bucer. After the Creed 'the elected Bishop' is presented by two other bishops, all wearing surplices and copes (unlike the deacons and priests, who wore albs). The King's Mandate is read, the Oath of the King's Supremacy is administered, followed by the Oath of due obedience to the Archbishop. The Archbishop or officiating bishop then moves the congregation to prayer, and the Litany follows, if not said before. It was traditional that a bishop should be examined before consecration, so that here the questions owe as much to Sarum as to Bucer; the prayer before laying-on of hands is likewise an amalgam of the two sources. The old ceremony is retained of laying the Bible on the bishop's neck, and so is the tradition of the staff, though unction of hands and tradition of the ring and the mitre are omitted. In each of the three ceremonies retained, the accompanying formula consists of words translated from the Latin, welded on to verses from the New Testament. The rest of the Communion follows, with a final collect composed by the process just described.

The ordination services show Cranmer already departing from the methods he had employed in the preparation of the book of 1549. Nowhere in that book did he follow a Reformed form of service so closely as in the Ordering of Priests, nor did he introduce scriptural quotations into medieval collects with the same freedom as in the Consecration of a Bishop. Even his handling of the traditional structure shows a greater readiness to alter as well as to abbreviate.

5 The Second Prayer Book of Edward VI

A book has now been published a month or two back, which the English churches received with the greatest satisfaction. . . . You will see that the summary of doctrine cannot be found fault with, although certain ceremonies are retained in that book which may appear useless, and perhaps hurtful, unless a candid interpretation be put upon them.

DRYANDER to Bullinger, 5 June 1549[1]

I am so much offended with that book . . . that if it be not corrected, I neither can nor will communicate with the Church in the administration of the Supper.

HOOPER to Bullinger, 27 March 1550[2]

REACTIONS to the Prayer Book of 1549 ranged from one end of the ecclesiastical spectrum to the other. Princess Mary simply continued to have Mass said by her chaplains in the old way. Edmund Bonner took no steps to introduce the new book into the diocese of London until ordered to do so by the Council in August, after which he 'did the office . . . sadly and discreetly'.[3] Many priests used the book, but disguised it in all the external trappings and gestures of the Mass, converting the popular 'Lady Mass' into a 'Communion of Our Lady'.[4] Stephen Gardiner found the book's eucharistic doctrine 'not distant from the Catholic faith',[5] and would have been prepared to use it, if incarceration in the Tower had not prevented him. The feelings of the ordinary worshipper received their most vigorous expression in the West Country, where the first use of the book was the signal for a rising which spread with surprising rapidity. The rebels compared the Communion Service to a 'Christmas game', and demanded the restoration of all the old ways.[6] The refugee divines were thankful for such reformation as had been effected, while obviously hoping for and expecting a

The beginning of Vespers, from a Book of Hours, 1407

Pater

ᴪOVRE FATHER, ᴪc.

℟ Then lykewyse he shall saye.

O God make spede to saue me.

Aunswere.

O Lorde make haste to helpe me.

Priest.

Glory be to the father, ⁊ to the sonne: and to the holy gost.

As it was in the begynnyng, is nowe, and euer shalbe:
worlde without ende. Amen.   Prayse ye the Lorde.

And from Easter to Trinitie Sonday.

Alleluya.

As before is appoynted at Mattyns.

Then Psalmes in ordre as they be appoynted in the Table
for Psalmes, except there be propre Psalmes appointed for
that daye. Then a lesson of the olde testamente, as it is appoynted lykewise in the kalender, excepte there be proper
lessons appointed for that daye. After that (*Magnificat anima
mea dominum*) in Englishe, as foloweth.

*Magnificat
Luc. i.*

My soule doeth magnifie the Lorde.

And my spirite hath reioysed in God my sauiour.

For he hath regarded the lowelynesse, of his had-
maiden.

For beholde, from henceforth all generacions shall call
me blessed.

For he that is myghtie hath magnifyed me : and holy
is his name.

And his mercy is on them that feare him : throughout
all generacions.

He hath shewed strength with his arme : he hath scate-
red the proude in the imaginacion of their heartes.

He hath put downe the mightie from their seate : and
hath exalted the humble and meke.

He hath filled the hungry, with good thynges : and the
ryche

further instalment; they were prepared to tolerate the retention of ceremonies only as a temporary expedient. Even this was unacceptable to John Hooper, the leading English disciple of Zwingli, who pronounced the book 'very defective, and of doubtful construction, and, in some respects indeed, manifestly impious'.[7]

The fall of the Protector, Somerset, in the autumn of 1549 gave rise to a rumour that the book would be withdrawn, and some of the Oxford colleges actually reintroduced the Mass. The Council, now led by Warwick, reacted vigorously, and issued an Order calling in all copies of the medieval service-books (with the exception of the pontificals, which had not yet been superseded), to be defaced and abolished.[8] *The King's Primer* was allowed to continue in use, provided that prayers to the saints were deleted; and a new edition was published, in which this had been done. A third edition, in 1551, omitted the 'Hail, Mary' and various other unacceptable passages. Any statues still standing were to be destroyed.

Gradually the older bishops were replaced by men of the New Learning. Gardiner and Bonner had been sent to prison for preaching against the new doctrine of the Eucharist; Rugg resigned; Heath was deprived for refusing to accept the Ordination Services, and Day for refusing to remove the altars. One of the new men was Hooper, who, appointed to preach before the king in Lent 1550, used the opportunity to deliver some trenchant criticisms of the Prayer Book services, more especially of the oaths and vestments required in the Ordination Services, which had appeared only a day or two before the sermon in question was delivered.[9] He was soon after nominated to the bishopric of Gloucester, but refused to take the oaths in the statutory form or to wear vestments for his consecration. The oath was altered by the king's own hand, but a long controversy ensued over the vestments.[10] Cranmer and Ridley were probably quite ready to abolish these by law, but they took their stand on the duty

D

of obeying the law while it remained unaltered. They were supported in this attitude by Bucer and Peter Martyr, while Hooper was encouraged by Bullinger and John à Lasco, a fellow-Zwinglian. Hooper was sent to prison, and eventually agreed to wear the vestments for the occasion, so long as he was not expected to wear them in his diocese. It was the first skirmish in a campaign which was to last more than a hundred years.

Meanwhile Ridley had led a drive against various practices which tended to perpetuate the ethos of the Mass. First, he carried out a visitation of the diocese of London, to which he had been translated in April 1550. This was accompanied by the issue of a set of Injunctions forbidding, among other things, a detailed list of gestures intended to 'counterfeit the popish Mass, as to kiss the Lord's Table; washing his fingers at every time in the Communion; blessing his eyes with the paten or sudary; or crossing his head with the paten; shifting of the book from one place to another; laying down and licking the chalice of the Communion; holding up his fingers, hands, or thumbs, joined towards his temples; breathing upon the bread or chalice; showing the sacrament openly before the distribution of the Communion; ringing of sacring bells; or setting any light upon the Lord's board at any time; and finally to use no other ceremonies than are appointed in the King's *Book of Common Prayers*, or kneeling otherwise than is in the said book'.[11] He also exhorted incumbents and churchwardens to replace their high altar by a table set in the place 'thought most meet by their discretion and agreement'; he himself carried out this procedure at St Paul's in June. By November the Council was ready to order this substitution everywhere. The table was placed in a diversity of positions: Ridley himself had it standing east and west 'in the midst of the upper quire', with the minister on the south side. At the same time he had the iron grates of the quire bricked up, to prevent anyone watching the communion without communicating.[12] Throughout the country, churches were being limewashed, with the Royal Arms and texts from Scripture taking the place of the medieval wall-paintings.

While the supporters of the old religion were being brought into line, pressure was building up for further revision. Already in September 1549 Calvin had written to Somerset, urging the removal of prayers for the dead, the chrisom, and unction.[13] The Zwinglians, few but influential, were pressing for the utmost simplicity of dress, furnishing, and movement. Bucer had been studying the Prayer Book at Cambridge, and submitted a detailed and closely argued criticism in a document now known as the *Censura*, which he presented to Bishop Goodrich of Ely on 5 January 1551. He sent a copy to Peter Martyr, by then Regius Professor at Oxford, where he had been defending a doctrine of the Eucharist very similar to Bucer's own. He had been asked for his suggestions, but had not enough English to read the book in the original language, and was compelled to rely on an incomplete Latin translation by Sir John Cheke. His ideas had agreed with Bucer's as far as they went, so he summarized Bucer's criticisms of the portions which he had not read himself, and sent them on to Cranmer as a supplement to his own comments, which, with two exceptions, have not survived. Cranmer, who had been pressing him for them, then told him that the bishops had already agreed in conference that many changes should be made. What the changes were to be, Cranmer did not tell him, nor did Martyr dare to ask. Cheke, however, told him that, if the bishops were reluctant, the king would use his authority to get the changes through Parliament.[14]

The two points which are known to be due to Martyr are, first, an exhortation against non-communicating attendance, the Latin original of which is to be found in his *Loci Communes* ;[15] and secondly, he urged that the whole of the Communion Service should be said in the presence of the sick man, instead of the priest bringing the consecrated elements from the service in church. He believed that the Words of Institution 'apply rather to men than either to the bread or to the wine', and therefore also disapproved of the rubric directing reconsecration.[16] The latter, of course, is not included in the 1549 service: had Martyr seen it done in Christ Church, or was he working from a translation of *The Order of the Communion*?

The influence of Bucer's *Censura* on the Book of 1552 is extremely difficult to assess. Bishop Goodrich certainly informed Cranmer of the contents. But some of Bucer's points had already been made by Peter Martyr in his own *censura*; and, of the points that were dealt with as Bucer desired, some had probably been decided upon already in order to cut the ground from under Gardiner's feet, others were also being urged by Hooper, others again are complaints made by all eager reformers of the time. Bucer submitted approximately sixty criticisms, of which certainly twenty-three, perhaps twenty-five, were embodied in the Book, and an equal number simply ignored. At seven points Bucer offers an alternative form of words, but this is never adopted: the point is taken, but dealt with in some other way. In four cases his suggestions are definitely rejected, and one of these is the matter to which he attached the greatest importance of all, the retention of the words 'whomsoever shall be partakers of this Holy Communion may worthily receive the most precious Body and Blood of thy Son Jesus Christ, and be fulfilled with thy grace and heavenly benediction, and made one body with thy Son Jesus Christ, that he may dwell in them and they in him'. Although warned by both Poullain and à Lasco not to 'raise any controversy on the matter of the Eucharist',[17] he devotes five pages out of forty-eight to this one point, beginning with the words 'I pray the Lord to grant that these words may be so kept as they are placed, for they are thoroughly pure and in agreement with the words of the Holy Spirit'. He goes on to defend them against all Zwinglian objections, states his own position, and ends with an appeal to those concerned to remember that the eyes of the whole world are upon them, and to show 'how carefully you cherish both the integrity of God's Word and the universal consensus of the true Church, and that you will not rashly and irreligiously admit any novelty, as men of ill-will report'. The words, however, were removed.

But if the influence of the *Censura* can be overestimated, it remains of unique interest as a critique of 1549. Bucer speaks appreciatively of the Communion Service, 'so pure and religiously conformed to the Word of God, especially for the time at which it was made', and he finds many points to commend in the Occasional Offices. There are also interesting sidelights on current practice, as for instance the comment that 'the congregation does not usually gather for Mattins and Evensong'. He confirms that the popish Mass is still counterfeited ; and he includes an impassioned attack on 'the great and unseasonable abuse of bells' and 'the inane sound of tintinnabulation'.[18] Various points in which his advice was taken will be noted below. But any further chance of his influencing the course of events was ended by his death within a few weeks of handing over the *Censura*.

Gardiner's approach was very different. At his trial in December 1550 he handed in *An Explication and Assertion of the true Catholic Faith,* in which he replied to Cranmer's *Defence of the true and Catholic Doctrine of the Sacrament of the Body and Blood of our Saviour Christ,* an exposition of the doctrine underlying the 1549 Book. Gardiner's method was both ingenious and irritating : he picked out various passages in 1549 which appeared to express the Catholic doctrine rather than Cranmer's, and warmly commended them.[19] The only way to deal with this situation was to alter the text at these points. The effect of Gardiner's criticisms was to make the next revision more narrowly Reformed in doctrine, and harder for a well-disposed Catholic to accept.

Revision of the text of 1549 had begun at once : in the

'Clerk's Book' of August 1549 the translation of *Te Deum* is improved, and the Litany has been placed between Mattins and Holy Communion. Merbecke, in 1550, inserts an Amen at the end of the first section of the Canon. The oath in the Ordination Services was altered within months of publication, as mentioned above. Two influential foreigners published forms of service early in 1551, which seem to have left some mark upon the 1552 Prayer Book. They were Poullain's *Liturgia Sacra*, a Latin translation of the 1545 version of Calvin's Strasbourg rite, itself derived from Bucer; and à Lasco's *Forma ac Ratio*, in the main Zwinglian tradition. But although the bishops had agreed on 'many changes' by January 1551, it was not until April 1552 that a new Act of Uniformity was passed, which referred to 1549 as 'a very godly order, agreeable to the Word of God and the primitive Church, very comfortable to all good people . . . and most profitable to the state of this realm', and explained that, because 'in the use and exercise' of the book doubts had arisen about 'the fashion and manner of the ministration of the same', it had been 'faithfully and godly perused, explained, and made fully perfect'. The two purposes of 'more plain and manifest explication' (an echo of *Certain Notes*), and 'more perfection of . . . some places where it is necessary to make [it] more earnest and fit to stir Christian people to the true honouring of Almighty God' cover a number of the changes made, but by no means all, unless the second purpose is very liberally interpreted.[20]

'Explication' may be the reason for printing the essay 'Of Ceremonies' as a second preface, and providing 'A Table of Proper Psalms and Lessons' and 'An Almanack for 19 Years'. Directions for saying the Litany are now placed at its head, instead of in the Communion Service, and the procedures for the Second Sunday after Christmas and the Twenty-Sixth Sunday after Trinity are explained. The services for 'the Purification of Women' and 'Ash Wednesday' have new titles; the priest is relieved of the duty of throwing dust into the grave; but there is little else that can be included in this category.

Changes designed 'to stir Christian people' include the requirement of saying the Office daily, with a bell to summon the people; more congregational participation, especially in the Creeds and the Lord's Prayer, though not, as Bucer suggested, in the Prayers of Humble Access and Thanksgiving; communion at least three times a year, instead of once (though even Zwingli required four times!); and above all, a new introduction to both the Holy Communion, and Mattins and Evensong. In pursuance of a general policy of dropping the old names, the latter are now called Morning and Evening Prayer, while 'the Mass', 'anthems', and 'Ash Wednesday' no longer appear anywhere in the book. There is also a certain diminution of seasonal material: the Easter Procession is incorporated into Morning Prayer, 'Alleluia' is no longer said in Eastertide, nor is *Benedicite* confined to Lent. Morning and Evening Prayer are to be said where 'the people may best hear', not necessarily in the quire; but the chancels are to 'remain as they have done', not be shut up, as Hooper wished.[21]

Some changes come under the heading of making the book 'fully perfect': the Athanasian Creed is to be said thirteen times a year instead of six; and psalms are provided as alternatives to the gospel canticles. Four new occasional prayers are added, one of which, 'In the time of any common plague or sickness', was obviously prompted by the 'sweating sickness' which swept across the country in the summer of 1551.

The penitential introduction prefixed to Morning and Evening Prayer represents the largest accession of new material since *The Order of the Communion*, to which it is very similar. The Sentences of Scripture are read first instead of last, and the Invitation is longer than 'Ye that do truly . . .'; but the Confession and Absolution have a distinct resemblance to those in the Communion. The idea of beginning the Office with confession is already found in Quiñones, though there only at Mattins, and *after* the Lord's Prayer; but the Strasbourg services, from the earliest onwards, always began with a confession; and Bucer introduced this feature into Hermann, the only form which provides a newly composed Absolution, all the others being content with a sentence of Scripture. Poullain and à Lasco have also been suggested as sources, but their influence seems to have been confined to stray phrases. In the Invitation, 'our manifold sins and wickedness' comes from the Confession in the Communion Service; the second sentence seems to be an expansion of Hermann's rubric: 'it is accordance with true piety that whenever we appear before God in his church, before everything we should acknowledge and confess our sins'; the Exhortation before the 1544 Litany includes the words 'infinite mercy, grace, and goodness' and 'our necessary food and sustenance, both of body and soul'. 'Wherefore I pray and beseech you, as many as are here present' echoes Hermann's baptism sermon: '*Quapropter* . . . *hortor et obsecro vos, quotquot adestis*', but a similar phrase is also found in Martyr's Exhortation; it is impossible to say who borrowed it from whom. Martyr also begins: 'Dearly beloved brethren . . .'. Brightman points out further similarities with *The King's Book*, Poullain, and à Lasco.[22]

In the Confession the phrase 'Spare thou them, O God, that confess their faults' seems to be derived from the Commination, which also shares three of the scriptural quotations in the new section. 'We have offended against thy holy laws' is paralleled in Poullain; 'we have left undone . . .' goes back to Strasbourg 1524 (had Bucer brought it with him?); 'but thou, O Lord, have mercy upon us' takes us back to the Breviary: '*Tu autem, Domine, miserere nostri*'. The Absolution begins with a quotation from Ezekiel found in Hermann, à Lasco, and the Commination, and goes on with part of Hermann's Absolution: 'hath left this power . . . I, the minister . . . declare and pronounce remission of sins . . .

which, being repentant . . . all them which be sorry for their sins . . . do truly believe . . .' (quoted from the English translation of 1547 and 1548). Hermann's Confession, with its 'give and increase thy Holy Spirit in us' may be the origin of 'grant us . . . his Holy Spirit'.

From all these references it may be concluded that Cranmer (if he was the author, which some would deny)[23] was, as so often, relying on a very retentive memory, rather than deliberately copying any one model. The reason for the addition of this section was probably the growing realization that there would be many occasions on which there were no communicants, and hence (since the service would end with the Offertory) no expression of penitence and forgiveness. By adding this at the beginning of Morning Prayer, the need was met, and all weekdays were also provided for, when there was not even an Ante-Communion.

The changes in the Communion Service were of three kinds, of structure, of language, and of ambience. Gardiner's arguments had made it necessary to remove the Prayer for the Church and 'We do not presume . . .' from the Canon, because in that context they suggested respectively a propitiatory sacrifice for living and dead, and adoration of the consecrated elements. So the Prayer for the Church was placed immediately after the Offertory, and 'We do not presume . . .' before the consecration. As long ago as 1523 Zwingli had laid down that the most objectionable feature of the Canon was that communion did not follow consecration immediately.[24] This failing was now remedied. The Lord's Prayer was placed after the Communion as a congregational response, followed by the Prayer of Oblation (which had been detached from the residue of the Canon) as an alternative to the Prayer of Thanksgiving, where it also was in no danger of suggesting propitiatory sacrifice. The Invitation, Confession, Absolution, and Comfortable Words were placed before *Sursum corda* ; and the Exhortation which preceded them in *The Order of the Communion*, but had been detached and made optional in 1549, was restored to its original context and made invariable once more. It was preceded by Peter Martyr's new Exhortation and the other from *The Order of the Communion*, each now for optional use. Martyr's piece is directed against non-communicating attendance, which was being actively discouraged in 1551.

In the course of these changes the short catena 'Christ, our paschal Lamb ...' disappeared altogether. *Gloria in excelsis* was moved to the end of the service to build up the 'sacrifice of praise and thanksgiving'; this may have been a late change, as a manuscript plainsong setting of the Communion Service, while including all the other changes, still has *Gloria* in its 1549 position.[25] The Ten Commandments had been recited in English after the Gospel since 1547, but their insertion at the beginning of the service was in all probability due to Hooper, who regarded them as 'the abridgment and epitome of the whole Bible, compendiously containing the whole law and the gospel', and urged his clergy to rehearse them to their parishioners.[26] Bucer, Calvin, and Poullain had all adopted this position; and both Luther and Calvin had produced metrical versions with *Kyrie eleison* as a refrain after each verse. There was thus ample precedent for the procedure adopted in 1552. 'Write all these thy laws in our hearts' is another borrowing from the earliest Strasbourg services (see p. 37).

The changes in language were nearly all dictated by doctrinal controversy. The Prayer for the Church was not only moved, but, as both Bucer and Hooper wished, shorn of any reference to the saints or the departed; it is now only for the 'Church militant here in earth'. A whole series of changes were aimed at removing any suspicion of transubstantiation. New words of administration were provided, and the Prayer of Thanksgiving was altered from 'hast vouchsafed to feed us in these holy mysteries' to 'dost vouchsafe to feed us which have duly received these holy mysteries'. There is a similar example in the Third Exhortation

THE ORDER OF 1552

1549	1552
Lord's Prayer	Lord's Prayer
Collect for Purity	Collect for Purity
Kyrie eleison	Ten Commandments, with *Kyrie*
Gloria in excelsis	
Salutation	
Collect of the day	Collect of the day
Collect for the King	Collect for the King
Epistle	Epistle
Gospel	Gospel
Creed	Creed
Sermon *or* Homily	Sermon *or* Homily
Exhortation II or III*	
Offertory	Offertory
	Prayer for the Church
	Exhortation I or II*
	Exhortation III
	You that do truly . . .
	Confession
	Absolution
	ComfortableWords
Sursum corda	*Sursum corda*
	We do not presume . . .
Canon: Prayer for the Church	
Consecration	Consecration
Oblation	
Lord's Prayer	
Christ, our paschal Lamb . . .	
You that do truly . . .	
Confession	
Absolution	
Comfortable Words	
We do not presume . . .	
Communion	Communion
Agnus Dei	
Post-Communion Sentence	
	Lord's Prayer
Thanksgiving	Oblation *or* Thanksgiving
	Gloria in excelsis
Blessing	Blessing

* Optional.

(First of 1549), and the phrase 'holy mysteries' is removed altogether, despite Bucer's commendation, from 'We do not presume . . .' Instead of praying that the bread and wine 'may be unto us the body and blood', the prayer now asks that we 'may be partakers of the body and blood'. This change was provoked by Gardiner, though Bucer also disliked the phrase. In fact the whole epiclesis disappears, and the gap is patched up with phrases from the next section of the Canon. The *Benedictus* was removed from the *Sanctus*, presumably because it might suggest a corporeal presence. The words quoted on p. 100 also disappeared, despite Bucer's plea, 'let no-one shrink from the words of the presence of the Lord'.[27] The elements are no longer referred to as 'gifts', and the ministry of angels is no longer prayed for (Bucer said it had been misinterpreted). Finally, three changes relate to the Christian life: it is no longer 'our duty . . . to come to these holy mysteries'; self-examination is to be 'by the rule of God's commandments' (Hooper again?); and confession is not to be secret.

The remaining changes are concerned with the actual performance of the service. Vestments are forbidden, and for all services the only permissible garments are the rochet for bishops and the surplice for priests and deacons : this change was demanded by all Reformers. The prototype is no longer High Mass, but Low Mass. Singing is virtually abolished, being only permitted for *Gloria in excelsis* as an alternative to saying it. As a result, the Introit Psalms are suppressed, even at ordinations ; so is the *Agnus Dei* and the Post-Communion ; and the Kyrie, Creed, and *Sanctus* may only be said. In September 1552 the organ in St Paul's was silenced.[28] The deacon is no longer allotted a share in the service. The table is to stand in the best place for audibility, with a fair white linen cloth upon it (Hooper's phrase) ; and the priest is to stand at the north side. Instead of the people coming up with their alms, the churchwardens are to collect them, as in Hermann ; and there are no longer any directions about placing the elements on the table. What Bucer described as 'those little black crosses' have gone, and so have the manual acts, again for fear of suggesting transubstantiation, though Hooper would have liked to retain the fraction.[29] Ordinary bread is to be used, and put into the communicants' hands, not their mouths; the latter point was made by both Bucer and Hooper, and had already been put into practice by Ridley.[30]

Scholars, such as Gregory Dix and C. C. Richardson, who hold that Cranmer was a Zwinglian can make out a much more plausible case in respect of the 1552 service. For Dix, Cranmer was 'a Zwinglian, not of the left wing like Megander, nor of the right like Calvin and Farel, but of the centre like Bullinger'.[31] Richardson admits that there is a difference between Cranmer and Zwingli. 'For Cranmer the Eucharist is more important than it is for Zwingli'; 'a quarterly communion suited Zwingli very well, but Cranmer wanted it daily'; Cranmer can describe the sacraments as 'effectual signs of grace' in the *45 Articles* of 1551, a phrase 'no parallel to which can be found in Zwingli'.[32] For C. H. Smyth, Cranmer is a Bucerian: 'the doctrine that Cranmer maintained consistently ... from his conversion in 1546 to his martyrdom ten years later, may be identified with that of Bucer, but also distinguished from it';[33] while G. B. Timms sees Cranmer as 'what has been called a "dynamic receptionist" ',[34] having close affinities with both Calvin and Bucer. C. W. Dugmore prefers to set him in a long tradition going back to Ratramnus and, ultimately, to Augustine, though he agrees that Bucer comes very close to Ratramnus. As he well points out, the exposition of the threefold sacrifice in 1549 (see p. 79) is preserved intact in 1552, despite the rearrangement of the Canon.[35] P. N. Brooks traces Cranmer's evolution through a Lutheran phase to a position not unlike that of Oecolampadius, who provided many of his patristic quotations, though Cranmer was never 'a blind disciple'.[36] Whatever conclusion may be reached about Cranmer's

private beliefs, 1552 certainly comes very near to Zwing-
lianism, but it has not yet been shown that this is the only
doctrine which can justifiably be found in it.

'Public Baptism' is vigorously remodelled. To begin with,
the whole service takes place at the font. Bucer suggested
this, but he also suggested that baptism should take place at
the Communion Service (in which he was some four hundred
years before his time as far as the Church of England was
concerned); on the other hand the Burial Service is also
confined to one place, though he had not made any such
suggestion. The superstitious ceremonies of exorcism, giving
the chrisom, and unction were removed, together with the
blessing of the font, and the godparents' repetition of the
Creed and Lord's Prayer; all this with Bucer's approval,
except for the exorcism, which he would have kept in the
form of a prayer.[37] The prayers at the blessing of the font
were incorporated into the service, and the questions were
addressed to the godparents instead of the child, as Bucer
wished. The godparents now offer, not their own vicarious
faith, but a promise of the child's future faith. Signing with
the cross was kept, as it had a useful role to play; Hooper
would have liked it dropped, but Bucer commended it.

The next step was to make the service illustrate the
purpose of baptism as set forth in 1549: that the children
'may be baptized with water and the Holy Ghost, and
received into Christ's holy Church, and be made lively
members of the same'. Reception into the Church is suitably
associated with the sign of the cross, which is therefore made
on the child's forehead immediately *after* baptism, with its
accompanying form, 'Receive the sign . . .' Bucer pointed
out that it was useless to address the words 'thou shalt not be
ashamed to confess thy faith in Christ crucified' to an infant,
and suggested turning them into a prayer to God, but
Cranmer preferred to make them into a statement on behalf
of the congregation.

Lastly, the conclusion of the service was built up in the

same way as that of the Communion. After the signing comes a congregational recitation of the Lord's Prayer, and a thanksgiving by the priest which echoes the Prayers of Oblation and Thanksgiving :

Communion, 1549	*Baptism, 1552*
very members incorporate in thy mystical body . . .	grafted into the body of Christ's congregation . . . incorporate him into thy holy congregation . . .
most humbly beseeching thee to grant . . .	and humbly we beseech thee to grant . . .
heirs through hope of thy everlasting kingdom . . .	inheritor of thine everlasting kingdom . . .
most hearty thanks for the innumerable benefits . . .	give thanks unto God for these benefits . . .

There is also an echo of the Collect for Christmas Day. The rest of the prayer, a paraphrase of Romans 6 : 4–6, may perhaps have been suggested by Hermann's use of the passage. Luther's widely adopted 'Flood Prayer' at the beginning of the service is much altered, and greatly improved, affording a rare glimpse into Cranmer's workshop. Normally only the original and Cranmer's final form have survived, but here we can see the process by which Cranmer gradually refined and clarified the clumsy and wordy compositions of the continental Reformers.

'Private Baptism' is little altered ; it won an unusually warm commendation from Bucer ('everything is set forth in a holy manner ; may it be kept so'). Now that signing follows baptism, it might have been included in the reception of children already baptized in emergency. Instead, it is stated that the child is 'received into the number of the children of God' 'by the laver of regeneration in Baptism'. The transfer of the questions to the godparents is here carried a stage further by including the words 'in the name of this child' (compare Hermann's '*infantis nomine*'). The Lord's Prayer is

THE ORDER OF 1552

1549	1552
Dearly beloved . . .	Dearly beloved . . .
Almighty and everlasting God . . .	Almighty and everlasting God . . .
Receive the sign of the holy Cross . . .	
Almighty and immortal God . . .	Almighty and immortal God . . .
I command thee, unclean spirit . . .	
The Lord be with you.	
Gospel : Mark 10.	Gospel : Mark 10.
Friends, you hear . . .	Friends, you hear . . .
Lord's Prayer	
Creed	
Almighty and everlasting God . . .	Almighty and everlasting God . . .
The Lord vouchsafe . . .	
Well-beloved friends . . .	Well-beloved friends . . .
Dost thou forsake . . .	Dost thou forsake . . .
	O merciful God . . .
I baptize thee . . .	I baptize thee . . .
	We receive this child (cross)
Take this white vesture . . .	
Almighty God (unction)	
	Seeing now, dearly beloved . . .
	Lord's Prayer
	We yield thee hearty thanks . . .
Forasmuch as these children . . .	Forasmuch as these children . . .

Henry VIII, by Holbein

Thomas Cranmer in 1546, aged 57, by G. Flicke

still said in its old place (but not the Creed, though the minister's invitation to recite this is still left in!); there is already a thanksgiving at the end, so that there is no need for the alteration made in Public Baptism.

The Catechism is only altered to gratify Hooper's enthusiasm for the Ten Commandments, which are now given in the fuller version of Exodus 20, complete with reference. In Confirmation, however, the signing with the cross and its prayer are removed; and God is asked, not to send down the Holy Spirit upon the candidates, but merely to strengthen them with him. The laying-on of hands is accompanied by a new prayer based on Hermann. Matrimony is unaltered, except for the removal of all reference to gold and silver 'tokens of spousage', and to the apocryphal Book of Tobit, which is also expelled from the Communion Offertory Sentences and from the Visitation of the Sick.

The last-named service loses the last trace of the Penitential Psalms, and the two antiphons are no longer so described, though they are still not 'cut off'. Unction, with its prayer and psalm, is suppressed, and, in accordance with Peter Martyr's suggestion, reservation is replaced by fresh consecration. Following continental custom, the whole service for 'Burial of the Dead' is to be said at the graveside. Two prayers of commendation and all the psalms are omitted, and committal (with a new exordium from Hermann) is followed immediately by the Lesson; after which the service ends with the Lord's Prayer, a prayer made up of phrases from the suppressed prayers and from Hermann, and the collect from the Communion 'when there is a burial'. Even this is a lengthy service by continental standards. The Communion, of course, disappears altogether, as Bucer desired.

'The Purification of Women' is now renamed 'The Thanksgiving of Women after Childbirth, commonly called the Churching of Women'; and takes place near the table, instead of at the quire door, which in practice may not have made much difference. The woman cannot now 'offer her chrisom', since none has been given. The 'Declaration of Scripture' is now called 'A Commination against Sinners', and is not restricted to, or even appointed on, Ash Wednesday (Bucer had suggested quarterly use); the only other change is the removal of the word 'anthem'. 'Of Ceremonies' has been moved to the beginning of the book, and 'Certain Notes' has been superseded.

The Ordination Services are now included in the book, though still with a separate title-page. Hooper's influence has dictated such changes as were made: he specially mentions the invocation of 'all saints and the holy Evangelist' in the Oath of the King's Supremacy, the wearing of albs, and the tradition of the chalice and paten.[38] In keeping with this approach, there is no tradition of the pastoral staff, nor do the presenting bishops carry them, nor do they wear surplices and copes; the Bible is delivered to the bishop-designate, not laid upon his neck.

At the last moment an additional note was added on kneeling at the Communion, the so-called 'Black Rubric'. Kneeling had been one of Hooper's grievances,[39] and had been raised also by à Lasco; but it was a sermon by John Knox in September 1552 which brought matters to a head. Cranmer was required by the Council to reconsider the Prayer Book rubric on the subject, which newly enforced kneeling, in consultation with Ridley, Peter Martyr, and others. He refused to alter what had been decided upon after long deliberation by 'a great many bishops and others of the best learned', and approved by Parliament.[40] Instead, a short note was appended to the rubrics after the Communion Service, explaining that kneeling is meant to express gratitude, and to avoid profanation and disorder, but does not imply any adoration of 'the sacramental bread or wine' or of 'any real and essential presence there being of Christ's natural flesh and blood'.

The Prayer Book of 1552 was to come into use from All

Saints' Day. It was only one of a number of official documents issued or in preparation during that year. A corpus of doctrine, ritual, ceremonial, and law had been formed during the last years of King Henry with *The King's Book*, the emended Breviary, Cranmer's second scheme, *The King's Primer*, the *Rationale of Ceremonies*, the Six Articles, and the Canon Law as modified by Act of Parliament; this was now to be replaced by a reformed version of each several part. *A short Catechism . . . set forth by the King's Majesty's authority, for all Schoolmasters to teach*, written by John Ponet, bishop of Winchester, and *Forty-two Articles*, drawn up by Cranmer, were printed together in English and in Latin, and appeared in May 1553. As Brightman says, these two formularies 'whether intentionally or not, answered in some sort to Bucer's aspiration for a longer Catechism and a Confession of faith'.[41] The same year there also appeared *A Primer, or Book of Private Prayer* (as opposed to Common Prayer), also 'set forth by the King's Majesty'. This is totally different in content from *The King's Primer*, even in the latter's purified state, and might be called the first completely reformed Primer. It contains the Catechism, some graces, a form of self-examination, the Prayer Book services of Morning and Evening Prayer with proper psalms and lessons for each day of the week, the Litany, the collects after the Communion, the proper collects, and a large number of 'godly prayers for divers purposes'. Seven of the proper lessons are, surprisingly, taken from Ecclesiasticus; and at the end of Morning Prayer stands 'The Fourth Collect, for the King'. This familiar prayer, which had originally appeared in the *Psalms* of John Fisher in 1544 and the *Prayers* of Queen Katharine in 1545, now received official recognition for the first time, though in a longer form than that which eventually reached the Prayer Book.

Cranmer had also prepared *Fifty-four Articles* 'for an uniform order to be observed in every church within this realm', which have disappeared without trace, and a new body of Canon Law, the *Reformatio Legum Ecclesiasticarum*. But before this could be authorized, Edward VI died, in July 1553, and the succession passed to the Catholic Princess Mary.

6 Rome, Canterbury, and Geneva

It appears indeed most extraordinary to me, if I may be allowed, most accomplished and very dear brethren, to speak my sentiments without offence, that you can persuade yourselves that you cannot with a safe conscience subject yourselves and your churches to vestiarian bondage.

BULLINGER to Humphrey and Sampson, 1 May 1566[1]

Our excellent Queen, as you know, holds the helm, and directs it hitherto according to her pleasure. But we are awaiting the guidance of the divine Spirit, which is all we can do.

BISHOP HORNE to Bullinger, 8 August 1571[2]

MARY's first step towards the restoration of the Catholic liturgy was to repeal all the Edwardine legislation, and restore the position as it was in the last year of Henry VIII. This allowed the continuance of the 1544 Litany, and at some time after Mary's marriage to Philip of Spain in July 1554, an edition was printed which still kept the text of 1552. There is also a copy of the 1553 Primer extant with Mary's name substituted for Edward's, but these issues can only be regarded as attempts to salvage something from otherwise worthless stock. Later in 1554 the full Sarum rite was restored, and the history of the Book of Common Prayer during the rest of Mary's reign must be sought outside England. North of the Border the Book of 1552 continued in general use until 1559. On the Continent its history was more eventful.[3] In June 1554 about two hundred exiles arrived at Frankfurt am Main, where Poullain had already established himself and his congregation of Walloon Calvinists. The exiles had to have their form of service licensed, and they began by perusing the English order, and decided to omit the Litany and all answering aloud after the minister, 'and many other things also', such as the use of the surplice. This modified Prayer Book soon gave place to a Calvinistic form, consisting of a new Confession, 'of more effect'; a metrical psalm 'in a plain tune' (i.e. in unison); prayer for the assistance of the Holy Spirit; the sermon; a general prayer for all estates and for our country of England, leading into the Lord's Prayer; the Creed; another psalm; and the blessing, 'The peace of God . . .' Of this service, only the blessing was derived from the Book of Common Prayer. It was severely criticized by a group of exiles at Strasbourg on the grounds that to alter the 1552 Book was 'to condemn the chief authors thereof, who as they now suffer, so are they ready to confirm that fact with the price of their blood'.

In December, after John Knox had become a minister of the congregation, it was proposed to adopt Huycke's translation of Calvin's service-book; but Knox refused to do this until other congregations of exiles had been consulted. He equally refused to use the Prayer Book Communion Service. A form produced by Thomas Lever was rejected as not 'fit for a right reformed church'. Meanwhile, a Latin synopsis of the Book of Common Prayer was sent to Calvin, phrased in terms designed to elicit a condemnation.[4] Calvin, however, replied with counsels of reconciliation, and only said of the Prayer Book that it lacked 'that purity which was to be desired', since there had been in it many ineptitudes which could be tolerated (*'multas video fuisse tolerabiles ineptias'*). Thereupon a committee consisting of John Knox, William Whittingham, Anthony Gilby, John Foxe, and William Cole, drew up a 'Form of Prayers'. But by now more adherents of the Prayer Book had arrived from England, and the proposed form was so Calvinistic that 'such as were bent to the book of England could not abide it'. So a compromise was attempted.

Knox, Whittingham, Parry, and Lever were appointed to draw up a form, and on 6 February produced what has been named 'The Liturgy of Compromise', 'some part taken forth of the English book, and other things put to'. The Preface contained a phrase which was to be a bone of contention for many years: 'We have omitted ... certain rites and ceremonies ... as things of their own nature indifferent'. Morning Prayer begins with a psalm; the first Lord's Prayer is said by the people; *Venite* is omitted; after *Te Deum* or *Benedicite* follows the Creed; then the Suffrages and Prayers, or sometimes the Litany. Evensong also had only one lesson (several of the exiles objected to liturgical reading from Scripture). In Holy Communion, there was no Collect, Epistle, or Gospel, their place being taken by 'a prayer for the time and for the whole state'. The Exhortations all followed after the Offertory Sentence, and the penitential section was retained complete, with 'We do not presume ...' restored to its 1549 position after the Comfortable Words. Preface and *Sanctus* omitted, the rest of the service went according to the book. In Baptism, Luther's 'Flood prayer' and the sign of the cross were dropped, and the final charge is addressed to the father as well as to the godparents, a sign of Calvinist influence. Private Baptism and Confirmation were abandoned; there was no ring in Matrimony; Visitation of the Sick and Burial were to be as in the book (this marks a considerable concession by the Calvinists); Churching and Commination were ignored. The manuscript ends with rules of discipline, and prayers for England and for Philip and Mary.

This first solution of an intractable problem had been used for a month, when Richard Cox arrived from England with a party of Prayer Book supporters. They began answering aloud, and said 'they would do as they had done in England, and would have the face of an English Church'. The ensuing strife led to the temporary imposition of Poullain's *Liturgia Sacra*, and in May to the final authorizing of the English book. Even so, it was not used in its entirety. 'Private baptisms, confirmation of children, saints' days, kneeling at the Holy Communion, the linen surplices of the ministers, crosses, and other things of the like character' were given up, 'not as being impure and papistical', but in order not to 'offend the minds or alienate the affections of the brethren'.[5]

By the end of March 1555 the Prayer Book party had succeeded in driving Knox out of Frankfurt. With others of his way of thinking, he went to Geneva, where the rejected *Form of Prayers* was printed, in English and Latin, in 1556. It is largely based on Calvin's *La Forme des Prières*, certainly as translated by Huycke, probably also in the original and in Poullain's Latin translation, *Liturgia Sacra*.[6] There are also slight borrowings from the Book of Common Prayer, such as the Exhortation in the Communion Service (itself ultimately derived from the same Strasbourg source as Calvin's service), and the charges at the beginning of Matrimony. The book also included fifty-one metrical psalms, in the version of Thomas Sternhold and John Hopkins, Calvin's Catechism, and a number of Private Prayers. Both Psalms and Prayers were often bound up with the Prayer Book in Queen Elizabeth's reign, and the *Form of Prayers* itself enjoyed a widespread, if unofficial, popularity in England.

In November 1558 Elizabeth came to the throne. Her immediate purpose, she assured the Spanish Ambassador, was to restore religion to the form it had had under her father, Henry VIII. A royal proclamation allowed the use of the English Litany, and a new edition promptly appeared, combining the text of 1552 with additions from 1544. The proclamation also restored Henrician practice in allowing the liturgical Epistles and Gospels, the Creed, the Lord's Prayer, and the Ten Commandments to be read in English.[7] These latter were included in a further edition of the Litany prepared for use at the Coronation, so that it could serve as a sort of interim Primer.[8] But Henrician Catholicism 'had by 1558 virtually disappeared, partly by death, partly by conversion';[9] and the return of the exiles made further steps towards Protestantism inevitable. A survey of the likely results of a change of 'religion' refers to the need for peace with France, for the removal of Catholics from all posts of importance, and for the firm handling of those who, 'when they shall see peradventure that some old ceremonies shall be left still, or that their doctrine which they embrace is not allowed and commanded only, and all other abolished and disproved, shall be discontented, and call the alteration "a cloaked papistry" or "a mingle-mangle" '. Special attention is needed for the universities and 'such colleges where children be instructed to come to the university, as Eton and Winchester'.[10]

When Parliament was opened in January 1559, the preacher was Richard Cox, the leader of the Prayer Book party at Frankfurt, a sign that both Catholics and extreme Reformers were indeed out of favour. If Sir John Neale's interpretation of the scanty evidence be accepted, the Queen did not intend to authorize a Prayer Book during the first session.[11] The plan was to follow the Edwardine pattern by permitting communion in both kinds, and by the holding of a disputation, after which a new Act of Uniformity would be passed, perhaps in the autumn, with a Prayer Book attached. But this was much too slow for the returned exiles. The first alternative to Sarum that was offered was 'the former order of King Edward';[12] but this also was unacceptable to the exiles. An unsigned letter to William Cecil (usually, though improbably, attributed to Edmund Guest) lists a number of points in 'the first book' which were altered in 'the new service', and thus rendered the latter preferable. They included ceremonies, processions, vestments, prayers for the dead, the petition for consecration (quoted on p. 100), and the leaving 'indifferent' whether the bread is placed in the communicants' hands, and whether they stand or kneel (1552 said firmly: 'in their hands, kneeling').[13] The queen must have realized that, if she did not accept the 1552 Book, she would face a demand for the Genevan *Form of Prayers*. The signing of peace with France removed the need to

attach much weight to the wishes of papal Catholics, and on
18 March a Bill was brought into Parliament providing that
'no persons shall be punished for using the religion used in
King Edward's last year'. Communion in both kinds was
permitted in time for Easter by a clause added to the Act of
Supremacy; the disputation was duly held; and at the end of
April an Act of Uniformity was passed. Annexed to it was
the Prayer Book of 1552 with a few small but important
alterations. Papal Catholics were placated by the omission of
references to the Bishop of Rome and his 'detestable
enormities' in the Litany, and his 'usurped power and
authority' in the Ordination Services. Adherents of 1549
were encouraged by the restoration of the Words of
Administration from that book, which were now combined
with those of 1552; by the quiet dropping of the 'Black
Rubric' on kneeling at communion; and by a new rubric
prefixed to Morning Prayer, directing the use of 'such
ornaments in the church as were in use by authority of
Parliament in the second year of the reign of King Edward
the Sixth'. The imprecise phrasing of this addition, apparently designed to restore eucharistic vestments, caused
untold trouble to the Church of England for the next
four hundred years. It was added, it seems, in the House
of Lords, where the Act was passed by only a small
majority.

Proper First Lessons were provided for Sundays. For the
most part these are simply selected chapters in biblical order,
but here and there care has been taken to fit them to the day.
Genesis is begun at Septuagesima, as in the Breviary. On
Lent IV, Joseph makes a feast for his brethren, which
foreshadows the feeding of the 5000 in the Gospel of the day.
Exodus 12 is reached on Easter Day, for which it was already
appointed, and chapter 14 follows equally appropriately at
Evensong. The Lessons for Whit-Sunday had no seasonal
reference, and were replaced in 1561. Those holy days which
had not already been allotted proper Lessons were fitted on

to the Sunday scheme. The Kalendar was at first unaltered, but in 1561 a large number of saints' days were restored, though distinguished from the major feasts by being printed in black letters, and without any liturgical provision being made for their observance.[14] New prayers were added at the end of the Litany, as in the Coronation edition: after the collect 'We humbly beseech thee . . .' there now follows a prayer for the queen, taken over from the Primer of 1553, and much improved by abbreviation; the prayer for the Clergy from 1544, discarded in 1549; and, after 'A Prayer of Chrysostom', the text from 2 Corinthians 13 which we now call 'the Grace', here making a first unobtrusive appearance in the Prayer Book. The occasional prayers follow the Grace as an appendix, with one prayer 'in time of dearth' omitted, and 'O God, whose nature and property . . .' restored from 1544. The Ordination Services were not included in the book, but were issued simultaneously.

The Prayer Book party had triumphed, but at a cost. The returned exiles contended earnestly for the reduced version of the book which they had used at Frankfurt, but instead they were given the book in its entirety, and slightly modified in the opposite direction. While these changes might make the alteration of religion easier for Catholics and for 'Lutherans' such as Richard Cheney, bishop of Gloucester, no concessions were made to those whose ideal was represented by the 'Form of Prayers . . . used in the English Congregation at Geneva, and approved by the famous and godly learned man, John Calvin'.[15]

But the ethos of the Elizabethan Settlement is not fully reflected in the actual text of the Book of Common Prayer. This has to be taken in conjunction with other official ecclesiastical publications; with a series of directives which took the place of the medieval Consuetudinary, though in much less detail; and, not least, with the queen's own practice. The year 1560 saw the publication of a Latin version of the Prayer Book. This was the normal procedure for reformed service-books, and the English books were no exception. In 1548 a translation of *The Order of the Communion* was made by Alexander Aless, who was also responsible for translating the book of 1549 when that appeared. The latter is by no means a reliable version. Aless simply incorporated his rendering of *The Order of the Communion* regardless of the changes that had been made in the Absolution. Some of the collects are copied directly from the Sarum text, ignoring Cranmer's alterations. Some renderings are so free as to be rightly called 'compositions of the translator'. These defects, however, did not prevent Aless's version from being taken as the basis of the new, official translation, which is commonly ascribed to the elegant Latinist Walter Haddon. This was intended for use in the universities, and so did not include Baptism, Confirmation, or Matrimony; these were added in an edition for use in Ireland. Haddon overlooked the Collect for St Andrew's Day newly composed for 1552; at other points he went behind Aless to 1549. The main interest of the 1560 version lies in two offices added after the Burial Service. One is for a 'Celebration of the Lord's Supper at funerals, if the friends and neighbours of the departed wish to communicate'; it simply revives the form in 1549, with a new alternative Gospel. The other office, a 'Commendation of Benefactors', follows a precedent set in the 1549 Visitation of Cambridge,[16] though the actual form then enjoined is not used; the new office, to be said at the end of every term, consists of the Lord's Prayer; Psalms 144, 145, and 146; Ecclesiasticus 44; a sermon declaring the virtues of the benefactors; *Benedictus*; *preces*; and a collect. It has been suggested that the Latin book was intended to introduce the members of the universities to some of the ideas of 1549; it certainly aroused opposition, and in 1571 a new and accurate translation appeared, without the additional offices, but still with the 1549 Collect for St Andrew.

Though no further alterations or additions were made to

the Prayer Book itself for the rest of the reign, supplementary material appeared in large quantities. One necessary item was the Book of Homilies, and in 1563 a second book was added, comprising twenty further sermons 'on subjects including some of those promised in 1547, some of those suggested by Bucer, and some of those proposed by the *Interpretations*'.[17] At regular intervals throughout the reign there appeared official forms of prayer and thanksgiving, usually in connection with plague, war, or attempts on the queen's life. They were usually designed to fit into Morning Prayer or the Litany. A typical example, of more than ephemeral interest, is the service for the anniversary of the queen's accession, first printed, apparently by private enterprise, in 1576, and repeated yearly thereafter.[18] At Morning Prayer there are three Proper Psalms and a choice of three Proper Lessons from 2 Kings and 2 Chronicles, dealing with kings Jehoshaphat, Hezekiah, and Josiah. After the Second Lesson (Romans 13) comes *Jubilate*; there is a special set of suffrages, and the Prayer for the Queen replaces the Collect of the day. The Litany ends with a cento psalm (i.e. a selection of verses from different psalms) and a new prayer for the queen. From 1578 onwards the latter was followed by the Prayer for the Clergy, the Prayer in time of Plague, the Prayer of Chrysostom, and the Grace. Proper Epistle and Gospel are provided, and psalms *in metre* are appointed before and after the sermon. This is probably their first appearance in an official form of service, though in 1564 a service had specified 'Psalms which may be sung or said before the beginning or after the ending of public prayer', in accordance with the *Injunctions* of 1559, and these were almost certainly metrical psalms. From 1578 the psalm after the sermon is replaced by a metrical Thanksgiving of fourteen verses, each of eight lines. After Evening Prayer an 'Anthem', also in metre, is provided and 'A Song of Rejoicing', to the tune of Psalm 25. The latter is an acrostic on 'God saue the Queene'. In general the style of these services is incredibly prolix, much more akin to that of the Genevan form than to Cranmer's.

As early as 1559 royal initiative led to the issue of a set of *Injunctions*, themselves needing to be read in the light of the bishops' *Interpretations* (1560–1), and taking final form in the *Advertisements* of 1566. According to the *Injunctions*, once every month a sermon is to be preached, or failing that, a homily is to be read, 'leisurely, plainly, and distinctly' ; and one bell is to be rung before the sermon. On holy days when there is no sermon, the Lord's Prayer, the Creed, and the Ten Commandments are to be read, as Edward VI had directed. Perambulations are to be retained once a year, including 'at certain convenient places' an admonition to thanksgiving; Psalm 103; and Deuteronomy 27: 17, 'Cursed be he which translateth the bounds and doles of his neighbour'. Instruction in the Catechism is enjoined on 'every second Sunday', and a new bidding prayer is provided, to be read before the sermon ; and reverence is to be made at the name of Jesus. At the Visitation of 1559, the Visitors introduced a new form of service into the western cathedrals, to be said at 6 a.m. and consisting of the Litany, preceded by the General Confession and Absolution, and with a chapter of the New Testament inserted before the end.[19] The *Interpretations*, which only circulated in MS, without official recognition, reduced the requirement of a monthly sermon to once a quarter, and revised the Perambulation to consist of Psalms 103 and 104, the Litany, and Archbishop Parker's *Homily of Thanksgiving to God*.[20] Private Baptism may in an emergency be administered by a layman ; the age of confirmation is fixed at twelve or thirteen ; and the passing-bell is restricted to 'one short peal ; and one before the burial, and another short peal after the burial'.

Church furnishings and vestments came in for a good deal of attention. A Royal Order of 1561 directs that the screen is to remain, or be replaced, as far as the upper beam ; all above is to be removed, and its place taken by 'some convenient crest', usually in practice the royal arms.[21] This eliminated the rood, and the Last Judgment on the tympanum, but maintained the division of the church into two rooms, the chancel for Holy Communion, the nave for Morning and Evening Prayer. Consequently the minister's seat was to be 'without the chancel door' in smaller churches, and 'in the body of the church' in greater. The Ten Commandments are to be hung up on the east wall over the holy table, which is to be set 'where the altar stood, and there commonly covered', which the *Advertisements* explain as 'decently covered with carpet, silk, or other decent covering'. Disused vestments were often converted for this purpose, and old albs provided the 'fair linen cloth' required in time of service. For the Communion, the table is to be moved to a suitable position in the chancel and replaced after the service; the *Interpretations* add that it may be moved into the body of the church if the chancel is small, or at great feasts. The original intention was that copes should be worn for the Lord's Supper, but by 1566 their use can be enforced only in cathedrals, where it is still expected that the celebrant will have two assistants, epistoler and gospeller; in parish churches the surplice is to be used at all services. 'The sacramental bread' is to be 'plain, without any figure thereupon', like that formerly used in private masses, but bigger and thicker. The walls of the church were usually whitewashed; the font stood in its ancient place by the door; the choir was in a musicians' gallery at the west end; stalls were provided in the chancel for communicants, pews in the nave for the other services, and a special pew near the screen for churchings.[22]

These successive directives show the bishops enforcing the queen's determination to hold the position to which she had been forced back in 1559. Having accepted the 1552 Book as the basis of the settlement, she resisted pressure to reform after the manner of Geneva by taking small steps in the opposite direction, in externals if not in forms of words. Not all these steps were successful: she was compelled to abandon her attempts to reintroduce the crucifix, whether on the rood-screen or the Holy Table.[23] The bishops carried out the enforcement of her wishes only with extreme reluctance, and by 1565 it must have been clear to the queen that she could not regain any more lost ground. Indeed, the strongest efforts would be needed to enforce the use of the Prayer Book and obedience to the moderate requirements of the various supplementary documents.

The absence of further official revision did not save the Prayer Book from modification in practice : some Injunctions issued in 1571 by Edmund Grindal, then Archbishop of York, show the process at work. All parishioners are to receive the Communion three times in the year besides Ash Wednesday, namely, on one of the two Sundays before Easter, Pentecost, and Christmas ; the Epistle and Gospel are to be read in the pulpit or stall ; and the minister is to make no pause between Morning Prayer, the Litany, and the Holy Communion, so that nobody should go out without attending 'the whole divine service'.[24]

Church music was officially encouraged, though greatly disliked by the Genevan party. The *Injunctions* of 1559 direct that choral foundations should remain, while in parish churches there should be

a modest and distinct song so used in all parts of the common prayers in the church that the same may be as plainly understanded as if it were read without singing; and yet nevertheless, for the comforting of such that delight in music, it may be permitted that in the beginning or in the end of the common prayers, either at morning or at evening, there may be sung an hymn or suchlike song to the praise of Almighty God, in the best sort of melody and music that may be conveniently devised, having respect that the sentence of him may be understanded and perceived.

The publisher John Day brought out a book of services set for four voices in 1565, including three in which the whole of the congregational part of the Communion Service is set to music. This is true also of Thomas Tallis's 'Dorian' and five-part services. It soon became the custom, however, to set only the *Kyrie* and Creed, presumably because the practice of ending the morning service with Ante-Communion on three Sundays out of four was becoming general. At Mattins and Evensong all the canticles were frequently set by the leading composers. The psalms were normally sung in unison to the old Sarum tones, though the proper psalms for the great festivals were sometimes given a harmonized setting. The permission given in the *Injunctions* soon produced compositions to English texts which acquired the name of 'anthem', the medieval version of 'antiphon'. The choice of text included the Collect, Epistle, and Gospel of the day; the Psalms were freely drawn on, and many passages of Scripture were chosen for their intrinsic appeal, rather than any liturgical reference. The organist was given his opportunity during the Offertory at the Communion, when the Sentence was followed by an organ solo. Short voluntaries were also sometimes inserted between the lessons and canticles. Metrical psalms had been included in the Genevan form, and the complete version by Sternhold and Hopkins became very popular throughout the Church of England. At first these psalms were sung in unison unaccompanied, but the familiar four-part harmonizations began to appear before the end of Elizabeth's reign. An attempt by Archbishop Parker to produce an Anglican competitor, though equipped with tunes by Tallis, was never actually put on sale.[25]

The publication of a corpus of doctrine, discipline, and devotion to accompany the public worship of the church followed the lines marked out by Henry VIII and Edward VI. Private devotion was the first to be provided for, with the issue in September 1559 of a Primer, which was largely a reprint of *The King's Primer* in the mildly reformed state it had reached by 1551. This was followed the next year by a companion volume in Latin entitled *Orarium* (i.e. Book of

E

Hours), similar, but by no means identical, in content: the *Dirige* and Commendations are only in the Primer, the Catechism only in the *Orarium*. But the canonical Hours were now too closely associated with medieval Catholicism to be widely acceptable, and the fully reformed Primer of Edward VI was reissued in 1560, and again in 1568. A collection of *Preces Privatae* put out by authority in 1564 for the benefit of students provided an interesting attempt to combine the services of the Breviary and the Prayer Book. Morning and Evening Prayer are given in full, translated into Latin; but the Absolution is turned into a prayer; the office hymn precedes the psalms, which are the invariable ones usual in Primers; and the Beatitudes are used as antiphons. The Lauds psalms follow *Te Deum*, with the heading *Laudes*; and another hymn follows the Second Lesson. The Prayer for the Queen is placed after the Collect of the day; and the services end with *Benedicamus Domino: Deo gratias*. Next comes a series of *Psalms, Lessons, and Prayers* for Christmas Day, Good Friday, Easter Day, Ascension Day, Whit-Sunday, and Trinity Sunday, which, it has been suggested above, may possibly be the propers referred to in *Certain Notes* of 1549; the *Prayers* are the Prayer Book Collects in Latin. The place of the *Dirige* customary in books of this kind is taken by a translation of the Burial Service. This book belongs with the Latin Prayer Book of 1560 as an attempt to retain a little more of the traditional ethos than had been possible in the Prayer Book passed by Parliament. It was also the last official appearance in print of the Hours. Thenceforward books of devotion, though numerous, were unofficial and increasingly Reformed in character.

The doctrinal basis of the Settlement was indicated by the reappearance of the *42 Articles* of 1553, reduced to 38 in 1563, and finally reaching the familiar number of 39 in 1571. Ponet's Catechism, which had formerly accompanied them, was replaced by the Catechism (largely based on it) of

Alexander Nowell, which was approved by Convocation in 1563, but held back from publication until 1570.[26] This was followed in 1572 by a Latin expansion of the Prayer Book Catechism, also the work of Nowell. Church discipline was dealt with in the Canons of 1571, supplemented in 1575 and 1584.[27] This completed the official documentary programme for the establishment of the Church of England. Much had been approved by Parliament or by Convocation, but much rested on the queen's authority, and much was very far from universally acceptable.

In fact, no-one really wanted the Prayer Book that they had been given. Those of the exiles who were prepared to use the 1552 Book opposed the retention of even the few ceremonies that remained in it, and many wished to abandon the book altogether. Appeals for help were despatched to Zurich and Geneva at frequent intervals, and in these the standpoint that was soon called 'puritanism' is already clearly set out. There are two main principles : nothing is admissible that is not actually enjoined by Scripture ; and nothing is admissible, even if mentioned in Scripture, that is tainted with popery. These principles rule out the use of the surplice, wafer bread, the sign of the cross in baptism, kneeling for communion, the ring in marriage, the veil in churching, bowing at the name of Jesus, and the use of organs and 'effeminate and over-refined' music. In Baptism it is an usurpation of the father's responsibility that the minister addresses the infant and the godparents answer in its name. Other reprehensible practices include emergency baptism by women, confirmation, the preaching of sermons at funerals, and, unexpectedly, the reading of the Bible in church.[28] In the first decade there is little criticism of the Prayer Book text beyond what is involved in the practices just mentioned.

None of these criticisms could be levelled against the Anglo-Genevan *Form of Prayers*. This had been introduced into Scotland by John Knox on his return there in 1559, and had soon been accepted as the official form of worship, gradually becoming known as *The Book of Common Order*. Any book associated with Knox would have been totally unacceptable to the queen, but its use in Scotland provided perpetual encouragement to those who desired its adoption in England. About 1567 it was being unofficially used in London in secret conventicles.[29] In 1563 an attempt had been made in Convocation to meet some of the Puritan points, but it was scotched by the queen. Then it was hoped that Bullinger would intervene, but, to the great disappointment of the Puritans, he took the line (like Bucer and Martyr before him) that the surplice, though objectionable, was unimportant compared to the need for preaching the gospel. If wearing the surplice was made a condition of exercising ministry, then the surplice should be worn.[30] This encouraged the bishops who had to enforce its use, but did not satisfy the extremists.

The thunders of Zurich having been invoked in vain, the 'ambitious morosity'[31] of the Puritans drove them to seek other means of effecting further reform. In 1571 Foxe the martyrologist published the *Reformatio Legum Ecclesiasticarum*, Cranmer's stillborn attempt at replacing the Canon Law, which in some respects, such as sitting for communion, went beyond the Book of 1552 in a Protestant direction. With this backing, two Members of Parliament, William Strickland and Thomas Norton, introduced a Bill the same year for the reformation of the Prayer Book, which proposed the abolition of copes, surplices, kneeling at communion, sacraments in private houses, questions put to infants in baptism, the whole service of confirmation, and the ring in marriage. It was promptly quashed by the queen.[32] The next year a Bill about rites and ceremonies recommended that the use of the Prayer Book should be made optional, and that the service-book used by the French and Dutch congregations in England should be authorized. This tactful way of introducing the Genevan form met with no more success.

Meanwhile two Puritan clergymen, John Field and

Thomas Wilcox, published *An Admonition to the Parliament*, which immediately became a best-seller. This delivers a detailed attack on the Prayer Book, going through the Communion Service and comparing it point by point with the practice of 'the old time', appealing to primitive usage against the perversions of the popes and the mass-book. It is the great weakness of the Prayer Book that it preserves so much pre-Reformation material, being 'culled and picked out of that popish dunghill, the portuise and mass-book, full of all abominations'. A section headed 'A view of popish abuses yet remaining in the English Church' specifies reading services instead of preaching ('as evil as playing upon a stage, and worse too'); observance of saints' days, 'contrary to the commandment of God'; the half-Communion'; kneeling at communion rather than sitting; the word 'priest'; private baptism; questions to infants, godparents' promises, and signing with the cross; the ring and the nuptial mass; confirmation; prayers for the dead; churching of women; the Gospel canticles; antiphonal recitation of the psalms; reverence at the name of Jesus; organs and 'curious singing'; and numerous smaller points.[33] All this is set forth in a vivid, racy style which makes the *Admonition* the most readable of all documents connected with the Prayer Book. Its authors were soon in prison, and a sequel published anonymously a few months later adds only a few details. Its chief criticism is that 'reading prayers' are formal and do not touch the heart. Here we first meet the pedantic literalness of Puritan criticism of the Prayer Book, which objects to 'this day' in the Christmas collect because it is to be said on seven different days, and suchlike small points. Ash Wednesday, the Easter Anthems, the Athanasian Creed, and *Benedicite* all fall into condemnation.[34]

Attempts to reform the Prayer Book by legislation having failed, the Puritans turned to making their own unofficial revision. In 1578 an edition appeared in which 'minister' is substituted for 'priest' throughout, except in *Benedicite*, which they were unlikely to use. Like their forerunners at Frankfurt, they omitted Private Baptism, Confirmation, and Churching of Women altogether, with the rubrics elsewhere referring to them, and also the rubrics about excommunication at the beginning of the Communion Service. The following year Private Baptism and Churching were restored, but with the word 'priest' left in as a silent warning of the true nature of these services. In subsequent editions Confirmation reappears, and smaller changes are gradually abandoned, as the attempt at compromise gave way to complete conformity or outright opposition, until the last editions are almost indistinguishable from the official text.[35]

The Puritans had still not given up hope of reform through Parliament, and in 1584 the Genevan form was reprinted under the title *A Book of the Form of Common Prayers*, to accompany a Bill for its authorization put forward by Dr Peter Turner.[36] A second edition, printed abroad and known as the Middelburgh Prayer Book, was attached to a Bill of 1586, introduced by Anthony Cope with an attack on the Book of Common Prayer on familiar lines, and praise of the Presbyterian system. In reply Sir Christopher Hatton defended the use of 'set prayer' on the ground that the common people became familiar with it 'by often hearing', and were able to use it at home. Both Bills were defeated.[37]

Soon afterwards the defeat of the Armada removed any serious danger from the papists, and the Queen felt free to take a stronger line with the Puritans. Legislation enabled judicial action to be taken against their illicit organizations and their doctrinal position was controverted by the massive reasoning of Richard Hooker's *Laws of Ecclesiastical Polity*, which began to appear in 1594. Book V (1597) deals particularly with the Prayer Book. In it Hooker sets out to rebut the criticisms of the *Admonitions*, a task which had already been undertaken by John Whitgift, Elizabeth's third archbishop of Canterbury, in a prolonged controversy with Thomas Cartwright, a Puritan who made Cambridge too hot to hold him. Whitgift relied largely on the writings of Bucer, Zwingli, and other Reformers normally regarded as authoritative by the Puritans. Hooker, however, writing at leisure, is able to deploy an enormous armoury of patristic learning, reinforced by effective appeals to pastoral experience. The argument is no longer between two university professors : Hooker has in mind the needs of the ordinary worshipper, and can draw on the experience of a further twenty years' use of the book.

The last years of Elizabeth's reign saw the established Church in the ascendant, resting on the foundations that had been well and truly laid in the sixties and seventies. Papists and Puritans were both vigorously repressed, but neither were finally crushed. They could only await in patience the accession of a more favourably disposed monarch.

7 The Grand Debate

> Prayer, confession, thanksgiving, reading of the Scriptures, and administration of the sacraments in the plainest and simplest manner were matter enough to furnish out a sufficient liturgy, though nothing either of private opinion, or of church-pomp, of garments, or prescribed gestures, of imagery, of music, of matter concerning the dead, of many superfluities which creep into the Church under the name of *order* and *decency* did interpose itself.
>
> JOHN HALES, quoted in the *Exceptions*, section I

> I shall only crave leave that I may remember Jerusalem, and call to mind the pleasures of the Temple, the order of her services, the beauty of her buildings, the sweetness of her songs, the decency of her ministrations, the assiduity and economy of her priests and Levites, the daily sacrifice, and that eternal fire of devotion that went not out by day nor night.
>
> JEREMY TAYLOR, *A Collection of Offices*, Preface, 3

FOR the first time for nearly a century the accession of a new sovereign involved no change of religion. There was no need for James I to proceed cautiously by reissuing the Litany. But he followed precedent to the extent of summoning a conference before producing a new edition of the Prayer Book. The immediate occasion was the presentation of the Millenary Petition, an attempt by the Puritan party to secure James's support, which conveniently collects the points at issue in the half-century of controversy:

That the cross in baptism, interrogatories ministered to infants, confirmations, as superfluous, may be taken away; baptism not to be ministered by women, and so explained; the cap and the surplice not urged; that examination may go before the Communion; that it be ministered with a sermon; that divers terms of priests and absolution and some other used, with the ring in marriage, and other suchlike in the book, may be corrected; the longsomeness of service abridged; church songs and music moderated to better edification; that the Lord's Day be not profaned; the rest upon holidays not so strictly urged; that there may be an uniformity of doctrine prescribed; no popish opinion to be any more taught or defended; no ministers charged to teach their people to bow at the name of Jesus; that the canonical scriptures only be read in the Church.[1]

James wisely neither accepted nor rejected the petition, but referred the whole subject to a conference which met at Hampton Court in January 1604. Eight bishops, seven deans, and two doctors of divinity represented the established Church; the Puritans were allowed only four speakers, the most able of their persuasion.

James confined the agenda to six points, three in the Prayer Book, namely the general Absolution, confirmation of children, and private baptism by women. The Puritans also complained that the Prayer Book Catechism was too short and Dean Nowell's too long; that the existing translation of the Bible was inaccurate; that twice the Prayer Book had 'Jesus said to his disciples' when it is plain that he was speaking to the Pharisees; that the Apocrypha was included in the Lectionary; and various other matters in the Petition. After three days' discussion it was agreed that:

to the Absolution shall be added the word of pronouncing remission of sins.

That to Confirmation shall be added the word of catechizing, or examination of the children's faith.

That the Private Baptism shall be called the Private Baptism by the ministers and curates only . . .

That an uniform short and plain catechism be made . . .

That a translation be made of the whole Bible, as consonant as can be to the original Hebrew and Greek; and this to be set out and printed without any marginal notes, and only to be used in all churches of England in time of divine service.

That such apocrypha as have any repugnance to canonical scripture shall be removed and not read . . .

The words of marriage to be made more clear.

The cross in Baptism was never counted any part in baptism, nor sign effective, but only significative.[2]

E2

The changes actually made were set out in a letter from the archbishop of Canterbury and the bishops of London and Chichester, and enjoined by the king in a proclamation prefixed to the Prayer Book. They do not exactly correspond with the decisions listed above, and it has been suggested that the bishops managed to secure a more favourable result from the conference than was intended at its conclusion. Of the eight decisions of the conference, the first was carried out literally ; the title of Confirmation was enlarged, but without reference to examination ; the title *Of them that be baptized in private houses* became *The Ministration of Private Baptism*, and the rubrics were altered to rule out baptism by women or laymen. The Catechism was enlarged by the inclusion of a section on Baptism and Communion, based on two catechisms by Nowell, which are by no means slavishly followed. A new translation of the Bible was put in hand immediately, though not completed until 1611. Four lessons from the Apocrypha were replaced by passages from the Old Testament. No change was made in Matrimony. A Puritan point not included in the eight decisions was met by altering the beginnings of the two liturgical Gospels complained of. Some further additions were made : a prayer for the royal family at Mattins and Evensong, and a suffrage for them in the Litany ; and six thanksgivings 'for diverse benefits, by way of explanation'. No request for the latter appears in the records of the conference, but criticism of their absence goes back as far as Cartwright and the *Admonitions* ; the statement that they were 'added upon the complaint of Dr Reynolds and others ... saying "that we wanted particular thanksgivings for particular benefits received" '[3] may come from John Overall, dean of St Paul's, who was present at the conference.

Of the supplementary publications issued by James's predecessors, no book of doctrine was now necessary ; the expansion of the Prayer Book Catechism removed the need for additional instruction ; and the Articles required no alteration. Provision for private devotion had long since ceased to depend on royal initiative. Only the Canons needed attention, and a new series was enacted in March 1604, consolidating the various Elizabethan directives. The Common Prayer is to be said on all holy days appointed in the Prayer Book and their Eves (Canon 13); reconsecration is provided for (21); and godparents must have received the Holy Communion (29). A long explanation of the significance of the cross in Baptism is included (30), carrying out the decision of the conference. The Elizabethan Bidding Prayer is continued (55), and the surplice once more enforced (58). The furniture of a church must include a font of stone (81); a decent communion table, covered with a carpet of silk, and a fair linen cloth at the time of the ministration, and placed for convenience of hearing and communion; the Ten Commandments on the east wall, with other chosen sentences (82); a pulpit (83), a chest for alms (84), a Bible and Prayer Book (80), and the Table of Prohibited Degrees of Marriage (99). Canon 67 restricts the obligation to use the Prayer Book Order for the Visitation of the Sick to those who are not licensed preachers; those who are may 'instruct and comfort' the sick as they 'shall think most needful and convenient'. With the issue of the Canons the Jacobean Settlement was complete.

The discovery of Guy Fawkes's 'most traitorous and bloody-intended massacre by gunpowder' made an impact on the life of the nation which was reflected in liturgical practice. A service of thanksgiving was appointed by Act of Parliament to be used yearly on 5 November. It assumes the normal morning service to consist of Mattins, Litany, and Ante-Communion. A cento psalm takes the place of *Venite*, and there are proper psalms, lessons, collect, Epistle, and Gospel, with extra prayers to be added 'in the end of the Litany' instead of the 'Prayer in time of war and tumults', and after the Prayer for the Church militant. In the absence of a sermon, 'one of the six Homilies against Rebellion' is to be read.[4] The form is in line with the Elizabethan occasional services, but its yearly repetition is an innovation : hitherto this had been confined to the Accession Service. A yearly commemoration was also issued for the Gowrie conspiracy, but this lapsed at James's death.

The Puritans were far from content with the meagre results of the Hampton Court Conference, and began to examine the text of the Prayer Book with a new thoroughness. The ministers of Lincoln diocese put in a petition, in which they brought to bear a tremendous battery of Reformed divines, quoted at length with chapter and verse. This was published in 1605, and the following year appeared an anonymous *Survey of the Book of Common Prayer*, in which the Book is subjected to a careful comparison with the books of 1549 and 1552, and the Canons of 1604, with the object of pointing out inconsistencies and superfluities, and a plea is made for the substitution of the *Book of Common Order*, to unify the worship of the two kingdoms. Among minor details it is interesting to learn that 'most marriages are upon Sunday', and that the recent additions to the Catechism are not thought to have anything to do with Nowell's Catechisms, but are regarded as 'intricate', and therefore inferior to them. Granted the Puritan premiss that everything in the Book ought to be taken from 'the pure word of God, or evidently grounded in the same', these two publications present a formidable indictment.

The long-continued Puritan pressure was bound to produce a reaction. The Catholic strain which had lain dormant since the early years of Elizabeth's reign came to the surface again in Cambridge in the 1580s, and blossomed out into a school of thought generally, if inaccurately, known as 'Laudian'. Just as the Puritans began by objecting to the surplice, so the Laudians found their first expression in outward adorning. Lancelot Andrewes at Winchester provides the best-known example, but the movement was not confined to bishops : noblemen's chapels and cathedrals were similarly enriched. Even John Williams, bishop of Lincoln, who was certainly no admirer of Laud, furnished his chapel at Buckden with extraordinary sumptuousness.[5] With lavish expenditure on copes, frontals, woodwork, and fine bindings went a less marked increase in ceremonial. The four ceremonies to which the Puritans specially objected were not only retained but elaborated : infants were not only signed with the cross, but carried up to the altar ;[6] and kneeling at communion tended to become one gesture in a series of bowings and genuflexions.

As regards the text of the Prayer Book, the earlier Laudians were content to conserve it intact, and made little effort to conform it to their doctrinal views. The earliest suggestion of change comes from Overall, who always used the Prayer of Oblation 'in its right place, when he had consecrated the sacrament, as being the true public sacrifice of the Church ... and when that was done, he did communicate the people, and so end with the Thanksgiving'.[7] The authority for this practice, and its inspiration, was the Prayer Book of 1549. Andrewes made various innovations in practice. He drew a clear distinction between alms and oblations, made explicit by having the congregation bring their oblations to the altar rails after the Creed, while the celebrant read a new set of Sentences, in which the theme of offering is paramount. The people were to remain in the chancel until the end of *Gloria in excelsis*, and only then return to their seats, on their way putting their alms into the 'poor man's chest', while the priest read the Prayer Book Sentences.[8] The practice was widely imitated and as widely disliked. The new Sentences were widely circulated in manuscript. Andrewes also drew up his own forms for Visitation of the Sick, in accordance with Canon 67, and for consecrating churches, cemeteries, and church plate. Several bishops, including Matthew Wren, a former chaplain of Andrewes, followed his lead.

It was a commonplace of Puritan polemic that Laud had

tampered with the text of the Prayer Book, but only two instances were produced : that he had changed the opening of the Prayer for the Royal Family, and that he had substituted '*at* the name of Jesus' for 'in'.[9] As archbishop he concentrated his attention, liturgically speaking, on placing the altar against the east wall of the chancel, fencing it with rails, making the communicants come to the altar to receive, and reading the Ante-Communion at the altar, not in the reading-pew. These directions combined with the Canons to produce the typical Laudian sanctuary, the altar with a silk or velvet carpet falling loose at the corners, richly carved altar-rails, and the floor paved with marble in black and white squares.

John Cosin, a second-generation Laudian, was employed in correcting the text of the Prayer Book at the king's printers, a task for which his enthusiasm and meticulous accuracy fitted him. Charles I, soon after his accession, commissioned him to compile a book of devotions for the ladies of the Court, thus providing the first opportunity for revision of the text in a Laudian direction. The king expressly asked for something like the 'pocket Offices' of the French ladies-in-waiting, 'with regard to the ancient forms before Popery'.[10] Cosin based his *Collection of Private Devotions* on the *Orarium* of 1560. For Mattins he prints the Prayer Book Service, but with the traditional psalms, and inserting the *Laudes* (Psalms 148–50) after *Te Deum*. Terce, Sext, and None follow ; and Evensong reverts to its original form of Vespers and Compline. A prayer to be said privately 'at the Consecration' in the Communion Service draws significantly upon the Canon of 1549, which now reappears in print for the first time since 1552. This is also the source of a 'Prayer and Thanksgiving for the whole estate of Christ's Catholic Church, with a commemoration of the Saints before us'. Among a number of special prayers is one 'for the Ordination of Priests and Deacons' which found its way into the Prayer Book at the next revision. Not unnaturally,

Cosin's book aroused bitter hostility from the Puritans, and Cosin himself joined Laud and Wren as the especial target of their attacks.

The next move came from Scotland. From 1616 onwards James had been pushing the Scottish bishops towards the introduction of a new service book. Little came of it, because of the intense opposition aroused by James's insistence on kneeling at communion.[11] The only result was the publication in 1620 of a form for ordaining ministers and consecrating bishops, but with no provision for the diaconate. Charles soon resumed his father's project. In 1629 a draft originally drawn up in 1619 was brought to London and presented to the king by John Maxwell, later bishop of Ross. No definite steps were taken until 1634, when Maxwell again came south, and a number of proposals were recorded in a Prayer Book now known as the Haddington Book. It was 'rather an English revision of the English Prayer Book than a book for Scotland'.[12] The Authorized Version was used throughout, and much freedom was allowed in the observance of saints' days. In May 1635 Maxwell returned once more with a full manuscript which was approved by the king, and printing began that autumn.

This, however, proved to be premature, as further changes, restoring the Communion Service to something very like its 1549 form, were suggested by James Wedderburn, soon to be bishop of Dunblane. After consideration by Laud and Wren, now Laud's right-hand man, the new version was approved by the king in April 1636, and entered by Laud himself in another Prayer Book (the Christ Church Book). Printing was finally completed in the spring of 1637. The introduction of the book led to rioting, and it was quickly dropped. Its later influence, however, was so great that it deserves close study.

The general substitution of the Authorized Version and the removal of the Apocrypha were both to be expected in the light of the Hampton Court Conference. The word 'priest' gives way to 'presbyter' throughout, and fifteen Scottish saints are added to the Kalendar. At Mattins *Benedicite* is replaced by Psalm 23, and the doxology is added to the second Lord's Prayer. A rubric directs the saying of the Prayers for the King, Royal Family, and Clergy at the end of Mattins when the Litany is not said, and always at Evensong. New collects are added for the Ember weeks and Easter Even. In the Communion Service, the Collect for the King precedes the Collect of day. Six of Andrewes's 'Peculiar Sentences for the Offertory' are included, and ten of the existing Sentences omitted, including, naturally, those from Tobit (but for Laud, all twenty would have been dropped). The collection is to be presented and the elements offered up 'upon the Lord's Table'. The thanksgiving for the departed omitted in 1552 is restored, though without mentioning the Blessed Virgin Mary, the Patriarchs, Prophets, Apostles, and Martyrs, or commending to God's mercy those that are departed 'with the sign of faith' and 'rest in the sleep of peace'. The Prayer of Consecration (now so named, at Laud's suggestion) restores the 1549 epiclesis and the manual acts. The Words of Institution are followed immediately by the 'Memorial, or Prayer of Oblation', again restoring the 1549 anamnesis. Next follows the Lord's Prayer with what a Scots divine called 'that naughty preface', and the Doxology; and after it the Prayer of Humble Access. The Words of Administration are shorn of the 1552 sentence, which seemed to Wedderburn 'to relish somewhat of the Zwinglian tenet, that the sacrament is a bare sign taken in remembrance of Christ's Passion';[13] and the communicant replies 'Amen'. Reconsecration, veiling, and consumption of the elements are directed by rubric. Wedderburn would have gone even further back towards 1549 by restoring the penitential section and the *Sanctus* to the position they held in that book. In Baptism a brief invocation of the Holy Spirit on the water in the font is added to the 'Flood Prayer', and a blessing of the water immediately before baptism. Psalm 27 is added as an alternative in Churching, and Ash Wednesday is restored as the special occasion for the Commination.

Here the Laudian programme is in full flower, though the flowering was indeed ephemeral. In the circumstances of the time the changes were, to say the least, injudicious, and Laud had to spend much time at his trial both in defending them and in disclaiming responsibility for originating them. To the Scots the book reeked of popery. The new position of the Prayer of Oblation, they said, was enjoined 'for no other end but that the memorial and sacrifice of praise mentioned in it may be understood according to the popish meaning . . . not of the spiritual sacrifice, but of the oblation of the body of the Lord'.[14] They also found 'the corporal presence of Christ's body in the sacrament' through the restoration of the epiclesis. Little as they liked the Prayer Book, they were highly sensitive to any change in its text.

Meanwhile the Laudians in England had been encountering increasing opposition. Proposals for new Canons and an English Pontifical both proved abortive. As the threat of civil war drew near, a committee of lay peers and moderate divines was appointed by the House of Lords to try to find a basis for a settlement of religious differences. Among them were Archbishops Williams and Ussher, Bishop Wren, and Robert Sanderson, afterwards bishop of Lincoln. A document printed as their *Proceedings* provides an interesting compendium of unpopular Laudian practices and mildly Puritan criticisms of the Prayer Book. Among the twenty-one 'Innovations in Discipline', six concern the furnishing of the church, chiefly of the altar; eight concern posture and movement; and the remainder deal with restrictions on commendable practices. The Committee put their finger unerringly on the original source of the Laudian movement with a comment about 'putting-to the Liturgy printed *secundo, tertio Edwardi sexti*, which the Parliament hath reformed and laid aside'.[15] They had no complaint to make of any attempt to alter the text of the Prayer Book, and themselves offered thirty-five 'Considerations' for revision. Most of these had already appeared in one or other of the Puritan manifestos, and some are quite trivial; but they had every reason to recommend the full implementation of the Hampton Court decisions by setting out 'the reading Psalms, Sentences of Scripture . . . hymns, Epistles, and Gospels . . . in the new translation', and the complete removal of the Apocrypha. A suggestion for the 'mending' of the Ornaments Rubric would have avoided much future controversy.

The Committee's reference to Parliament was significant. From now on Parliament was to enter more and more into the picture. The Committee failed to save the Laudians from disaster, though its recommendations were not forgotten. The Puritans were now in the ascendant, and they were well beyond wanting revision of the Prayer Book: 'root and branch' was the order of the day, whether for bishops or liturgies. Cosin went into exile, Wren to the Tower; Laud was executed, Wedderburn was dead. In January 1645 the use of the Prayer Book was declared illegal. Its place was taken by *A Directory for the Public Worship of God*. This is 'not so much a prayer book as a rubric book, a corpus of liturgical suggestions and directions'.[16] The Lord's Day Service follows the tradition of Bucer, Calvin, and Knox, with an occasional concession to the more radical Independents, who were now asserting themselves against the moderate Puritans, or Presbyterians. Baptism and the Lord's Supper, when administered, follow the prayer after the sermon. The Lord's Supper begins with a 'fencing of the Table' and a prayer for 'the effectual working of his Spirit in us' and for the sanctification of the elements, so that 'we may receive by faith the Body and Blood of Jesus Christ'. Fraction follows the eucharistic prayer. Baptism also reproduces Knox's order, with a prayer for the sanctifying of the water. A brief marriage service is allowed, but no rite for burial; nor is there any Kalendar.

Those who wished to continue using the Prayer Book

during the Commonwealth had to find ways and means of doing so. There was a certain amount of clandestine use, even of the Ordinal (as the ordination services now began to be called). Sanderson, who had had to leave his Oxford professorship for the obscure living of Boothby Pagnell in Lincolnshire, took the middle path. His method was to follow the Prayer Book outline, abbreviating freely and varying a phrase here and there. The result was certainly not the Prayer Book within the meaning of the Act, but produced the effect of the Prayer Book forms. The Sunday morning service followed Mattins as far as the first Lesson, after which there is a choice of psalms, including a metrical psalm and a thanksgiving from various sources; then, apparently without a New Testament Lesson, comes the Creed and a large selection of prayers and seasonal collects. No provision is made for Evensong. The Communion Office begins at the Exhortation, and reproduces the Prayer Book order, omitting the Comfortable Words and the Prayer of Thanksgiving, and inserting 'Prevent us, O Lord' before the Blessing. Each section of the service is given a heading : the Absolution is called 'The Benediction', and the Blessing 'The Mission'. Presumably this service followed Mattins, and the Epistle and Gospel were read immediately after the seasonal collect ; hence no need for a Second Lesson. In any case Sanderson had always to aim at brevity to avoid detection.

Churching, Baptism, Burial, and Matrimony follow, in that order. They adhere closely to the Prayer Book services, with the exception of Burial, which is remodelled as shown in the table on p. 148. The service in church is assimilated to Mattins by the insertion of the Lord's Prayer and the psalms ; the interment follows the Lesson, as was apparently often the custom ; and the service ends at the graveside.

Many clergymen were employed as private chaplains to noblemen, among them Jeremy Taylor, chaplain to the Earl of Carbery at Golden Grove in Wales. Here he compiled a *Collection of Offices . . . taken out of the Scriptures and the ancient*

PRAYER BOOK	SANDERSON
At the church stile Sentences	*At the church gate* Sentences
	In the church Lord's Prayer Psalms 39 and 90 Lesson : 1 Corinthians 15

At the grave
'Man that is born of a
    woman'
'Forasmuch as it hath
    pleased'
'I heard a voice from heaven'
	At the grave
	Prayer
	
	'Forasmuch . . .'

(*In the church*) Lesson : 1 Corinthians 15 Lesser Litany Lord's Prayer 'Almighty God' 'O merciful God'	 Lesser Litany Lord's Prayer 'Almighty God' The Grace

Liturgies ; the latter are those of 'the Greek Church, with some mixture of the Mozarabic and Ethiopic and other liturgies'. Taylor's eminence lies in his devotional and doctrinal writing, and the *Collection of Offices*, though not without influence in detail, and a fruitful quarry for anthologists of prayers, was too far removed, especially in the Communion Service, from Prayer Book language and structure to make a wide appeal in its own generation. It did, however, herald a new approach to the early liturgies.

This also found expression in a new species of literature, the Prayer Book commentary. Explanation of the Prayer

Book services began with their defence against Roman and Puritan attacks, but, once the main lines of defence had been laid down, the time was ripe for historical study and devotional exposition. This was provided during the Commonwealth by the *Rationale* of Anthony Sparrow, which borrows the title of a famous medieval liturgical treatise ; and the *Alliance of Divine Offices* of Hamon L'Estrange, a devout and well-read layman. The latter sets out the text of the 1604 Book with the variations of 1549, 1552, 1559, and the Scottish Liturgy of 1637 in parallel columns or marginal notes. He also points out discrepancies in the Latin translations of the Prayer Book, and appends the *Order of the Communion* of 1548. These texts are then discussed in eleven chapters of 'Annotations, vindicating the Book of Common Prayer from the main objections of its adversaries, explicating many parcels thereof hitherto not clearly understood, showing the conformity it beareth with the primitive practice, and giving a fair prospect into the usages of the ancient Church'.[17] The work, which was reprinted in 1690 and 1699, put the historical study of the Prayer Book on a serious footing, and pointed the way towards further investigation and utilization of the primitive rites.

Meanwhile, Bishop Wren, shut away in the Tower, reflected that 'Never could there have been an opportunity so offenceless on the Church's part for amending the Book of Common Prayer as now, when it hath been so long disused that not one of five hundred is so perfect in it as to observe alterations.'[18] Accordingly, he occupied much of his eighteen years' enforced leisure in preparing his own suggestions for amendment. These are embodied in a manuscript document whose title-page has been damaged by fire ; since Wren himself refers to 'these Advices', it is convenient to refer to it as the *Advices*. He begins by suggesting a royal proclamation inviting all men of quality to submit proposals for revision, and then sets forth his own. He is greatly, and professedly, concerned with the removal of Latinisms and archaisms, with the explanation of obscurities, and with the defence of the monarchy against sedition. His guiding principle was that 'Whatsoever is not very perfect and right, be it never so small, should now be set right, to prevent all after quarrels; yet all care to be had that, in setting it right, it be done with as little alteration as well may be.'

Another rule is: 'Leave nothing ambiguous.' He notes over three hundred points to be set right, many of them no more than 'hast' for 'didst' and suchlike, but here and there branching out into a scholarly comment. He likes to give chapter and verse, underlining the scriptural origin of much of the Prayer Book text. Some of his suggestions are repeated from his own *Particular Orders for the Diocese of Norwich* (1636), the Scottish Liturgy, and the *Proceedings* of the Lords' Committee. In the Communion Service he joins with Cosin, Wedderburn, Taylor, and L'Estrange in wanting to restore the Thanksgiving for the Departed, and the *Amen* after the Words of Administration; but he makes no suggestion of inserting an epiclesis or moving the Prayer of Oblation. He had agreed to these changes in the Scottish Liturgy, and had seen the result. His most drastic suggestion is the removal of the Exhortations.

It is highly probable that Cosin saw the *Advices* soon after his return to England in 1660, and set to to produce his own proposals. These are contained in a paper headed *Particulars to be considered, explained, and corrected in the Book of Common Prayer*, whose title and method of giving reasons for each suggestion are almost certainly derived from the *Advices*. In his early years Cosin had been strongly influenced by Overall, and had made a detailed study of the Sarum books and such Roman writers as Maldonatus. He also worked through Bucer's *Censura* and the *Survey* of 1606, and rebutted their criticisms. During his exile he had come into contact with the French Reformed Church, and he returned to England much more tolerant of Presbyterian ideas than were most of his colleagues. His suggestions differ from the

Advices in being more concerned with the rubrics than with the text, though the latter is not by any means neglected. The former archdeacon and future bishop lays monotonous stress on legality and uniformity, and the avoiding of disputes and questions. Exactitude of statement and the removal of ambiguity are his chief concerns. Several times he appeals to 1549, but the only major change he advocates is the transfer of the Prayer of Oblation. The 1549 position is 'more consonant to the nature of this holy action', and for the same reason he would like the words 'a perpetual memory of that his precious death' to continue 'and sacrifice'.[19] He held that the celebration of the sacrament was commemorative *and* propitiatory, a view which in 1660 was, to say the least, controversial.

In that year the very existence of the Prayer Book was still not assured. Even before Charles II returned to England a deputation of ministers had asked him to abstain from using it in his chapel. He replied that he thought that form of service the best in the world, and refused their request.[20] He had, however, issued the Declaration of Breda, which contained a phrase that soon became a proof-text: 'We do declare a liberty to tender consciences.' Returning to the subject in July 1660 the Presbyterians, who were now the dominant party among the Puritans, complained that the Prayer Book contained 'many things that are justly offensive and need amendment',[21] and this complaint led to the issue of the Declaration of 25 October. As drafted by Clarendon, this promised to appoint 'some learned divines of different persuasions to review [the book], and to make such alterations as shall be thought most necessary, and some such additional prayers as shall be thought fit for emergent occasions'.

It was probably in preparation for this review that Cosin and Wren combined their suggestions in the volume called the *Durham Book*, a Prayer Book dated 1619 in which Cosin entered the bulk of the alterations and additions proposed by himself and Wren, besides a good deal of other material, much of it now added by Cosin himself. Most notably, whereas neither had previously so much as mentioned the Scottish Liturgy, it is quite obvious that they now had it open on the table in front of them. Although they still made good use of 1549, preference is now given to Wedderburn's revision. Its influence can be seen most clearly in the Communion Service. This is to be celebrated at a table standing 'always at the upper end of the chancel', and decently furnished for 'the high mysteries'. The priest's movements are more fully indicated than in 1604, though not as fully as by Andrewes, and provision is made for epistoler and gospeller in addition to the celebrant. Singing is permitted for the Creed and *Sanctus*, and enjoined for *Agnus Dei* and the Post-Communion Sentences which are now added. Andrewes's Offertory Sentences make another appearance; the alms are to be presented upon the Holy Table, and after them the elements. 'Christ's Church militant here in earth' becomes 'Christ's Catholic Church', and every reference to Christ's death becomes his 'death and sacrifice'. The Scottish Book is followed exactly in the introduction of a thanksgiving for the departed; in the rearrangement of the Canon; and in the restoration of the epiclesis and of the memorial of Christ's passion, resurrection, and ascension, 'now represented' to God. Provision is made for reconsecration; an assistant may follow with the chalice; the residue of the consecrated elements is to be veiled, and consumed after the Blessing. Wafer bread may be used, provided it has no figure on it.

Another important source is the Prayer Book itself: many entries are remodellings of material from elsewhere in the book, or the turning of a rubric into a form of words. The Canons of 1604, and occasionally the Elizabethan *Injunctions* and *Advertisements*, are quoted in the rubrics, and thereby made more effective. Cosin's *Devotions* supply a number of smaller matters. Little use, if any, is made of Sparrow or L'Estrange, Sanderson or Taylor. Many of the changes are routine improvements such as would have been made by any reviser. The compilers showed a certain degree of caution in controversial matters : the Scottish Liturgy is never mentioned by name. They also remained silent about the unpopular Laudian practice of making the people come up to the altar rails to receive communion : indeed the words 'Draw near' are spiritualized into 'Draw near with a true heart in full assurance of faith'. But even so the *Durham Book* is unmistakably Laudian at heart. To take only two examples, the Baptism Service now has a blessing of the water, while the duty towards God in the Catechism includes the clause 'to honour and worship him with the outward reverence of my body',[22] a deliberate renewal of two practices to which the Puritans objected most vigorously, the blessing of inanimate things and bowing to the altar.[23] The Puritan demand for more thanksgivings was neatly met by the addition of one headed 'For victory over rebels'. The book was in no way intended to meet the Puritans 'in the midway',[24] as the king had promised their leader, Richard Baxter. Rather it was put forward in the belief held by some of the Scottish bishops in the 1630s that 'if they did not then make that book as perfect as they could, they should never be able to get it perfected after'.[25]

Meanwhile events in the political sphere led to the calling of the promised synod, known to posterity as the Savoy Conference. Although exclusively concerned with revising the Prayer Book, the Conference was an important part of the Restoration Settlement, and as such was managed by politicians rather than by liturgical scholars. In 1661 power lay largely in the hands of a group of Oxford men. Clarendon, the lord chancellor, Gilbert Sheldon, bishop of London, and George Morley, bishop of Worcester, had all been members before the Civil War of the brilliant circle around Lord Falkland at Great Tew. In religion they were latitudinarian, with little interest in liturgy. As against the Laudians, Clarendon held that ceremonial was 'not in itself of that important value to be either entered upon with that resolution, or to be carried on with that passion' ; as against the Puritans, that 'no reformation is worth the charge of a civil war'.[26] Evidence of the intentions of those in power is provided by the Royal Warrant for the Conference, which authorizes the Commissioners 'to advise upon and review the said Book of Common Prayer, comparing the same with the most ancient liturgies which have been used in the Church, in the primitive and purest times. ... And if occasion be, to make such reasonable and necessary alterations, corrections, and amendments therein, as ... shall be agreed upon to be needful or expedient for the giving satisfaction unto tender consciences, and the restoring and continuance of peace and unity ... but avoiding, as much as may be, all unnecessary alterations of the forms and liturgy wherewith the people are already acquainted, and have so long received in the Church of England'.[27] This runs counter to Wren's belief that nobody would now notice any changes, but was certainly truer to the facts, at any rate as far as Parliament was concerned.

There were twelve commissioners on each side, mostly chosen for their moderation. The bishops included Cosin and Sanderson, the Presbyterians were led by Richard Baxter and Edward Reynolds, bishop of Norwich. When the Conference began on 15 April 1661, Sheldon took control of the business, using Morley as his mouthpiece. He took the line that the bishops were content with the book as it stood, and that it was for the other side to produce proposals for revision. This move, aimed at the Presbyterians, also boded ill for the sponsors of the *Durham Book*. The Presbyterians, however, were willing to comply, though the comparison with ancient liturgies remained a dead letter, for lack of texts acceptable to both sides. The Presbyterian proposals took two forms. Baxter was entrusted with the composition of a completely new alternative liturgy, and a sub-committee was appointed to draw up a list of criticisms of the Prayer Book.

The criticisms, or *Exceptions*, as they were entitled, were divided into General (eighteen) and Particular (seventy-eight). They form a bulky document, occupying, with the bishops' *Answer*, some sixty pages in the modern reprints. It shows signs of the haste with which it was compiled; much is copied from earlier sources, and the classification is sometimes misleading. But when rearranged according to subject-matter, it provides an excellent summary of Puritan criticism of the Prayer Book as it had been developed over a century of controversy. Three main groups may be distinguished: general principles, defects in wording, and objectionable usages.

The general principles begin with the premises that the book should be doctrinally acceptable to all Protestants. The gift of conceived prayer should be allowed free exercise. There should be no readings from the Apocrypha (hence no *Benedicite* and no Offertory Sentences from Tobit). There are only two sacraments, so alterations are required in Confirmation and Matrimony where the text seems to hint that they are sacraments. There have been no godparents since 1645, and the practice should not be revived. It must not be presumed that all worshippers are regenerate, as the language of the Prayer Book so often suggests, particularly in the contexts of Baptism and Burial. Formal observance of religious duties is not to be required, as in the communion of newly married couples. A stricter discipline should be exercised in admitting to Baptism and Communion.

The defects in wording, besides many points too slight to be enumerated, include a general objection to the people's participating in the prayers: their part is 'to be only with silence and reverence to attend thereunto, and to declare their consent in the close by saying, Amen'. This applies especially to the Litany. 'Minister' is to be substituted throughout for 'priest', and 'Lord's Day' for 'Sunday'. No portions of the Old Testament or the Acts of the Apostles are to be called 'Epistles'. The Collects are disorderly, and need revision. The new translation of the Bible is to be used for all readings from Scripture. A purer version of the metrical Psalms should be provided; and all obsolete words, such as 'worship' and 'depart', should be altered.

Under the heading of usages, the four ceremonies duly appear: kneeling for communion, the surplice, the cross in baptism, and the wedding ring. Ante-Communion is not to be said at the Holy Table (an echo of the Laudian persecutions). There is to be no observance of Lent or of saints' days. Movement in the course of services is to be avoided as far as possible. On wet days the whole of the Burial Service may be said in church. (This provoked the bishops to reply: 'being not pretended to be for the ease of tender consciences, but of tender heads, [this] may be helped by a cap better than a rubric'.)

These suggestions far overstepped the limits laid down in the Warrant, and the bishops conceded only seventeen points out of ninety-six, three general and fourteen particular. Only one is of any significance, the substitution of the Authorized Version, and this in no way affects the structure or doctrine of the services. The only area in which anything like agreement was attainable was the removal of archaisms. Of the other concessions, six are concerned with general principles, seven with wording, and two with usages. They apply only to single phrases, often in a rubric; one of them is barely intelligible; and several are so far from being characteristically Puritan that they had already been put forward as proposals in the *Durham Book*. Apart from the concessions, each 'exception' is carefully but firmly rebutted by the bishops. Neither side will budge an inch. The bishops, in fact, still maintained the intransigent attitude they had adopted at the beginning of the Conference. Even so inoffensive a suggestion as a change of psalm in the Churching of Women was peremptorily refused with the words 'fit and pertinent ... and therefore not to be changed'. Yet a few months later, in Convocation, a change was adopted.

It is clear that to have accepted the whole, or even the bulk, of the *Exceptions* would have produced something much more like the Genevan service book than the Book of Common Prayer, and so would have changed the whole character of the Church of England. It was not for this that the bishops had suffered exile, impoverishment, and persecution. Baxter's alternative liturgy proved equally unacceptable. The Sunday morning service was an attempt to carry out the suggestions of the *Directory* in a set form, while including a certain amount of inoffensive material from the Prayer Book. The Lord's Supper, when celebrated, is appended to the ordinary service in the same way as in the *Directory*, and shares with the latter the prayer for the sanctification of the elements, here placed before the Words of Institution. Fraction likewise follows the prayer. The service also originally contained 'a few lines . . . where the word "offering" was used', but Baxter's fellow-commissioners removed them. A compromise that pleased nobody, it was rejected without hesitation by the bishops.[28]

The Conference broke up on 25 July without achieving anything, and the bishops found themselves committed to preserving the Prayer Book virtually unaltered. Meanwhile a Bill 'for the Uniformity of Public Prayers' had been given its third reading in the House of Commons, and annexed to it was 'a Book of Common Prayer . . . imprinted at London in the year 1604'.[29] It went up to the Lords, where it remained until January 1662 before being read, but the date of the edition chosen shows that the memory of the charges against Laud still lingered. Parliament, at any rate, saw no need for changes in any direction, Puritan or Laudian.

During the succeeding months, while Cosin was in Durham, his chaplain, William Sancroft, was left in charge of the *Durham Book*. He first added the concessions made at the Savoy Conference, and then carried out a thorough revision in detail, improving the rubrics in about eighty places, and in sixty-six restoring the printed text. These latter had been alterations like those of the *Exceptions*, 'so nice, as if they that made them were given to change'. In this process there is very little fresh material associated with Cosin, whereas there are a dozen changes obviously derived from Wren. There are new proposals of some importance : for instance, Cosin had introduced an Ember Collect of his own composition, to which Sancroft now added the note, 'Or, that of the Scottish Liturgy'. The indiscreet reference was then hastily crossed out, and the text of the collect substituted. Two points made by the Presbyterians are now conceded : the Tobit Sentences are omitted, and the sick man is only to be absolved 'if he shall humbly and heartily desire it'. Up to this point the *Durham Book* had been merely a private manifesto ; it had yet to be submitted to authority. At some point about the beginning of September 1661, Wren must have taken up the matter with Sheldon, or *vice versa*, with the result that the two bishops wrote urgently to Cosin, asking him to return to London by the beginning of November, which he promised to do.[30]

Meanwhile, Sancroft had a further task. As the *Durham Book* had no Ordinal, Cosin had begun to correct The Ordering of Deacons in a Prayer Book of 1634, and Sancroft completed the rest of the Ordinal. This was only a matter of going through the text with Wren's suggestions (most of which have been subsequently lost), for none of the other sources previously used were concerned with the Ordinal. The next step was to copy the contents of the *Durham Book* into the main body of the new book. Quite apart from the advantage of having all the proposals under one cover, the crucial pages of the *Durham Book* had become almost undecipherable. The text of the 1634 edition was also free from a number of errors found in the *Durham Book* text, having benefited from Cosin's supervision of the printers. The resultant book is known as the *Fair Copy*. It was by no means a carbon copy. Besides twenty more improvements to rubrics and twenty-eight further rejections of alterations, there is one change of supreme importance. In addition to the *Durham Book* version of the Canon, which is written out in full on a separate sheet ('Paper B'), there is a new, much more conservative revision, indicated by marginal annotations to the printed text. It retains the old order and text of the prayers intact, though admitting the *Durham Book* rubrics and Words of Administration. Sancroft adds a note that both versions 'are left to censure'. In the *Durham Book* he later recorded the result of that 'censure', namely that 'My lords the bishops at Ely House ordered all in the old method', after which he outlines an order which corresponds in every detail to the newer Canon.[31]

Its authorship will probably never be known. The first initiative must surely have come from Sheldon; Cosin can have had no part in it. He may have been prevailed upon to accept it at the meeting of the three bishops at the beginning of November, or he may have insisted that the final 'censure' be left to Convocation. In either case the responsibility for the suppression of the *Durham Book* Canon must rest with Sheldon, for, when Convocation met, a committee of eight bishops was at once appointed to carry on the work of revision between the full sessions; and of the eight, four were staunch supporters of Sheldon in the persons of Morley, Sanderson, Henchman, and Nicholson. Besides Cosin and Wren, the other two members were Skinner and Warner, both in disfavour and anxious to please Sheldon. In this committee, if not before, the *Durham Book* Canon was finally buried. Its fate is not surprising. At a time when efforts were being made to win over the dissenting brethren, it would have created a new stumbling-block of formidable dimensions.

On 21 November the final revision began. Official policy was to rush the book through with the minimum of debate. Sheldon is said to have remarked before the session began that 'what should be, was concluded on or resolved'; and Clarendon complained that 'the consideration of it took up much time', although in fact the whole business was concluded in twenty-two days. The bulk of the work must have been done in committee. The Convocation records are disappointingly sketchy, but they do at least show that consideration of the proposals in full session of both Upper and Lower Houses must have been rapid and superficial. According to James Parker's calculation, changes involving the erasure of approximately 4500 words and the addition of 10,500 were passed in sixteen hours' sitting.[32] These debates were only held from 8 to 10 a.m., and the committee thus had considerably more time in which to prepare the next day's portion. Much of the preparatory work had already been done by Cosin and Wren; and it is clear that the *Fair Copy* was carefully examined, and many of its less controversial suggestions accepted. Most of the additional services required had been prepared during May and June, and only needed revising; and such items as the Table of Moveable Feasts were allotted to experts. Even so, they must have been pressed for time: the greatest debate 'was between the Cambridge professor Dr Gunning and the Oxford professor Dr Creed, about . . . the age of children to be confirmed'.[33]

As the work progressed, a number of scribes prepared a full manuscript text, which was eventually signed by the proctors in Convocation and annexed to the Act of Uniformity. It preserves a number of readings which were subsequently discarded, and must have been copied from some otherwise unknown source.[34] Some are completely new, and must have originated in the committee. Four of them are definitely attributable to Sanderson. The final text was entered by Sancroft in a 1636 Prayer Book, known as the *Convocation Book*; from this the Annexed Book was corrected. The outstanding figures on the committee were clearly Sanderson, Cosin, and Wren. Wren secured the inclusion of a number of points in his *Advices* which had not been included in the *Durham Book*, and Cosin the reinstatement of a number of his suggestions which had been omitted from the *Fair Copy*.

Elizabeth I in her coronation robes, by Nicholas Hilliard

Effigies D. Joannis Corin Episcopi
Dunelmensis &c

W. Dolle Sculp

John Cosin (1594–1672): a portrait published shortly after his death

The friends of the Presbyterians kept up their pressure, with help from Robert Sanderson. *Benedicite* was dropped; plainsong is no longer allowable; the sick man is to be moved, not required, to make a confession; it is no longer stated that 'the flood Jordan' was sanctified by Christ's baptism; and newly married couples are only recommended, not obliged, to make their communion the same day. The complaint about the disorderliness of the Collects was now taken seriously, and a large number were given more point by introducing direct quotations from Scripture or new phrases, among which are some of the most memorable in the whole Book. In some of these there is a definite hint of Sanderson; others could equally well be Cosin's. Although no concession was made over the four ceremonies, an olive branch was held out in the form of a reference to Canon 30 as an 'explication' of the cross in Baptism, and the restoration of the Declaration on Kneeling. The latter was not added until after the book had been signed, possibly at the Privy Council meeting of 24 February 1662. It was proposed by John Gauden, bishop of Exeter, and opposed by Sheldon; but since Gauden was supported by Morley, who had always been a Calvinist in matters of doctrine, and by the Earl of Southampton, always eager for reconciliation, on this occasion at least Sheldon was defeated.[35]

In other matters the Presbyterians had less success. They were unable to secure the removal of the Apocrypha: 'after a long tug at the Convocation House about that matter, a good Doctor came out at last with great joy, that they had carried it for *Bel and the Dragon*'.[36] Back came *Benedicite* and the Tobit Sentences. Out of some ninety-six points raised in the *Exceptions*, thirty-eight were granted at one stage or another; but eight were withdrawn again, so that in the end about one in three was conceded. Many of those granted were insignificant, and they were granted in a grudging spirit. The collation of the Psalms with the Great Bible was carried out in the Annexed Book, but quietly suppressed in the printing.

The Declaration on Kneeling was modified by the substitution of 'corporal' for 'real and essential', a change attributed to Gunning.[37] The Prayer for All Conditions of Men might seem to meet the request that the Litany be 'composed into one solemn prayer', but it is to be read, not instead of the Litany, but only 'when the Litany is not appointed to be said.'

A more substantial result of Presbyterian influence was the whittling away of the definitely Laudian elements in the *Durham Book*. In the rubric about the Holy Table the word 'always' was removed at once, 'the upper end' after discussion. The words 'offer' and 'sacrifice' were systematically rejected, even to the extent of changing 'the money offered' into 'the money given at the offertory'. Cosin's bidding, 'Let us offer up our prayers and praises for the good estate of the Catholic Church of Christ', was supplanted by the familiar version of 1552, another eleventh-hour gesture after the signing of the Book. One insertion of 'sacrifice' slipped through, probably because it was hidden away in the Exhortation to the Negligent. The Thanksgiving for the Departed, still redolent of 1549, was replaced by an unexceptionable excerpt from the Bidding Prayer of Canon 55. A last-minute intervention by Cosin failed to save the congregation's 'Glory be to thee, O Lord' at the Gospel, though it had remained in constant use even after its omission in 1552.[38] A new rubric, 'When the communicants have conveniently placed themselves', perhaps aroused memories of Laudian insistence on 'coming up', and was altered to 'the communicants being conveniently placed'.

Even the *Fair Copy* version of the Canon was not left as 'my lords the bishops ordered'. Its rubrics and Words of Administration, which had survived from the *Durham Book*, were given a thorough working-over. The rubric allowing an assistant for the chalice was dropped, and the others were brought closer to the 1604 text. 'The sacrament of the Body of Christ' becomes 'the consecrated bread', and then simply 'the bread'. Any idea of preserving 1604 intact must have been abandoned long before Convocation reached the Communion Service, but the principle remained, and was often applied. Originally aimed at the Presbyterians, it did equal harm to the Laudians. It caused the rejection of three new suggestions by Sanderson, one of which had already appeared in the *Exceptions*. A last casualty was the rubric allowing the use of wafers. All that remained of the Laudian programme was the manual acts, the rubrics for reconsecration, veiling, and consumption, and watered-down versions of the Offertory and the Thanksgiving for the Departed.

They had some compensation when the revisers reached the Ordinal. The need in these services was to dispose once and for all of the puritan doctrine of the parity of all ministers. In this the Government agreed with the extremest Laudian. First, the phrase in the Preface, 'every man which is to be consecrated a bishop' was altered to '. . . be ordained, or consecrated bishop', implying a fresh ordination. The Epistles in the Ordering of Priests had to be changed, because both had been used, by Ussher and Burgess respectively, to argue that there was only one order. They were transferred to the Consecration of Bishops, and replaced by the present passage from Ephesians, which speaks of varying gifts of grace for the ministry. In the bishop's charge to the candidates, the word 'pastors' was omitted from the list which now runs 'messengers, watchmen, and stewards of the Lord', in deference to Cosin's theory that in antiquity the word was applied only to bishops. Lastly, and most importantly, the Lower House, led by Gunning and Pearson, clarified the formula accompanying the imposition of hands.[39] In the Consecration of Bishops this had run, 'Take the Holy Ghost, and remember that thou stir up the grace of God, which is in thee, by imposition of hands', which was dangerously similar to the form for Priests. An unmistakable differentiation was now made : 'Receive the Holy Ghost, for the office and work of a Bishop in the Church of God, *now* committed unto thee by the imposition of our hands . . . and remember that thou stir up the grace of God, which is *given* thee, by *this* imposition of *our* hands.' Besides the specifying of the order conferred, the words here italicized are all intended to make the same point. The priesthood is also defined as dependent on episcopal ordination, and the sermon is to declare the esteem in which priests should be held. A new question to bishops-elect, 'Will you be faithful in ordaining, sending, or laying hands on others?' reflects conditions during the Commonwealth, when the number of bishops had sunk dangerously low, despite repeated adjurations from Clarendon, though one of the committee, Bishop Skinner, had a good record in the ordination of priests and deacons.[40]

Other changes were made for their practical value, rather than from doctrinal considerations. Some codified contemporary custom, as in printing the 'State prayers' at the end of Morning and Evening Prayer. Various rubrics are changed into forms of words, notably the Preface at Confirmation. The series of collects appended to the Communion Service is drawn on for prayers to conclude other services. The language is modernized to the extent of substituting 'are' for 'be', and 'who' or 'that' for 'which' (except in the Lord's Prayer). Scripture references are completed by the addition of verse numbers. Rubrics are revised in the interests of clarity and precision, as for instance the Ornaments Rubric. In the Communion Service the Prayer for the King is placed before the Collect of the day, as in the Scottish Liturgy, and the notices before the sermon. The Exhortations are rearranged so that timely notice is placed before rebuke to the negligent. In Baptism, the number of godparents is made definite; the promises are made in the name of the child (hitherto only in Private Baptism); and the Scottish petition for sanctifying the water is inserted. Private Baptism is printed out in full, and Confirmation is all in one piece, where previously the Catechism divided the introductory rubrics from the service. The latter is given more substance by the addition of the Preface and a renewal of the baptismal vows, while the insertion of the Lord's Prayer immediately after the laying-on of hands brings it into line with all the other occasional offices. Burial is remodelled in accordance with Sanderson's scheme; Churching is given a better choice of psalms, despite the bishops' *Answer* to the *Exceptions*; and the Commination is restored to Ash Wednesday. In the Ordinal, a special Gospel is provided for Deacons; Cosin's translation of *Veni, creator Spiritus* is substituted for the old version; and the Ordering of Priests is assimilated to that of Deacons in order to facilitate the conferring of both orders at one service.

Having completed the process of making alterations, Convocation turned to the additions. These were more substantial. Proper Psalms were provided for Ash Wednesday and Good Friday, as were a Collect, Epistle, and Gospel for Epiphany VI, an Epistle for the Purification, an extra Easter Anthem, and a Collect for Easter Even (from the Scottish Liturgy, but much improved). The section headed *Prayers* was enlarged by a second prayer 'in time of dearth' (from 1552, omitted in 1559), two Ember prayers (from Cosin's *Devotions* and the Scottish Liturgy), a prayer for Parliament first printed in 1625 and now revised, and the Prayer for All Conditions of Men. The latter was probably composed by Reynolds, who was also the author of the new General Thanksgiving, though both were thoroughly worked over by Sanderson in Convocation.[41] Wren contributed a thanksgiving 'for restoring public peace at home', and an appendix of four prayers was added to the Visitation of the Sick, in which the hand of Sanderson is once more clearly visible.

Various new services had been drawn up during the summer session of 1661. On 16 May forms for the king's return and the martyrdom of Charles I were allotted to two committees. The former was prepared at once, and used on

29 May. It follows exactly the outline of the form for 'Gunpowder Treason', and was probably mainly the work of Wren, who introduced it in Convocation on 18 May. The Martyrdom service has a complicated history, beginning with the forms of prayer issued for the Cavalier army in the 1640s. A form said to have been drawn up by Bishop Duppa and revised by Sancroft was printed and used on 30 January 1661, but was 'in too high a strain' to be acceptable. The final version was first printed on 7 January 1662, and again follows 'Gunpowder Treason', but differs from that and the 29 May service in providing for Evensong. On 18 May a committee was appointed to prepare 'a form for the baptizing of adult persons'. The composition of the service, attributed mainly to George Lloyd, bishop of St Asaph, took little time, as it is a straightforward adaptation of Public Baptism, and it was approved on 31 May. In November it needed revision in order to incorporate the changes made in its prototype, and some traces of the older version still remain unaltered. Sanderson again contributed some of the phrasing. The 'Forms of Prayer to be used at sea' first appear in the Convocation records on 5 December. Isaak Walton says that they were altered and added to by Sanderson, and internal evidence supports his statement.[42] They are not so much services as selections of prayers and psalms. The last addition, again ascribed by Walton to Sanderson, was the Preface, debated on 6 and 7 December. His authorship would not have been obvious from the language, and it was actually committed to Wren, Henchman, and Lloyd, as well as Sanderson. Certainly its advocacy of keeping 'the mean between the two extremes' is characteristic of him. 'Our general aim', the Preface says, 'was not to gratify this or that party in any of their unreasonable demands; but to do that which . . . might most tend to the preservation of peace and unity in the Church.' It was not enough that alterations should be desirable; they must be requisite or expedient; none are, in the last resort, actually necessary. This needs to

be read in the light of the numerous changes that were in fact made, many of them at Sanderson's own suggestion ; but it shows why so few of them were of any importance.

On 21 December 1661 the Book was signed by the Convocations ; with a few alterations it was annexed to the Act of Uniformity, which received the royal assent on 19 May 1662 ; and by the terms of the Act it was to come into use not later than St Bartholomew's Day, 24 August, of the same year. Neither Laudians nor Presbyterians had achieved more than a small part of their desires ; they had compelled an administration which would have preferred to reprint the 1604 text intact to make concessions to both sides ; but in the end it is the same book that emerges with only minor alterations. Sheldon had a more accurate sense of the nation's religious temper than either Cosin or Baxter.

8 Branching off the *Via Media*

And now, what remains but that we rejoice and joy together in our exceeding great happiness, and that in the best of things, our religious worship, an happiness far superior to what other churches and sects enjoy, or rather, fancy they enjoy.

THOMAS BISSE, *The Beauty of Holiness in the Book of Common Prayer*, 1716[1]

I myself so far allow the force of several of those objections [at the Savoy Conference] that I should not dare to declare my assent and consent to that book in the terms prescribed.

JOHN WESLEY to Samuel Walker, 20 November 1755[2]

As to the controverted points (for the sake of which only we thought it necessary to alter the Communion Office), we have followed the first Liturgy of King Edward VI, excepting where we found it not so agreeable as we could wish to the ancient liturgies.

THOMAS BRETT, *A Collection of the Principal Liturgies*, 1720[3]

FEW of those who signed the *Annexed Book* can have imagined that the rite was to remain in force for three hundred years. Even before it had become law, Convocation was looking farther afield. In March 1662 Cosin was asked to prepare a form for consecrating churches, which he duly presented in June; but it contained, according to Sheldon, 'something amiss', and was never approved.[4] Being closely based on Andrewes's form, it was probably thought too definitely Laudian in tone. In 1712 Convocation, faced with the prospect of fifty new churches being built in London, authorized a greatly simplified form, and revised it in 1714.[5] When James II came to the throne, a service was needed for the anniversary of his accession, and the form used in the reigns of Elizabeth, James I, and Charles I was revived. The service for Charles II's restoration still continued in use, but now adapted to commemorate the restoration of the royal family. A cento psalm was substituted for *Venite*, new proper psalms and Second Lesson were appointed, and several collects were added. The service for 30 January was similarly treated, with the further addition of the first two parts of the *Homily against Rebellion*. William III's landing in England took place on 4 November ; he therefore had the 'Gunpowder Treason' service revised to celebrate this new event as well, and did not have a separate Accession Service. This revision was the work of Bishop Simon Patrick, and followed the lines of the 1688 revisions. Anne revived James II's Accession Service : as usual, a cento psalm replaced *Venite*, and new proper psalms were appointed. After the Prayer for the Church, a Prayer for Unity was inserted, which, alone among the collects of the period, is still in use today.

Throughout the eighteenth century occasional forms continued to appear with great regularity. The list in the British Museum Catalogue reads like the battle honours of an infantry regiment. For example :

for the prosperity of the Christian arms against the Turks, and especially for taking the city of Buda (1686);
for restoring the greatest part of the Spanish Netherlands to the possession of the House of Austria (1706);
for the suppression of the late unnatural rebellion, and deliverance of these kingdoms from the calamities of an intestine war (1746);
for putting an end to the late bloody, extended, and expensive war in which we were engaged (1784, revived 1802).

These and many others, often specifying the exact scene of the victory concerned, helped to link Church and State. Other forms were occasioned by non-military matters, such as one

upon occasion of the Queen's being with child (1688);

while a thanksgiving for the harvest, to be said after the General Thanksgiving, first appeared in 1796, and continued to be reissued until 1847. The Church of Ireland not only showed more imagination in the provision of supplementary services, but printed them as appendixes to the Prayer Book. A form for consecration of churches, attributed with great probability to Jeremy Taylor, was so printed from 1666. In 1700 it was joined by a *Form for receiving lapsed Protestants, and reconciling converted Papists*; and a *Form of Prayer for the Visitation of Prisoners*, agreed on in 1711, was added to the Prayer Book in 1721, and remained there until 1926.[6]

The Commonwealth period had interrupted the musical tradition of the cathedrals, and the efforts made to deal with this situation produced music which could be widely used in parish churches. The Psalms, which in the sixteenth century had been sung to plainsong tones, or said (so that the contemporary name for them is 'the reading psalms'), were provided after the Restoration with simplified versions of the tones set in four-part harmony. These chants were rapidly assimilated to a regular metrical scheme, and musicians began to compose new chants on this basis. The 'Anglican Chant' reached its prime in the eighteenth century: the earliest example of a 'double chant' still in general use was first published about 1715. At the same period Tallis's five-part setting of the Responses at Mattins and Evensong was arranged for four voices, and a simple four-part harmonization of Merbecke's setting came into use; these came to be known respectively as the 'Festal' and 'Ferial' Responses. Tallis's music for the Litany was treated similarly. The new generation of composers, led by Henry Purcell and John Blow, drew their texts for anthems chiefly from the Psalms, and in Purcell's case there are clear indications that he chose the Proper Psalms when any were appointed. William Croft made a setting of the Burial Service which became almost inseparably associated with it.

The metrical psalms had been a fertile field for music publishers as early as 1561, when Sternhold and Hopkins's version first appeared 'with apt notes to sing them withal', followed by a series of psalters with four-part harmonizations, culminating in Thomas Ravenscroft's collection of 1621.

After the Restoration John Playford issued *The Whole Book of Psalms* (1677), which remained the standard edition of Sternhold and Hopkins as long as they continued in use. The 'Old Version', however, was gradually superseded by a new versification undertaken by Nahum Tate and Nicholas Brady. This appeared in 1696, with a supplement four years later containing the music, versions of the Canticles, Creeds, and Lord's Prayer, and six hymns, including 'While shepherds watched their flocks by night'. The metrical psalms had at last become respectable, and the two Versions continued in general use throughout the eighteenth century, sometimes taking the place of the 'reading psalms', sometimes sung after the Second Lesson, and sometimes as an introit to the Holy Communion.[7] In 1724 Bishop Gibson issued to the clergy of the diocese of London *A Course of Singing Psalms for Half a Year*. The composite morning service demanded 'the intervention of psalmody, that the transitions from one service to another may not be too sudden and abrupt'. For this purpose he suggested metrical psalms, and provided a selection for twenty-six Sundays, three for each Sunday, under the headings 'Praise and Thanksgiving', 'Prayer to God and Trust in Him', and 'Precepts and Motives to a Godly Life'. For the first Sunday the psalms recommended were 8, 4, and 1 respectively. Each psalm was restricted to four or five verses, and fifty-four psalms were selected, with such surprising exclusions as 46, 104, 121, and 122. Gibson's course was widely adopted outside his diocese.[8] The Dissenters, meanwhile, had progressed beyond metrical psalms, and, under the leadership of Isaac Watts and Charles Wesley, perfected the vernacular congregational hymn.

Under the influence of Sir Christopher Wren, new churches were now built with audibility rather than mystery as the first consideration.[9] The chancel virtually disappeared, and the altar was placed against the east wall of the nave, or in a shallow recess. In this position the priest could be easily seen and heard all over the church. The large box-pew became general during the eighteenth century, and the windows were filled with plain glass. The three-decker pulpit provided a convenient rostrum for the priest and the parish clerk, and in the smaller churches a few instrumentalists supported the singing from a gallery at the west end. Where there was an organ, it was customary to play a short voluntary between the psalms and the First Lesson.[10]

The Prayer Book was fast becoming as much part of the national religious heritage as the Bible, and commentaries found a ready market. To name only the outstanding examples, Thomas Comber's *A Companion to the Temple* was a devotional exposition ; William Nicholls printed all Bishop Cosin's notes in *A Comment on the Book of Common Prayer* ; and Charles Wheatly combined exposition with historical comment in *A Rational Illustration of the Book of Common Prayer*. Most popular of all was Robert Nelson's *Companion to the Festivals and Feasts of the Church of England*. All were regarded as standard authorities, and all were heavily plundered by later writers.

Although the Prayer Book was already being called 'incomparable',[11] it was not regarded as unalterable. Despite the failure of the Savoy Conference, efforts at comprehension still continued, and these always involved revision of the Prayer Book. The accession of a Roman Catholic sovereign brought a new urgency into the matter, and in July 1688 a meeting was held to draw up fresh proposals which should attract the Dissenters. The work was divided : Sancroft, now archbishop of Canterbury, seems to have taken Prayers and Thanksgivings, Baptism, the Catechism, and Confirmation ; Simon Patrick was to revise the Collects ; and a committee including John Sharp and John Moore was entrusted with the Daily Office and the Communion Service.[12] Events, however, moved quickly, and the arrival of William of Orange completely changed the situation. Sancroft and eight other bishops, with about four hundred beneficed clergymen, felt themselves still bound by their oaths of allegiance to James II. They were eventually suspended, and came to be known as the Nonjurors. It was not until October 1689 that an official commission could start work on the project. The Commissioners were chosen from all parties : Gilbert Burnet, Richard Kidder, Edward Stillingfleet, Thomas Tenison, and John Tillotson were notable Latitudinarians, or Broad Churchmen; the High Church party had at least ten members, few of them well-known to posterity except William Beveridge. In the middle were Henry Compton, Simon Patrick, and John Sharp. Besides the work done under Sancroft's direction the previous year, the Commission was able to draw upon 'a complete list of all the exceptions that had ever been made to the Prayer Book, either by Puritans before the Civil War or by Nonconformists afterwards',[13] which had been collected by Tenison, who acted as secretary to the Commission. A revised translation of the Psalms had been prepared by Kidder, an able Orientalist. It seems probable that the Commission was intended to placate the Nonjurors as well as the Dissenters. However, about half of the High Church members boycotted the proceedings, and in the end Convocation's hostility became so obvious that the Commission never even produced a report.

Their proposals, entered in an interleaved Prayer Book now in Lambeth Palace Library, were studied throughout the following century in a rather inadequate summary printed in Edmund Calamy's *Abridgment of Mr Baxter's History of his Life and Times*, and deserve more attention from scholars than they have enjoyed. The influence of the High Churchmen may be seen in the addition of the Beatitudes as an alternative to the Ten Commandments, following the example of Jeremy Taylor's *Collection of Offices*, though modifying his response. The introduction of Psalm 8 at Evensong and the substitution of cento psalms in the Visitation of the Sick and the Churching of Women follow Taylor's methods, though not his actual words. The

Confirmation Service was expanded by inserting a verbatim renewal of baptismal vows, a suggestion of the *Durham Book* which had failed to get through Convocation.[14] 'A Prayer for Repentance' was written by 'A[rch] B[ishop] S[ancroft] &c in K[ing] James's time', and so perhaps was 'A preparatory prayer for the receiving of the Communion', based on the First Exhortation.[15] To Sancroft may well be due also the stress laid on the Ember Weeks and the provision of a proper for Rogation Sunday. Four of the Offertory Sentences are placed in a separate group, 'to be read only in those churches where the custom is that the minister has any share in the offerings'. This division had also been suggested in the *Durham Book*, at Wren's instance.[16] A Proper Preface was provided for Good Friday, and in the Prayer of Humble Access and in the Catechism a reference was inserted to 'the sacrifice' of Christ's Body and Blood. A rubric at the end of the Communion Service reads :

> And in every great town and parish there shall be a Communion once a month; and in every parish at least four times in the year, that is, on Christmas Day, Easter Day, Whit-Sunday, and some Lord's Day soon after Harvest at the minister's discretion. And all ministers shall exhort their people to communicate frequently.

A final example of High Church influence may be seen in the new title of the Commination, 'The Proper Office for Ash Wednesday'.

On the other hand, the *Exceptions* made at the Savoy Conference are met in at least twenty points, most of them verbal (for example, 'such as travel' for 'all that travel'). Though the four ceremonies are retained, they are now provided with a loophole. The Ornaments Rubric is removed, and any minister 'who cannot satisfy his conscience in the use of the surplice' or 'in baptizing any with the sign of the cross', may apply to his bishop for a dispensation, and the bishop shall appoint a curate, if required, who is not bound by such scruples. Likewise, parishioners, after discussion with their parish priest, may receive the communion 'in some convenient place or pew'. The wedding ring is declared in a rubric to be 'only used as a civil ceremony and pledge'. Complaints that regeneration is too lightly assumed in Baptism and Burial are adequately met; and the priest says to the sick man 'I pronounce thee absolved', instead of 'I absolve thee'. Godparents are no longer regarded as essential. All the black-letter saints' days are removed from the Kalendar. *Benedicite* and the Tobit Sentences disappear once again, the former replaced by Psalm 148, while *Magnificat* and *Nunc Dimittis* give way to Psalms 8 and 134; *Benedictus*, curiously, remains, though now as the second choice (in musical settings of this period *Jubilate* is almost always preferred). Conditional ordination is recommended for Dissenting ministers, leaving them 'the freedom of their own thoughts concerning their former ordinations'. For continental protestant ministers the deacon's formula would suffice.

Other changes would be equally acceptable to both parties. Improvement was aimed at, as well as the satisfaction of the parties. The Litany is to be used continuously with the Holy Communion, the prayer 'We humbly beseech thee' being followed directly by the Collect for Purity. The Collect for the King is then omitted; after the Creed follow the General Thanksgiving, the Prayer of St Chrysostom, the Grace, the notices, the 'singing psalm' ('Query, of what Translation?'), and the sermon. The desirability of including the Prayer for the Church before the sermon was raised, but no decision was taken. All is to be said in the reading-pew. On 'Sacrament Sundays', of course, the Communion Service would follow its normal course. In Confirmation an exhortation is 'to be read the Lord's Day before'; the doxology is added to the Lord's Prayer (though not in Baptism!); and a prayer and another exhortation are inserted before the Blessing. In Burial, a lesson from 1 Thessalonians 4 is provided as an alternative 'in colder or later seasons'; and Churching concludes with the Blessing, if the office is not used within another service.

Bishop Patrick's suggested alterations to the Collects were gone over by Stillingfleet, Burnet, and Tillotson, but not, apparently, by any of the High Church party. They consist chiefly in adding direct quotations from the Epistle and Gospel of the day, after the example of the 1662 revisers; they certainly add body and 'order' to the content of the Collects. Eight Collects for Sundays after Trinity, which were thought 'good but not suitable to the Epistle and Gospel', were transferred to the 'Collects to be said when there is no Communion', and completely new ones were composed in their stead. The answers in the Catechism are more precisely articulated, and a new preface to the Commination deals with the true purpose of fasting. Bishop Burnet wanted to remodel the formula of ordination in accordance with the findings of Jean Morin, published in 1655, but he was overruled. He would also have liked to insert a note in the Nicene Creed 'with relation to the Greek Church', and to omit the Athanasian Creed altogether, as being too Western in outlook. The latter was retained, but only on five days in the year, instead of thirteen.

As the legal position of the Dissenters improved, the desire for a comprehensive liturgy weakened. Proposals for revision still had an eye to comprehension, but the main motives lay elsewhere. A strong influence was exerted by the doctrinal temper of the age, which tended to Deism or Unitarianism. Early in the eighteenth century Dr Samuel Clarke made a private revision of the Prayer Book in which the Nicene Creed was replaced by a psalm, and all Trinitarian formulae were modified or completely removed. Other criticisms arose from pastoral needs and literary taste. There was a general feeling that the Prayer Book Office for the Visitation of the Sick was inadequate, and that the situation was not sufficiently covered by Canon 67, but should be met by the issue of a better official form.[17] Unofficial critiques of

Prayers.

Preparatory Prayer for ye Receiving of ye Communion, to be read on ye Lords day or some week day or days before.

O God who hast ordained holy mysteries for a commemoration of our Saviours wonderfull love in laying down his life for us, & for ye communication of ye benefits of his death & passion to us; we beseech thee to dispose all those, who intend to ~~receive this holy Sacrament~~ come to thy Table with such sincere repentance of all their sins, unfeigned Resolutions of better obedience, & with such an humble faith & ardent love unto thee & unto all men, that they may comfortably hope for thy gracious pardon, & for ye power of thy holy Spirit, to carry them, by patient continuance in well doing, into eternall life, through Jesus Christ o̅r̅ L̅d̅. AMEN.

For Repentance. A Prayer to be said in any time of Calamitie.

Almighty God & most mercifull Father: we miserable Sinners do here humbly acknowledge before thee, that we are unworthy of ye least of all thy mercies: we confess, o̅ L̅d̅, in ye bitterness of o̅r̅ souls yt we have grievously sinned against thee: that all orders of men amongst us have transgressed thy righteous Laws: that we have hitherto evaded both thy mercies & thy judgments in respect both to o̅r̅ amendment. It is of thy mere mercy, o̅ L̅d̅, that we are not consumed; for wch o̅ Lord do magnify & bless thy name. O God who hast hitherto spared us to ye end yt thy goodness might lead us to Repentance: Let it be thy good pleasure to give unto us all yt godly sorrow wch worketh repentance to salvation not to be repented of; That thou mayst turn ~~from~~ thy heavy displeasure against us, & mayst ~~rejoyce~~ over us to do us good, through ye merits & mediation of Jesus Christ our L̅d̅ & only Saviour. AMEN.

2. of Prayers for ye Army & Navy.

XX

Rubric.

Prayers from the Proposals of 1689, attributed to Archbishop Sancroft; handwriting of Thomas Tenison

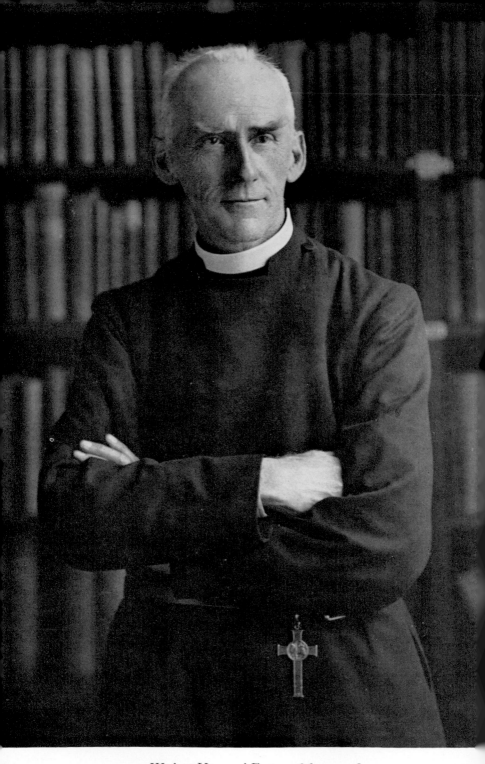

Walter Howard Frere, 1863–1938

the Prayer Book were numerous. A typical example is *An Essay for a Review of the Book of Common Prayer, to which is added a Specimen thereof* . . . *attempted by an Impartial Hand*, which appeared anonymously in 1734. The author is chiefly concerned with bringing the English style of the Prayer Book up to the level of contemporary taste. He commends the proposals of 1689, and follows them in his treatment of the canticles. The Ten Commandments are relegated to a footnote, because, it is interesting to learn, 'they are now never used as part of the Communion Service'. He places *Gloria in excelsis* immediately after communion, and omits the Blessing.

By 1749 interest in revision had become so widespread that John Jones, vicar of Alconbury, was able to fill a volume with suggestions collected from his contemporaries. The book, entitled *Free and Candid Disquisitions*, was widely read, and indeed studied by the authorities. No action was taken, except that one of Jones's requests, for more topical prayers, was met by the issue in 1759 of a form of prayer 'for the ceasing of the distemper which lately raged among the horned cattle in this kingdom', a subject which Jones had specifically mentioned. It would have been difficult to make any changes without the co-operation of Convocation, which had transacted only formal business since 1717. Jones begins by raising a subject which was destined to recur, the inordinate length of the Sunday morning service. There is much repetition, and Mattins is sufficient by itself if there is to be no Communion. There should be proper psalms for every Sunday, and hymns should be introduced, especially during communion. Sternhold and Hopkins should be discarded. The choice of lessons could be improved, and the Sunday psalms and lessons should be omitted from the weekday course. Jones reveals puritan leanings in asking for the Athanasian Creed to be omitted, and the cross in baptism to be made optional, while private baptism should be abolished altogether. He lists a number of supplementary offices which are needed : for excluding unworthy members, and their re-admission ; for receiving and re-ordaining of proselytes ; for prisoners at debt and criminals ; at executions ; for preparation for Holy Communion; and for family prayers. Forms for excommunication and reception had been drawn up by Convocation in 1714, but never passed into law.[18] Jones ends his book with an anthology of passages on Prayer Book revision from Lord Bacon down to 1748, including Edmund Calamy's summary of the 1689 proposals. Jones realizes the shortcomings of this summary and wishes a fuller account was available.

As he hoped and suggested, Jones's work led to the production of a number of unofficial schemes for revision, many of which acknowledge it as their inspiration. All those compiled by Church of England authors omit the Athanasian Creed, *Benedicite*, and the words 'and there is no health in us' ; most omit *Benedictus*, *Magnificat*, and *Nunc Dimittis*. There is also a marked tendency to leave out the second Lord's Prayer and the suffrages at Mattins and Evensong. Much the most influential was *The Book of Common Prayer reformed according to the plan of the late Dr Samuel Clarke*. This was the work of Theophilus Lindsey, an Anglican clergyman who had joined the Presbyterians. A copy of Clarke's suggestions which came into his hands so much impressed him that he expanded and published them in 1774. Apart from its strongly Unitarian tone, Lindsey's book contains many interesting ideas. In order to remove any suggestion that it is the priest who forgives sins, Lindsey replaces the Absolution at Mattins and Evensong by the Collect for Purity, and turns that at Holy Communion into a prayer to God to forgive 'us'. The canticles are variously treated : *Te Deum*, *Benedicite*, *Magnificat*, and *Nunc Dimittis* are dropped ; *Jubilate* is alternative to *Venite* ; *Benedictus* is reduced to verses 1–5, 7, and 8 ; and Psalm 145 takes the place of *Te Deum*. 'The Holy Ghost' gives way to 'the Holy Spirit'. The Prayer for all conditions of men is included in Mattins, the Prayer for the Church

Militant in Evensong, and the General Thanksgiving in both.

When there is a Communion, Mattins begins with the Ten Commandments and the Litany; after the First Lesson follow two parts of Psalm 119 or Psalm 103, after the Second, Psalm 19; after the Lord's Prayer, the Collect for Purity and the General Thanksgiving lead into the Communion Service, which begins at 'Ye that do truly'. The language is much altered, though the structure is basically unchanged. 'The burden of them is intolerable' is omitted, as is any suggestion of sacrifice, and the reference to Christ's coming again. The Prayer of Humble Access, the Lord's Prayer, and the Prayer of Thanksgiving are omitted, and the Blessing is replaced by the Grace. Fraction takes place after the Words of Institution, as in the *Directory* and Baxter's Liturgy. In Baptism the promises are to 'exhort this child' and 'instruct him in the gospel', and the service ends with a long exhortation. There are no services of Private Baptism, Baptism of those of Riper Years, or Confirmation. In Matrimony, the 'causes for which matrimony was ordained' are removed; there is no psalm, and only one prayer following, but again a lengthy exhortation is added. In Burial the 'sure and certain hope' is 'that there shall be a resurrection to eternal life', and the words 'as our hope is, this our brother doth' are omitted on the same grounds.

Puritan influence is clear in Lindsey's book, but the final realization of Baxter's ideals was achieved by John Wesley. In 1754 he also read Calamy's *Abridgment*, and found himself much in sympathy with the Presbyterian divines. Thirty years later he prepared a service book for the Methodists in America, and in 1786 a new edition was published for use in England, under the title *The Sunday Service of the Methodists, with other Occasional Services*. In this revision, Wesley adopted many of the Puritan suggestions of 1661,[19] but he was also much influenced by Lindsey's book, and possibly by other proposals, such as Jones's *Disquisitions*.

Wesley follows the *Exceptions* of 1661 in excluding the

Apocrypha from the lectionary; in discarding all holy days except Christmas Day, Good Friday, and Ascension Day; and in making no provision for Lent, the Sundays being numbered 'after Christmas' up to and including Passion Sunday. He does, however, retain 'all the Fridays in the year' as days of abstinence, a relic of his early High Church practices. Like Lindsey, he discards Private Baptism and Confirmation; unlike him, he also discards Visitation of the Sick (but not Communion of the Sick), Churching, the Commination, the State Services, and the Sea Service. All general rubrics are omitted, and throughout the book 'priest' is replaced by 'minister' or, in the Communion and Ordination Services, 'elder'. Wesley's view of the ministry was similar to Lindsey's, and he follows him in replacing the Absolution at Mattins by a collect (in his case, that for Trinity XXIV) and turning that at Holy Communion into a prayer. In the Ordaining of Elders, the words 'Whose sins thou dost forgive . . .' are omitted, and the Gospel in which they occur is not appointed for the Ordaining of a Superintendent.

Morning and Evening Prayer are shortened, in order to leave more room for preaching, by omitting the Exhortation at the beginning, the second Lord's Prayer, and the Suffrages. *Benedicite* disappears with the Apocrypha, and all the Gospel canticles are replaced by the psalms provided by the Prayer Book as alternatives. The Athanasian Creed is omitted, and the Litany is only to be read on Wednesdays and Fridays. On the other weekdays prayer was to be extemporary. All mention of singing the service is removed. Again following Lindsey, the Prayer for all conditions of men and the General Thanksgiving are transferred to Mattins and Evensong, and the other Prayers and Thanksgivings are discarded. In all these changes Wesley is in line with the general opinion of the time.

In the Communion Service changes are fewer. Wesley omits the first Collect for the King, the Nicene Creed, the three Exhortations, and the offering of bread and wine, but not the Tobit Sentences. A further debt to Lindsey is the omission of the phrase 'the burden of them is intolerable' in the Confession, and the whole of the Prayer of Thanksgiving. It was Wesley's practice to have hymn-singing at Holy Communion, and one of his brother Charles's hymns is based on the epiclesis of the 1549 Book.[20] The congregation is to stand for the Comfortable Words, but is not required to kneel for communion. Wesley allows extemporary prayer before the Blessing. If reconsecration is necessary, the whole of the Prayer of Consecration must be repeated. In this service Wesley's youthful enthusiasm for the Nonjurors and his High Church grounding have exerted a stronger pull than his later enthusiasm for the Puritans. Here he joins hands with Luther and Cranmer. The Puritan influence comes to the fore again in Baptism. Godparents are not required, though 'the friends of the child' are mentioned, so there is no need for the address and questions to the sponsors. All references to regeneration are removed except one, as is the rubric about baptized children dying in infancy. The minister is permitted to sprinkle the child with water. The sign of the cross is omitted, and the reception of the child into the Church. Again extemporary prayer is allowed at the end of the service. Emergency baptisms are covered by the words 'as many of the following prayers as time will permit'.

The ring disappears from Matrimony, with all allusions to it, and also the words 'with my body I thee worship', and the psalms. The commendation and another prayer are omitted from Burial on the usual doctrinal grounds. Many of the Psalms are abridged (Psalm 35 from 28 verses to 8), and thirty-three are entirely omitted, including Psalms 72, 122, and 132; the daily course is altered to allow for the omissions. The Thirty-nine Articles are reduced in number to twenty-five. Wesley, in fact, proceeded almost entirely by omission, and there is virtually no new matter in the *Abridgment*, as it was soon called. The positive contribution of

Methodism is to be found in separate publications such as the Covenant Service and the forms of prayer for private use, for families, and for children ; above all, in the hymns of the two brothers, an achievement unrivalled in any other communion.

The Laudian strain had already begun to bear fruit by the end of the seventeenth century. Edward Stephens produced two unofficial liturgies under the influence of L'Estrange, Sparrow, and Thorndike, and following the example of Jeremy Taylor. The first of the two is an attempted restoration of the ancient forms of service : in actual fact, of the so-called *Clementine Liturgy* which forms book VIII of the fourth-century work entitled *The Apostolic Constitutions.* Stephens' other liturgy is entirely composed of material from the Book of Common Prayer, restoring parts of 1549, which he esteemed highly, and adding parts of the Scottish Book of 1637, which he regarded as 'much the best of any modern form whatever'.[21] Though these liturgies remained a private venture, they blazed the trail for High Church revisions of the next hundred years, nearly all of which start from the assumption that the best models are 1549, 1637, and *The Apostolic Constitutions.*

Stephens' example was followed in conscious admiration by William Whiston, a mathematician and patristic scholar with tendencies towards Arianism. His *Liturgy of the Church of England reduced nearer to the Primitive Standards*, published in 1713, makes very generous use of the *Apostolic Constitutions.* Unlike Stephens, he revised the whole of the Prayer Book. At Morning Prayer he introduces such modern-sounding ideas as a wide choice of canticles, headings before the lessons, and exhortations after them. The Sundays after the Epiphany are continued right up to Passion Sunday, which may have suggested Wesley's treatment. In the Communion Service Whiston omits the first Lord's Prayer, the Ten Commandments, the Confession, and the Absolution. The Prayer for the Church comes after the Comfortable Words, and the Prayer of Oblation before the Communion (though not the Lord's Prayer). For the first time the words 'we offer and present unto thee, O Lord, these thy gifts' are restored to the eucharistic prayer in expression of primitive doctrine. An alternative consecration prayer is provided: described as 'the most ancient form', it is in fact that of the *Apostolic Constitutions*. Although Whiston borrows much of the language of 1549, the structure of his rite is still based on 1662. His Baptism Service is more drastically revised, being designed solely for adults, and combined with Confirmation (in later life Whiston became a Baptist). The candidates are to be 'decently put into the water', and the sign of the cross 'ought to be made with the holy ointment'. Unction is also restored in the Visitation of the Sick. Matrimony is 'a thing of civil nature, and not directly belonging to religious worship', yet 'the ordinary form' is not 'wholly improper'. Whiston's tamperings with the Nicene Creed and other minor eccentricities should not distract attention from his real importance as a pioneer of scholarly revision. On the other hand, the liturgy of John Henley (1726–7) deserves mention only because it has been recently reprinted, and as an example of the prevalent enthusiasm for revision.

Meanwhile the ranks of the Nonjurors, who had originally seceded in protest against the usurpation of William and Mary, were reinforced by those who could accept Mary and Anne, but not the House of Hanover. They were divided into two parties, those whose reasons for secession were purely concerned with oaths of loyalty, and those who were also dissatisfied with the eucharistic theology and liturgy of the Established Church. At first the model of the latter party was the Book of 1549, which they reprinted in 1717;[22] but they also decided to go ahead and produce their own forms of service, with special attention to four points known as 'the Usages': the mixed chalice, the invocation of the Holy Spirit on the elements, the transfer of the Prayer of Oblation, and prayers for the departed. The following year a service-book

appeared which had probably been compiled by Jeremy
Collier, Thomas Brett, and Thomas Deacon, three leading
'Usagers'.[23] It consists of offices for Communion, Con-
firmation, and Visitation of the Sick.

The book follows in the footsteps of Stephens and Whiston.
Further study of ancient liturgies had made its authors more
critical of 1549, which they now thought to be in some
respects as medieval as the Roman Missal. The sources of
their inspiration will become apparent from the contents of
the services. The Communion Office begins with an Introit
Psalm (appointed as in 1549) and the *Kyrie*. The Ten
Commandments are omitted because, first, their insertion
was 'altogether modern and unprecedented'; secondly, they
are 'comprehensively explained in the Church Catechism';
and thirdly, the fourth commandment 'looks somewhat
foreign to the Christian religion'.[24] Their place is taken by
the Summary of the Law (Matthew 22 : 37–40), an innovation that established itself over a very wide field. After the
Sermon come the Exhortations, the third of which is detached
from the penitential section. The Offertory Sentences follow,
'the people kneeling'; they include four of Andrewes's set.
After the presentation of the collection (described as 'the
oblations'), the priest is to mix the chalice 'in view of the
people', and, after 'setting both the bread and the cup upon
the altar', to say an offertory prayer 'abridged out of *St Basil's
Liturgy*', 'that we may be worthy to offer unto thee this
reasonable and unbloody sacrifice'. The Preface follows at
once (beginning with the Salutation), and then the eucharistic
prayer, starting with a recital of 'the most signal instances of
the divine providence and bounty' (from the *Liturgy of St
James*). This is followed by the 'Prayer of Oblation and
Invocation' from the *Apostolic Constitutions*, and the Prayer
for the Church, largely in its 1549 form. These prayers are
placed in the order of the ancient liturgies, other than the
Roman. The rest of the service is exactly as in 1549, with the
addition of *Gloria in excelsis* in the 1552 position.

THE 1718 COMMUNION OFFICE

Introit Psalm
Kyrie
Lord's Prayer
Collect for Purity
Summary of the Law
Collect for the King
Collect of the day
Epistle
Gospel
Creed
Sermon
Exhortation
Offertory Sentences
Presentation of Collection and Elements
Offertory Prayer (*St Basil*)
Sursum corda (with *Benedictus qui venit*)
Prayer of Consecration (*St James*)
Prayer of Oblation and Invocation (*Ap. Const.*)
Prayer for the Church
Lord's Prayer
The peace of the Lord . . .
Christ, our Paschal lamb . . .
Ye that do truly . . .
Confession
Absolution
Comfortable Words
Prayer of Humble Access
Communion
Prayer of Thanksgiving
Gloria in excelsis
Blessing

The changes in Confirmation and Visitation of the Sick are almost entirely concerned with the restoration of unction. The Confirmation Service begins with a prayer of consecration of the 'chrism, or ointment'; and the bishop anoints the candidates with the chrism, making the sign of the cross on their foreheads, and then lays his hands on their heads. At the end of the Visitation of the Sick another prayer of consecration is added, invoking the authority of the Epistle of James, and followed by the 1549 prayer accompanying the anointing. Unction may be repeated as often as desired, 'at the discretion of the priest'. A rubric after the Absolution prescribes its use 'in all private confessions'; alternatively, the Absolution in the Communion Service may be used with the sick.

The Nonjurors were few in number, and among them the 1718 Book was only accepted by the 'Usagers'. They themselves laid it aside in 1732, in an attempt at reconciliation with the 'Non-Usagers', though a splinter group continued to use it until 1748, when Thomas Deacon replaced it with a liturgy that he himself had published in 1734, much more closely modelled on the *Apostolic Constitutions*. By then the Nonjurors were dwindling rapidly, and eventually they died out altogether. But their liturgies, especially that of 1718, had an influence altogether disproportionate to the short time they were in use or the small numbers of those that used them. For the first time a deliberate attempt had been made by an organized body of Anglicans (for so they regarded themselves) to create a liturgy on truly primitive lines. They used the best patristic scholarship of their day to correct what they regarded as the errors of the Book of Common Prayer. In so doing they brought to maturity the work of the pioneers, from Taylor to Whiston, and opened the way for many liturgies of later years. Above all, they regained from the Fathers the conception of the eucharist as a sacrifice.

The immediate fruit of the Nonjurors' labours was

gathered in Scotland. The Scottish bishops were all Nonjurors from the political point of view, and the liturgically minded among them welcomed their colleagues' liturgy with open arms. Others looked rather to the book of 1637: this was reprinted in its entirety by the Earl of Winton in 1712, and the Communion Service alone was published in Edinburgh in 1722 and 1724, the first of a series of 'wee bookies'. Before long, under the leadership of Bishop James Gadderar, who had long been in close contact with the Nonjurors while resident in England, many who used the 1637 form began to alter the order of the prayers. In 1735 an edition appeared in which 'all the parts of this office are ranked in the natural order', and four further editions of this character appeared over the next thirty years. The 'natural order' is that of 1549, except that the Exhortation follows immediately after the Offertory, and the Prayer for the Church follows the Prayer of Oblation, instead of forming the first section of the eucharistic prayer. The Nonjurors had also detached the Exhortation from the penitential section, but placed it *before* the Offertory Sentences. To their example is also due the addition of the Salutation before *Sursum corda*, and the omission of the words 'militant here in earth'. Most significantly, the Scots took over the phrase 'which we now offer unto thee', thus taking a first step in the direction of the ancient liturgies.

Meanwhile Bishop Thomas Rattray, who had been much impressed by the Nonjurors' liturgy of 1718, had conducted a scholarly investigation of the text of the *Liturgy of St James*. The year 1744 saw the posthumous publication of a critical edition with the *Apostolic Constitutions* and other liturgies in parallel columns. An appendix contained *An Office for the Sacrifice of the Holy Eucharist*, closely modelled on *St James* with borrowings from 1637. This office was little used, but its influence may be seen in a further revision of 1637 published in 1755 by Bishop William Falconar. The changes he made may be due either to further study of the Nonjurors or directly to Rattray's work. Falconar places the Exhortation before the Offertory, as the Nonjurors did; the words 'which we now offer unto thee' are printed in capitals; and the epiclesis, which had previously been in the 1549 position before the Words of Institution, now follows the Oblation. Rattray probably suggested the Offertory Sentence from 1 Chronicles in connection with the actual presentation, though Falconar places it after, Rattray during the action; and Rattray's text of *Gloria in excelsis* may be responsible for a strange variant in Falconar's. Other variations are the addition of the Salutation, as in 1718 and 1735; the reading 'his *own* oblation', found in one edition of 1549, and sporadically down to 1735 (notably in Sanderson's Commonwealth form, where it cannot be a printer's error); and the omission in the same sentence of the word 'there', which seemed to restrict the sacrifice to the Cross and exclude the Supper. The phrase thus reads: 'who made by his own oblation of himself once offered'.

The edition of 1755 was due to Falconar's private initiative, but he soon obtained the agreement of his fellow-bishops to a further version prepared by himself and Bishop Robert Forbes, which appeared in 1764, and became the official service of the Episcopal Church of Scotland. To the changes already made in 1755 are added others which show that the compilers knew Thomas Deacon's liturgy of 1734, which had certainly been known to Rattray. From this or from Rattray they derived the phrase 'Let us present our offerings to the Lord with reverence and godly fear', and a bidding before the Prayer of Thanksgiving. The latter is chiefly from Deacon, with one phrase from Rattray and one added by the compilers, who also altered the 1755 wording 'that they may be unto us the Body and Blood of Christ' into 'that they may become the Body . . .'.

This service was the only one authorized officially by the Episcopal Church, though individual bishops drew up Confirmation offices which remained in manuscript.[25] It finally obtained recognition for the results of a century's study of the early liturgies, and created a new type of Communion Service, in which the Prayer for the Church followed the Prayers of Consecration and Oblation, and in which the epiclesis followed the Oblation instead of preceding the Words of Institution. Its influence was immediately felt in America, where the War of Independence had freed the Church from obedience to the Act of Uniformity. Dr Samuel Seabury was elected bishop of Connecticut, and crossed the Atlantic to seek consecration, which he received from the Scottish bishops. A proposed revision of the Prayer Book undertaken by Dr William Smith of Maryland in 1786 proved to be too radical in its outlook,[26] and Bishop Seabury 'set forth and recommended' a form which is virtually identical with the Scottish office of 1764. The following year William White and Samuel Provoost were consecrated at Lambeth, and in 1789 a revision of the English Prayer Book was carried out at a convention in Philadelphia.

The resultant book, published in 1790, with the Ordinal following in 1792, combines English and Scottish ideas. Many of the changes are made with the purpose of modernization. Archaisms are removed, minor abbreviations are permitted, and the Commination is discarded. New forms are provided for the Visitation of Prisoners (the Irish form of 1711), for Harvest Thanksgiving, for the Consecration of Churches (published in 1799 and based on Andrewes), and the Institution of Ministers (1804). Further occasional prayers and thanksgivings are added, including one by Jeremy Taylor in the Visitation of the Sick. The Psalms are freely abbreviated and combined, and hymns are officially recognized : one is to be sung after the Consecration, and as an optional alternative to *Gloria in excelsis* ; they are to be taken from a book entitled *A Selection for the Feasts and Fasts*. Parents may be accepted as godparents in Baptism, an innovation which was to be imitated by many subsequent revisions.

Changes in the Communion Service reflect the Scottish tradition : 'here in earth' is omitted from the Prayer for the Church Militant, and the rubric on kneeling disappears. The Summary of the Law is borrowed from the Nonjurors (to be said *after* the Ten Commandments, not as an alternative), and is followed by the second collect printed after the Blessing as a prayer for grace to keep the Commandments. Most important of all, the Scottish form of the eucharistic prayer was adopted at Bishop Seabury's instance, so that Oblation and epiclesis precede communion. The wording of the epiclesis, however, was restored to the form of 1637, and the Prayer for the Church was retained in the English position. In all other respects the English order was followed. Other changes seem to be influenced by the successors of the Puritans. *Benedictus* is reduced to four verses ; *Magnificat*, *Nunc Dimittis*, and the Athanasian Creed are omitted altogether ; so are the special Absolution in the Visitation of the Sick, and the Ornaments Rubric. The minister need not use the sign of the cross in Baptism. A final group of changes does not belong to any of the categories above : it allows the use of *Gloria in excelsis* as an alternative to *Gloria Patri* after the last psalm in Mattins ; likewise the Absolution from the Communion Service and the Nicene Creed may be used in Mattins. The object seems to have been the combination of Mattins and Ante-Communion.

Thus the end of the eighteenth century saw the principle firmly established that Churches in communion with the see of Canterbury were not committed to the use of the Book of Common Prayer in the exact form annexed to the Act of Uniformity of 1662.

9 Battle Rejoined

The church is larger than before;
You reach it by a carriage entry;
It holds three hundred people more,
And pews are fitted up for gentry.

W. M. PRAED, *The Vicar*

Let them, on the one side and the other, consider that men's judgments of perfection are very various, and what is imperfect, with peace, is often better than what is otherwise more excellent, without it.

Irish Prayer Book of 1877, Preface

It is now clear to me that all the Clergy, of whatever school, are equally stupid.

A. J. BALFOUR, 3 March 1904[1]

THE outbreak of the French Revolution created a great fear of reform in any sphere of national life, and religious practice was no exception. The first quarter of the nineteenth century was a period of inactivity in the Established Church, except for the small band of Evangelicals, who were not at that time interested in liturgical reform. There was, however, a revival of liturgical study. Richard Laurence, afterwards archbishop of Cashel, devoted his Bampton Lectures of 1804 to showing that our Reformation was Lutheran, not Calvinistic.[2] Though the text of the lectures makes little reference to the Prayer Book, they are supported by extremely full notes, in which Laurence points out similarities between Poullain's *Liturgia Sacra* and the Prayer Book of 1552. More important, he analyses in some detail the indebtedness of our Baptism Service to Hermann's *Consultation*, the influence of which had not previously been appreciated. Later, Laurence published the documents of the Visitation of Saxony in 1527 and 1528, thus opening up a line of inquiry which was not pursued for half a century.

Another pioneer was Charles Lloyd, Regius Professor of

Divinity at Oxford, who from 1823 gave a course of private lectures on the history of doctrine, including two on the Prayer Book services. Those who attended the lectures, among them J. H. Newman and E. B. Pusey, were pointed to the study of the medieval service-books. After Lloyd's death in 1829 his notes were utilized by William Palmer, whose *Origines Liturgicae*, published in 1832, brought to the attention of his generation the true ancestry of the Prayer Book. What was self-evident to Cosin, L'Estrange, and the Nonjurors, to say nothing of Puritan writers, had somehow been lost to sight, and was now made generally known once more.

Oxford became the source of a flood of liturgical reprints. Lloyd himself had edited *The Bishops' Book* and *The King's Book*; Edward Burton reprinted three of the Henrician primers; Edward Cardwell produced several indispensable volumes of documents; the works of Comber, Wheatly, and Sparrow were reissued, the last edited by Newman; and the *Library of Anglo-Catholic Theology* offered a very generous selection of the Caroline divines. The publisher Pickering produced some fine facsimiles; A. J. Stephens edited the Sealed Books and other Restoration texts; and William Keeling presented the various Prayer Books printed in parallel columns in *Liturgiae Britannicae* (1851). The fruits of all this labour were gathered by the Reverend Francis Procter in his *History of the Book of Common Prayer* (1854).

When the dammed-up forces of reform eventually burst the floodgates, the first essays at Prayer Book revision were surprisingly old-fashioned in manner. They still breathe the atmosphere of 1689, or at any rate of Jones's *Disquisitions*. Lindsey's Prayer Book continued to appear in edition after edition, and there were several other publications on similar lines, such as *The Common Prayer Book of the Sect of the Thirty-nine Articles, still whimsically enough styling itself the Church of England, made Scriptural in point of language* (?1820). The Athanasian Creed remains the critics' chief

target, while the Apocrypha, priestly absolution, and regeneration in Baptism and Burial continue to make regular
appearances. The chief new feature is a demand for the
separation of the three parts of the morning service (Mattins,
Litany, and Holy, or Ante-, Communion) into three independent services, or for their substantial abridgment. It was
already becoming customary to divide them, but the practice
lacked rubrical authority. The first pamphlets from within
the Establishment appeared in 1828, and were rapidly
followed by others.[3] They aroused considerable opposition,
expressed in 1834 by addresses presented to the archbishop
of Canterbury, signed by 6530 clergymen and 230,000
heads of families. Newman, who had begun the publication
of *Tracts for the Times* the previous year, urged the clergy
to resist all alterations. In *Tract 38* and *Tract 41* he pointed
out that all the changes suggested were intended to make the
book less Catholic; and in *Tract 75* he put Lloyd's teaching
to practical use by reprinting selections from the Roman
Breviary for private use as a supplement to the Prayer Book
Offices.[4]

At Cambridge two undergraduates, John Mason Neale
and Benjamin Webb, founded the Camden Society in 1839,
and 'by 1843 it had as its patrons two archbishops, sixteen
bishops, thirty-one peers and Members of Parliament, and
a membership of no less than seven hundred'. Through their
periodical *The Ecclesiologist* the romantic enthusiasm for the
Middle Ages kindled by the novels of Sir Walter Scott was
harnessed to the restoration of churches on medieval lines.
The altar was to be raised by the insertion of nine steps,
thus dividing nave from chancel, and centring attention on
the altar. Box-pews were censured because they prevented
the worshippers from being able to see the altar. Above all,
the three-decker pulpit was to be replaced by a simple
pulpit, a lectern, and a litany-desk. Stained-glass windows,
brass vases for flowers, and encaustic tiles complete the
typical Victorian interior. The choir was brought from the

western gallery, robed in surplices, and placed in the chancel, to distinguish it from the congregation, whose place was to listen to the singing of the services.[5]

Many parish churches began to adopt the cathedrals' repertoire of sacred music, and organs replaced orchestras in the remotest country churches. Psalters pointed for chanting came into general use, and settings of the canticles appeared without number. Hymns had received judicial sanction in 1792,[6] and were gradually ousting the metrical psalms. Reginald Heber was the first to compile a book deliberately intended 'to reinforce the lessons and scheme of the Prayer Book'. His book, published posthumously in 1827, follows the Church Year and consists, for the most part, of 'hymns illustrative of the Epistles and Gospels, and to be sung after the Nicene Creed' ; more than half of them were of his own composition.[7] Others followed Heber's lead. Neale's *Hymnal Noted* (1852 and 1854) consisted entirely of translations of Latin office hymns. John Keble's *Christian Year*, on the other hand, was original throughout. In 1860 appeared the first edition of *Hymns Ancient and Modern*, an eclectic volume also partly based on the Church Year, and closely related to the Prayer Book services. The modern hymnbook was fully fledged.

Meanwhile, there was a general movement towards a more faithful observance of the rubrics. This led to the adoption of 'such usages as preaching in the surplice, administering Baptism during Morning or Evening Prayer . . . vesting the choristers in surplices, the use of credence tables, the reading of the Prayer for the Church Militant when there was no Communion, the daily recital of Morning and Evening Prayer, and other orderly, and now ordinary, usages'.[8] The 'ultra-rubricians', as they were called, met with considerable opposition, and in 1851 the bishops signed a joint pastoral letter defending those who followed custom rather than the letter of the rubrics. They also rejected the principle that 'whatever form, or usage, existed in the Church before its

Reformation, may now be freely introduced and observed, unless there can be alleged against it the distinct letter of some formal prohibition'.[9] At a deeper level, controversy was raging over such subjects as baptismal regeneration and the Real Presence, which of course involved discussion of the text of the Prayer Book. The legality of the objects and practices introduced in obedience to the rubrics was first tested in 1854, when an action was brought against Robert Riddell, vicar of St Paul's, Knightsbridge, for the removal of 'the High Altar with the Cross elevated thereon or attached thereto, gilded candlesticks, and candles, a credence table, various altar coverings, a chancel screen, and a Cross upon it'. The case was taken to the Judicial Committee of the Privy Council, since 1833 the final court of appeal in ecclesiastical matters, and its judgment, delivered in 1857, authorized the two crosses, the credence table, and the frontals. The Committee also indicated that in their view the Ornaments Rubric allowed the use of vestments. In the years that followed, the latter were widely adopted, and so were altar lights, flowers, and incense.

As the Ornaments Rubric now takes the centre of the stage, it will be well to recall its wording :

And here is to be noted, that such ornaments of the Church, and of the Ministers thereof at all times of their ministration, shall be retained, and be in use, as were in this Church of England by the authority of Parliament in the second year of the reign of King Edward VI.

The first question at issue was the meaning of 'the second year' of Edward VI : was this before or after the publication of the Book of 1549? If before, then the full medieval range of vestments and furnishings was legal ; if after, those at any rate that were mentioned in the Book were legal. In either case, alb and chasuble were allowed. Those to whom this conclusion was unwelcome fell back upon the Elizabethan Act of Uniformity, which included the words of the rubric with the addition, 'until other order shall be therein taken by the authority of the Queen's Majesty'. The question then arose whether the *Advertisements* of 1566, which only enforced the surplice, constituted a taking of order; and if so, whether it was 'by authority of the Queen's Majesty'. Another line of attack was to maintain that the rubric itself lacked statutory authority. Both sides engaged in a great deal of historical research : inventories and visitation articles were combed for evidence on the actual use of vestments and other ornaments during the sixteenth century. A further refinement was the question already answered by the bishops, whether ornaments not mentioned in 1549, if not superseded by anything that was mentioned, were thereby tacitly allowed, the classic instance of such ornaments being the censer.

A new element had been brought into the situation by the revival, in 1852, of the Convocation of Canterbury, with York following suit in 1861. This at once became the obvious and natural forum for the discussion of Prayer Book revision, and in 1854 a committee was appointed to consider the church services. It recommended that 'the Prayer Book should be preserved entire and unaltered', and made various suggestions for dividing, shortening, and rearranging the services. Its report was poorly received, and any revision seemed out of the question.[10] In spite of this, Dean Milman of St Paul's raised the question of abolishing the State Services, which had already been severely censured by F. D. Maurice.[11] In 1858 Parliament debated the matter, and it was agreed to present an address to the Queen for the removal of the services from the Prayer Book. The Queen approved, and the services were withdrawn by royal warrant in January 1859. Convocation also took steps to provide for Harvest Festivals. The observance of harvest-time with one of the four yearly celebrations of the Holy Communion had been recommended in the eighteenth century, and Harvest Festivals in the modern sense had begun to appear in the 1840s. By 1854 the practice had reached St Paul's Cathedral, and in 1862 Convocation issued an official form of service. It consists of proper psalms, lessons, collects, epistle, and gospel, together with prayers for 'Grace and Glory', 'Christian Missions', and 'a joyful Resurrection', the General Thanksgiving, and a final harvest prayer.[12]

Meanwhile, feeling on the subject of 'ritualism', as the new movement was now generally called, was running high; no fewer than thirty-seven pamphlets on revision were published in the years 1859–61 alone; and 1859 saw the formation of an 'Association for Promoting a Revision of the Book of Common Prayer' (in a Low Church direction), under the leadership of Lord Ebury, who kept the subject continuously before the House of Lords,[13] and in 1873 produced *The Book of Common Prayer Revised*. This remarkable publication restores the petition against the enormities of the Bishop of Rome, and the whole of the Gunpowder Treason Service! The Anglo-Catholics, as the Ritualists called themselves, immediately retaliated by forming the 'English Church Union', pledged 'to resist all such charges' in the Prayer Book 'to the utmost'. The Evangelicals in turn founded the 'Church Association', 'to counteract the efforts now being made ... to assimilate [the Prayer Book] services to those of the Church of Rome'. This phrase pinpoints a change which became evident about 1860. Mere observance of the rubrics was no longer enough : many of the clergy were deliberately taking the worship of the Church of Rome in its contemporary form as their authoritative model. Dean Close had remarked as early as 1844, 'Romanism is taught analytically at Oxford; it is taught artistically at Cambridge',[14] and Romanism was now the real point at issue. But the Evangelicals were divided on the question of tactics : Lord Ebury's followers wanted a revision to remove all traces of sacerdotalism and Romanism; the Church Association defended the Prayer Book as a Protestant book by prosecuting those who did not see it in that light.

Harassed by the warfare of these private armies, the

bishops determined to find out exactly what was legal and what was not. In 1866 'four of the most eminent counsel of the day ... gave it as their opinion that the Eucharistic vestments, altar-lights, incense, the ceremonially-mixed chalice, and the use of wafer-bread, were all illegal'. The English Church Union promptly consulted nine equally distinguished lawyers, who pronounced all these usages legal, with the exception of incense, which all thirteen agreed to be illegal.[15] Something had to be done to clarify the position, and the same year, after a debate in the House of Lords had underlined the need to tackle the Ornaments Rubric, Convocation appointed a committee to report on 'the actual state of the law with regard to ritual'. Its report dealt with vestments, candles, incense, elevation, non-communicating attendance, and wafers, recommending that the first two 'should not be introduced into any parish church without reference to the Bishop', and expressing 'entire dis-approval' of the remainder.[16] The Upper House finally resolved that 'no alterations from long-sanctioned and usual ritual ought to be made in our churches until the sanction of the Bishop of the Diocese has been obtained thereto'. This resolution was reaffirmed by the Second Lambeth Conference in 1878.

In spite of this definite pronouncement, Lord Ebury and Lord Shaftesbury, the great social reformer, continued to put pressure on the Prime Minister and the archbishop of Canterbury, and in 1867 a royal commission was appointed. Its terms of reference were to inquire into differences of practice which 'have arisen from varying interpretations put upon the rubrics, orders, and directions for regulating the course and conduct of public worship, the administration of the Sacraments, and the other Services contained in the Book of Common Prayer, according to the use of the United Church of England and Ireland, and more especially with reference to the ornaments used in the churches and chapels of the said United Church, and the vestments worn by the ministers thereof at the time of their ministration ... with the view of explaining or amending the said rubrics, orders, and directions so as to secure general uniformity of practice in such matters as may be deemed essential'. The Commission began work on 17 June, and issued an interim report on 19 August, taking the view that vestments 'are by none regarded as essential, and they give grave offence to many' ; therefore 'it is expedient to restrain ... all variations in respect of vesture'. A second report, in 1868, declared it 'expedient to restrain all variations from established usage in respect of lighted candles and incense', and suggested that complaints should be heard by the bishop. This report was greatly influenced by the recently delivered Mackonochie Judgment, a ritualistic case which it prints in full. It also collected and printed a great number of Injunctions and Visitation Articles dating from 1561 to 1730, in an attempt to decide the meaning of the Ornaments Rubric from subsequent practice.[17]

The Commission's third report (1870) dealt with the Lectionary, which, though mildly revised in 1604 and 1662, was still in all essentials that of 1561. The Commission recommended changes which were accepted by Convocation and, ultimately, by Parliament, becoming law in July 1871. They have been summarized as follows :

1. Many lessons were shortened and chapter divisions were disregarded where the continuity of subject made it advisable.

2. Forty-two chapters from the Old Testament lessons were omitted, and 100 new chapters were added from 1 and 2 Chronicles and Ezekiel; while twelve chapters from the New Testament were omitted, and twenty-eight new chapters added, including the Revelation of St John. The number of lessons from the Apocrypha was reduced from 132 to 44. The New Testament was rearranged so as to be read twice a year – once in the morning and once in the evening – instead of three times a year.

3. Proper lessons on holy days were revised, and lessons for Ash Wednesday and the whole of Holy Week were provided.

4. A second set of evening lessons on Sunday was given, for use either as alternative lessons at Evensong or as lessons for a third service. At a third service the minister could choose his own second lesson from the Gospels: on other occasions he could substitute his own lessons with the bishop's approval.[18]

The 'third service' just referred to, 'by far the most popular service with the church-going poor', was 'an Evangelical innovation' dating from the close of the eighteenth century.[19] It should be noticed that there were still no proper New Testament lessons for Sundays.

The fourth (and last) report, which also appeared in 1870, dealt with the whole of the rubrics in the Prayer Book, proposing no change in the greater number. 'In the alterations which we have proposed', said the commissioners, 'we have endeavoured ... to explain and amend rubrics so as to secure general uniformity of practice in those matters which may be deemed essential: in other matters we have recommended alterations which may give facilities for adapting the services of the Church to the wants and circumstances of different congregations.' Here was the first official divergence from the ideal of 'one Use'. The Report proper takes up two pages, after which follow twenty-one pages of dissentient opinions, mostly relating to the Athanasian Creed and the Ornaments Rubric. The former was to be dealt with by the insertion of a note to the effect 'that the condemnations in this Confession of Faith are to be not otherwise understood than as a solemn warning of the peril of those who wilfully reject the Catholic Faith'. This was proposed only in March 1870, after lengthy debates in which no proposal commanded a majority, and was carried by eleven votes to seven, out of a commission of twenty-nine. Samuel Wilberforce, temporarily in the chair, in putting it to the vote, described it as an 'illogical and unsatisfactory' explanation, and it was generally felt that the question had been left 'in a very anomalous state'.[20] The treatment of the Ornaments Rubric, on the other hand, was not considered at all until April 1869, and was never thoroughly discussed. Alterations in the cause of general uniformity were few: there was to be no change in the Ornaments Rubric; the Athanasian Creed was to be retained, with its explanatory note; rules were given for the use of the propers of the Epiphany, Ascension Day, and Trinity xxv and xxvi; the Communion Service is to be said audibly; and 'wafers shall not be used'. Under the heading of adaptation, Mattins and Evensong may be shortened on weekdays, and need not be said at all. Mattins, Litany, and Holy Communion may be said together or separately; a sermon may be preached after the third collect, or at the end of the service, of Mattins and Evensong; hymns and anthems may be used if not 'disallowed by the Ordinary'. When a holy day falls on a Sunday, its Collect, Epistle, and Gospel may be used, except on Advent Sunday, Palm Sunday, Easter Day, Whit-Sunday and Trinity Sunday. The First Exhortation need not be said more than three times a year, and the Third may always be omitted. A pause may be made for non-communicants to withdraw. The Words of Administration may be said 'once to so many ... as the Minister ... shall see fit'. On occasions sanctioned by the Ordinary the service may begin at the Collect, and the Prayer for the Church may be omitted at Ante-Communion. Parents may be sponsors; if Matrimony is not followed by Communion, it may end with the Blessing. The minister may instruct and comfort the sick 'as he shall think meet and convenient'. Burial may be said over suicides in a shortened form and alternative lessons are provided (Mark 5: 35–42, Luke 7: 11–17, John 11: 30–45, 1 Thessalonians 4: 13–18, Matthew 24: 35–43).

The Report did nothing to remove the Athanasian Creed from the centre of controversy. Archbishop Tait, with the support of Lord Shaftesbury and his followers, strongly urged the complete exclusion of the creed from public worship. Some favoured making its use optional; some would have been content with removing the 'damnatory clauses' (verses 2 and 42), or with a new translation; some wanted merely an explanatory rubric. At the opposite extreme to the archbishop stood E. B. Pusey and H. P. Liddon, the acknowledged leaders of the Anglo-Catholic party, who threatened to resign their orders if the creed was 'degraded or mutilated'. After lengthy discussion, Convocation decided in 1872 against any alteration of the rubric, and in the following year issued a Synodical Declaration 'for the removal of doubts, and to prevent disquietude in the use of the Creed'.

Another sequel to the Fourth Report proved less controversial. The Act of Uniformity Amendment Act became law in July 1872.[21] Generally known as 'the Shortened Services Act', it allowed Morning and Evening Prayer to be shortened on weekdays by the omission of the Exhortation, *Venite*, one lesson and canticle, the second Lord's Prayer, and the State Prayers; and it permitted special services on special occasions, including anthems or hymns, but otherwise to be derived from the Bible or Prayer Book; and likewise additional services from these sources on Sundays. Mattins, Litany, and Holy Communion may be used together or separately 'in varying order', and the Litany may also be said after Evensong. Sermons without 'common prayers' must be preceded by a special service, or the Bidding Prayer from Canon 55, or a Prayer Book collect. The Act is chiefly notable as the first legal variation in the text of the main body of the Book of Common Prayer for 210 years; nearly another century was to pass before any further changes were officially authorized.

The Royal Commission had failed to solve its chief problem, the meaning of the Ornaments Rubric. Lord Shaftesbury made six attempts in successive years from 1867 to settle the question by Act of Parliament, none of which came to anything. A series of court cases ensued, in an attempt to secure a decisive ruling. In 1871 the Judicial Committee reversed its previous opinion, and declared vestments illegal; so also were the eastward position, the mixed chalice, and wafers. The Purchas Judgment, as it was known, caused widespread dissatisfaction: though vestments were not yet used by many, the eastward position was, and 4700 clergymen signed a protest.[22] The immediate result of the judgment was that the usages condemned were more widely practised. The First Report's formula of 'restraint' evidently needed clarifying. The Public Worship Regulation Act of 1874 was passed with the object of facilitating the enforcement of the law as now declared. It created a new court; 'directed that a monition should take the place of a penalty in the first instance, followed by suspension or deprivation in case of contumacy and, when there was contempt of court, allowing the possibility (quite unintended by those who framed the Act) of imprisonment'; and allowed the bishop of the diocese to veto any prosecution.[23] The first prosecution under the Act took place in 1877. The Ridsdale Judgment, delivered 'by a Court of exceptional strength', confirmed the illegality of vestments, modified the decision as to wafers, and declared the eastward position legal, so long as the manual acts were visible. Further prosecutions followed, as the result of which four clergymen were sent to prison during the years 1878–81. This only increased 'the general confusion, irritation, and unrest'.[24]

Convocation began a discussion of the Ornaments Rubric in 1875, and at first resisted any attempt to alter it at all. Eventually, after much debate, in 1879 a joint conference of the two houses of Canterbury accepted a composite rubric which ran:

And here is to be noted . . . [*as in the Prayer Book*] . . . King Edward the Sixth, until further Order be taken by lawful Authority.

In saying Public Prayers and ministering the Sacraments and other rites of the Church, every Priest and Deacon shall wear a surplice with a stole or scarf, and the hood of his degree, and in preaching he shall wear a surplice with a stole or scarf, and the hood of his degree, or if he think fit, a gown with hood and scarf; and no other ornament shall at any time of his ministrations be used by him contrary to the monition of the Bishop of the Diocese.

Provided always that this Rubric shall not be understood to repeal the 24th, 25th, and 58th of the Canons of 1604.

York Convocation, however, rejected the proposal, and no change was made.[25]

The 1880s saw a steady increase in 'ritualistic' practices, and in 1888 the Church Association brought a suit against Edward King, bishop of Lincoln, a High Churchman of saintly character, to test the legality of six usages. Archbishop Benson heard the case (exercising the jurisdiction of an archbishop over his suffragans), and gave judgment in November 1890 in favour of the mixed chalice, altar lights, the eastward position, the singing of *Agnus Dei*, and the ablutions, but forbidding the signing of the cross at the Absolution and Blessing. On appeal, the Judicial Committee in August 1892 confirmed the archbishop's decisions, and a short period of peace ensued.[26]

Meanwhile, Convocation had completed its consideration of the Fourth Report in 1879 and had prepared proposals for revision of the Prayer Book. These were printed in 1880, but were never sent to Parliament. The intention was to wait until a measure became law which would avoid discussion of the rubrics in Parliament. The measure, however, was rejected, and the proposals remained in a state of suspense. Though superficial in character, they are by no means without interest. The disciplinary purpose which led to the appointment of the Royal Commission plays remarkably little part. The contemporaneous Convocation rubric is attached to the Ornaments Rubric, and the Synodical Declaration of 1873 to the Athanasian Creed. The reader of the Gospel is to 'turn himself to the people', and York Convocation wanted the minister to receive communion kneeling. There is no other attempt to restrain ritualistic practices.

Of enrichment, such as had been urged by Anglo-

Catholic scholars, there is also very little. Proper Psalms are appointed for ten additional days; the Easter Anthems are to be said throughout the octave; the propers for The Epiphany and Ascension Day are to be used until the following Sunday; and the collects of St Michael and all Angels and of All Saints are to be repeated as memorials throughout the octave. The people's responses before and after the Gospel are restored, and permission is given for both the Prayer of Oblation and the Prayer of Thanksgiving to be said. A psalm, hymn, or anthem may be sung as an Introit and before the sermon (as Heber had suggested) in the Communion Service. A hymn and sermon may be added after the Third Collect at Morning and Evening Prayer, and, at Evening Prayer only, this may be done after the Grace.

The popular demand for abbreviation is met by the incorporation of the provisions of the Shortened Services Act, and by permission to omit the Ten Commandments and the Collect for the King at late celebrations and wedding communions. The sermon may be omitted from the Communion Service at any time; the third Exhortation need be read only once a month; and the Prayer for the Church may be omitted from Ante-Communion.

By far the greater part of the alterations were practical in character, and were no doubt designed to legalize what was already general usage. A table was provided 'to regulate the service' when two feasts clashed, though no provision was made for transference; and precise rules are given for the treatment of Trinity xxv and xxvi. The newly revived office of Reader is allowed for in the rubric governing the reading of the lessons. The Litany may be said after Morning or Evening Prayer, before Holy Communion, or on its own. The first and second Exhortations at Holy Communion are to be read (if at all) between the notices and the sermon. A pause may be made for non-communicants to withdraw before or after the Offertory Sentences, or after the Prayer for the Church. The collection may be placed on the Holy Table at any service, and the service ended with the Blessing from the Holy Communion. Parents may be sponsors at Baptism, and all sponsors should be communicants. Those who have never had godparents should make the vows themselves at Confirmation. The Burial service may be said in case of suicide 'while of unsound mind'; and when no service is allowable, the priest may conduct a service after interment, so long as it does not include any part of the Burial or Communion Services. A larger portion of the service may be said in church, or interment may take place without any service at all. Hymns and anthems are permitted, though no such provision is made at weddings.

These proposals, together with the new Lectionary, the Shortened Services Act, and a section in the Burial Laws Amendment Act of 1880, represent the entire result of the Royal Commission on Ritual, and a sufficiently meagre result it is. Neither Evangelicals nor Anglo-Catholics received any real consideration, a situation which Baxter and Cosin would have found familiar. Only in supplementary services was anything achieved. Besides the Harvest service already mentioned, revisions were produced of the service for consecrating churches and of the Accession Service. The former, the work of Bishop John Wordsworth of Salisbury, appeared in 1887, and, though never submitted to Convocation, was widely adopted in other dioceses.[27] In 1898 a committee was appointed to consider the Accession Service and, at the petition of a number of liturgical scholars, produced a new form. It provides propers for Mattins, Evensong, and Holy Communion, and an independent service consisting of *Te Deum*, the Lord's Prayer and suffrages, five prayers (including that for Unity), and the Blessing.[28]

Various Churches which had made their own contributions to the history of the Prayer Book text during the eighteenth century, namely the Irish, American, and

Methodist Churches, carried out further revisions in the nineteenth. The Church of Ireland, after the burst of activity described in the previous chapter, had settled down to a lengthy period of inaction, ended in 1871 by its disestablishment. A revision of the Prayer Book followed which was published in 1877. Some of the changes go right back to 1689, such as Psalm 148 at Mattins and 1 Thessalonians 4 at Burial, both as alternatives; also, black-letter saints' days and the Apocrypha are removed from the Kalendar, though otherwise the Lectionary is the English one of 1871. Other changes are probably derived from the Shortened Services Act or the Fourth Report of the Ritual Commission. The daily service is no longer obligatory, and may begin at the General Confession; the people's responses to the Gospel are restored; a pause is to be made after the Prayer for the Church; the Third Exhortation may sometimes be omitted; so may the Prayer for the Church at Ante-Communion; wafers are prohibited; the Words of Administration need not be said in full to every communicant; parents may be sponsors, and only one sponsor is required. In contrast to the Church of England, the Athanasian Creed is no longer to be recited, but remains as witness 'to the truth of the Articles of the Christian Faith therein contained' (a procedure recommended long ago by Bishop Seabury[29]). The General Thanksgiving may be said by the congregation, who also join in the third prayer in Baptism; propers are provided for two Communions on Christmas Day and Easter Day; the Communion Service may begin with the Collect; after the Gospel the people may say 'Hallelujah'; *Gloria in excelsis* is to be said standing; a question and answer derived from Article xxviii (Of the Lord's Supper) are added to the Catechism; 'O Almighty Lord and everlasting God' and the Grace end the Marriage Service. Among the additional services are Harvest Thanksgiving, the Consecration of Churches and Churchyards, and the 1711 form for Visitation of Prisoners. The Canons of

1871 and 1877 which conclude the Book reflect current English controversies by forbidding the sign of the cross, bowing to the altar, and placing a cross thereon.[30] In its concentration on practical points the Book resembles the English proposals of 1879, which indeed it may have influenced at the eleventh hour, but it differs from them in displaying a definitely Evangelical approach. Anglo-Catholicism was virtually unknown in Ireland at that time.

The American revision (1892) shows the influence of the Convocation Prayer Book in its concern with the relationship of Mattins, Litany, and Holy Communion; in the introduction of proper psalms for the same ten additional days; and in the treatment of the Epiphany Collect and the Third Exhortation. To the Irish Book may be due the propers for first Communions on Christmas Day and Easter Day, though the passages are those of 1549; and additions to the section of Prayers and Thanksgivings. Several changes represent a return to traditional ways: the Gospel canticles are restored, and the second part of the Commination has been reassembled as a Penitential Office for Ash Wednesday. A new set of propers is provided for The Transfiguration. The Nicene Creed is back in its place, to be used at least on the five great festivals of the year. Some of Andrewes's Offertory Sentences are adopted, and various phrases are reinstated in the Marriage Service. Among the innovations are seasonal Sentences at Mattins and Evensong; 'Give peace in our time, O Lord' is answered by 'For it is thou, Lord, only, that makest us dwell in safety'; a new petition is added to the Litany, 'That it may please thee to send forth labourers into thy harvest'; and Acts 8: 14–17 is used as a lesson at Confirmation. In the Burial Service, a hymn or anthem, the Apostles' Creed, and prayers may be inserted after the Lesson. Psalm 141 has been moved to Evensong, as J. M. Neale had suggested in 1856.[31]

The Methodists had never taken Wesley's *Abridgment* to their hearts – many actually preferred the 'genuine original' of 1662 – but it was frequently reprinted, in abbreviated and altered forms. The manual acts, for example, were omitted or replaced in almost every successive edition; and an unofficial revision of 1846 restored two prayers in Baptism, but omitted the Lord's Prayer and the Thanksgiving. The same year saw the issue of a new form 'for Ordaining Candidates for the Ministry'. From 1838 the Communion Service had also been printed separately, and in 1860 Conference initiated a revision which brought back the Nicene Creed and the first Prayer for the Queen, but omitted the Collect, Epistle, and Gospel, the sermon, the manual acts, the rubric on reconsecration, and the second Lord's Prayer (the doxology being transferred to the first). Methodism, no less than the Church of England, was fearful of the growth of Anglo-Catholicism in its midst, and in 1874, at the instigation of Dr J. H. Rigg, Conference appointed a committee to revise 'the Liturgy and the Book of Offices, especially with a view to the removal of all expressions which are fairly susceptible of a sense contrary to the principles of our Evangelical Protestantism'.[32] The result, which appeared in 1882, was called *The Book of Public Prayers and Services for the use of the People called Methodists.*

In some ways this marks a return from the *Abridgment* to the Book of Common Prayer. The Nicene Creed and the Third Exhortation are restored, though the latter is abbreviated; and the omissions of 1864 are replaced, except for the manual acts. The ring reappears in the Marriage Service, and the Commendation and the Lord's Prayer in Burial; and the names 'Epiphany', 'Septuagesima', and 'Lent' are brought back. But an alternative psalm and a new prayer are added in Burial, while in Baptism, which was the subject of violent controversy, the whole of the first Exhortation was removed, including the quotation of John 3 : 5, and the Mozarabic prayers were placed *after* the baptism as a 'denial of baptismal grace'. The Psalms are taken from the

Authorized Version, not from the Prayer Book; the Tobit Sentences disappear; and in the Ordinal no distinction is made between deacon, elder, and superintendent. Three occasional services are added to the book: the Covenant Service, 'The Public Recognition of New Members' (a substitute for Confirmation), and 'The Setting-Apart of Deaconesses'.[33]

The lull in party strife brought about by the Lincoln Judgment did not last long. During the 1890s a number of services from sources other than the Book of Common Prayer were being widely introduced, the most controversial being the Veneration of the Cross on Good Friday. Much opposition was aroused, and in 1898 the bishops took steps to discourage such services. Despite their action, the 'Ritual Question' remained very much in the public eye, and Church Discipline Bills were introduced in 1899 and in each of the four years following. Finally in 1904 a Royal Commission on Ecclesiastical Discipline was appointed. It was to 'inquire into the alleged prevalence of breaches or neglect of the Law relating to the conduct of Divine Service in the Church of England and to the ornaments and fittings of Churches; and to consider the existing powers and procedure applicable to such irregularities and to make such recommendations as may be deemed requisite for dealing with the aforesaid matters'.[34]

The Commission's Report, drafted by Sir Lewis Dibdin, the leading ecclesiastical lawyer, but owing much to Francis Paget, bishop of Oxford, was issued in 1906, and contains an exhaustive survey of customary or well-authenticated departures from the text of the Prayer Book. Among 'Non-significant breaches of the Law' it specifies omission of the First and Second Exhortations in Holy Communion, the publication of notices not covered by the rubric, special services such as Harvest Festivals, sermons by bishops at Confirmations, taking a collection at Morning or Evening Prayer, ending the latter services with a blessing, failure to read the Daily Offices, administration of baptism on week-days, failure to catechize at Evensong, omission of the whole of the Ante-Communion, or at least of the Ten Commandments, and insertion of the words 'Thanks be to thee, O Lord' after the Gospel. All these illegalities were well nigh universal, but had no doctrinal import.[35] Another group of 'breaches', however, were thought to 'lie on the Rome-ward side of a line of deep cleavage between the Church of England and that of Rome'.[36] They include vestments, the *Confiteor* and the 'last Gospel', ceremonial mixing of the chalice, wafers, the *Lavabo*, obscuring of the manual acts, the sign of the cross, the *Sanctus* bell, incense, portable lights, holy water, the Roman rites for Holy Week, the Stations of the Cross, the observance of saints' days other than the 'red-letter' days, celebrations without com-municants and children's Eucharists, elevation, genu-flexion, use of the Canon of the Mass, reservation, various forms of Mariolatry, veneration of images and roods, and prayers for souls in Purgatory.[37]

The Report thus builds up an authoritative picture of worship at the turn of the century, first in churches of all persuasions, then in Anglo-Catholic parishes. The raw material is set out in detail in four accompanying volumes of evidence. After a review of about thirty books of popular devotion, the Report summarizes all this mass of material with the remark :

The law relating to the conduct of Divine Service and the ornaments of churches is, in our belief, nowhere exactly observed; and certain minor breaches of it are very generally prevalent. The law is also broken by many irregular practices which have attained lesser, and widely different, degrees of prevalence. Some of these are omissions, others err in the direction of excess.[38]

Finally, it enunciates two main conclusions :

First, the law of public worship in the Church of England is too narrow for the religious life of the present generation. It needlessly condemns much which a great section of Church people, including many of her most devoted members, value. . . . Secondly, the machinery for discipline has broken down. . . . It is important that the law should be reformed, that it should admit of reasonable elasticity, and that the means of enforcing it should be improved; but, above all, it is necessary that it should be obeyed.[39]

The Report ends with ten Recommendations. They single out the last five in the list of doctrinally significant practices given above, and recommend that they 'should be promptly made to cease'; they enumerate various ways in which ecclesiastical discipline should be tightened up; they call for 'wider scope for the exercise of a regulative authority . . . for the sanction and regulation of additional and special services and collects in accordance with the teaching of the Holy Scriptures and the Book of Common Prayer, and for the forbidding of the use of hymns or anthems not in accordance with such teaching'. Most important of all, the Report recommends that

Letters of Business should be issued to the Convocations with instructions: (*a*) to consider the preparation of a new rubric regulating the ornaments (that is to say, the vesture of the ministers of the Church, at the times of their ministrations, with a view to its enactment by Parliament; and (*b*) to frame, with a view to their enactment by Parliament, such modifications in the existing law relating to the conduct of Divine Service and to the ornaments and fittings of churches as may tend to secure the greater elasticity which a reasonable recognition of the comprehensiveness of the Church of England and of its present needs seems to demand.

It would be most desirable for the early dealing with these important subjects that the Convocations would sit together, and we assume that they would take counsel with the House of Laymen.[40]

Letters of Business were duly issued, and the way was once more open for a revision of the Book of Common Prayer after the lapse of nearly 250 years.

10 The Royal Letters of Business

The ultimate failure of Prayer Book Revision had its root in the well-intentioned but intrinsically irrational attempt to serve two conflicting policies, of which the one was designed to satisfy the popular demand for order in the Established Church, and the other aspired to revise the system which was to be enforced. . . . I think few even of the Bishops, as they sate round the table in Lambeth Palace engaged in the task of revision, escaped an uncomfortable feeling of unreality and misgiving when they listened to the earnest and learned pleas of those members of their body (they were not many) who spoke as recognizably expert in liturgical science.

BISHOP HENSLEY HENSON, *Retrospect of an Unimportant Life*[1]

THE authorities of the Church cannot be said to have grasped the opportunity offered by the Letters of Business with eager hands. Archbishop Davidson was of the opinion that 'such changes as are made in the Rubrics should be reduced sternly to the smallest possible dimensions'.[2] This view, though widely held, was actively combated. The steady rise of the Anglo-Catholic party had produced a great desire for 'enrichment' of the Prayer Book services, usually by borrowing from the Roman Missal; and the publication in 1904 of *The English Liturgy* had shown what could be done in this direction without going outside the Anglican Communion. It was largely the work of two young men, Percy Dearmer and W. H. Frere, each of whom was to have a great influence on the worship of the Church of England during the next half-century. Dearmer concentrated on the externals, Frere on the text, but both stressed the continuity of the Church of England with the pre-Reformation Church. The Alcuin Club was founded to promote this approach to liturgiology and church furnishings. The so-called 'English altar' with its riddels was to become almost universal in churches where the celebrant did not stand at the north end, a position which the riddel-curtains rendered impossible. The Club produced over the years a large number of well-edited and beautifully printed liturgical texts, while an equally high standard of scholarship was maintained by the publications of the Henry Bradshaw Society, which operated in the same field. A number of important texts had already appeared during the latter half of the nineteenth century, notably from the Cambridge University Press and the Surtees Society, so that students of Prayer Book history were far better equipped than their predecessors.

The harvest of all these publications was reaped by Frere, in his revision of Francis Procter's work, now called *A New History of the Book of Common Prayer* (1901), and by F. E. Brightman, another learned member of the Alcuin Club, in *The English Rite* (1915). Frere's influence, however, was not confined to the study. He had made a considerable impression by his evidence before the Royal Commission, and was in much demand as a lecturer on Prayer Book revision, now that the subject had once more become a live issue. The content of his lectures was published in 1911 as *Some Principles of Liturgical Reform*. The book betrays its date by the amount of space given to the Ornaments Rubric; but, when read in the light of subsequent proposals, its importance becomes obvious. Numerous instances are recorded in the notes to this chapter. Especially significant is Frere's suggestion of an 'optional and experimental' rearrangement of the Canon, by placing the Prayer of Humble Access before *Sursum corda*, and the Prayer of Oblation and the Lord's Prayer before communion.[3]

The bishops' first step in preparing a reply to the Letters of Business was to divide themselves into three committees, to study the ornaments of the minister, the legal procedure to be adopted in giving effect to such proposals as should be made in the Reply, and changes needed in the rubrics. The first committee, headed by Bishop John Wordsworth, confined themselves to a re-examination of the historical evidence, and their report (no. 416), published in 1908, made no recommendation as to action. They concluded that 'the second year of King Edward VI' meant 1549, positively and exclusively. Anything not mentioned in the 1549 Book was illegal, as the book was 'intended by itself to be . . . a sufficient directory for public worship'; the words 'shall be in use' were correctly interpreted as 'the minister shall use'; and the *Advertisements* of 1566 did not constitute a taking of other order under the Act of Uniformity of 1559. The second committee deferred any discussion until the reports of the other two had been received. The third, under the chairmanship of G. F. Browne, bishop of Bristol, produced its report (no. 427) in February 1909. Four points were singled out as especially controversial: the Athanasian Creed, the repetition of the Words of Administration, Reservation, and the Ornaments Rubric. In actual fact, the vestments question, though still a sore point, gradually ceased to be at the centre of controversy, and the same is true of the Athanasian Creed. Administration never became a burning issue at all, but Reservation was destined to become the chief stumbling-block.

The same year the Lower House of Convocation began to discuss a report (no. 466) by a committee of their own. The wide interest aroused by the subject came as a surprise, and in April 1910 the archbishop told the Upper House that the preparation of the Reply was taking longer than he had expected, but that it was important to be deliberate. Part of the delay was caused by prolonged debates in both houses about the correct procedure to be followed. Throughout the period the archbishop's speeches reveal considerable uneasiness about the dangers of detailed discussion of the proposals in Parliament. By May 1911 the bishops' revision of Report no. 427 was completed, and in November 1912 the Lower House ended their considerations of Report no. 466. In February 1912 the archbishop announced the formation of an Advisory Committee on Liturgical Questions, which included Frere, Brightman, and Dearmer, as well as some prominent Evangelicals. It soon became known as the 'Committee of Experts'.[4] It was not until February 1914 that their criticisms of Report 427 were embodied in a new report (no. 481), which the bishops passed unanimously. In the process of revision it had grown from nineteen pages to forty, as 'enrichment' grew to 'very considerable dimensions'. A joint committee was then appointed to harmonize the proposals of the two Houses, and parallel action was taken in York Convocation. The Canterbury report (no. 487) was presented in February 1915 by Bishop Gibson of Gloucester, Frere's mentor, and was discussed in detail by the Advisory Committee, which was then allowed to fall into oblivion.

At this stage the changes recommended were to be for optional use for a limited period, and the text of 1662 was to remain unaltered and fully in force. Among the proposals of the Lower House was one for the rearrangement of the Canon, which they had passed by 79 votes to 8. This was rejected by the Upper House in April 1915 by 15 votes to 8. The bishops debated it 'at immense length', and were chiefly influenced by a speech from the bishop of London (Winnington-Ingram), who said that 'nothing was more hotly opposed by the whole Evangelical party', and that 'it would not satisfy the Catholic party'. In July 1917 the Lower House reaffirmed the resolution of 1914. When the bishops returned to the question in February 1918, the bishop of London said that the Catholic party 'had pointed out that he was quite wrong in what he said last time', and the bishops thereupon voted 13 to 7 in favour of the change. In York Convocation the Lower House also desired a rearrangement, but the bishops were adamantly opposed to anything of the sort.

The process of revision went on unhindered by the involvement of the nation in the First World War, but in

1918 a committee of inquiry set up by the archbishops produced a report, *The Worship of the Church*, in which the voice of the service chaplains made itself heard for the first time. In October of that year a conference of members of all four houses of Convocation was held, which reached agreement on all points except the rearrangement of the Canon. The conference's findings were embodied in Report no. 517. To complete the process, another conference, 'in which younger men and liturgical scholars should have full representation', was called for May 1919. As a result of prolonged previous discussion between Frere and Dr Drury, the Evangelical bishop of Ripon, an alternative order was agreed on with only five dissentients. The Prayer of Humble Access was to follow the Comfortable Words, and the Lord's Prayer to follow the Prayer of Consecration; but the Prayer of Oblation was to remain *after* communion; and after the Words of Institution an anamnesis and epiclesis were to be inserted.[5] Both Houses of Canterbury and the Lower House of York accepted these proposals, but the northern bishops still rejected any change.

It was now at least possible to send the Answer to the Royal Letters of Business, and it was signed in April 1920, with four schedules appended, containing proposals for revision, a Table of Lessons, and revised translations of the Psalter and the Athanasian Creed. But this was by no means the end of the process of revision. The National Assembly of the Church of England had recently come into existence, including a House of Laity; and the proposals, now known as N.A. 60, were duly submitted for the Assembly's consideration. It appointed a committee, which reported in June 1922, after making a number of changes. In the following October the bishops attached the report as it stood to a measure (N.A. 84), which received general approval (the Assembly's equivalent of the parliamentary 'first reading'). The Lectionary was detached from the other proposals, and was sent on to Parliament, where it was passed, and came into use in addition to that of 1871, which was not withdrawn. The Assembly passed on to the next stage, that of revision (the 'second reading').

Before it lay the proposals agreed upon by the whole of the clergy in 1918, its own committee's comments upon these, and also now a large number of external productions. The three most important of these were nicknamed, from the colour of their covers, 'the Green Book', 'the Grey Book', and 'the Orange Book' (the last sometimes oddly referred to as 'the Yellow Book'). The Green Book, which appeared in October 1922, was the work of the English Church Union; its scholarly and pronouncedly Anglo-Catholic tone is exemplified in its requests for feasts of St Joseph, the Falling Asleep of the Blessed Virgin Mary, and Corpus Christi. The Grey Book (1923) originated in the 'Life and Liberty' movement, which had led to the setting-up of the Church Assembly. Prefaced by a few words from William Temple, then bishop of Manchester, it was a remarkable combination of sound liturgical craftsmanship, modernist theology, and high-flown liberal sentiment, 'largely the work of the Revds Percy Dearmer, F. R. Barry, and R. G. Parsons'.[6] The Orange Book (1923–1924; chiefly written by Frere) attempted to harmonize the other two books with the text of the Measure. All these three books were considered with as much care as the official proposals. The Evangelicals produced no comprehensive scheme; they were content with 1662, and to have suggested improvements would have fatally weakened this position; they therefore contented themselves with opposition.

Revision was completed by the House of Clergy in March 1925, and by the House of Laity in July. The Clergy rejected the proposed alternative Canon, and substituted two Canons of their own composition. They also slightly widened the purpose of reservation, and attempted to remove the control of it from the individual bishop. The

Laity were content with the 1662 Communion Service, but were ready to accept *one* alternative form with 'provision for vestments and Reservations for the sick only', for the sake of 'peace and order in the Church'.[7] The bishops began their revision in October 1925. The archbishop had by then received 800 different memorials, including a statement by nine diocesan bishops against any change in the Communion Service after the Creed, or any alternative form of service.[8] The bishops spent forty-seven full days, working six or seven hours a day, making 'such a substantial remodelling that the result not unfairly produced the impression that they were addressing themselves to the improvement of the Prayer Book for the first time'.[9] For two-thirds of the Bench this was in fact the case. Since the Upper House completed its work in 1917, there had been twenty-six new consecrations,[10] of whom only Frere, now bishop of Truro, could claim any liturgical expertise, though Temple and Theodore Woods (Winchester) were eager supporters of revision. Gibson of Gloucester and Chase of Ely, who had borne the brunt of the work since 1914, had died, 'not having received the promises, but having seen them afar off'; and of the older bishops, the outstanding figure was Pollock of Norwich, who was hostile to the whole project. An immediate proposal that revision of the Communion Service should be left until the rest of the book had been passed was defeated by 24 votes to 9: unhappily, as events were to show.[11] The principle of having an alternative Canon was accepted by 29 votes to 5. Reservation, the other storm-centre, was to be dealt with 'by means of Rubrics prescribing the purpose, and of Rules settling the method', thus distinguishing between reservation for communion and reservation for adoration. The Rules, however, were not at first made public. Continuous reservation was to be recognized 'if the Bishop shall so permit'.

The bishops drew freely from the unofficial books, and added new material of their own, including a service for the

Ordering of Deaconesses. They also took it upon themselves to make certain alterations which might fairly be said to involve change of doctrine, removing the word 'obey' from the Marriage Service, and a reference to original sin from Baptism.[12] These alterations had not been passed by the Lower Houses, and therefore contravened Standing Orders. The result of the bishops' labours was placed before Convocation in February 1927. In deference to the Lower Houses the reference to original sin was restored and other minor concessions were made. The Ordering of Deaconesses was dropped altogether, as it had not been approved by the Assembly. The rubrics on reservation were altered to guard against arbitrary refusal by a bishop, but the Upper House still refused to include their rules in the book, though they were now at least circulated separately to members of Convocation. Frere made one last unsuccessful attempt to secure the provision of two alternative epicleses in the Canon.[13] In July the Assembly passed the book by 517 votes to 133, a majority of 59 per cent. Intense interest had been aroused throughout the country; an immense amount of propaganda was being produced; and Anglo-Catholics united with Evangelicals in opposing the book, though for diametrically opposite reasons.

In December the Measure reached Parliament, where it was carried in the Lords by 214 votes to 88, but defeated in the Commons, after an acrimonious debate, by 238 to 205. A majority of English members was in favour of the book, so that its defeat was due to members representing constituencies to which the Measure did not apply. The bishops decided 'to reintroduce the Measure into the Church Assembly as soon as possible, with such changes . . . as may tend to remove misapprehensions'.[14] These included the restoration of prayers for the king, and the rubric on kneeling, the publication of the rules for reservation, and the insertion of a rubric declaring fasting before communion to be optional.[15] These changes merely 'lost the support of certain Anglo-Catholics without much pacifying of Evange-licals'.[16] Continuous reservation was the burning question, and Anglo-Catholics were offended by the tightening-up of conditions imposed, Evangelicals by the bishops' refusal to omit it altogether. Bishop Frere withdrew his support from the book he had done so much to shape, and abstained from voting. The book in its new form passed the Assembly in April 1928 by 396 votes to 153, the majority dropping to 44 per cent. Two months later the book again came before the House of Commons; but, after a debate on a consider-ably higher level, it was rejected once more, this time by 266 votes to 220, a slightly higher majority than before.

The bishops were faced with a paradoxical situation : here was a book which still commanded the votes of 72 per cent of the members of the Church Assembly, but had been twice rejected by Parliament by a comparatively small majority. They met the situation by issuing a statement declaring the Church's 'inalienable right . . . to arrange the expression' of its faith 'in its forms of worship'.[17] The book was published at the end of the year with a note to the effect that publica-tion did not imply authorization for use in churches.[18] The following year the bishops defined the attitude which they would adopt towards the use of the 1928 Book. They could not, they said, 'regard as inconsistent with loyalty to the principles of the Church of England the use of such additions or deviations as fall within the limits of these proposals. For the same reason they must regard as incon-sistent with Church Order the use of any other deviations from or additions to the Forms and Orders contained in the Book of 1662.' They would endeavour to secure that practices consistent neither with 1662 nor with 1928 should cease ; and permission to use any part of 1928 would require 'the good will of the people as represented in the Parochial Church Council'.[19] Under these conditions the Book of 1928 began to come into use.

A number of reasons have been adduced for the defeat in

Parliament. There is a general feeling that the archbishop of Canterbury, who was nearing the end of his life, failed either to give a firm lead to the bishops, or to give clear replies to Evangelical politicians who raised questions about discipline and Reservation. The Anglo-Catholics saw the book as a curb to their hard-won gains ; liberal Evangelicals reluctantly made concessions to the Anglo-Catholics, only to find them actually opposed to the book ; for conservative Evangelicals, the book meant surrender to Anglo-Catholicism, and Anglo-Catholicism meant popery. Fear of Rome was undoubtedly the largest single factor in Parliament. Both extremes could claim that the revision involved some change of doctrine, whether by introducing explicit prayer for the dead, or by abandoning the traditional 'moment of consecration'. These difficulties might have been surmounted by a different approach. 'The restoration of discipline and the revision of the formularies were excellent objects, but in the actual circumstances of modern England not easily harmonized'.[20] There was a widespread desire among the laity for firmer repression of Anglo-Catholic innovations, but little enthusiasm for alteration of the Prayer Book. The man in the pew, like the archbishop, wanted as little change as possible, and consequently was undisturbed by the Commons' votes. Not enough had been done to educate the ordinary congregation in the understanding of the liturgy, while 'the influence of the chaplains was out of all proportion to their pastoral experience, learning, or wisdom'.[21] The suggestion of taking the revision in two stages was repeatedly but invariably rejected ; and it was authoritatively stated that the revision was intended to be 'final' for many years to come.[22] Later experience suggests that a piecemeal revision of an explicitly experimental and optional character would have had a far greater chance of success.

The Book of 1928 is a cumbrous production. By the desire of the House of Laity, the whole of the 1662 Book is included, with each service followed by the proposed alternative. Exceptions are made in the case of the Visitation of the Sick, where only the new form is printed (the old, which no-one used as it stood, 'being, for the most part, contained' in the new); the Psalter, where the revised translation was quietly suppressed, as its inclusion would have raised the bulk of the volume to an intolerable size; and the Ordinal where the changes were minimal. Before each group of services is placed a set of 'General Rubricks', applying to the performance of both the forms following, 1662 and 1928. This idea originated at a late stage in the bishops' final revision, though the phrase is used in the Orange Book.

A new preface opens the book, from the hand (on internal evidence) of archbishop Davidson.[23] The Table of Proper Psalms now includes all Sundays, as Frere had suggested in *Some Principles of Liturgical Reform*:[24] it sets a precedent by omitting six psalms altogether. First published in a report of 1920, it had already come into widespread use. The Lectionary is that of 1922 'as revised in 1927', 'though a diligent search [by Dr Lowther Clarke] has failed to reveal any differences'.[25] This Lectionary, which originated in the Lower House in 1913, departs from Cranmer's scheme based on the civil year, and follows the ecclesiastical year, again as suggested by Frere.[26] Compared with that of 1871, it adds proper Second Lessons for all Sundays, alternative lessons on most Sundays, and lessons for the First Evensongs of Holy Days;[27] and the proportion of passages from the Apocrypha is noticeably increased.[28] On weekdays after Trinity, material from the Synoptic Gospels is arranged to form a composite life of Christ. The compilers were much influenced by Vernon Staley's *Revision of the Lectionary* (1910) in general, and by W. Herschel's *The Gospel Monogram* (1911) for the life of Christ.[29] The Kalendar is greatly improved: St Mary Magdalen and The Transfiguration are added to the red-letter days; sixteen 'black-letter' saints are ejected and twenty-seven new ones admitted, in accordance with the criteria applied by Frere, namely historicity, or, failing that, popularity in church dedications; the new ones are mostly great teachers and English saints.[30] A Table of Transference, mainly compiled by Frere, was one of the fruits of the 'Committee of Experts'.[31]

A page of General Rubrics which apply to the whole book begins with the Ornaments Rubric intact, though a General Rubric before the Communion Service allows either surplice with stole or scarf, or alb with vestment or cope. The Rubrics go on to allow hymns and anthems at the beginning or end of any service, and, subject to episcopal control, in the course of any service. Collections may be taken at any service, and may be presented upon the Holy Table. All this is merely codification of existing practice. Complete paragraphs from 1928 may be substituted for the corresponding sections of 1662. Changes 'should not be made arbitrarily or without the good will of the people'.

The alternative forms of Mattins and Evensong return to the 1549 limits. They are preceded by 'An Introduction to Morning or Evening Prayer', which begins with seasonal Sentences on the Scottish model, followed by a new Exhortation and Confession (taken with very little alteration from the Grey Book), and the Absolution from Compline, all as alternatives to the old forms, which must still be used on the First Sundays in Advent and Lent. The Irish sentence 'Let us humbly confess our sins to Almighty God' forms a third option. The first Lord's Prayer is omitted,[32] and the Office begins at 'O Lord, open thou our lips'. *Venite*, which ends with verse 7,[33] is provided with invitatories for ten special occasions; these had been suggested by Frere and successfully put forward by the Advisory Committee,[34] though it is doubtful whether the bishops really envisaged the effect of combining these with the seasonal Sentences, which had been recently added by the Clergy. Psalm 51 was inserted by the Clergy as a further alternative to *Te Deum* (mainly for use in Lent[35]), and the bishops added Psalm 40; the response 'Because there is none other that fighteth for us' becomes '. . . that ruleth the world'. The Athanasian Creed is given in the revised translation and its use is optional. The 'State Prayers' are incorporated in the section of Prayers and Thanksgivings, so that they are no longer of obligation, though, to appease the Laity, a rubric ensuring *some* use of the Prayer for the King was added after the first rejection. Two new petitions (from the Scottish proposals) are added to the Litany, which ends with the Lord's Prayer, the remainder being headed 'A Supplication which may be used' on certain occasions.[36] The missing antiphon is restored after *Gloria Patri*, but the superfluous repetition before it still remains.

Prayers and Thanksgivings are enormously increased in number, and now total forty-five. All are provided with a bidding, a versicle, and a response.[37] Besides the 'State Prayers' and others brought from different parts of the book, there are new prayers for such subjects as the British Empire, Missions, the observance of Sunday, Confirmation candidates, Convocation, the Church Assembly, universities, schools, hospitals, the League of Nations, industrial peace, and the faithful departed. Their authors include R. M. Benson, St Francis Xavier, George Cotton, Francis Paget, John Dowden, John Wordsworth, Frere, Armitage Robinson, and J. H. Newman.[38] Ten are taken as they stand from the Scottish proposals, and two more are adapted from the same source. Three or four had come into general use during the First World War. At least ten were added by the Clergy in their last revision. Four alternative endings are provided for the intercessory section of the Office, including an ascription derived from Bishop Ken. This, and other borrowings noted above, mark the introduction of a new approach. In previous revisions new material came almost entirely from existing service-books or from the pens of the revisers: now, the private compositions of well-known divines of all periods were freely laid under contribution, a development pioneered by the Canadian revisers of 1922.

H

Surprisingly little work was done on the Collects, Epistles, and Gospels. Propers were provided for the Second Sunday after Christmas (including an Epistle of one verse) and the two new red-letter days; a collect referring to the New Year was added to 1 January (from the Scottish proposals), and a second collect for Easter Week. Provision was made for reading the whole Passion at the Communion on Palm Sunday and Good Friday, with alternative Lessons and Gospels for this purpose; and the observance of the octaves of The Epiphany and Ascension Day was enjoined. Alternative Epistles were provided for The Circumcision, Lent IV, Trinity XIII, and St Simon and St Jude; and alternative Gospels for Ascension Day, Trinity IX, and St Luke. The bishops removed the provision made in the Measure of 1923 for second Communions on Christmas Day and Easter Day, deleted St Joseph's Day altogether, and relegated a number of suggested new feasts to the Appendix. A large number of minor improvements were made in the text of the Epistles and Gospels.

The General Rubrics of the Holy Communion provide that the service is to be 'said throughout in a distinct and audible voice', and not 'supplemented by additional prayers'; 'nor shall the private devotions of the Priest be such as to hinder, interrupt, or alter the course of the service', an obvious reference to the practice of interpolating parts of the Roman rite, whether silently or audibly. This rubric originated in the Green Book, and must be regarded as an eirenic gesture by the Anglo-Catholic party. Non-communicating attendance is discouraged, and fasting before communion is commended, at the request of the Clergy and Laity in 1928. Vestments, as has already been said, are now explicitly allowed, in a rubric taken from the Orange Book, and so are wafers. The interchange of 1662 and 1928 allowed by the General Rubrics of the Book is suspended for this service; after the Absolution, one book or the other must be followed without variation until the Blessing, except that the 1928 proper prefaces may be used with 1662. If the Parochial Church Council so desires, 1662 shall continue to be used at least once a month.

The service is divided by headings into eight parts: Introduction, Ministry of the Word, Offertory, Intercession, Preparation, Consecration, Communion, and Thanksgiving. The direction 'at the north side of the Table' was omitted by the Clergy; the bishops substituted the 1549 phrase 'at God's Board'. The Ten Commandments are printed in the shortened form of the 1549 Catechism, with three alternatives: the Summary of the Law, and the three-fold *Kyrie* in either English or Greek;[39] but they must still 'be rehearsed at least once a month on a Sunday in each month'. The Collect for the King is omitted, and the Salutation is restored before the Collect of the day. All the changes made in the Introduction are found in the Green Book, and most of them are also supported by the Green and Grey Books. This section of the 1662 service has clearly been found unsatisfactory, without a generally acceptable substitute having been forthcoming. The restoration of the people's responses to the Gospel, and permission to omit the Nicene Creed on weekdays and the sermon at any time, were universally desired. Four of the Offertory Sentences are omitted, and six new ones added, three of which are applicable to the elements;[40] one with a missionary reference was added by the bishops. The mixture of water with the wine is recognized in a rubric as 'the ancient tradition of the Church'.

The Prayer for the Church is enlarged by phrases from the Grey Book which introduce 'all nations', missionaries, and 'places of learning'. The insertion of a petition for the departed is common to all the unofficial books: the eventual form is closest to the Green Book. All likewise desire a 'more explicit statement of our fellowship with the saints': the Clergy produced a form combined from three separate suggestions deriving from the wording of 1549, but the bishops preferred one which comes much closer to the less exuberant phraseology of the Grey Book. The first two Exhortations are removed to the end of the service, and the third is shortened by one sentence. An alternative penitential section is provided for weekdays : the second half of 'Ye that do truly . . .', and the Confession and Absolution from Compline. The latter were adopted by the Clergy from the alternative form in the Orange Book, though there it stands at the beginning of the service. The Prayer of Humble Access is placed before *Sursum corda*, as agreed at the Conference in 1919, being thus reunited with the rest of the 1548 devotions for the first time since their separation in 1552. There was a general desire for the restoration of the Salutation and *Benedictus qui venit* (printed after the service as 'An Anthem'); new proper prefaces for The Epiphany, Maundy Thursday, Whitsunday, Trinity Sunday, Saints' Days, and other occasions had been recommended by the Advisory Committee, once again chiefly at the suggestion of Frere.[41] They were mostly taken from the Scottish proposals, and were wisely placed at the end of the service.

The Prayer of Consecration now begins '*All glory be to thee*, Almighty God, our heavenly Father, *for that thou* of thy tender mercy . . .', thus linking it to the end of *Sanctus*, though the connection is obscured if *Benedictus* is inserted. The third clause is omitted ('Hear us, O merciful Father, we most humbly beseech thee ; and grant that we, receiving thy creatures of bread and wine, according to thy Son our Saviour Jesus Christ's holy institution, in remembrance of his death and Passion, may be partakers of his most blessed Body and Blood') ; its content is now expressed later in the prayer, and it has become redundant. After the Words of Institution follows a prayer consisting of the anamnesis from 1549 with the phrases rearranged to form an easier sequence of thought ; the 1549 epiclesis, somewhat enlarged by a phrase from the Catechism ; and the Prayer of Oblation.

This brings the Consecration to a conclusion, 'and all the people shall answer *Amen*'. The Lord's Prayer precedes communion, as all proposals desired. The Clergy suggested a Fraction following the Lord's Prayer, but the bishops unanimously struck it out. Five methods of saying the Words of Administration are permitted. The service ends, as in 1662, with the Prayer of Thanksgiving, *Gloria in excelsis* (which may be omitted on weekdays), and the Blessing.

The first proposals for rearrangement of the Canon, as put forward by the Lower House in February 1914, had been:

That the Prayer of Humble Access be removed from its present position and be placed immediately before the Communion of Priest and People; that the *Amen* at the end of the present Prayer of Consecration be omitted, and that the Prayer of Oblation follow at once (prefaced by the word *Wherefore*), and then the Lord's Prayer.

The bishops, in conceding this suggestion, were led by Bishop Burrows, then of Truro, to add the anamnesis from 1549 as a stronger link than the single word 'Wherefore'. As a result of the 1919 conference, agreement was reached on placing the Prayer of Humble Access immediately after the Comfortable Words; the Prayer of Consecration was to be followed by an anamnesis and epiclesis and the Lord's Prayer; and the Prayer of Oblation was not to be moved, but might be said in addition to the Prayer of Thanksgiving. However, the Canon in the Measure (proposed by the Church Assembly Committee) departed from the 1919 agreement by omitting the epiclesis and including the Prayer of Oblation before communion, with the 1919 form of anamnesis as link. The Clergy, however, felt that, though everyone would prefer to have one form only, it appeared impossible to devise a form that would be accepted by all; and to carry such a form 'in the face of a very considerable and important minority . . . would be disastrous'.

Therefore there would have to be two forms; and an un-official conference in the Jerusalem Chamber produced two, one 'which would be acceptable to those who represented the Green Book', and another 'which was accepted by those who represented the Grey Book'.[42] Neither party raised any objection to the other's proposals. In the first of these Canons the epiclesis was placed before the Words of Institution; in the second, after. The second made explicit reference to the work of the Holy Spirit; the first had none. The first included the whole of the Prayer of Oblation; the second retained the words of self-offering after communion, joined to the Prayer of Thanksgiving (a concession to Evangelical feeling made in the course of debate). In April 1926 another unofficial conference combined these two Canons to produce what was known as 'the Farnham Canon'. This followed the first of the 1923 Canons with regard to the epiclesis; the second in the treatment of the Prayer of Oblation; the anamnesis is in a new form (that finally adopted); and there is a second epiclesis at the end of the prayer. Frere constantly advocated the insertion of two epicleses, but he intended them to be indicated as alternatives;[43] the bishops rejected this solution as no better than having two complete Canons, which nobody wanted. The version finally printed in 1927 and retained without change in 1928 adopts the anamnesis of the Farnham Canon, and places the epiclesis after the Words of Institution (in the new form proposed by archbishop Lang), followed by the whole of the Prayer of Oblation.[44] If reconsecration is necessary, the epiclesis is to be recited in addition to the Words of Institution; this Frere regarded as 'the irreducible minimum'.[45] The successive suggestions are set out in a Table on p. 397.

The 1928 Canon was a compromise that pleased nobody: Evangelicals could not accept the offering of ourselves before communion, and neither they nor the Anglo-Catholics wished to give up the 'Western' view that consecration was effected by the recital of the Words of Institution. Frere's argument that 'the primitive Church regarded the prayer as consecrating, not any particular words of it',[46] fell on deaf ears. As Baxter observed of the bishops in 1661, 'antiquity is nothing to them when it makes against them'. Many Anglo-Catholics preferred to go on using a translation of the Roman Canon.

The General Rubrics for Baptism allow parents to be sponsors, and a deacon to baptize in the absence of a priest. Due notice must be given by the parents, so that the minister may appoint the time for the Baptism. The language is altered in various places to make it clear that it is original sin, not actual sins, that is washed away in baptism. 'Remission of sins' becomes 'remission of sin', though this change is not carried through into Baptism of Adults and Confirmation, where it would be more questionable. The phrase suggested in the Measure 'by nature born in a state of sinfulness', itself a toning-down of 1662, was further softened by the bishops into 'from their birth prone to sin', which drew a vigorous protest from Frere.[47] Noah and the Red Sea are banished from the 'Flood prayer', leaving the second half of the prayer without its key figure. This and the next prayer are now given as alternatives; the prayer preceding the promises is said by the congregation, as was already the general custom; and the Creed is said by the godparents in full, instead of their assenting to the priest's questions. The last two questions are transposed, and are answered explicitly 'in the name of this child'. The prayer over the font is turned into an eucharistic preface, as suggested in the Orange Book; the thanksgiving after the Lord's Prayer is divided into two; and a prayer for the home was added by the bishops. The final charge is recast, and the service may end with the Aaronic blessing.

Private Baptism now includes a rubric permitting lay baptism in an emergency; as in earlier revisions, the service was not brought completely into line with the revised public service. The same is true of the service for those of Riper Years; here the godparents are replaced by 'witnesses', as in Confirmation. In spite of a desire felt by the Clergy for the revival of the chrisom and the candle, neither of these ceremonies was restored. The Catechism was left untouched, but for the transfer of the last two rubrics to Confirmation. The General Rubricks of Confirmation begin with the Preface from the 1662 service; the ages of the candidates have now to be brought or sent to the bishop, presumably to help the enforcement of diocesan rules. The service begins with a new Preface, incorporating Acts 8 : 4, 5, 14–17, and stating that Scripture here teaches that 'a special gift of the Holy Spirit is bestowed through laying-on of hands with prayer'. This phrase was inserted by the bishops in place of the more cautious statement found in previous stages of revision, 'in Confirmation there is an outward sign, the laying-on of hands with prayer, the effectual token of an inward grace which is the strengthening gift of the Holy Spirit to those who rightly receive it'. An alternative renewal of vows is borrowed from Scotland for 'candidates who have not been baptized in infancy'. No address may be introduced into the latter part of the service (the bishops' milder version of the phrase in the Measure, 'without any interruption by preaching'). The doxology was added by the bishops to the Lord's Prayer, and the service ends with a catena of texts taken from the Grey Book, and the Blessing.

Matrimony authorizes the saying of Banns after the Third Collect of Mattins and Evensong. The language of the introduction is refined, and the old Puritan plea for 'honour' instead of 'worship' is at last granted. The bride is no longer to obey her husband (another last-minute change by the bishops), and he shares his worldly goods with her instead of endowing her with them. A third choice of Psalm is added (37 : 3–7). The Old Testament couples, Isaac and Rebecca, Abraham and Sarah, Adam and Eve, are all expelled, and the post-nuptial prayers are otherwise slightly shortened. A proper is provided for a communion, chosen by the bishops in place of the more traditional passages proposed in the Measure, which are found in most other revisions ; the new Gospel comes from the Grey Book.

The Visitation of the Sick is the service of 1662 abridged and rearranged (by Frere) in five sections: Visitation, Exhortation to faith and prayer, Exhortation to repentance, Act of prayer and blessing, and Special Prayers. One ancient prayer has been added in section iv. The rehandling makes the best possible use of the old material, but probably came too late to bring it into use. A request from the Clergy for a form for Unction was rejected by the bishops by a very narrow majority, and a rubric was inserted putting the matter in the hands of the diocesan bishop. Alternative propers are added to The Communion of the Sick, whose rubrics raise the thorny question of Reservation. The bishops' original draft rubric of 1911 had allowed the priest at an 'open Communion' to set apart some of the consecrated elements, and to 'go and minister the same'. If 'for any urgent cause' they were not taken to the sick person immediately, they were to be kept as directed by the bishop, 'so that they be not used for any other purpose whatsoever'.[48] What the bishops directed was 'a secluded chapel not accessible for worship', and under these conditions continuous reservation was permitted in a few churches. The conditions soon became unacceptable to Anglo-Catholics, who claimed that refusal of access 'cannot rightly be demanded and will not be given'.[49] The mounting casualty lists of the First World War widened the demand for reservation beyond the ranks of extreme Anglo-Catholics, but in 1918 the bishops declared that the rubric was not intended to cover perpetual reservation.[50] The 1911 rubric was included in the Measure of 1923, with an additional clause allowing 'further provision' with the bishop's permission or in accordance with future rules made by the Upper House. In the 1927 Book the bishops made it clear that there was to be 'no service or ceremony in connexion with the Sacrament so reserved'. A good deal of opposition was aroused by the phrase 'if the Bishop shall so permit', which was altered in 1928 to 'if licensed by the Bishop to do so'. The 'future rules' alluded to in the Measure, which were drawn up by Bishop Garbett of Southwark,[51] were not included in the 1927 Book. After the first defeat in Parliament the bishops incorporated them in the rubrics of 1928, and made 'the conditions of continuous reservation more definite'.[52]

The Burial Service is greatly altered in tone, though not in shape, by the provision of alternatives largely stressing the note of comfort for the mourners. Six new introductory sentences are added (from the Grey Book), and the Penitential Psalms ('if need so require', as suggested in the Green Book). Psalms 23 and 130 are added to those said in church, and an antiphon is provided (the only one to be restored in the main services of the book : Frere believed that this was the best place at which to reintroduce the use of antiphons[53]). Alternative lessons are taken from 2 Corinthians and Revelation, and part of Psalm 103 is appointed as an alternative to 'In the midst of life'. A second form of commendation is provided, which can be used in the case of suicide. The committal is rounded off with an ascription. New versicles and responses, and additional prayers from the Grey Book, complete the service. Permission is given for the universal practice of saying the Prayers in church before the committal; cremation is provided for; three lessons may be read, each 'preceded by one of the psalms'; and a proper is provided for a Requiem. There follows an Order for the Burial of a Child, the sole survivor of three services in the Measure. The other two were 'An Order which may be used when the Prayer Book Service may not be used', and 'An Order for the Burial of an Unbaptized Child'. The latter was the work of Frere and Bishop Ryle, then Dean of Westminster,[54] but was rejected by the Assembly.

The bishops added two further prayers to the Churching

of Women. The first part of the Commination is completely rewritten; the latter part is untouched; and an alternative rewriting of the first part submitted by the Clergy was printed in the Appendix as 'An Exhortation'. The Ordinal was little altered: the Litany was made optional; the eucharistic preface-form was restored;[55] the 1550 translation of *Veni creator Spiritus* was omitted; and an attempt was made to rephrase the question about the Scriptures so that it did not appear to imply a fundamentalist attitude.

After the Ordinal and the Accession Service follows an Appendix containing Prime, Compline, A Devotion before Communion, the propers for black-letter saints' days, and the Exhortation just mentioned. These are presumably grouped together and placed at this point as being additional rather than alternative, and perhaps also as appealing to a particular party. Prime was added by the Clergy from the Green Book, Compline was already in the Measure (in the main body of the proposals); both were intended for family prayers.[56] The 'Devotion' originally included the Sarum Confession and Absolution, but these were struck out by the bishops, leaving only Psalm 43, with versicles and responses; the idea of printing it separately from the Communion Service is put forward in the Green Book, where the mutual confession is still included. The blackletter propers begin with all the weekdays in Lent, Easter Week, the Rogation Days, and Whitsun Week; most of these are derived from Sarum, which provided for Lent a notable anthology of Old Testament teaching about forgiveness, while part of Lent is devoted to serial reading of Hebrews and Colossians (the first instance of continuous reading in the eucharistic lections on any scale). The other days include St John *ante portam Latinam*, the Beheading of John the Baptist, and the Saints, Missionaries, and Doctors of the Church of England. Commons are provided for Martyrs, Bishops, Abbots, and so forth. Dedication and Harvest Festivals are catered for, and also special intentions, such as Thanksgiving for the Institution of Baptism and of Holy Communion, and the Guidance of the Holy Spirit. The literary taste of the bishops (to whom this section is largely due) has not escaped criticism.

It was by no means only in England that revision had been going on. In 1908 the Fifth Lambeth Conference appointed a committee to discuss 'Prayer Book adaptation and enrichment', and among its members were several bishops who were closely concerned in the English revision, including Bishops Browne (Bristol), Chase (Ely), Drury (Sodor and Man), and Gibson (Gloucester), as well as the Scottish bishops Dowden (Edinburgh) and Maclean (Ross and Moray), and Bishop Hall of Vermont.[57] The committee pointed to various universal deviations, such as the insertion of 'Glory be to thee, O Lord' before the Gospel, and the omission of the Third Exhortation. Parts of the Preface to Matrimony were usually omitted, which suggested a need for revision. Undue repetition, as of the Lord's Prayer, should be avoided. More occasional prayers were needed, and more alternative forms, such as anthems instead of *Venite* on Great Feasts other than Easter. Morning and Evening Prayer should be shortened, so that they could be combined with Holy Communion and Baptism respectively, and shorter Words of Administration were desired. Revision of the Kalendar and Tables was urgently needed, including the insertion of some national saints; Proper Psalms should be appointed for every Sunday; and the Lectionary should be further revised, allowing more choice, and following the church year. The committee received a proposal that the Revised Version should be permitted for all liturgical use of Scripture: they were not prepared to 'recommend this proposal in its entirety, but they regard the subject as worthy of consideration'. They did not deal with the Ornaments Rubric or 'the structure and contents of the Prayer of Consecration', as time was insufficient.

The Conference laid down seven principles for revision :

(*a*) The adaptation of rubrics in a large number of cases to present customs as generally accepted ;

(*b*) the omission of parts of the services to obviate repetition or redundancy ;

(*c*) the framing of additions to the present services in the way of enrichment ;

(*d*) the fuller provision of alternatives in our forms of public worship ;

(*e*) the provision for greater elasticity in public worship ;

(*f*) the change of words obscure or commonly misunderstood ;

(*g*) the revision of the Calendar and Tables prefixed to the Book of Common Prayer.[58]

The Report touched off an explosion of revisions. Scotland and Ireland began work in 1909, Canada and South Africa in 1911, America in 1913. The process was long-drawn-out, which allowed the revising committees to become acquainted with each other's proposals. The South Africans in 1919 borrowed a phrase in the Prayer of Consecration from the Scottish draft of 1912, and contributed another to the final Scottish form of 1929. The Scottish 'Additional Prayers upon several Occasions', first published in 1912, were drawn on for all the other books, including the English, from which latter the Scots in their turn derived several features. The influence of the seven principles of the Lambeth Conference is everywhere manifest.

The Scottish Episcopal Church had made an abortive attempt at revision in 1889, but now its proposals were completed in two years, and were authorized for experimental use in 1912. At this stage, they consisted solely of the Scottish Liturgy of 1764, slightly revised, and a 'schedule of permissive additions to and deviations from' the Book of Common Prayer. The latter, mainly from the pen of Bishop Dowden, who was the leading figure at that stage, included the influential collection of prayers referred to above; seven additional proper prefaces; and a series of seasonal post-communion prayers. The Liturgy had always previously begun at the Offertory, the first part of the service being supplied from 1637, 1662, or the Nonjurors' form. This lacuna was now officially filled. In 1918 work was resumed, and widened to cover the whole book. Several contributions were derived from the English reports, but 'surprisingly little' was found in the Green, Grey, and Orange Books.[59] The Provincial Synod of 1925 decided to wait for the passing of the English Book; when that was defeated, revision was completed in June 1928, and approval was given in 1929. In these later stages the chief role was played by Bishop Maclean, a close friend of Frere, and a member of the 'Committee of Experts'.

Among the notable features of the book are the inclusion in the Kalendar of several Scottish saints, as recommended by Lambeth 1908 (Kentigern, Patrick, Columba, Ninian, and Margaret), and an independent Lectionary with a three-year cycle for Sundays. Seasonal Sentences for Mattins and Evensong included in the 1912 schedule were imitated by most of the other revisions. A new alternative to *Te Deum*, the canticle *Benedictus es* (Song of the Three Holy Children 29–34), was borrowed from the American proposals. Compline was included, in a different form from the English; Prime was not. The Litany is judiciously improved, and also printed in a shorter version; and an entirely new short litany based on the *Liturgy of St James* has been widely admired and borrowed. The Communion Service is printed in two forms: the Scottish Liturgy, and a very slightly revised version of 1662. In both the opening Lord's Prayer is omitted. The eucharistic prayer of the Scottish Liturgy already had both anamnesis and epiclesis, but the latter was now rewritten to include the congregation in the blessing of the Holy Spirit, and the former had an eschatological phrase added to it. *Agnus Dei* may precede communion. The new proper prefaces and post-communions have already been mentioned. The remainder of the book is very close to the English book of 1928, though in Confirmation a signing with the cross is restored before the laying-on of hands ; and in Matrimony there is a prayer for blessing the ring, while the proper is that of the English Measure of 1923, subsequently altered in England. Reservation is permitted without conditions, 'according to long-existing custom in the Scottish Church', and Visitation of the Sick includes unction. In Burial the choice of psalms and lessons is slightly different from the English, and the committal is placed at the end of the service.

The Protestant Episcopal Church in the United States of America had carried out a conservative revision as recently as 1892, but by 1913 the desire for enrichment was making itself felt, just as in England, and caused the appointment of a revising commission, whose work was approved in 1928. As with the Scottish book, many of the changes made in England in 1928 had already been made in America in previous revisions. Of the changes now made which were not also made in England, the following are the most important. The Lectionary is different, and the daily ration of psalms is reduced to one or two at each service. *Benedictus es* is added to the canticles at Mattins, *Gloria in excelsis* is restricted to Evensong, and further alternative psalms are provided at Evensong. The Communion Service is placed before the Collects, Epistles and Gospels ; new collects are added for Holy Week ; and a Gradual hymn or anthem is allowed. The Prayer for the Church retains its 1662 form, except for a petition that the departed may be granted 'continual growth in thy love and service'. The Prayer of Consecration is not altered (it already had an anamnesis and an epiclesis), but the Prayer of Humble Access is now placed immediately before Communion. As in England, the Lord's Prayer now follows the Prayer of Consecration.

Baptism is treated more vigorously : the service is so

arranged that it may be used either for children or adults. The 'Flood prayer' is omitted altogether, and so is the first reference to original sin; Matthew 28 : 18–20 forms a third alternative Gospel. The sponsors do not recite the Creed, but merely profess their belief in 'all the articles of the Christian Faith, as contained in the Apostles' Creed'. The final charge is reduced to two questions, which are appended to the four that evoke the promises. In the case of adults these questions are replaced by two relating to belief in Jesus Christ and desire to follow him. For the first time in America, signing with the cross is made obligatory. The Catechism is turned into two 'Offices of Instruction', in which the succession of questions and answers is varied by the inclusion of prayers and hymns. In Confirmation the Preface is replaced by a simple reading of Acts 8 : 14–17. The prayer for blessing the ring and the proper for the nuptial communion found in the Scottish book are also added here. Visitation of the Sick restores provision for unction, and Burial has yet other alternative psalms (27, 46, and 121).

The Irish revision began in 1909 and was approved in 1926. It was even more conservative in character than the Scottish and American revisions; not, however, because much of the work had already been done, but because the general tone of Irish Anglicanism demanded few alterations. The outstanding feature is a more logical arrangement of the contents. The Psalter is placed after the Prayers and Thanksgivings, the Collects, Epistles, and Gospels after the Communion Service, and Churching after Matrimony. Three yearly services, Commination, Harvest Thanksgiving, and the Accession Service, are placed in the middle of the book, and at the end are added 'The Publick Institution of a Minister', 'The Service to be used on the first Sunday' on which he officiates, and forms for consecration of churches and churchyards. The form for Visitation of Prisoners, a special feature of the Irish book since 1711, is now discarded. The occasional prayers show the usual Scottish influence, and Visitation of the Sick is set out in Frere's arrangement. *Urbs fortitudinis* (Isaiah 26 : 1–4, 7, 8) is added as yet another alternative to *Te Deum*. Alternative forms of Evensong were added in 1933.

The Canadian and South African revisions started from a different liturgical background from that obtaining in Scotland and America. The book in use in those two Dominions was, as in England, still that of 1662, though the Churches concerned were free from the necessity of obtaining the consent of Parliament. In Canada the revision began in 1911 ; a draft was authorized by the House of Bishops in 1915, amended and approved in 1918, finally confirmed in 1921, and brought into use in 1922. The book is chiefly notable for the addition of new occasional offices, for Dominion Day, Children, Missions, Harvest (based on the Convocation form of 1862), Induction, Laying a Foundation Stone, Consecrating a Church, and Family Prayers. The Kalendar was revised after comparison with the suggestions of John Wordsworth (in *The Ministry of Grace*), Frere (in *Some Principles of Liturgical Reform*), and one of the Convocation reports.[60] Much of the work done, such as the new introductory Sentences, is independent of British proposals, but the section of Prayers borrows freely from the Scottish schedule. The Lambeth Report's suggestion is followed, of additional seasonal anthems, which are provided for Christmas Day, Good Friday, Ascension Day, and Whitsunday, in place of *Venite*, an innovation peculiar to this book. The only change in the Communion Service is the introduction of the Summary of the Law and the people's responses to the Gospel ; the 'Flood prayer' is kept untouched ; and the bride still promises to obey her husband. The Confirmation Service, however, has unusual features : after a presentation of the candidates modelled on that in the Ordinal, follows the Preface, expanded by Bishop Williams of Huron,[61] and three passages of Scripture

(Acts 8, Acts 19, and Hebrews 6). Throughout the book there are numerous small alterations which show that the revision, though conservative, was carried out with extreme thoroughness.

The South African approach was very different, reflecting the predominance of a different type of churchmanship. Here revision began in 1911 with a schedule of permitted modifications and additions, which collates existing practice and adds new suggestions, apparently much influenced by Frere's *Some Principles of Liturgical Reform*. As in England the next step was a demand for the rearrangement of the Canon. Two young priests published a pamphlet which aroused widespread interest, and in January 1918 the bishops issued a *Proposed Form*, which adopts the order of 1549 (except for the Prayer for the Church, which remains in its 1662 position); the wording is that of 1662 with the inclusion of anamnesis and epiclesis in the Prayer of Oblation. A copy was sent to Frere, who submitted a detailed criticism, concentrating particularly on the epiclesis, with which he was closely concerned at that time in England.[62] Almost all of his points were embodied in an *Alternative Form* issued in February 1919. In this the penitential section (except for the Prayer of Humble Access) is put back to its 1662 position, and the wording of the Canon after the anamnesis is altered to:

we offer here unto thy divine majesty *these sacred gifts and creatures of thine own*, this holy Bread of eternal life and this Cup of everlasting salvation; and we humbly beseech thee to pour thy Holy Spirit upon us and upon these thy gifts, *that he may hallow this oblation, and* that all we who are partakers of this Holy Communion . . .[63]

This second epiclesis, based on the newly revised Scottish Liturgy but much altered in accordance with Frere's suggestions, aroused a storm of protest among those who held strongly to the Western theory that consecration is effected by the Words of Institution. In November 1921 the words printed above in italics (all suggested by Frere) were withdrawn by the bishops, and with this alteration the *Alternative Form* was approved in 1924 and finally authorized in 1929. Throughout the whole controversy the bishops held firmly to the belief (by no means usual at that time) that consecration is effected by the whole of the prayer, and that the essence of the prayer is thanksgiving and offering, the corporate act of the Church.[64]

In the first part of the service the sermon may follow the Gospel, and in 1924 seasonal offertory sentences and an offertory prayer were provided, all for the first time in an English Prayer Book, innovations which have since been widely copied. The sentences were suggested in the Grey Book, but the suggestion was not accepted in England. The Prayer for the Church has a further new petition for common welfare, good will, and brotherhood, and ends with the 1549 thanksgiving for the Blessed Virgin Mary and the Patriarchs, Apostles, and Martyrs. The Prayer of Consecration has one unique feature, a double epiclesis, one before and one after the Words of Institution. This Canon was eagerly studied in England : a phrase translated from the Roman Canon, 'this holy Bread of eternal life and this Cup of everlasting salvation', was quoted as a precedent by the Green Book, and an insertion in the first sentence, 'to take our nature upon him' was borrowed by the Grey Book, while other phrases are used in the Orange Book. A new versicle and response is added before the Prayer of Thanksgiving.

The revised Occasional Offices first appeared in 1926, and again, after further revision, in 1930. The entire book did not appear as a single entity until 1954. A number of New Testament saints are added to the Kalendar, such as Timothy and Philip the Deacon. In Baptism the chrisom and candle are restored for optional use, and at Confirmation the bishop declares that the newly confirmed are admitted to Holy Communion ; signing with the cross is permitted, with or without unction. All these points are suggested in the Orange Book; the renewal of the baptismal vows is also found in other contemporary revisions. The prayer for blessing the ring is included, and Visitation of the Sick includes unction. A new pastoral need is met by a Form of Admitting Catechumens.

The six revisions of the 1920s bear a strong family resemblance, but do not form a homogeneous group. Theologically speaking, Scotland, America, and South Africa are on the Catholic side, Ireland and Canada on the Evangelical, while the English book stands in the centre, though expressing a movement in the Catholic direction. Scotland and America had conservative revisions because most of the work had been done already, Ireland and Canada from choice; England and South Africa each introduce a great deal of change. The South African Communion Service was generally regarded as the most satisfactory of the six, even by supporters of the English book. It certainly represented the ideals of the Anglo-Catholics more accurately than did the English book, just as the Irish revision would have been perfectly acceptable to the Evangelicals.

11 New Paths

There is only the fight to recover what had been lost
And found and lost again and again: and now, under conditions
That seem unpropitious. But perhaps neither gain nor loss.
For us, there is only the trying. The rest is not our business.

T. S. ELIOT, *East Coker*, V

AFTER the débâcle of 1928, interest in revision naturally slackened, at any rate in England. In 1936 Convocation approved a form of Administration of Unction and the Laying-on of Hands, which brought English provision for the sick into line with other recently revised books.[1] Two years later the archbishop of Canterbury (Dr Lang) said in Convocation that he was not 'prepared at present to introduce a new Prayer Book Measure into Parliament'.[2] In spite of this declaration, a 'Round Table Conference' was called in 1938 to prepare a workable liturgy, but it did not survive the outbreak of war.[3]

Meanwhile, the newly united Methodist Church had produced a *Book of Offices* in 1936, which follows the Wesleyan *Book of Public Prayers* of 1882 in reproducing the Prayer Book Mattins almost intact, but makes no provision for Evensong. The Communion Service borrows from 1928 the Summary of the Law (to which it adds a third commandment) and the Proper Preface for All Saints' Day, though no other saints' days are allowed propers of any kind. Also as in 1928, the Collect for the King is omitted. Two further phrases disappear: 'provoking most justly thy wrath and indignation against us' from the Confession, and 'oblation and satisfaction' from the Prayer of Consecration. The latter is justified on the ground that 'the historical protest has done its work', and anti-Roman polemic is out of place here.[4] An alternative order was included for the benefit of whose who were unaccustomed to set forms of prayer, so that they could be brought gradually to the full service. Baptism adopts the 1928 'Prayer for the Home', and Matrimony also incorporates some minor alterations. The Churching of Women is restored under the name of 'The Thanksgiving of Mothers' (originally 'of Parents'), and includes some Prayer Book elements.

The 1922 Lectionary, though widely used, was also widely criticized, and in 1947 a new set of Sunday Lessons appeared, arranged in two tables for use in alternate years. Tables A and B, as they were generally known, met with considerable criticism on the ground that the gradual unrolling of sacred history was sacrificed to the reading of 'purple passages'. A further Lectionary appeared in 1955, reverting to a more traditional approach, but retaining the division into two years, a practice which is rapidly becoming universal. Unlike Tables A and B, it also included a rearrangement of the weekday lessons.

In 1947 the archbishops of Canterbury and York (Dr Fisher and Dr Garbett) issued *A Shorter Prayer Book*, which, according to its preface, had been prepared

in response to a growing demand from the clergy and laity of the Church, and more recently from service chaplains.

In 1943 the archbishops and bishops of the Provinces of Canterbury and York commissioned some of their number to prepare such a book. From time to time they have been consulted about its contents and have given general approval to its form and arrangement.

The purpose of the Book is to provide for congregational use an edition of the Book of Common Prayer, limited to the parts most often required, simplified in arrangement, and generally made easier to follow. The Orders of Service and the wording of prayers and psalms are unchanged, except for some of the variations in the Deposited Book of 1928. Rubrics have been re-worded for the sake of simplicity, and some page references and directions as to posture have been inserted. Otherwise the only new material is the explanatory Preface on the Christian Year . . .

The book incorporated most, but by no means all, of the

1928 changes that had been brought into general use. Outstanding among these were the seasonal Sentences at Mattins and Evensong, the occasional prayers, the Prayer for the Church, the new Proper Prefaces, and, above all, the entire services of Baptism, Confirmation, Matrimony, and Burial. The Canon which had caused so much controversy was very little used, and was not included in the *Shorter Prayer Book*. The latter itself caused a good deal of controversy because of its lack of statutory authority, but it was very widely used.

By the year 1900 *Hymns Ancient and Modern* had become thoroughly entrenched as the leading Anglican hymnal, but its position was challenged in 1906 by the appearance of *The English Hymnal*, which gave open expression to such advanced Anglo-Catholicism as led to its being banned by Bishop Gore, the acknowledged leader of the Anglo-Catholics. It enjoyed a rapid success, however, owing to the very high quality of the music, edited by Ralph Vaughan Williams, then almost unknown. It brought an entirely new atmosphere of vigour and objectivity into Anglican church music, allied to a most rigorous musical taste. Much the same could be said of the choice of words, largely controlled by Percy Dearmer. *Songs of Praise*, issued in 1929, continued even further along the same musical path, but bowdlerized the words in the interests of liberal theology. *Hymns Ancient and Modern Revised* (1950) took over many of the *English Hymnal* favourites without losing its own flavour. If there were ever such a thing as an official Anglican hymn-book, it would probably be very like this book. After the First World War various attempts were made to improve the chanting of the Psalms, under the leadership of the Poet Laureate, Robert Bridges. The new approach can be summarized as 'fitting the music to the words, not the words to the music'. The new methods of pointing were designed to reproduce the rhythms of speech as far as was consistent with the metrical form of the Anglican chant.

The Psalter Newly Pointed (1925) led the way followed by *The Parish Psalter* (1932), while *The Oxford Psalter* (1929) took the principle to the limits of what is practicable with the average congregation.

Throughout the first half of the twentieth century the Roman Catholic Church in Europe has been greatly renewed by the teaching and practice of the Liturgical Movement. The leaders of this movement have insisted on the understanding of the Eucharist as the corporate act of the whole church. This has to some extent been accepted in the Church of England since 1549, and the movement came too late to have any influence on the 1928 Book; but the appearance in 1935 of A. G. Hebert's *Liturgy and Society* set the Communion Service in a new perspective for Anglicans, and a volume of essays edited by the same author, *The Parish Communion* (1937), had a profound effect on the practice of worship in England. The pattern of Holy Communion at 8 and Mattins at 11, which had become almost universal since about 1860, varied only by the substitution of the Sung Eucharist at 11 in 'high' parishes, was now shown to put the emphasis in the wrong place. A celebration at 9 or 9.30 (the time has tended to get steadily later), with hymns and sermon, and with everyone communicating, combines the purposes of both '8' and '11' in a single service, and restores the Eucharist to the central position that it should occupy in Sunday worship. Further, such a service is neither 'high' nor 'low' in itself. In the conduct of a Parish Communion great importance is attached to the participation of the laity, who are encouraged to join in some of the prayers hitherto said by the celebrant alone, to make responses to the various petitions in the Prayer for the Church, to bring up the elements at the Offertory, and to assist with the chalice. The virtual disappearance of Mattins makes the inclusion of an Old Testament lesson and a psalm highly desirable, the latter usually following the Epistle; and the large number of communicants of necessity restricts the length of the sermon. These trends all affect the text of the service.

The architectural implications of the Parish Communion include the placing of the altar in a position where it can be clearly seen by everyone present. In a new church this will often be in the centre of the building; in older churches it usually means the provision of a nave altar in front of the chancel step. In either case, it is possible for the celebrant to face westwards, thus adding a visual association with the Last Supper, and emphasizing that the real celebrant is Christ himself. The position also has the incidental merit of resolving the ancient controversy about the 'north end' and the 'eastward position' by superseding both. There has been a consequent reaction against the 'English altar', and a tendency to move the choir out of the chancel. This kind of arrangement was given strong historical support in *The Architectural Setting of Anglican Worship*, by G. W. O. Addleshaw and F. Etchells, which appeared in 1948. In this seminal work the ground-plan and furniture of churches were analysed from the point of view of their suitability for the services of the Prayer Book. A church was seen as a set of rooms for different services; the traditional post-Reformation interior, so despised by the Victorians, was rehabilitated, along with Wren's 'auditory' churches; and the retention of the chancel screen was powerfully advocated.

In 1945 a new era in English liturgical studies was opened by the publication of Dom Gregory Dix's *The Shape of the Liturgy*, a study of the 'ritual pattern' of the Eucharist. Abandoning the search for an archetypal eucharistic prayer, Dix set out to show that underlying all the older liturgies is to be found 'a single normal or standard *structure* of the rite as a whole'. This he called the 'shape' of the liturgy, and it is based on our Lord's actions at the Last Supper.

Our Lord (1) took bread; (2) 'gave thanks' over it; (3) broke it; (4) distributed it, saying certain words. Later He (5) took a cup; (6) 'gave thanks' over that; (7) handed it to His disciples, saying certain words. We are so accustomed to the liturgical shape of the eucharist as we know it that we do not instantly appreciate the fact that it is not based in practice on this 'seven-action' scheme, but on a somewhat drastic modification of it. With absolute unanimity the liturgical tradition reproduces these seven actions as four: (1) The offertory; bread and wine are 'taken' and placed on the table together. (2) The prayer; the president gives thanks to God over bread and wine together. (3) The fraction; the bread is broken. (4) The communion; the bread and wine are distributed together.[5]

This thesis is worked out in detail in a book of 752 pages which reached an unexpectedly wide public and made its influence felt on all subsequent revisions. Some of Dix's enthusiasms, such as the theory that the Last Supper was a *chabûrah* meal, have not withstood further examination; but his advocacy of the importance of Hippolytus's *Apostolic Tradition* certainly established that text in a commanding position in the estimation of English liturgists; and his argument that the Communion Service of 1549, no less than that of 1552, was intended to express a Zwinglian theology of the eucharist has not been demolished by the searching counter-attacks that it has undergone.

In 1947 the united Church of South India came into being, and its constitution included a skeleton outline of the necessary elements in a communion service. As one of the uniting churches was the Church of England (the others were Congregational, Methodist, and Presbyterian), it is not surprising that when the infant Church produced its new liturgy in 1950 it should be strongly influenced by the Book of Common Prayer in its various revisions; but, equally naturally, it also draws on the *Book of Common Order* of the Church of Scotland, the *Liturgy of St James* as used in the Syrian Churches of Malabar, the Methodist *Book of Offices*, and other non-Anglican sources.[6] It is, in fact, the first ecumenical liturgy, based on the principle of faithfulness to the Scriptures, and intended to be 'an act of the whole people of God in the place where it is used'.[7] The Liturgy is divided into three sections: Preparation, Ministry of the Word of God, and Breaking of the Bread; these are more clearly articulated than in the Prayer Book service. The first two sections may be used by themselves as an Order of Service for Morning or Evening Prayer. The second section ends with the Grace, and 'those who leave shall leave' at that point. As will be seen from the table (p. 252), the order of 1662 has been greatly altered, and the numerous additions and alternatives give the impression of a completely new service. The penitential section has been moved to the beginning; and extemporary prayer is allowed at the Intercession. The influence of *The Shape of the Liturgy* is clearly seen in the place of the Offertory immediately before *Sursum corda*, and the separate Fraction *after* the eucharistic prayer. The 1662 Prayer of Consecration is kept, with modifications at the start, because its emphasis on the uniqueness of Christ's sacrifice is especially needed in India, as a contrast to Hindu sacrificial practice. Where it ends, however, an anamnesis and epiclesis are added, whose carefully ambiguous wording owes little to Anglican models. The westward position is enjoined, and communion is by 'tables', in Methodist fashion. Self-offering was originally included in the Offertory, but was placed after communion in deference to Swiss theologians. The Lord's Prayer and *Gloria in excelsis* are back in their 1549 positions, but may alternatively be said in their 1662 places.

This introduces a new element of flexibility: previously, variation in the Prayer Book had been confined to a choice of prayers at a fixed point, but now a choice of places was allowed for a single prayer. This principle had already been applied by South Africa to the sermon, and by the Colombo Liturgy (see p. 259) to *Gloria in excelsis*; here it is applied generally. Another extension of Prayer Book practice is found in the propers, to which psalm and Old Testament lesson are now added: each Sunday is allotted a specified subject, which forms the theme of collect, psalm, and all

The South Indian Liturgy

THE PREPARATION
Collect for Purity
Gloria in excelsis
    or Holy God (*St James*)
    or *Revelation* 5 & 7
Ye that do truly . . .
    or Holy Father (*Book of Common Order*)
Comfortable Words
Absolution

THE MINISTRY OF THE WORD OF GOD
Salutation
Collect of the day
Old Testament Lesson
Psalm
Epistle
Gospel
Sermon
Nicene Creed
    or Apostles' Creed
Prayer for the Church, as a litany (*Colombo*)
    or Litany (*Scottish Episcopal*, from *St James*)
Collects
Grace

THE BREAKING OF THE BREAD
Sentences
The Peace (*St James*)
Offertory: elements and alms
Offertory Prayer (Scripture phrases)
Prayer for Presence (*Mozarabic* and *Didache*)
Salutation and *Sursum corda*
Preface (*Book of Common Order*)
Sanctus and *Benedictus* (latter in *St James* version)
Prayer of Consecration
Response (*Bombay Liturgy*, from *St James*)
Anamnesis and Response
Epiclesis (*Book of Common Order*)
Lord's Prayer
Prayer of Humble Access
Fraction
Communion
Agnus Dei
O almighty God (Prayer Book phrases)
    or Almighty and everlasting God (*Book of Common Prayer*)
Blessings

three Scripture readings. In the Prayer Book this had only been done systematically on the Great Festivals and on saints' days, less thoroughly in Advent and on certain isolated Sundays, such as Easter II; but here it is carried out to its logical conclusion.

Other services followed at intervals: Confirmation in 1950, Baptism in 1955, a Covenant Service in 1956, Morning and Evening Prayer and the Ordinal in 1958, Marriage and Burial in 1960, the whole series finally appearing in 1963 as *The Book of Common Worship*. The services follow the same method as the Liturgy, that is, to take the Book of Common Prayer as the starting-point, and freely abbreviate, add, and alter. There are interesting points in Confirmation, where the renewal of vows is made explicitly and in detail; and in Baptism, where the profession of faith is made by the whole congregation, not only by the sponsors for themselves or in the name of the child. The Ordinal goes behind the Prayer Book service to a more primitive procedure. Most original of all is the treatment of the Morning and Evening Services. After the First Order mentioned above, the Second Order combines Mattins and Evensong into one service, so that the canticles and collects may be used either in the morning or in the evening. *Benedictus* and *Te Deum* are transposed, thus giving *Benedictus* a more appropriate place between the Testaments, and producing the following scheme:

> *Venite* or *Jubilate*
> First Lesson
> *Benedictus* or *Benedicite* or *Magnifica*
> Second Lesson
> *Te Deum* or *Nunc Dimittis*

The evening lessons are always related to the theme of the Sunday, and on weekdays the amount of psalmody and the length of the lessons is noticeably smaller than in the English tables. In general, the other services have not aroused nearly as much interest as the Liturgy, which has been frequently celebrated in this country. It is not too much to say that it started Anglicans thinking of revision in entirely different terms. 1928 was seen to be a dead-end, and exciting new possibilities were offered.

One consequence of this new interest in liturgy was the appointment in 1954 of a Liturgical Commission, in response to a request from Convocation, 'to consider questions of a liturgical character submitted to them by the archbishops of Canterbury and York : and to report thereon to the archbishops'. The first services the Commission produced were contained in the report *Baptism and Confirmation*, which appeared in 1959. The administration of baptism had raised practical problems in an increasingly secular society, which was nevertheless reluctant to discard the traditional outward observances, while the relation between baptism and confirmation had been since the Second World War the subject of a flood of controversial theological writing. The Commission tried to get behind Reformation debates to the services of the primitive Church. Taking the baptism and confirmation of adults in one service as normative, the Commission also provided separate services of Baptism and Confirmation derived from 'the archetypal service'. This was to take the form of a communion service into which baptism and confirmation were inserted in place of the Nicene Creed. The proper included an Old Testament Lesson and four psalms. The Blessing of the Water preceded the Promises, so that they might be followed immediately by the baptism. The giving of a lighted candle after baptism was allowed, but not made compulsory. Confirmation followed without any interruption, and then the bishop resumed the Communion Service. The forms for Infant Baptism and Confirmation on its own were similar, but with different propers and simpler promises. The services proved to be too much in advance of their time – the omission of Mark 10: 13–16 was quite

unacceptable – and they never came into use. A Table of
Proper Psalms which slightly reduced the amount of
psalmody on Sundays was generally adopted, except by the
Lower House of York, always at this time the odd man out.
On the other hand, an experimental form of baptism devised
by Dean Milner-White of York had been authorized by
York Convocation, but never received official recognition
in the province of Canterbury.

The Liturgical Commission did not include the Catechism
in its proposed services of Christian initiation, because this
had been allotted to a separate commission, which reported
in 1962. *The Revised Catechism*, after reinstatement of the
devil, was authorized for seven years' use. A third committee
produced a revision of the Psalter, going a good deal further
than that of 1916, but still retaining the bulk of Coverdale's
wording. This was published and approved in 1963, and
an edition with pointing followed in 1966, thus providing
the Church of England with its first official pointed psalter.

Meanwhile, the Anglican Communion had been displaying a similar interest in Prayer Book revision at its rep-
resentative gatherings. A Congress at Minneapolis in 1954
heard two notable addresses on liturgical subjects which
went into some detail in discussing new ideas and trends.
They prepared the way for the Lambeth Conference of
1958, which gave more attention to the Book of Common
Prayer than any of its predecessors for half a century. A
sub-committee's report listed 'essential' and 'effective
features' in the Prayer Books, and also 'suggested modifications or additions for the further recovery of other elements
of the worship of the Primitive Church' :

1. Exhortations have a legitimate function in the liturgy but they
   should be shorter and fewer.
2. The present corporate expressions of penitence need to be modified
   both in length and language.
3. More extensive provision of litanies, with shorter clauses, for
   corporate intercession, thanksgiving, and adoration; with the

discouragement of long strings of collects or other prayers for this purpose.

4. The recovery of the 'People's Prayers' at the Eucharist by breaking up the Prayer for the Church into sections, each followed by congregational response, or into a litany with short clauses.

5. The Offertory, with which the people should be definitely associated, to be more closely connected with the Prayer of Consecration.

6. The events for which thanksgiving is made in the Consecration Prayer are not to be confined to Calvary but include thanksgiving for all the principal 'mighty works of God', especially the resurrection and the ascension of our Lord, and his return in glory.[8]

The ideal of the recovery of primitive practice, neglected in England since the Nonjurors in favour of the restoration of Sarum or 1549, or of the imitation of contemporary Rome, was reaffirmed in the Conference's *Resolutions*,[9] and clearly formed one of the guiding principles in the services prepared by the Liturgical Commission, whose first chairman, Bishop Dunlop, was a member of the Lambeth sub-committee. The Conference also recommended the development of the Ante-Communion, and desired to see a new approach to the Eucharistic Sacrifice which would end controversy and produce a liturgy acceptable to all Anglicans.[10]

The bishops also listed twelve elements which should appear in any baptismal service:

1. The Ministry of the Word declaring the teaching of Scripture concerning baptism, e.g. Matt. 28: 19; John 3: 5; Acts 2: 38; Rom. 6: 3, 4; 1 Cor. 12: 13; Col. 2: 12.

2. A renunciation of the former way of life, the putting off of the old man (Col. 3: 8–10).

3. A profession of faith in Christ with the reciting of the baptismal creed.

4. The promises: to hold fast to the Christian faith; to obey God's commandments; to bear witness to Christ.

5. Blessing of the Water, with a thanksgiving for Christ's baptism

and the benefits of his redeeming work and prayer for the fruits of baptism in those to be baptized, which might well be expressed in litany form.

6. Baptism with water in the threefold Name, thereby uniting the baptized person to Christ (John 15: 1–8).

7. The signing with the Cross as a sign that we have been bought with a price, that we belong to Christ (1 Peter 1: 18, 19).

8. The reception of the baptized person into the fellowship of the Church (Gal. 3: 26–8).

9. Thanksgiving for having been sealed by the Holy Spirit for ever unto the day of redemption (Eph. 4: 30; cf 2 Cor. 1: 21, 22 and Eph. 1: 13, 14). [This is the reason why, according to the universal doctrine of Christendom, baptism cannot be repeated.]

10. Prayer for growth in the Christian life.

11. An Exhortation to the congregation reminding them that the newly baptized person has been brought into the life of the family of God and is to be encouraged by its fellowship, supported by its prayers, and strengthened by its example.

12. An Exhortation to the baptized person to live the new life in the power of the Holy Spirit (Col. 3: 1).[11]

Not all of these elements can be easily recognized in the Liturgical Commission's services, though the most important are clearly present.

The 1958 Conference, like that of 1908, was followed by an outburst of revised books. A complete revision was authorized for Canada in 1959, after sixteen years' preparation, while the Church of India, Pakistan, Burma, and Ceylon, which had published *A Proposed Prayer Book* in 1951, produced a definitive version in 1960. Japan and the West Indies each produced a revised Communion Service in 1959. The Canadian revision was conservative in character, though not as conservative as that of 1922. The Communion Service has special features arising from its attempt to combine Evangelical doctrine with sound liturgical structure. Thus it places the Prayer of Humble Access immediately before communion, but keeps the

Lord's Prayer after, as in 1662, a unique combination. The Prayer of Oblation is divided into two, the first part attached to the Prayer of Consecration, and the second part taking the place of the final sentence of the Prayer of Thanksgiving, thus avoiding the charge of Pelagianism which is levelled against self-offering before reception. The anamnesis is worth quoting as a typical example of the Canadian approach:

Wherefore, O Father, Lord of heaven and earth, we thy humble servants, with all thy holy Church, remembering the precious death of thy beloved Son, his mighty resurrection, and glorious ascension, and looking for his coming again in glory, do make before thee, in this sacrament of the holy Bread of eternal life and the Cup of everlasting salvation, the memorial which he hath commanded . . .

At this crucial point the balance between Catholic and Evangelical doctrine is equitably held. The prayer concludes with a petition for the Holy Spirit to fill the communicants with grace, thus producing a Trinitarian pattern for the whole prayer.

The Kalendar shows a remarkable degree of enterprise in the addition of post-Reformation commemorations: for example, William Laud, John Horden ('first bishop of Moosonee, 1893'), George Herbert, Caedmon ('first recorded Christian Poet in England'), John and Charles Wesley, Thomas Ken, Thomas Cranmer, John Keble, Henry Budd ('first North American Indian to be ordained to the ministry, 1850'), Florence Nightingale, Charles Inglis ('first Anglican Bishop in Canada, consecrated 1787'), and Robert McDonald ('Missionary in the Western Arctic, 1913'). As elsewhere, the Lectionary has been completely remade, and the daily psalmody diminished. The 1928 Invitatories are now introduced, though they had been little used in England; and Isaiah 42 : 10–12 and 60 : 1–3, 11, 14, 18, 19 are appointed as alternative canticles. The

Litany has been skilfully pruned of redundancies such as the repeated 'That it may please thee', and the occasional prayers have been very thoroughly revised, as in the previous revision. The Collects, Epistles, and Gospels are sensibly placed after the Communion Service, and break new ground for Anglicans by including a proper for The Baptism of our Lord. The Psalter follows, in a slightly emended version. Private Baptism is reduced to a single page, and a further page is devoted to The Public Receiving of such as have been Privately Baptized. The Catechism is divided into headed sections, and provided with a Supplementary Instruction on the Church, the Ministry, and the Bible. The Visitation of the Sick is renamed The Ministry to the Sick, and rearranged as in 1928. A valiant attempt to render the Commination acceptable to modern ears by drastic abbreviation is probably a forlorn hope.

A long history lies behind the Indian Communion Service. An experimental liturgy compiled by J. C. Winslow and E. C. Ratcliff was authorized in 1922 for the diocese of Bombay, and in 1933 for the whole province. Though never widely used, it was included in the *Proposed Prayer Book* of 1951, but not in the final edition of 1960, though it was to appear in a Supplementary Book. It was designed as 'a distinctive liturgy for the Indian Church', and differs from all its contemporaries in being, not a revision of the Prayer Book service, but an 'enormously shortened' adaptation of the Syriac version of the *Liturgy of St James*. The latter has been in use in Malabar since 1665, when it supplanted the *Liturgy of SS. Addai and Mari*. The Bombay Liturgy also draws on the Byzantine *Proskomide* and the *Liturgies of St Basil* and *St John Chrysostom*, and imports a Western element of 'variableness'. One phrase, a congregational response to the Words of Institution, was adopted in the South Indian Liturgy: 'Thy death, O Lord, we commemorate; thy resurrection we confess; and thy second coming we await.' In 1938 the diocese of Colombo produced a revision of 1662 which was well ahead of its time. The Confession and Absolution are placed at the beginning of the service; *Gloria in excelsis* may be sung either at the beginning or at the end; and the Prayer for the Church is turned into a litany. The Prayer of Consecration begins with a thanksgiving for creation from *St James* via the Bombay Liturgy, then, reverting to Prayer Book phraseology, includes anamnesis, epiclesis, and self-offering.

The Indian Prayer Book of 1960 includes two Communion Services, one a modern recension of 1662, and the other a revision which first appeared in 1951 and was further revised in 1955 and 1959. The latter is an eclectic service which benefits from the experience of several other countries. It includes an Old Testament lesson (the first Anglican revision to do so), and follows the Colombo Liturgy in its treatment of the Prayer for the Church, though this may also be said as a continuous prayer. The Prayer of Humble Access is placed after the consecration and the Lord's Prayer. The Prayer of Consecration begins with the same ancient phrase as Colombo, 'Holy in truth art thou', then borrows 'to take our nature upon him' from South Africa. The anamnesis follows the Scottish text, but omits the controversial phrase 'which we now offer unto thee' and substitutes 'we entirely desire thy fatherly goodness mercifully to accept *on high* this our sacrifice of praise and thanksgiving'. Indians regard it as essential to have some form of epiclesis, and that of the South Indian Liturgy is adopted, followed, after an amen, by 'here we offer and present unto thee . . .'

Other sources contributed new material to other parts of the book. The Scottish Episcopal Church supplied the *Shorter Litany* also adopted by South India; the American book furnished material for the Catechism and the Litany at ordinations; and Dean Milner-White's *Memorials upon several Occasions* provided many additional prayers and improved versions of prayers from 1928. In Baptism the lead given by South Africa has been followed, in restoring the 1549 three-fold renunciation and three-fold profession of faith.[12] Distinctive Indian features are also to be found. Great emphasis is laid on the duty of bearing witness, a theme whose presence is due to Bishop Azariah of Dornakal. This is expressed in some of the collects, and in an additional question at ordinations and consecrations; most prominently, in the Preface at Confirmation, where the conclusion is rewritten to relate to our Lord's words in Acts 1 : 8, 'Ye shall be my witnesses', and a fourth question is added to the Renewal of Baptismal Vows, in answer to which the candidates pledge themselves to bear witness in word and deed.[13] Another unique feature is an entire section headed The Ministry of Reconciliation. This has four parts, two public services and two private. The first is the Commination, 'recommended for use during Lent'; since the discipline referred to in the 1662 service is still in force in India, there is nothing anachronistic in retaining this form. Next comes a special service for the Renewal of Vows, particularly for use on Easter Eve and after a parochial mission. The private forms are for confession 'alone or after counsel with a fellow-Christian', and for confession and absolution in the presence of a priest. An Indian custom is christianized by permission to substitute the *mangalasutra* ('lucky thread') for the ring in Matrimony.[14]

The Japanese Church had already begun revision by 1897, but the Communion Service adopted in 1959 goes back only to 1953. It is chiefly remarkable for its handling of the penitential section, which 'may be used on the evening before a celebration', or if not, after the Creed (the sermon having followed the Gospel). It is said mutually by priest and people, as in the Missal, the first appearance of the procedure within an official Anglican service. The Prayer of Consecration begins with thanksgiving for creation, and has an epiclesis before the Words of Institution, as in 1549. The note of offering is strongly sounded with the words 'we do celebrate and make here the memorial which thy Son hath commanded us to make, and in the Lord's presence offer this holy Bread of Heaven and Cup of Salvation'; but there is no offering of ourselves until the Prayer of Thanksgiving.

The West Indian Liturgy allows variation in the position of *Gloria in Excelsis*. The Prayer of Consecration is very similar to the Japanese, but does not make any explicit mention of the Holy Spirit. Like the Scottish rite, it restores the penitential devotions to their 1549 position immediately before communion.

This efflorescence of local rites had become somewhat disruptive of the unity of the Anglican Communion, and the Lambeth Conference expressed the hope that it would be possible 'to work towards a liturgy which will win its way throughout the Anglican Communion'.[15] In 1961 the archbishops of Africa suggested that a liturgy should be compiled which might be used all over that continent, and a service entitled *A Liturgy for Africa* appeared in 1964. The compilers make acknowledgment to the South Indian Liturgy, an unusual procedure which eases the task of the historian. The marked structural similarity between the two services is probably to be ascribed to the presence of Bishop Leslie Brown on both committees, though the *Liturgy for Africa*, being purely Anglican in origin, naturally uses much more Prayer Book material. This is handled with considerable originality. As in South India, the penitential section is part of the Preparation, and the South Indian forms are alternative to the traditional Latin; the latter may also be said mutually. *Venite* (as far as verse 7) may be said as an introit; Gloria in excelsis may be said at the beginning or end of the service, or not at all; *Benedicite* may be said after the Old Testament lesson, and *Te Deum* or *Benedictus* after the Epistle. 'The Intercession' is an entirely new litany, which may be replaced on weekdays by the Prayer for all conditions of men; then follows the Prayer of Humble Access. This prayer had hitherto always been associated

with the Comfortable Words, or with communion, or both;
now it is isolated. After the Peace and the Offertory, 'The
Great Thanksgiving' begins without the Salutation, a
peculiarity shared only with the Irish revision of 1926. The
Preface is very fully developed, in trinitarian form, and
covers the themes of all the Great Festivals; accordingly,
there are no Proper Prefaces at all. The anamnesis makes a
gallant attempt to combine two points of view in the phrase
'offering to thee, with this holy Bread and Cup, our praise
and thanksgiving'. A final (optional) note of praise is
sounded by the use of part of Psalm 103, *Gloria in excelsis*,
part of *Te Deum*, *Nunc dimittis*, or another psalm. This is
followed by a prayer for Christian discipleship. If there is no
celebration, the Intercession is followed by the General
Thanksgiving, the Lord's Prayer, and the Grace.

In 1964 the ghost of the Ornaments Rubric was finally
laid by the passing of the Vestments of Ministers Measure,
which allowed the use of vestments or surplice and scarf,
without intending any doctrinal significance thereby.
Similarly, in 1965, the Prayer Book (Alternative and Other
Services) Measure made it possible at last to give full
parliamentary authority to the proposals of 1928.[16] They
were brought forward in a form entitled *Alternative Services:
First Series*, and were authorized by the Church Assembly
for seven years from November 1966. Like the *Shorter
Prayer Book* of 1947, 'Series I' tacitly drops a number of
features in the 1928 Book which had been little used. It also
includes some new ideas not to be found in 1928, but
paralleled in other recent revisions. The Table of Psalms is
that put out by the Liturgical Commission in 1959. The
1928 Introduction to Morning and Evening Prayer is
retained in full, though not typographically separated from
the rest of the office; but the Invitatories have been dropped.
The Litany is printed exactly as in 1928, but the section of
Prayers and Thanksgivings is omitted completely. In Holy
Communion, which follows next, *Gloria in excelsis* is now

allowed before the Collect of the day, and an Old Testament lesson may be read (from a Table taken from the Indian Prayer Book of 1960). The sermon may follow the Gospel. For the remainder of the service, the 1662 text and the alternative are printed in parallel columns. The Prayer for the Church may be treated as a litany, with the response 'Hear us, we beseech thee'. The alternative Confession and Absolution are retained, and the Prayer of Humble Access may be said either as in 1662 or as in 1928. The Offertory may be presented immediately before the Preface. The Prayer of Consecration is only printed in the 1662 form, and does not even begin with the 1928 phrase linking it with the end of *Sanctus*; however, permission is given for the Fraction to take place after the end of the prayer, so that the four actions can be brought closely together in the proper order. The prayer may end at the Words of Institution, or after the whole of the Prayer of Oblation (at the insistence of the House of Clergy), or after a shortened version omitting the self-offering. The Lord's Prayer may follow, with or without the doxology, and then *Agnus Dei*. After communion may be said the whole of the Prayer of Oblation, or the part containing the self-offering, or the Prayer of Thanksgiving, or both the two latter.

The Collects, Epistles, and Gospels are now printed after the Communion Service. Only the references are given, to allow for the use of different translations. The 1928 distinction between red- and black-letter days has been abolished, the latter being inserted in their calendrical places without any difference or inequality. Baptism of infants and of adults are repeated without change, but Private Baptism is omitted entirely. Confirmation was rejected by the House of Laity, which objected to the phrase 'The Scripture here teacheth us that a special gift of the Holy Spirit is bestowed through laying on of hands with prayer'; this was thought to be an unwarranted inference from Acts 8. In Matrimony both the 1662 and 1928 forms of the vows are printed, and a blessing of the ring is inserted. In Burial the lesson from 1 Corinthians has been skilfully shortened, and the Committal follows the Prayers instead of preceding them. The first part of the Commination is retained, in the 1928 version, but not the second; The Visitation of the Sick and The Churching of Women are entirely omitted; and so are Prime and Compline. Some of the changes not found in 1928 were derived from new forms prepared by the Liturgical Commission, which began to appear at the same time.

Sixty years have been needed to take full advantage of the opportunity offered by the Letters of Business issued in 1906; but justice has now been done to the proposals of 1928 and the widespread recognition they had obtained; the lapse of time has allowed some of the less well-advised proposals to be discarded; and a new chapter begins.

Documents

Mass of the First Sunday in Advent

When Mass is to be said, while the priest robes himself in the sacred vestments, he shall say the hymn:
Come, Holy Ghost, our souls inspire . . .   (in full)
V. Send out thy Spirit, and they shall be created.
R. And thou shalt renew the face of the earth. (Ps. 104 : 30)
  O God, unto whom every heart is open and every wish speaks, and whom no secret escapes, cleanse the thoughts of our hearts by the infusion of the Holy Spirit; that we may deserve to love thee perfectly and praise thee worthily; through Jesus Christ. . . .
Antiphon. I will go in to the altar of God,
to God who makes glad my youth.   (Ps. 43 : 4)
Psalm. Give sentence with me, O God, and defend my cause against the ungodly people: O deliver me from the deceitful and wicked man. . . .   (Ps. 43 : 1–6 and *Gloria*)
Antiphon. I will go in to the altar of God,
to God who makes glad my youth.
  Lord, have mercy. Christ, have mercy. Lord, have mercy.
  Our Father . . .
  Hail Mary . . .

Introit. Unto thee have I lifted up my soul; my God, I trust in thee, let me not be put to shame, nor my enemies mock me: for all they that wait for thee shall not be confounded.   (Ps. 25 : 1–3a)
Psalm. Show me thy ways, O Lord, and teach me thy paths.
(Ps. 25 : 4)
Introit. Unto thee . . . be confounded.

Glory be to the Father . . .
Introit. Unto thee . . . be confounded.

During the singing of the Introit, the priest with his ministers shall approach the step of the altar and himself say the Confession, the deacon on his right and the subdeacon on his left, beginning thus:
V. And lead us not into temptation.
R. But deliver us from evil. Amen.
V. O give thanks unto the Lord, for he is good.
R. For his mercy endureth for ever.   (Ps. 107 : 1)
Priest. I confess to God, to Blessed Mary, to all the Saints, and to you : I have sinned exceedingly in thought, word, and deed, through my fault. I pray Holy Mary and all the Saints of God and you to pray for me.
Ministers. May God Almighty have mercy upon you, deliver you from all evil, preserve and confirm you in goodness, and bring you to eternal life.
Priest. Amen.
Ministers. We confess to God . . . to pray for us.
Priest. May God Almighty . . . eternal life.
Ministers. Amen.
Priest. May Almighty and merciful God grant you absolution and remission of your sins, time for true repentance, amendment of life, and the grace and comfort of the Holy Spirit.
Ministers. Amen.
V. Our help is in the name of the Lord.
R. Who made heaven and earth.   (Ps. 124 : 8)
V. Blessed be the name of the Lord.
R. From this time forth, now, and for evermore.
                                                      (Ps. 113 : 2)
When the prayers are finished, the priest kisses the deacon and then the subdeacon, saying:
Receive the kiss of peace and love, that you may be fit for the holy altar, to perform the divine duties.
This done, the candle-bearers shall set down the candlesticks on

the altar step, and the priest shall approach the altar and say in a
low voice, bowing and joining his hands:

Take away from us, O Lord, all our iniquities, that we
may be found worthy to enter the holy of holies with pure
minds ; through Jesus Christ . . .

Then shall the priest stand up and kiss the altar in the middle,
and cross himself on the face, saying:

In the name of the Father, and of the Son, and of the
Holy Spirit. Amen.

Lord, have mercy.	Christ, have mercy.
Lord, have mercy.	Christ, have mercy.
Lord, have mercy.	Christ, have mercy.

Lord, have mercy.
Lord, have mercy.
Lord, have mercy.

(Gloria in excelsis *was omitted in Advent, but is printed here*
to show the normal order of service.)

Priest. Glory be to God in the highest.

Choir. And on earth peace to men of good will. We praise
thee, we bless thee, we worship thee, we glorify thee, we
give thanks to thee for thy great glory, O Lord God,
heavenly King, God the Father Almighty. O Lord the
only-begotten Son, Jesu Christ ; O Lord God, Lamb of
God, Son of the Father ; thou that takest away the sins of
the world, have mercy upon us. Thou that takest away the
sins of the world, receive our prayer. Thou that sittest at
the right hand of the Father, have mercy upon us. For
thou only art holy, thou only art the Lord ; thou only,
Jesus Christ, with the Holy Spirit, art most high in the
glory of God the Father. Amen.

Then shall the deacon put incense in the censer and say to the priest:
Bless

Priest. The Lord. May it be blessed by him in whose
honour it shall be burnt ; in the name of the Father. . . .

Then the deacon, giving him the censer, shall kiss his hand; and
the priest shall cense the altar . . .; then he shall himself be censed

*by the deacon; and then he shall kiss the Gospel Book brought by
the subdeacon.*

This done, the priest shall say the Introit, Kyrie, *and* Gloria
(*if not omitted*). *When* Gloria *is sung, after beginning it, he and
the ministers shall say it together in a low voice. Then he shall
cross himself on the face, and, turning to the people with arms a
little raised and hands joined, shall say:*

The Lord be with you.

Choir. And with thy spirit.

Priest (*turning to the altar*). Let us pray.

Stir up, we beseech thee, O Lord, thy power, and come; that by
thy protection we may be rescued, and by thy deliverance may be
set free from the dangers that hang over us from our sins; who
livest and reignest with God the Father, in the unity of the Holy
Spirit, God, throughout all ages. Amen.

Let us pray.

O God, who wast pleased that thy Word should take flesh in the
womb of the Blessed Virgin Mary, through the message of an
angel; grant unto us thy suppliants that, as we believe her to be
truly the mother of God, so we may be aided by her intercession
before thee; through . . .

*When there are more collects to be said, all that follow are said
with a single 'Let us pray' and 'through our Lord'; according to
the Use of Sarum, the number should not exceed seven.*

*One of the candle-bearers shall bring the bread, wine, and
water which are set for the ministering of the Eucharist; the
other shall carry a basin with water and a towel.*

*When the last collect before the Epistle has been begun, the
subdeacon shall go through the middle of the quire to the pulpit to
read the Epistle.*

The Reading of the Epistle of Blessed Paul the Apostle to the
Romans.

Brothers, knowing that now it is time to awake out of sleep: for
now is our salvation nearer than when we believed. The night is far

spent, the day is at hand: let us therefore cast off the works of darkness, and let us put on the armour of light. Let us walk honestly, as in the day; not in rioting and drunkenness, not in chambering and wantonness, not in strife and envying. But put ye on the Lord Jesus Christ. (Rom. 13: 11–14)

While the Epistle is being read, two boys in surplices shall bow to the altar before the quire step and go through the middle of the quire to the pulpit, and prepare to begin the Gradual and sing its Verse.

Gradual. All they that wait for thee shall not be confounded, O Lord.
(Ps. 25: 3a)
Verse. Make thy ways known unto me, O Lord, and teach me thy paths. (Ps. 25: 4)
Gradual. All they that wait for thee shall not be confounded, O Lord.

While the Gradual-Verse is being sung, two men of superior rank shall put on silk copes to sing the Alleluia, and go through the middle of the quire to the pulpit.

Clerks. Alleluia.   *Choir.* Alleluia.
Clerks. O Lord, show thy mercy upon us.   (Ps. 85: 7)
Clerks. Alleluia.
Sequence. Eternal Salvation, never failing, life of the world, Light everlasting, truly our redemption,
    Grieving that the human race was perishing through the power of the tempter,
    Without leaving the heights, thou didst descend to the depths, of thine own mercy.
    Quickly putting on human nature by thy spontaneous grace,
    All the earthly things that had been lost thou didst save, bringing joy to the world.
    Do thou, O Christ, cleanse our souls and bodies, that thou mayest have us as bright dwellingplaces.
    By thy first advent justify us; at thy second, deliver us;
    That, when the great light shall shine and thou shalt judge all things,
    Clad in imperishable robes, we may swiftly follow thy footsteps, wherever we see them.

The deacon shall cense the middle of the altar before going to read the Gospel. Then he shall receive the Gospel Book, bow to the priest, and say, facing south:

> Sir, bid a blessing.

Priest. The Lord be in thy heart and in thy mouth to proclaim the holy Gospel of God ; in the name of the Father, and of the Son, and of the Holy Spirit. Amen.

The deacon shall go through the quire to the pulpit, solemnly carrying the Gospel Book in his left hand, preceded by the thurifer and candle-bearers. . . . And the Gospel shall always be read facing north.

Deacon. The Lord be with you.

Choir. And with thy spirit.

The deacon shall make the sign of the cross with his thumb on the book, on his forehead, and on his breast.

The Continuation of the holy Gospel according to Matthew.

Choir. Glory to thee, O Lord.

At that time, when Jesus drew nigh unto Jerusalem and was come to Bethphage, unto the mount of Olives, then sent he two disciples, saying unto them, Go into the village over against you, and straightway ye shall find an ass tied, and a colt with her: loose them, and bring them unto me. And if any man say ought unto you, ye shall say, The Lord hath need of them, and straightway he will send them. All this was done, that it might be fulfilled which was spoken by the prophet, saying, Tell ye the daughter of Zion, behold, thy King cometh unto thee, meek, and sitting upon an ass, and a colt the foal of an ass. And the disciples went, and did as Jesus commanded them, and brought the ass, and the colt, and put on them their clothes, and they set him thereon. And a very great multitude spread their garments in the way; others cut down branches from the trees, and strawed them in the way. And the multitudes that went before and that followed, cried, saying, Hosanna to the son of David: Blessed is he that cometh in the name of the Lord.

(Matt. 21: 1–9)

When the Gospel is finished, he shall kiss the book . . . The

*priest, standing at the altar, shall begin the Creed, to be sung by
the whole Choir, not in alternation.*

Priest. I believe in one God.

Choir. The Father Almighty, maker of heaven and earth,
and of all things visible and invisible. And in one Lord
Jesus Christ, the only-begotten Son of God, born of his
Father before all ages, God from God, light from light,
true God from true God, begotten, not made, of one
substance with the Father, by whom all things were made ;
who, for us men and for our salvation, descended from
heaven and was incarnate by the Holy Spirit, of the Virgin
Mary, and became man. Crucified also for us under
Pontius Pilate, he died and was buried. And the third day
he rose again according to the Scriptures, and ascended
into heaven, and sits at the right hand of the Father. And
he shall come again in glory to judge the living and the
dead. His kingdom shall have no end. And in the Holy
Spirit, Lord and lifegiver, who proceeds from the Father
and the Son, who with the Father and the Son is worshipped
and glorified together, who spoke by the prophets. And in
one holy, catholic, and apostolic Church. I acknowledge
one baptism for the remission of sins. And I await the
resurrection of the dead and the life of the age to come.
Amen.

Priest. The Lord be with you.

Choir. And with thy spirit.

Priest. Let us pray.

Offertory. Unto thee, O Lord, have I lifted up my soul: my God, I
put my trust in thee, let me not be put to shame, nor my enemies
mock me; for all they that wait for thee shall not be confounded.

(Ps. 25: 1, 2a)

Verse. Lead me forth in thy truth and teach me; for thou art the God
of my salvation; in thee hath been my hope all the day long.

(Ps. 25: 4)

Look upon me and have mercy upon me; O Lord, guard

my soul and deliver me; let me not be confounded, for I have called upon thee. (Ps. 25 : 16)

After the Offertory the deacon shall hand the priest the chalice with the paten and the sacrifice, kissing his hand each time. The priest shall take the chalice from him and carefully put it in its proper place in the middle of the altar; and after bowing, he shall slightly raise the chalice in both hands, offering the sacrifice to God, and saying:

Receive, O holy Trinity, this offering which I, an unworthy sinner, offer in thy honour and in that of Blessed Mary and of all thy saints, for my sins and offences, for the salvation of the living, and for the repose of all the faithful departed.

In the name of the Father, the Son, and the Holy Spirit, may this new sacrifice be acceptable to Almighty God.

Then he shall put down the chalice and cover it with a corporal, and place the bread reverently upon the corporal in front of the chalice, which contains the wine and water. He shall kiss the paten and place it on the altar to the right of the sacrifice, covering it slightly with the corporal. Then he shall take the censer from the deacon, and cense the sacrifice, saying:

May my prayer be directed to thee, O Lord, as incense in thy sight. (Ps. 141 : 2)

Then the priest himself shall be censed, and then go to the right corner of the altar and wash his hands, saying:

Cleanse me, O Lord, from all defilement of soul and body, that I may be clean to carry out the holy work of God.

Then he shall turn and, standing before the altar with bowed head and body, and hands joined, shall say:

May we be accepted by thee, O Lord, in the spirit of humility and with a contrite heart; and may our sacrifice be so made in thy sight that it may be accepted by thee today and be pleasing to thee, O Lord my God.

He shall stand up and kiss the altar on the right of the

sacrifice, and give a blessing over the sacrifice; then he shall cross himself, saying:

In the name of the Father, and of the Son, and of the Holy Spirit.

Then he shall turn to the people and say in a low voice:

Pray for me, brothers and sisters, that the sacrifice, which is yours as well as mine, may be acceptable to the Lord our God.

A clerk may reply privately:

May the grace of the Holy Spirit enlighten your heart and your lips; and may the Lord accept meetly this sacrifice of praise from thy hands for our sins and offences.

The Bidding of the Bedes.

Priest. You shall stand up and bid your bedes to our Lord Jesu Christ, and to our Lady Saint Mary, and to all the company of heaven, for the state of Holy Church and for our mother Church of Rome, for our Lord the Pope, for the patriarch of Jerusalem, for the cardinals, for the archbishop of Canterbury, for all archbishops and bishops, and namely for the bishop of *N.*, for the patron of this church, and for your ghostly father, and for priests and clerks that herein serve or have served, for all men and women of religion, and for all other men of Holy Church, and for all them that have the state of Holy Church in keeping; that God for his mercy grant them such grace so to maintain and keep it that God be therewith repaid. You shall bid for the Holy Land and the Holy Cross, that God send it into Christian men's hands when his will is.

You shall bid also for the peace of this land, and for our lord the king, and for the queen, and for dukes, earls, and barons, and for all them that have the peace of this land to keep, that God for his mercy send them good counsel and grace thereafter to work.

You shall bid for the mayor of this town, and for all the community, and for all our parishioners that be here or elsewhere, on water or on land, that God for his mercy grant them grace safe to go and safe to come, and speed them in all their needs.

You shall bid for the good man and the good wife that this day brought the loaf and the candle, and for all them that first it began and longest held on.

And for all women that be in our Lady's binds that God for his mercy so them unbind as it be best to life and to soul; and for all that do truly their tithes and their offerings to God and to Holy Church; and for all that do not, that God for his mercy send them grace to come to amendment.

You shall bid for all the sick of this parish here or elsewhere, and principally for all that lie in deadly sin bound, that God send them such health as it be best to life and to soul; and for all those that be in good life, that God grant them grace to hold them therein; and them that be not, to turn them to amendment.

You shall also bid that God for his mercy such weather us send on earth that the fruit that is therein thrive, and that is for to do, turn Christian men to help.

You shall also bid specially for all that this church help with any thing whereby God and Saint *N.* the fairer are served and worshipped.

You shall also bid for yourself, that God for his mercy grant you grace so your life here to lead, him for to please our soul to save, and that it might be so for you and for us and for all Christian people, say a *Pater noster* and *Ave Maria* for charity.

Psalm 67 and *Gloria.*

Lord, have mercy upon us. Christ, have mercy upon us. Lord, have mercy upon us.

Our Father . . .

V. O Lord, show thy mercy upon us.

R. And grant us thy salvation.

V. Endue thy ministers with righteousness.

R. And let thy saints rejoice.

V. O Lord, save the king.

R. And hear us when we call upon thee.

V. Save thy servant.

R. My God, who trusteth in thee.

V. Save thy people, and bless thine heritage.

R. Govern them, and lift them up for ever.

V. Peace be within thy stronghold.

R. And plenteousness within thy towers.

V. Lord, hear my prayer.

R. And let my cry come unto thee.

V. The Lord be with you.

R. And with thy spirit.

Priest. Let us pray.

O God, who pourest the gifts of charity into the hearts of thy faithful through the grace of the Holy Spirit, grant unto thy servants and handmaids for whom we pray thy clemency, health of mind and body, that they may love thee with all their power, and perfect what is pleasing to thee with all love; and give peace in our time, through Jesus Christ our Lord.

You shall kneeling bid for your fathers' souls, for your mothers' souls, for your brothers' souls, for your sisters' souls, for your godfathers' souls, for your godmothers' souls', and for all your kin's souls.

You shall also bid for all the souls whose bones rest in this church or churchyard, or in any other holy place; and for all the souls that have given in their life or bequeathed any manner good to this place, wherefore God's service is the fairer done in this holy stead.

You shall also bid for all the souls that be in pain of purgatory, that God for his mercy for your bedes the rather bring them to bliss and to rest, and for all the souls you have had of their goods, wherefore you be in debt for to bid, and for all Christian souls, *Pater noster* and *Ave Maria.*

Psalm 130 and *Gloria.*

Lord, have mercy upon us. Christ, have mercy upon us. Lord, have mercy upon us.

Our Father . . .

V. Grant them eternal rest, O Lord.

R. And let perpetual light shine upon them.

V. From the gates of hell.

R. O Lord, deliver their souls.

V. I believe to see the goodness of the Lord.

R. In the land of the living.

V. The Lord be with you.

R. And with thy spirit.

Priest. Let us pray.

Absolve, we beseech thee, O Lord, the souls of thy servants the pontiffs and priests, and the souls of thy servants and handmaids our parents, fellow-parishioners, friends, and benefactors, and the souls of all the faithful departed, from every bond of their sins, that in the glory of the resurrection they may be revived and live among thy holy elect, through Jesus Christ our Lord.

May they rest in peace. Amen.

The Sermon.

Turning to the altar, the priest shall say the Secrets according to the number and order of those previously said before the Epistle, beginning thus:

Let us pray.

Secret. May these sacred gifts, O Lord, make us, being cleansed by their powerful virtue, come more pure to him who gave them; through our Lord Jesus Christ . . .

Secret of the Blessed Virgin. Strengthen, we beseech thee, O Lord, our minds in the mysteries of the true faith; that we who stedfastly confess him who was conceived of a virgin to be very God and very man, may by the power of the same saving incarnation be found worthy to attain unto everlasting happiness; through . . .

Then he shall say aloud:

For evermore. Amen.

The Lord be with you.

Choir. And with thy spirit.

Here he shall raise his hands.

Lift up your hearts.

Choir. We have them with the Lord.

Let us give thanks unto the Lord our God.

Choir. It is meet and right.

It is truly meet and right, fitting and profitable, that we should at all times and in all places give thanks unto thee, O holy Lord, almighty Father, everlasting God, through Jesus Christ our Lord, through whom angels praise, dominions worship, powers fear, the heavens and the heavenly hosts and the blessed seraphim joining in exultation do celebrate thy majesty. Praying that thou wouldest command our voices to be admitted with them, we say in suppliant confession :

Choir. Holy, holy, holy is the Lord, the God of hosts. The heavens and the earth are full of thy glory ; hosanna in the highest. Blessed is he that cometh in the name of the Lord ; hosanna in the highest.

The priest immediately, joining his hands together and lifting up his eyes, beginneth these words:

Therefore, most gracious Father, through Jesus Christ, thy Son, our Lord, we humbly beseech thee,

Let him bow down his body while he saith:

And we desire

Here the priest, standing upright, must kiss the altar on the right hand of the sacrifice, saying:

That thou accept and bless

Here let him make three crosses upon the chalice and the bread, saying:

These ✠ gifts, these ✠ presents, these ✠ holy and unspotted sacrifices

When the signs are made upon the chalice, let him lift up his hands, saying thus:

Which first of all we offer unto thee for thy holy

catholic Church, that thou vouchsafe to pacify, keep, unite, and govern it throughout the whole world, with thy servant our Pope *N.*, and our King *N.*, and all true believers, and such as have the catholic and apostolic faith in due estimation.

Here let him pray for the living:

Remember, O Lord, thy servants and handmaids *N.* and *N.*, and all that stand hereby round about, whose faith and devotion unto thee is known and manifest; for whom we offer unto thee, or which themselves offer unto thee, this sacrifice of praise for them and theirs, for the redemption of their souls, for the hope of their salvation and health, and render their vows unto thee, the eternal, living, and true God.

Communicating and worshipping the memorial, first of the glorious and ever-Virgin Mary,

Bowing down a little, let him say:

the mother of our God and Lord Jesu Christ, and also of thy blessed apostles and martyrs, Peter, Paul, Andrew, James, John, Thomas, Philip, Bartholomew, Matthew, Simon and Thaddaeus, Linus, Cletus, Clement, Sixtus, Cornelius, Cyprian, Laurence, Chrysogonus, John and Paul, Cosmas and Damian, and of all thy saints; by whose merits and prayers grant thou that in all things we may be defended with the help of thy protection, through the same Christ our Lord. Amen.

Here let him behold the host with great veneration, saying:

Therefore, Lord, we beseech thee that thou, being pacified, wilt receive this oblation of our bound service and of all thy household; and order our days in thy peace, and command us to be delivered from eternal damnation, and to be numbered in the flock of thine elect, through Christ our Lord. Amen.

Here again let him behold the host, saying:

Which oblation we beseech thee, O Almighty God, in all things to make blessed, ✠ appointed, ✠ ratified,

reasonable, and acceptable ; that unto us it may be the ✠
body and ✠ blood of thy most dearly beloved Son our
Lord Jesu Christ ;

*Here let the priest lift up his hands and join them together, and
afterward wipe his fingers, and lift up the host, saying:*

Who, the next day afore he suffered, took bread into
his holy and reverend hands, and, his eyes being lift up to
heaven

Here let him lift up his eyes.

unto thee, God Almighty his Father,

*Here let him bow down, and afterward erect up himself a
little.*

rendering thanks unto thee, he ✠ blessed, he brake,

Here let him touch the host.

and gave unto his disciples, saying, Take ye and eat of
this ye all, for this is my body.

*And these words must be pronounced with one breath and
under one prolation, without making of any pause between.
Afterwards let him bow himself to the host, and afterward lift it
up above his forehead, that it may be seen of the people; and let
him reverently lay it again before the chalice, in manner of a
cross made with the same. And then let him uncover the chalice,
and hold it between his hands, not putting his thumb and forefinger
asunder, save only when he blesseth, saying thus:*

Likewise after they had supped, he, taking this excellent
cup into his holy and reverend hands, rendering thanks
also unto thee,

Here let him bow himself.

blessed and gave unto his disciples, saying, Take and
drink of this ye all,

Here let him lift up the chalice a little.

for this is the cup of my blood, of the new and everlasting
testament, the mystery of faith, which for you and for
many shall be shed to the remission of sins.

*Here let him lift the chalice to his breast or further than his
head.*

As oft as ye do these things, ye shall do them in remembrance of me.

Here let him set down the chalice again, and rub his fingers over the chalice. Then let him lift up his arms and cover the chalice. Then let him lift up his arms crosswise, his fingers being joined together until these words 'of thy own rewards'.

Wherefore, O Lord, we also thy servants and thy holy people, being mindful as well of the blessed passion and resurrection as of the glorious ascension of the same Christ, thy Son, our Lord God, do offer unto thy excellent majesty of thy own rewards and gifts ✠ a pure host, ✠ a holy host, ✠ an undefiled host, the holy ✠ bread of eternal life, and ✠ cup of eternal salvation. Vouchsafe thou also with a merciful and pleasant countenance to have respect hereunto and to accept the same, as thou didst vouchsafe to accept the gifts of our patriarch Abraham, and the holy sacrifice, the undefiled host, that the high priest Melchizedek did offer unto thee.

Here let the priest with his body bowed down and his hands holden across, say:

We humbly beseech thee, O Almighty God, command thou these to be brought by the hands of thy holy angel unto thy high altar in the presence of thy divine majesty, that as many of us as

Here erecting up himself, let him kiss the altar on the right side of the sacrifice.

of this participation of the altar shall receive thy Son's holy ✠ body and ✠ blood may be replenished with all

Then let him make a sign in his own face.

heavenly benediction and grace through the same Christ our Lord. Amen.

Here let him pray for the dead.

Remember, Lord also the souls of thy servants and handmaidens *N.* and *N.* which are gone before us with the mark of faith, and rest in the sleep of peace. We beseech thee, O Lord, that unto them and unto all such as rest in

Christ thou wilt grant a place of refreshing, of light, and of peace, through the same Christ our Lord. Amen.

Here let him smite once upon his breast.

Unto us sinners also, thy servants, hoping of the multitude of thy mercies, vouchsafe to give some portion and fellowship with thy holy Apostles and Martyrs; with John, Stephen, Matthias, Barnabas, Ignatius, Alexander, Marcellinus, Peter, Felicitas, Perpetua, Agatha, Lucia, Agnes, Cecilia, Anastasia, and with all thy saints; within whose fellowship, we beseech thee, admit us, not weighing our merit, but granting us forgiveness, through Christ our Lord, by whom, O Lord, all these good things thou dost ever create,

Here let him make a sign over the chalice three times.

thou ✠ sanctifiest, thou ✠ quickenest, thou ✠ blessest, and givest unto us.

Here let him uncover the chalice and make a sign of the cross with the host five times. . . .

Through ✠ him, and with ✠ him, and in ✠ him is unto thee, God, Father ✠ Almighty, in the unity of the Holy ✠ Ghost, all honour and glory,

Here let him cover the chalice, and hold his hands still upon the altar.

world without end. Amen.

Let us pray.

Being advertised by wholesome precepts and taught by God's institution, we are bold to say:

Here let the deacon take the paten and hold it uncovered on the right side of the priest, his arm being stretched out on high. Let the priest lift up his hands, saying:

Our Father . . .

Choir. But deliver us from evil.

(*Priest.* Amen.)

Deliver us, we beseech thee, O Lord, from all evil, past, present, and for to come; and by the intercession of the blessed, glorious, and ever-virgin Mary, the mother of

God, and thy blessed apostles Peter and Paul and Andrew, with all saints,

Here let the deacon commit the paten to the priest, kissing his hand, and let the priest kiss the paten. Afterward let him put it to his left eye and then to the right. After that let him make a cross with the paten above upon his head, and so lay it down again into its place, saying:

give peace graciously in our days, that we, being helped through the succour of thy mercy, may both be always free from sin and safe from all trouble ;

Here let him uncover the chalice and take the Body, doing reverence, shifting it over in the hollow room of the chalice, holding it between his thumbs and forefingers; and let him break it into three parts, while there is said:

through the same our Lord Jesus Christ, thy Son,

The second breaking.

who with thee, in the unity of the Holy Ghost, liveth and reigneth God,

Here let him hold two pieces in his left hand and the third piece in the right hand upon the brink of the chalice saying thus with open voice:

world without end.

Let the choir answer:

Amen.

Here let him make three crosses within the chalice with the third part of the host, saying:

The peace of the Lord ✠ be always ✠ with ✠ you.

Let the choir answer:

And with thy spirit.

To say Agnus Dei, let the deacon and subdeacon approach near unto the priest . . . and let them say privately:

O Lamb of God, that takest away the sins of the world, have mercy upon us.

O Lamb of God, that takest away the sins of the world, have mercy upon us.

O Lamb of God, that takest away the sins of the world, grant us peace.

Here making a cross, let him put down the said third part of the host into the sacrament of the blood, saying:

This holy ✠ mingling together of the body and blood of our Lord Jesu Christ be unto me, and to all that receive it, salvation of mind and body, a wholesome preparation both to deserve and to receive eternal life, through the same Christ our Lord. Amen.

Afore the pax be given, let the priest say:

O Lord, holy Father, almighty eternal God, grant me so worthily to take this holy Body and Blood of thy Son, our Lord Jesu Christ, that by this I may merit to receive forgiveness of all my sins, and be replenished with thy holy Spirit, and to have thy peace ; for thou art God alone, neither is there any other without thee, whose glorious kingdom and empire endureth continually, world without end. Amen.

Here let the priest kiss the corporal on the right side, and the brink of the chalice, and afterward let him say to the deacon:

Peace be unto thee and to the Church of God.

Answer : And with thy spirit.

On the right hand of the priest let the deacon receive the pax of him, and reach it to the subdeacon. Then to the step of the quire let the deacon himself bear the pax unto the rectors of the choir; and let them bring it to the choir, either of them to his own side, beginning at the eldest . . . After the pax given, let the priest say the prayers following privately, before he communicate, holding the host with both his hands.

O God, Father, thou fountain and original of all goodness, who, being moved with mercy, hast willed thine only-begotten Son for our sake to descend into the lower parts of the world and to be incarnate, whom I unworthy hold in my hands :

Here let the priest bow himself to the host.

I worship thee, I glorify thee, I praise thee with whole

intention of mind and heart ; and I beseech thee that thou fail not us thy servants, but forgive our sins, so as with pure heart and chaste body we may be able to serve thee, the only living and true God, through the same Christ our Lord. Amen.

O Lord Jesu Christ, thou Son of the living God, who according to the will of the Father, the Holy Ghost working withal, hast quickened the world through thy death, deliver me, I beseech thee, through this thy holy body and this thy blood, from all my iniquities and from all evils ; and make me to alway obey thy commandments, and never suffer me to be separated from thee for evermore, thou Saviour of the world, who with God the Father and the same Holy Ghost, livest and reignest God, world without end. Amen.

O Lord Jesu Christ, let not the sacrament of thy body and blood which I receive (though unworthy) be to my judgment and damnation, but through thy goodness let it profit to the salvation of my body and soul. Amen.

To the Body let him say with humiliation before he receive:

Hail for evermore, thou most holy flesh of Christ, unto me afore all things and above all things the highest sweetness ! The Body of our Lord Jesu Christ be unto me, sinner, the way and life, in the name ✠ of the Father, and of the Son, and of the Holy Ghost. Amen.

Here let him take the Body, a cross being first made with the same Body afore his mouth, saying:

Hail for evermore, thou heavenly drink, unto me before all things and above all things the highest sweetness. The Body and Blood of Christ profit me, sinner, for a remedy everlasting unto life eternal. Amen. In the name ✠ of the Father, and of the Son, and of the Holy Ghost. Amen.

Here let him take the Blood, which when it is received, let him bow himself and say the prayer:

I render thanks to thee, O Lord, holy Father, almighty

eternal God, which hast refreshed me out of the most holy
Body and Blood of thy Son our Lord Jesu Christ; and I
beseech thee that this sacrament of our salvation which I,
unworthy sinner, have received come not to my judgment
nor condemnation after my merits; but to the profit of my
body and to the salvation of my soul into life everlasting.
Amen.

*Which prayer being said, let the priest go to the right side of
the altar, with the chalice between his hands, his fingers being yet
joined together as afore, and let the subdeacon approach near and
pour out wine and water into the chalice. And let the priest rinse
his hands, lest any parcels of the Body or Blood be left behind in
his fingers or on the chalice . . .*

After the first ablution is said this prayer:

That we have received with the mouth, O Lord, let us
take with a pure mind, and out of a temporal gift let it be
to us a remedy everlasting.

*Here let him wash his fingers in the room of the chalice with
wine being poured in by the subdeacon; which when it is drunk
up, let the prayer follow:*

Lord, let this communion purge us from sin, and make
us to be partakers of the heavenly remedy.

*After the receiving of the ablutions, let the priest lay the chalice
upon the paten, that if aught remain behind, it may drop. And
afterward, bowing himself, let him say:*

Let us worship the sign of the cross, whereby we have
received the sacrament of salvation.

*Afterward let him wash his hands. In the mean season let the
deacon fold up the corporal. When his hands are washen, and the
priest returneth to the right end of the altar, let the deacon reach
the chalice to the priest's mouth, that, if aught of that which was
poured in do remain behind, he may receive it. After that let him
say the Communion with his ministers.*

The Lord shall show loving-kindness: and our land
shall give her increase. (Ps. 85 : 12)

Then making a sign of the cross in his own face, let the priest

K

turn himself to the people, and with his arms somewhat lifted up and his hands joined together, let him say:

The Lord be with you.

Choir. And with thy spirit.

And turning him again to the altar, let him say:

Let us pray.

Then let him say the Postcommon, according to the number and order of the aforesaid prayers before the Epistle.

May we wait for thy mercy, O Lord, in the midst of thy temple: and may we carry out the coming solemnities of our restoration with fitting honours; through our Lord Jesus Christ.

We beseech thee, Lord, pour thy grace into our hearts, that, as we have known the incarnation of Christ thy Son by the message of an angel, so by his cross and Passion we may be brought unto the glory of his resurrection, through the same Christ our Lord.

When the last postcommon is ended, and the priest hath made a sign of the cross in his forehead, let him turn him again to the people and say:

The Lord be with you.

Choir. And with thy spirit.

Then let the deacon say:

Let us bless the Lord.

Choir. Thanks be to God.

At another time is said:

Ite, missa est.

As oft as 'Ite, missa est' is said, it is always said in turning to the people. And when 'Let us bless the Lord' must be said, let it be said in turning to the altar. When these things are spoken, let the priest (with his body bowed down and his hands joined together) in the midst before the altar say with a still voice this prayer:

O holy Trinity, let the office of my bond-service please thee, and grant that this sacrifice which I, unworthy, have offered in the eyes of thy majesty, may be acceptable unto thee; and that unto me and all them for whom I have offered it, it may avail to obtain remission, thou being

merciful, who livest and reignest God, world without end.
Amen.

*Which prayer being ended, let the priest stand upright, crossing
himself in his face, saying:*

In the name of the Father, and of the Son, and of the
Holy Ghost. Amen.

*And so, when obeisance is made, they shall return after the
same order wherein they came afore to the altar at the beginning
of the Mass; so having on their apparel, with the censer-bearer
and other ministers, let them go their way again.*

*And immediately after 'Thanks be to God', the Office of None
shall be begun in the quire, when it is said after Mass. But the
priest, as he returns, shall say the Gospel:*

In the beginning was the Word ... full of grace and
truth.   (John 1 : 1–14)

*If a bishop were present, he would give his blessing at the end
of the Canon, thus:*

May Almighty God, the coming of whose only-begotten Son in
the past you believe in and await in the future, sanctify you by the
illumination of that coming, and enrich you with his blessing. Amen.

May he in the course of this present life defend you from all
adversity, and show himself merciful to you in judgment. Amen.

May you be delivered from all the contagions of sin in this
present life, be found worthy with the holy souls through his mighty
intercession, and await without fear the day of that dread trial.
Amen.

May he vouchsafe to grant this, whose kingdom and rule endures
without end throughout all ages. Amen.

The blessing of God Almighty, the Father, the Son, and the
Holy Spirit, descend upon you and remain with you always. Amen.

(The text translated is that printed by Procter and Frere, 282–94, supplemented
from F. H. Dickinson's edition of the Sarum Missal. The Bidding of the Bedes is a
typical vernacular form printed by Brightman, II 1050–6; the language is here
modernized. The translation of the Canon, from 'The priest immediately' to 'go their
way again' (pp. 281–91), is that of Miles Coverdale [J. Foxe, *Acts and Monuments*,
ed. J. Pratt (n.d.) VI 362–8].)

Office of the First Sunday in Advent

MATTINS

Priest. Our Father . . .[1]
Hail, Mary . . .[1]
O Lord, thou shalt open my lips.
Choir. And my mouth shall tell forth thy praise.

(Ps. 51 : 15)

Priest. O God, make speed to my help.
Choir. O Lord, hasten to help me.   (Ps. 70 : 1)
Glory be to the Father, and to the Son, and to the Holy Spirit.
As it was in the beginning, is now, and ever shall be, world without end. Amen. Alleluia.

Invitatory. Behold, the King cometh : let us run to meet our Saviour.   (cf Matt. 25 : 6)
Venite. O come, let us sing unto the Lord : let us heartily rejoice in the strength of our salvation.
Let us come before his presence with thanksgiving ; and show ourselves glad in him with psalms.
Behold, the King cometh : let us run to meet our Saviour.
For the Lord is a great God ; and a great King above all gods.
In his hand are all the corners of the earth ; and the strength of the hills is his also.
Let us run to meet our Saviour.

[1] Said privately.

The sea is his and he made it : and his hands prepared the dry land.

O come, let us worship and fall down : and kneel before the Lord our Maker.

For he is the Lord our God : and we are the people of his pasture and the sheep of his hands.

Behold, the King cometh: let us run to meet our Saviour.

Today, if ye will hear his voice, harden not your hearts ; as in the provocation and as in the day of temptation in the wilderness,

When your fathers tempted me : proved me, and saw my works.

Let us run to meet our Saviour.

Forty years long was I grieved with this generation and said : it is a people that do err in their hearts, for they have not known my ways.

Unto whom I sware in my wrath : that they should not enter into my rest.

Behold, the King cometh: let us run to meet our Saviour.

Hymn

O Word, that goest forth on high
From God's own depths eternally,
Who in these latter days art born
For succour to a world forlorn ;

Our hearts enlighten from above,
And kindle with the fire of love,
That we who hear the call today
At length may cast our sins away.

And when as judge thou drawest nigh,
The secrets of all hearts to try ;
When vengeance falls on hidden sin,
And Saints their promised reign begin ;

O let us not through evil past
Be driven from thy face at last,
But with the saints in glory be
To endless ages pure and free.

To God the Father, God the Son,
And God the Spirit, Three in One,
Praise, honour, might, and glory be
From age to age eternally. Amen.

FIRST NOCTURN

Antiphon. The sceptre shall not be taken away from Judah, nor a leader from his loins, until he come who must be sent.

(Gen. 49: 10)

Psalms 1, 2, 3, 6.[1]

Antiphon. He shall be the expectation of the nations, and he shall wash his robe in wine, and his cloak in the blood of the grape.

(Gen. 49: 11)

Psalms 7, 8, 9, 10, 11.

Antiphon. His eyes are fairer than wine, and his teeth whiter than milk.

(Gen. 49: 12)

Psalms 12, 13, 14, 15.

V. Out of Zion is the appearance of his glory.
R. Our God shall manifestly come. (Ps. 50: 2, 3)
Choir (privately). Our Father . . .
I believe in God . . .
Priest. And lead us not into temptation.
Choir. But deliver us from evil. Amen.
Reader. Lord, bid a blessing.
Priest. May the eternal Father bless us with eternal blessing.[2]

FIRST LESSON: ISAIAH I: I, 2[3]

Reader. The vision of Isaiah the son of Amoz, which he saw concerning Judah and Jerusalem in the days of Uzziah, Jotham, Ahaz,

---

[1] When a psalm is said by itself, it is always followed by 'Glory be to the Father . . .'; when two or more are said, 'Glory be . . .' is repeated only after the last one.

[2] The first three blessings invoke the three Persons of the Trinity; so also in the Second Nocturn.

[3] The Lessons vary in different editions; Dickinson gives here Isaiah 1: 1–4, 5–9, 10–15.

and Hezekiah, kings of Judah. Hear, O heavens, and give ear, O earth: for the Lord hath spoken, I have nourished and brought up children, and they have rebelled against me.

Thus saith the Lord : turn to me and be saved.

Respond. Looking from afar, behold I see the power of God coming, and a cloud covering the whole earth. Go to meet him and say, Tell us if thou art he who shall reign among the people of Israel.

(cf Ezek. 38 : 15, 17)

V. Ye inhabitants of the world, and sons of men, rich and poor, one with another. (Ps. 49 : 1, 2)

Choir. Go to meet him and say: Tell us if thou art he who shall reign among the people of Israel.

V. Give ear, O ruler of Israel, who leadest Joseph like a sheep.

(Ps. 80: 1)

Choir. Tell us if thou art he who shall reign among the people of Israel.

V. Stir up thy strength and come, to save us. (Ps. 80: 2)

Choir. Who shall reign among the people of Israel.

Glory be to the Father ...

Among the people of Israel.

Looking from afar, behold I see the power of God coming, and a cloud covering the whole earth. Go to meet him and say, Tell us if thou art he who shall reign among the people of Israel.

Reader. Lord, bid a blessing.

Priest. May God, the Son of God, vouchsafe to bless and help us.

SECOND LESSON : ISAIAH I : 3, 4

Reader. The ox knoweth his owner, and the ass his master's crib: but Israel doth not know, my people doth not consider. Ah, sinful nation, a people laden with iniquity, a seed of evildoers, children that are corrupters: they have forsaken the Lord, they have provoked the Holy One of Israel to anger, they are gone away backward.

Thus saith the Lord : turn to me and be saved.

Respond. I saw in a night-vision, behold, the son of man cometh in the clouds of heaven. And a kingdom and honour was given to him; and all peoples, tribes, and tongues shall serve him.

V. His power is an eternal power, which shall not be taken away; and his kingdom one which shall not be destroyed. (Dan. 7 : 13, 14)

Choir. And a kingdom and honour was given to him; and all peoples, tribes, and tongues shall serve him.

Reader. Lord, bid a blessing.

Priest. May the grace of the Holy Spirit shine upon our hearts and bodies.

THIRD LESSON: ISAIAH I : 5, 6

Reader. Why should ye be stricken any more? Ye will revolt more and more: the whole head is sick, and the whole heart faint. From the sole of the foot even unto the head there is no soundness in it, but wounds, and bruises, and putrefying sores; they have not been closed, neither bound up, neither mollified with ointment.

Thus saith the Lord : turn to me and be saved.

Respond. The angel Gabriel was sent to Mary, a virgin espoused to Joseph, to tell her the word, and the virgin was frightened of the light: Fear not, Mary; thou hast found favour before God: lo, thou shalt conceive and bring forth; and he shall be called son of the Most High.   (Luke 1 : 26, 27, 30, 31, 32a)

V. And the Lord God shall give him the seat of David his father, and he shall reign in the house of Jacob for ever.   (Luke 1 : 32b, 33)

Choir. Glory be to the Father ...

And he shall be called son of the Most High.

SECOND NOCTURN

Antiphon. Bethlehem, thou art not least among the princes of Judah: for out of thee shall come a leader who shall rule my people Israel: for he shall save his people from their sins.

(Micah 5 : 2; Matt. 1 : 21)

Psalm 16.

Antiphon. Behold, a virgin shall conceive and bear a son, and his name shall be called Emmanuel. (Isa. 7. 14)

Psalm 17.

Antiphon. In his time shall righteousness flourish and abundance of peace: and all kings shall worship him, all nations shall do him service. (Ps. 72: 7, 11)

Psalm 18.

V. A rod shall come out of the root of Jesse.
R. And a flower shall grow out of his root. (Isa. 11 : 1)
Reader. Lord, bid a blessing.
Priest. May the almighty God bless us with his grace.

FOURTH LESSON: FROM A HOMILY OF MAXIMUS[1]

Reader. Therefore, since we ought to refresh ourselves after a time with spiritual feasts, let us see how the gospel lesson goes on. The Lord said about the time of his coming (as we heard), 'As lightning shining from under heaven, so shall be the coming of the Son of Man'. And he added in later verses, 'In that night there shall be two men in one bed: one shall be taken and the other left; two women grinding at a mill: one shall be taken and the other left'.

But thou, O Lord, have mercy upon us.
R. Thanks be to God.

Respond. Hail, Mary, full of grace, the Lord is with thee. The Holy Spirit shall come upon thee, and the power of the Most High shall overshadow thee; for the holy thing which shall be born of thee shall be called the Son of God. (Luke 1: 28, 35b)
V. How shall this be, seeing I know not a man? And the angel answered and said unto her: (Luke 1: 34, 35a)
Choir. The Holy Spirit shall come upon thee, and the power of the Most High shall overshadow thee; for the holy thing which shall be born of thee shall be called the Son of God.

Reader. Lord, bid a blessing.
Priest. May Christ give us the joys of eternal life.

[1] *Homilia* II of Maximus, bishop of Turin; also attributed to St Ambrose: Migne, *Patrologia Latina*, LVII, cols 225–8.

K2

FIFTH LESSON: CONTINUED FROM THE FOURTH

Reader. Brothers, perhaps we wonder why the Lord, telling of his coming, revealed that he would come in the night-time, and that his coming will be received by all in bright daylight, with fear and trembling. We have often heard it foretold in the holy Scriptures that, before the Lord Jesus Christ comes, Antichrist will reign, who shall so pour the darkness of his wickedness over the human race that almost no-one shall see the light of truth; and, covering the minds of men with his own darkness, shall affect their spiritual eyes with blindness.

But thou, O Lord, have mercy upon us.
R. Thanks be to God.

Respond. Receive the word, O Virgin Mary, which was sent to you from God by the angel: thou shalt conceive through hearing, thou shalt bear God and man, that thou mayest be called blessed among women.
V. Thou shalt bear a son, but shalt not suffer loss of thy virginity; thou shalt be made with child, and shalt be a mother ever untouched.
Choir. That thou mayest be called blessed among women.

Reader. Lord bid a blessing.
Priest. May the kind Spirit cleanse us within and without.

SIXTH LESSON: CONTINUED FROM THE FIFTH

Reader. No wonder the devil emits the darkness of wickedness, since he himself is the night of all sins. Therefore Christ will come, as it were, like lightning, to dispel the foul darkness of this night. And as night is removed by the dawning of day, so Antichrist will be routed by the rays of the Saviour. Nor will he be able to spread the darkness of his wickedness any further, when the light of truth has shone out.

But thou, O Lord, have mercy upon us.
R. Thanks be to God.

Respond. We wait for a Saviour, the Lord Jesus Christ, who shall

change the body of our low estate, made like unto his glorious body.
(Philipp. 3: 20, 21)

V. Let us live soberly and righteously and devoutly in this world,
waiting for the blessed hope and the coming of the glory of our
great God. (Titus 2: 12, 13)

Choir. Who shall change the body of our low estate, made like unto
his glorious body.

Glory be to the Father....

Made like unto his glorious body.

THIRD NOCTURN

Antiphon. The night is far spent, but the day is at hand; let us therefore cast off the works of darkness and put upon us the armour of
light.[1] (Rom. 13: 12)

Psalm 19.

Antiphon. It is time now for us to awake out of sleep; and our eyes
are open to rise to Christ; for he is the true light that shineth in
heaven.[1] (Rom. 13: 11)

Psalm 20

Antiphon. Rejoice in the Lord always: let your moderation be known
to all men. The Lord is at hand. Be fearful for nothing, but in every
prayer let your requests be made known before God.
(Philipp. 4: 4–6)

Psalm 21.

V. The Lord shall come out of his holy place. (Mic. 1 : 3)

R. He will come to save his people from their sins.
(Matt. 1 : 21)

Reader. Lord, bid a blessing.

Priest. May the gospel-reading be salvation and protection
to us.

SEVENTH LESSON: MATTHEW 21: 1–9[2]

Reader. The Reading of the holy Gospel according to Matthew.
At that time ... (see p. 274) ... in the name of the Lord.

[1] Based on the Epistle of the day.   [2] The Gospel of the day.

The Homily is taken from various treatises.[1]

'Bethphage' means the house of the mouth, or the house of the jaws; it was a village of the priests, and bore the meaning of 'Confession'. It was situated in mount Olivet, where is the light of learning, and rest from toil and grief. 'Then he sent two of his disciples': by those two disciples, sent to bring animals to the Lord, it is not unreasonable to understand two orders of preachers: one sent to the Gentiles, the other to the Jews. It was right to send two, as well for the knowledge of the truth and for pureness of action, as on account of the sacrament of twofold love (of God and of one's neighbour) to be preached in all the world.

But thou, O Lord, have mercy upon us.

R. Thanks be to God.

Respond. Hear the word of the Lord, ye nations, and proclaim it in the ends of the earth, and say in the far-off islands: our Saviour will come.   (Jer. 31 : 10)

V. Proclaim it and make it heard: speak and shout.

Choir. Our Saviour will come.

Reader. Lord, bid a blessing.

Priest. May the help of God remain with us always.

EIGHTH LESSON, CONTINUED FROM THE SEVENTH

Reader. 'Go into the city which is over against you'. For it was 'against' the Apostles, and did not wish to accept the yoke of their teaching. The disciples who were sent stand for teachers, whom he destined to penetrate the untaught and barbarous places of the whole world (like the walls of the city set 'against' them). 'And straightway ye shall find an ass tied, and a colt with her; loose them and bring them unto me'. Going into the world, the holy preachers found the 'colt', that is, the Gentiles enmeshed in the bonds of perfidy; for everyone was tied by the bonds of his sins. Nor only the Gentiles, but the Jews also; 'for all have sinned and fallen short of the glory of God'.

[1] From an anonymous homiliary containing *Expositiones Evangeliorum*. It has affinities with Haymo of Halberstadt's *Homily for the First Sunday in Advent*: Migne, *Patrologia Latina*, xix, cols 11–14.

But thou, O Lord, have mercy upon us.
R. Thanks be to God.

Respond. Behold, a virgin shall conceive and bear a son, saith the Lord; and his name shall be called Wonderful, the Mighty God.
V. He shall sit on the throne of David and on his kingdom for ever.
Choir. And his name shall be called Wonderful, the Mighty God.

(Isa. 7: 14; 9: 6, 7)

Reader. Lord, bid a blessing.
Priest. May the Father and the Son bless us in the unity of the Holy Spirit.

NINTH LESSON, CONTINUED FROM THE EIGHTH

Reader. The ass, which was tamed and subdued, means the synagogue, which bore the yoke of the Law; the colt of the ass, which was free and wanton, the peoples of the Gentiles. 'On which no man yet sat'; because none of the reasonable teachers had brought the bridle of correction which should 'keep the tongue from evil', or make them go in the narrow way of life. No-one had brought the clothes of salvation, in which they might wax spiritually warm in giving useful advice to the peoples of the Gentiles. For a man would sit on it, if he were to use his reason and correct its folly by suppressing it.

But thou, O Lord, have mercy upon us.
R. Thanks be to God.

Respond. Let the heavens rejoice, and earth exult: let the mountains shout praise; for our Lord will come, and have mercy on his poor.

(Ps. 96: 11)

V. In his time shall righteousness flourish and abundance of peace.

(Ps. 72: 7)

Choir. And have mercy on his poor.
Glory be to the Father . . . And have mercy on his poor.

(*At other seasons* Te Deum *would be sung instead of the repetition of the Respond.*)

V. Send out the Lamb, O Lord, the ruler of the earth.

R. From the rock of the desert to the mountain of the Daughter of Zion. (Isa. 16 : 1)

LAUDS[1]

Priest. O God, make speed to my help.

Choir. O Lord, hasten to help me.

Glory be to the Father, and to the Son, and to the Holy Spirit.

As it was in the beginning, is now, and ever shall be, world without end. Amen. Alleluia.

Antiphon. In that day the mountains shall drop sweetness, and the hills shall flow with milk and honey. Alleluia. (Amos 9: 13)

Psalm 93.

Antiphon. Rejoice, O daughter of Zion; shout, O daughter of Jerusalem. Alleluia. (Zech. 9: 9)

Psalm 100.

Antiphon. Behold, the Lord will come, and all his saints with him, and in that day there will be great light. Alleluia. (Zech. 14: 5)

Psalms 63 and 67.[2]

Antiphon. All ye thirsty, come to the waters: seek the Lord while he may be found. Alleluia. (Isa. 55: 1, 6)

Benedicite. O all ye works of the Lord. . . .

Antiphon. Behold, a great prophet shall come, and shall renew Jerusalem. Alleluia.

Psalms 148, 149, 150.[2]

Capitulum. It is time now for us to awake out of sleep: for now is our salvation nearer than when we believed.[3]

---

[1] Lauds follows Mattins without a break.

[2] When a psalm is said by itself, it is always followed by 'Glory be to the Father . . .'; when two or more are said, 'Glory be . . .' is repeated only after the last one.

[3] Based on the Epistle of the day.

R. Thanks be to God.

Hymn.   Hark, a thrilling voice is sounding;
                   'Christ is nigh', it seems to say;
                   'Cast away the dreams of darkness,
                   O ye children of the day !'

                   Wakened by the solemn warning,
                   Let the earthbound soul arise;
                   Christ her Sun, all ill dispelling,
                   Shines upon the morning skies.

                   Lo, the Lamb, so long expected,
                   Comes with pardon down from heaven;
                   Let us haste with tears of sorrow,
                   One and all, to be forgiven;

                   That, when next he comes with glory,
                   And the world is wrapped in fear,
                   With his mercy he may shield us,
                   And with words of love draw near.

                   Honour, glory, might, and blessing
                   To the Father and the Son,
                   With the everlasting Spirit,
                   While eternal ages run. Amen.

V. The voice of him that crieth in the wilderness,
R. Prepare ye the way of the Lord ; make straight the paths
    of our God.   (Isa. 40 : 3)

Antiphon. The Holy Spirit shall descend upon thee, Mary; fear not,
    though you have the Son of God in your womb. Alleluia.
                                                   (Luke 1 : 35)

Benedictus. Blessed be the Lord God of Israel . . .
        Psalm 123.
    (*On weekdays* Kyrie, Lord's Prayer, *and* preces *follow here.*)
V. The Lord be with you.
R. And with thy spirit.
Priest. Let us pray.

Collect. [1] Stir up, we beseech thee, O Lord, thy power, and come; that by thy protection we may be rescued and by thy deliverance may be saved from the dangers that hang over us from our sins; who livest and reignest with the Father and the Holy Spirit, ever one God, world without end. Amen.

V. The Lord be with you.

R. And with thy spirit.

V. Let us bless the Lord.

R. Thanks be to God.

MEMORIAL OF SAINT MARY

Antiphon. The angel Gabriel was sent to Mary, a virgin espoused to Joseph.

V. A rod shall come out of the root of Jesse.

Antiphon. The angel Gabriel was sent to Mary, a virgin espoused to Joseph.

Collect. O God, who wast willing to take flesh from the womb of the Blessed Virgin Mary, when the angel announced thy word : grant to thy suppliants who believe her to be truly the Mother of God that we may be helped in thy sight by her intercession ; through the same. . . . Amen.

V. The Lord be with you.

R. And with thy spirit.

V. Let us bless the Lord.

R. Thanks be to God.

PRIME

Priest. Our Father . . .[2]

    Hail, Mary . . .[2]

    O God, make speed to my help.

Choir. O Lord, hasten to help me.

    Glory be to the Father, and to the Son, and to the Holy Spirit.

---

[1] The Collect of the day.   [2] Said privately.

As it was in the beginning, is now, and ever shall be, world without end. Amen. Alleluia.

Hymn.   Now that the daylight fills the sky,
We lift our hearts to God on high,
That he, in all we do or say,
Would keep us free from harm today;

Our tongues would bridle, lest they sin
By waking anger's hateful din;
With tender care would guard our eyes
From giving heed to vanities.

O may our inmost hearts be pure,
From thoughts of folly kept secure;
And pride of sinful flesh subdued
Through sparing use of daily food.

So we, when this new day is o'er,
And shades of night return once more,
The path of holy temperance trod,
Shall give the glory to our God.

All praise to God the Father be,
All praise, eternal Son, to thee,
Whom with the Spirit we adore,
For ever and for evermore. Amen.

Antiphon. [1] In that day the mountains shall drop sweetness, and the hills shall flow with milk and honey. Alleluia.   (Amos. 9: 13)

Psalms 22 and 23.
Psalms 24 and 25.
Psalms 26 and 54.
Psalms 118 and 119 : 1–16.
Psalm 119 : 17–32.[2]

---

[1] The first antiphon of Lauds.
[2] 'Glory be . . .' is repeated after Psalms 23, 25, 54, 119: 16, and 119: 32.

Antiphon. With heart and mouth we acknowledge, praise, and bless thee as God, the Father unbegotten, the only-begotten Son, the Holy Spirit the Paraclete, the holy and undivided Trinity: to thee be glory for evermore.

St Athanasius' Creed. Whosoever will be saved . . . he cannot be saved.

Capitulum. To the King of ages, immortal, invisible, the only God, be honour and glory from generation to generation. Amen. (I Tim. 1 : 17)

R. Thanks be to God.

Respond. O Jesu Christ, Son of the living God, have mercy upon us. (Matt. 16 : 16)
　　　Alleluia, Alleluia.

V. Thou that sittest at the right hand of the Father.
　　　　　　　　　　　　　　　　　　　　　(Col. 3 : 1)

Choir. Have mercy upon us.
　　　Glory be to the Father . . .
　　　O Jesu Christ, Son of the living God, have mercy upon us.

V. Arise, O God, and help us.

R. And deliver us for thy name's sake. (Ps. 44 : 26)

Lord, have mercy.	Christ, have mercy.
Lord, have mercy.	Christ, have mercy.
Lord, have mercy.	Christ, have mercy.

　　　　　Lord, have mercy.
　　　　　Lord, have mercy.
　　　　　Lord, have mercy.

Priest. Our Father . . . And lead us not into temptation.

R. But deliver us from evil. Amen.

V. My soul shall live and praise thee.

R. And thy judgments shall help me.

V. I have gone astray as a sheep that is lost.

R. Seek thy servant, for I do not forget thy commandments.
　　　　　　　　　　　　　　　　(Ps. 119 : 175, 176)

Priest. I believe in God . . . the resurrection of the flesh.

R. And life everlasting. Amen.

V. Let my mouth be filled with thy praise.

R. That I may sing of thy glory and thy greatness all the day long. (Ps. 71 : 8)

V. Lord, turn thy face from my sins.

R. And blot out all mine iniquities.

V. Make me a clean heart, O God.

R. And take not thy Holy Spirit from me.

V. Give me the comfort of thy help again.

R. And stablish me with thy chief Spirit. (Ps. 51 : 9–11)

V. Deliver me, O God, from the wicked man.

R. Deliver me from the ungodly man. (Ps. 140 : 1)

V. Deliver me from my enemies, O my God.

R. And free me from those that rise up against me.

V. Deliver me from them that work wickedness.

R. And save me from the bloodthirsty men. (Ps. 59 : 1, 2)

V. So will I always give thanks unto thy name.

R. That I may daily perform my vows. (Ps. 61 : 8)

V. Hear us, O God of our salvation.

R. The hope of all the ends of the earth and in the far sea.

(Ps. 65 : 5)

V. O God, make speed to help me.

R. O Lord, hasten to help me. (Ps. 70 : 1)

V. Holy God, holy and strong, holy and immortal.

R. O Lamb of God, that takest away the sins of the world, have mercy upon us.

V. Bless the Lord, O my soul.

R. And all that is within me praise his holy name.

V. Who forgiveth all thy sins.

R. Who healeth all thy infirmities.

V. Who saveth thy life from destruction.

R. Who crowneth thee with mercy and lovingkindness.

V. Who satisfieth thy desire with good things.

R. Thy youth shall be renewed as an eagle's.

(Ps. 103 : 1, 3–5)

Priest. I confess to God, to Blessed Mary, to all the Saints, and to you : I have sinned exceedingly in thought, word, and deed, through my fault. I pray Holy Mary and all the Saints of God and you to pray for me.

Choir. May God Almighty have mercy upon you, deliver you from all evil, preserve and confirm you in goodness, and bring you to eternal life.

Priest. Amen.

Choir. We confess to God . . . to pray for us.

Priest. May God Almighty . . . eternal life.

Choir. Amen.

Priest. May Almighty and merciful God grant you absolution and remission of your sins, time for true repentance, amendment of life, and the grace and comfort of the Holy Spirit.

Choir. Amen.

V. O God, thou wilt turn again and quicken us.

R. And thy people shall rejoice in thee.

V. Show us thy mercy, O God.

R. And grant us thy salvation. (Ps. 85 : 6, 7)

V. Vouchsafe, O Lord, this day.

R. To keep us without sin.

V. O Lord, have mercy upon us.

R. Have mercy upon us. (Ps. 123 : 3)

V. O Lord, let thy mercy be upon us.

R. As we have hoped in thee. (Ps. 33 : 22)

V. Turn us again, O Lord God of hosts.

R. Show thy countenance, and we shall be whole.

(Ps. 80 : 19)

V. O Lord, hear my prayer.

R. And let my cry come unto thee. (Ps. 102 : 1)

V. The Lord be with you.

R. And with thy spirit.

Priest. Let us pray.

1 In this hour of this day, fill us, O Lord, with thy

---

1 The first collect is said on all double feasts, the second on ordinary Sundays and Saints' Days.

mercy; that, rejoicing all the day, we may delight in thy praises; through . . .

Or,

O Lord, holy Father, almighty, everlasting God, who hast safely brought us to the beginning of this day, save us today by thy power; and grant that in this day we may fall into no sin, nor run into any danger; but that all our doing may be ordered by thy government to do always thy righteousness; through . . .

V. The Lord be with you.
R. And with thy spirit.
V. Let us bless the Lord.
R. Thanks be to God.

TERCE

Priest. O God, make speed to my help.
Choir. O Lord, hasten to help me.

Glory be to the Father, and to the Son, and to the Holy Spirit.

As it was in the beginning, is now, and ever shall be, world without end. Amen. Alleluia.

Hymn. Come, Holy Ghost, who ever one
Art with the Father and the Son;
Come, Holy Ghost, our souls possess
With thy full flood of holiness.

In will and deed, by heart and tongue,
With all our powers, thy praise be sung;
And love light up our mortal frame,
Till others catch the living flame.

Almighty Father, hear our cry,
Through Jesus Christ, our Lord most high,
Who with the Holy Ghost and thee
Doth live and reign eternally. Amen.

Antiphon. [1] Rejoice, O daughter of Zion; shout, O daughter of Jerusalem. Alleluia.

Psalm 119 : 33–80 (*sung as three psalms*).

Capitulum. [2] It is time now for us to awake out of sleep: for now is our salvation nearer than when we believed.

R. Thanks be to God.
Respond. Come to deliver us, O Lord God of hosts.
V. Show thy countenance, and we shall be whole.
Choir. O Lord God of hosts.
    Glory be to the Father . . .
    Come to deliver us, O Lord God of hosts.
V. The nations shall fear thy name.
R. And all the kings of the earth thy glory.   (Ps. 102 : 15)

Collect. [3] Stir up, we beseech thee, O Lord . . . (p. 272) world without end. Amen.

SEXT

Priest. O God, make speed to my help.
Choir. O Lord, hasten to help me.
    Glory be to the Father, and to the Son, and to the Holy Spirit.
    As it was in the beginning, is now, and ever shall be, world without end. Amen. Alleluia.

Hymn.   O God of truth, O Lord of might,
        Who orderest time and change aright,
        Arraying morn with joyful gleams,
        And kindling noonday's fiery beams;

---

[1] The second antiphon of Lauds.
[2] Based on the Epistle of the day.
[3] The Collect of the day.

Quench thou on earth the flames of strife ;
From passion's heat preserve our life ;
Our bodies keep from perils free,
And grant our souls true peace in thee.

Almighty Father, hear our cry,
Through Jesus Christ, our Lord most high,
Who with the Holy Ghost and thee
Doth live and reign eternally. Amen.

Antiphon. [1] Behold, the Lord will come, and all his saints with him, and in that day there will be great light. Alleluia.

Psalm 119 : 81–128 (*sung as three psalms*).

Capitulum. [2] The night is far spent, but the day will draw near: let us therefore cast off the works of darkness and put upon us the armour of light.

Respond. Show us thy mercy, O Lord.
V. And grant us thy salvation.
Choir. Thy mercy, O Lord.
 Glory be to the Father . . .
 Show us thy mercy, O Lord.
V. Remember us, O Lord, in caring for thy people.
R. Visit us with thy salvation.   (Ps. 106 : 4)

NONE

Priest. O God, make speed to my help.
Choir. O God, hasten to help me.
 Glory be to the Father, and to the Son, and to the Holy Spirit.
 As it was in the beginning, is now, and ever shall be, world without end. Amen. Alleluia.

---

[1] The third antiphon of Lauds.   [2] Based on the Epistle of the day.

Hymn.   1 O God, the world's sustaining force,
Thyself unmoved, all motion's source,
Who from the morn till evening's ray
Dost through its changes guide the day.

O grant us light at eventide,
That life may unimpaired abide,
And that a holy death may be
The door of immortality.

Almighty Father, hear our cry,
Through Jesus Christ our Lord most high,
Who with the Holy Ghost and thee
Doth live and reign eternally. Amen.

Antiphon. 2 Behold, a great prophet shall come, and renew Jerusalem. Alleluia.

Psalm 119 : 129–76 (*sung as three psalms*).

Capitulum. 3 Let us walk honestly, as in the day; not in rioting and drunkenness, not in chambering and wantonness, not in strife and envying; but put ye on the Lord Jesus Christ.

Respond. Upon thee, O Jerusalem, shall the Lord arise.
V. And his glory shall be seen upon thee.   (Isa. 60 : 2)
Choir. Shall the Lord arise.
         Glory be to the Father . . .
         Upon thee, O Jerusalem, shall the Lord arise.
V. Turn us, O Lord God of hosts.
R. Show thy countenance, and we shall be whole.

---

1 This hymn is better known in the translation 'O strength and stay, upholding all creation', which does not preserve the metre of the original.

2 The fifth antiphon of Lauds.

3 Based on the Epistle of the day.

VESPERS

Priest. O God, make speed to my help.
Choir. O Lord, hasten to help me.

Glory be to the Father, and to the Son, and to the Holy Spirit.

As it was in the beginning, is now, and ever shall be, world without end. Amen. Alleluia.

Antiphon. The Lord said unto my Lord: Sit at my right hand. (Ps. 110 : 1)

Psalm 110.

Antiphon. All his commandments are true, standing fast for ever and ever. (Ps. 111 : 7, 8)

Psalm 111.

Antiphon. He delighteth greatly in his commandments.
(Ps. 112 : 1)

Psalm 112.

Antiphon. Blessed be the name of the Lord for ever.
(Ps. 113 : 2)

Psalm 113.

Antiphon. We who live bless the Lord. (Ps. 115 : 18)

Psalms 114 and 115.

Capitulum. [1] It is time now for us to awake out of sleep: for now is our salvation nearer than when we believed.

Respond. Thou shalt arise, O God, and have mercy upon Zion.
V. For it is time to have mercy upon her, for the time has come. (Ps. 102 : 13)

Choir. Have mercy upon Zion.

Glory be to the Father. . . .

Thou shalt arise, O God, and have mercy upon Zion.

Hymn.   Creator of the starry height,
             Thy people's everlasting light,
             Jesu, Redeemer of us all,
             Hear thou thy servants when they call.

[1] Based on the Epistle of the day.

Thou, sorrowing at the helpless cry
Of all creation doomed to die,
Didst save our sick and helpless race
By healing gifts of heavenly grace.

When earth was near its evening hour,
Thou didst, in love's redeeming power,
Like bridegroom from his chamber, come
Forth from a Virgin Mother's womb.

At thy great name, exalted now,
All knees in lowly homage bow;
All things in heaven and earth adore,
And own thee Lord for evermore.

To thee, O Holy One, we pray,
Our Judge in that tremendous day,
Ward off, while yet we dwell below,
The weapons of our crafty foe.

To God the Father, God the Son,
And God the Spirit, three in one,
Praise, honour, might, and glory be
From age to age eternally. Amen.

V. Drop down, O heavens, from above.
R. And let the clouds rain righteousness : let the earth open
and bring forth a Saviour.   (Isa. 45 : 8)
Antiphon. [1] Fear not, Mary, thou hast found favour with the
Lord : behold, thou shalt conceive and bear a son.
Alleluia.   (Luke 1 : 30, 31)
Magnificat. My soul doth magnify the Lord . . .
    (*On weekdays* Kyrie, Lord's Prayer, *and* preces *follow here.*)

Collect. [2] Stir up, we beseech thee, O Lord . . . (p. 272) world without
end. Amen.

---

[1] Cf the third respond at Mattins.   [2] The Collect of the day.

V. The Lord be with you.
R. And with thy spirit.
V. Let us bless the Lord.
R. Thanks be to God.

MEMORIAL OF SAINT MARY[1]

Antiphon. Blessed art thou, Mary, who hast believed, for those things shall be accomplished in thee which were told thee by the Lord. Alleluia. (Luke 1 : 45)
V. A rod shall come out of Jesse.
R. And a flower shall grow out of his root.
Collect. O God, who wast willing . . . (p. 304) through the same . . .
V. The Lord be with you.
R. And with thy spirit.
V. Let us bless the Lord.
R. Thanks be to God.

COMPLINE

Priest. Our Father . . .[2]
 Hail, Mary . . .[2]
 Turn us, O God our Saviour.
Choir. And turn thine anger from us. (Ps. 85 : 4)
Priest. O God, make speed to my help.
Choir. O Lord, hasten to help me.
 Glory be to the Father, and to the Son, and to the Holy Spirit. As it was in the beginning, is now, and ever shall be, world without end. Amen. Alleluia.
Antiphon. Have mercy upon me, O Lord, and hearken unto my prayer. (Ps. 4 : 1b)
 Psalm 4. Glory be to the Father. . . .

---

[1] Also said after Lauds.   [2] Said privately.

Psalm 31 : 1–6.

Psalm 91.

Psalm 134. Glory be to the Father . . .

Antiphon. Have mercy upon me, O Lord, and hearken unto my prayer.

Capitulum. Thou, O Lord, art in the midst of us, and thy holy name has been invoked upon us : leave us not, O Lord our God. (Jer. 14 : 9)

Choir. Thanks be to God.

Hymn.   To thee before the close of day,
Creator of the world, we pray ;
As thou art wont, in mercy keep
Thy watch around us while we sleep.

Put every evil dream to flight,
And haunting visions of the night ;
Keep far our ghostly foe, that we
Thy temples undefiled may be.

Almighty Father, hear our cry
Through Jesus Christ our Lord most high,
Who with the Holy Ghost and thee
Doth live and reign eternally. Amen.

V. Keep us, O Lord.

R. As the apple of an eye ; hide us under the shadow of thy wings. (Ps. 17 : 8)

Antiphon. Come, O Lord, to visit us in peace, that we may rejoice before thee with a perfect heart.

Nunc dimittis. Lord, now lettest thou thy servant depart in peace . . .

Lord, have mercy.	Christ, have mercy.
Lord, have mercy.	Christ, have mercy.
Lord, have mercy.	Christ, have mercy.

Lord, have mercy.
Lord, have mercy.
Lord, have mercy.

Priest. Our Father ... And lead us not into temptation.

R. But deliver us from evil. Amen.

V. In peace likewise.

R. I will sleep and rest. (Ps. 4 : 8)

Priest. I believe in God ... the resurrection of the flesh.

R. And life everlasting. Amen.

V. Let us bless the Father and the Son with the Holy Spirit.

R. Let us praise and exalt him above all for ever.

V. Blessed art thou, O Lord, in the firmament of heaven.

R. And worthy of praise, and glorious, and exalted above all
for ever. (Song of the Three Children 34)

V. May the almighty and merciful God bless and keep us.

R. Amen.

Priest. [1] I confess to God ... (p. 307) ... the Holy Spirit.
Amen.

Priest. O God, thou wilt turn again ... (p. 308). ... And
with thy Spirit.

(*At Compline* this night *is said instead of* this day.)

Priest. Let us pray.

Collect. Lighten our darkness, we beseech thee, O Lord, and
mercifully defend us against the perils of all this night;
through our Lord ...

V. The Lord be with you.

R. And with thy spirit.

V. Let us bless the Lord.

R. Thanks be to God.

(The text translated is that printed by Procter and Frere, 257–68, supplemented
from F. H. Dickinson and C. Procter's edition of the Sarum Breviary.)

[1] Confession, Absolution, and *preces* as at Prime.

The *Taufbüchlein* of 1526

(Luther's Baptism Service)

The baptizer shall say:

Depart, thou unclean spirit, and give place to the Holy Spirit.

Then he shall make a cross on the (child's) forehead and breast, and say:

Receive the sign of the holy Cross, both on the forehead and on the breast.

Let us pray.

O almighty, everlasting God, I call upon thee over this *N.* thy servant, who asks thy gift of baptism, and seeks thy eternal grace through spiritual rebirth. Receive him, O Lord; and, as thou hast said, 'Ask, and ye shall receive; seek, and ye shall find; knock, and it shall be opened unto you', so grant him now that good thing that he asks, and open the door to him that knocks; that he may enjoy the eternal blessing of thy heavenly washing, and receive the promised kingdom of thy gift, through Christ our Lord. Amen.

Let us pray.

Almighty, everlasting God, who of thy stern justice didst destroy the unbelieving world by the Flood, and saved faithful Noah among eight persons according to thy great mercy, and didst drown in the Red Sea hard-hearted Pharaoh and all his men, and led thy people Israel through it dry; whereby thou didst foreshadow this washing of thy holy Baptism, and through the baptism of thy dear child, our Lord Jesus Christ, didst sanctify and ordain Jordan and all water to be a holy flood and plentiful washing away of sins; we beseech thee through thy same infinite mercy that thou wouldest look graciously on this *N.*, and sanctify him in spirit with true faith; that, through this saving flood, all that is born in him of Adam, and that he himself has done besides, may be drowned and submerged; and that he may be separated from the number of the unbelievers, and preserved dry and safe in the holy Ark of Christianity, ever fervent in spirit and joyful through hope, and serve thy name; that he, with all the faithful, may be worthy to receive the eternal life of thy promise, through Jesus Christ our Lord. Amen.

I adjure thee, thou unclean spirit, in the name of the Father, and of the Son, and of the Holy Spirit, that thou come forth and vanish from this servant of Jesus Christ. Amen.

Let us hear the holy Gospel of Saint Mark.

At that time they brought the children to Jesus, that he should touch them, but the disciples rebuked those that brought them. But when Jesus saw it, he was displeased, and said to them, 'Let the children come to me, and forbid them not, for of such is the kingdom of God. Verily I say to you, whosoever does not receive the kingdom of God as a little child, shall not enter therein'. And he embraced them, and laid his hands upon them, and blessed them.

Then shall the priest lay his hands on the child, and pray the Lord's Prayer with the godparents, kneeling.

Our Father, which art in heaven, hallowed be thy name. Thy kingdom come, thy will be done, on earth as it is in heaven. Give us this day our daily bread, and forgive us our trespasses, as we forgive them that trespass against us. And lead us not into temptation, but deliver us from evil. Amen.

Then shall they bring the child to the font, and the priest shall say:

The Lord preserve thy coming in and thy going out, henceforth and for evermore. (Ps. 121 : 8)

Then shall the priest cause the child to renounce the devil through its godparents, saying:

Dost thou renounce the devil? *Answer.* Yes.

And all his works? *Answer.* Yes.

Then shall he ask:

Dost thou believe in God, the Father almighty, maker of heaven and earth? *Answer.* Yes.

Dost thou believe in Jesus Christ, his only Son, our Lord, born and suffered? *Answer.* Yes.

Dost thou believe in the Holy Spirit, a holy Christian Church, communion of saints, forgiveness of sins, resurrection of the flesh, and after death eternal life?

Answer. Yes.

Dost thou desire to be baptized? *Answer.* Yes.

Then shall he take the child and dip it in the water and say:

And I baptize thee in the name of the Father, and of the Son, and of the Holy Spirit. Amen.

Then shall the godparents of the child remain by the font, and the priest shall say, while he puts the chrysom on it:

May the almighty God and Father of our Lord Jesus Christ, who hath given thee new birth through water and the Holy Spirit, and hath forgiven thee all thy sins, strengthen thee with his grace unto eternal life. Amen.

Peace be with thee. *Answer.* Amen.

The *Trau-Ordnung* of 1534
(Luther's Marriage Service)

THE CALLING OF THE BANNS

Hans *N.* and Grete *N.* desire according to God's ordinance to enter the holy estate of matrimony ; they seek a common spiritual prayer for them, that they begin it in the name of God and advisedly. And if any man has anything to say about it, let him do so forthwith, or keep silence hereafter ; God give him his blessing. Amen.

THE CHURCH SERVICE

Hans, wilt thou have Grete to thy wedded wife?
Answer. Yes.
Grete, wilt thou have Hans to thy wedded husband?
Answer. Yes.
Then shall he cause them to give each other the wedding rings, and shall join their right hands together, and say:
What God joins together, let no man put asunder.
(Matt. 19 : 6)

Since Hans *N.* and Grete *N.* seek each other in wedlock, and acknowledge it here openly before God and the world, in that they have given each other their hands and wedding rings, I pronounce them married, in the name of the Father, and of the Son, and of the Holy Spirit. Amen.
Before the altar he shall read God's Word over the bridegroom and the bride.

The Lord God said, It is not good that the man should be alone ; I will make a help meet for him. And the Lord

L

caused a deep sleep to fall upon Adam, and he slept; and he took one of his ribs, and closed up the flesh instead thereof; and the rib, which the Lord God had taken from man, made he a woman, and brought her unto the man. And Adam said, This is now bone of my bones and flesh of my flesh : she shall be called Woman, because she was taken out of Man. Therefore shall a man leave his father and his mother, and shall cleave unto his wife : and they shall be one flesh.   (Gen. 2 : 18, 21–4)

Since you have given yourselves to each other in marriage in the name of God, hear first God's commandment on this estate. Thus saith Saint Paul :

Wives, submit yourselves unto your own husbands, as unto the Lord. For the husband is the head of the wife, even as Christ is the head of the Church; and he is the saviour of the body. Therefore as the Church is subject unto Christ, so let the wives be to their own husbands in everything. Husbands, love your wives, even as Christ also loved the Church, and gave himself for it, that he might sanctify and cleanse it with the washing of water by the word, that he might present it to himself a glorious Church, not having spot or wrinkle or any such thing, but that it should be holy and without blemish. So ought men to love their wives as their own bodies. He that loveth his wife loveth himself. For no man ever yet hated his own flesh; but nourisheth and cherisheth it, even as the Lord the Church.   (Eph. 5 : 22–9)

Further, hear the cross which God hath laid on this estate. God spake thus to the woman :

I will greatly multiply thy sorrow and thy conception; in sorrow thou shalt bring forth children; and thy desire shall be to thy husband, and he shall rule over thee.
                              (Gen. 3 : 16)

And to the man God spake :

Because thou hast hearkened unto the voice of thy wife, and hast eaten of the tree of which I commanded thee, saying, Thou shalt not eat of it : cursed is the ground for thy sake; in sorrow shalt thou eat of it all the days of thy life. Thorns also and thistles shall it bring forth to thee; and thou shalt eat of the herb of the field. In the sweat of thy face shalt thou eat bread, till thou return unto the ground; for out of it wast thou taken; for dust thou art, and unto dust shalt thou return.   (Gen. 3 : 17–19)

Thirdly, it is your comfort that you know and believe that your estate is pleasing to God and blessed by him.

God created man in his own image, in the image of God created he him; male and female created he them. And God blessed them, and God said unto them, Be fruitful and multiply, and replenish the earth and subdue it; and have dominion over the fish of the sea, and over the fowl of the air, and over every living thing that moveth upon the earth. And God saw everything that he had made; and behold, it was very good.   (Gen. 1 : 27, 28, 31a)

Solomon also speaks of this :

Whoso findeth a wife findeth a good thing, and obtaineth favour of the Lord.   (Prov. 18 : 22)

Here he shall extend his hands over them, and pray thus:

Lord God, who hast created man and woman, and ordained them to matrimony, hast blessed them with the fruit of the body and the sacrament of thy dear Son Jesus Christ, and signified therein the Church his bride; we beseech thine infinite goodness that thou wouldest not let thy creation, ordination, and blessing be reversed or destroyed, but graciously preserved in us, through Jesus Christ, thy Son, our Lord. Amen.

(For references, see Bibliography.)

The Lord's Supper at Strasbourg, 1524

(as described by Martin Bucer)

When the congregation come together on Sunday, the
minister exhorts the people to confess their sins and to pray
for pardon; and on behalf of the whole congregation he
makes confession to God, prays for pardon, and pronounces
absolution to the believers. Thereupon, the whole congregation sing a few short psalms and hymns. Then the minister
says a short prayer, reads to the congregation a passage from
the writings of the Apostles, and as briefly as possible
expounds the same. Then the congregation sing again, this
time the Ten Commandments or something else. After that,
the minister reads the Gospel, and preaches the sermon
proper. The sermon ended, the congregation sing the
Articles of our Belief; and the minister says a prayer for the
magistrates and for all men, and specially for the congregation
there present, beseeching an increase of faith, love, and grace
to hold in reverence the memory of Christ's death. Then he
admonishes those who wish to observe the Lord's Supper
with him that they are to do so in memory of Christ, to die to
their sins, and bear their cross willingly, and be strengthened
in faith for what must come to pass when we contemplate
with believing hearts what measureless grace and goodness
Christ hath shown to us, in that for us he offered up to his
Father his life and blood upon the Cross. After this exhortation, he reads the Gospel concerning the Lord's Supper, as
the three Evangelists and Paul in 1 Corinthians 11 have
described it. Then the minister distributes the Bread and
Cup of the Lord among them, having partaken of them also

himself. The congregation then sing a hymn of praise ; and afterwards the minister closes the Supper with a short prayer, blesses the people, and lets them go in the peace of the Lord. This is the manner and custom with which we now celebrate the Lord's Supper on Sundays only.

(From *Grund und Ursach*, as translated by W. D. Maxwell, *An Outline of Christian Worship*, 100–1.)

Mass at Nuremberg in Lent, 1532

(as described by Sir Thomas Elyot)

The priest, in vestments after our manner, singeth everything in Latin, as we use, omitting suffrages. The Epistle he readeth in Latin. In the meantime the subdeacon goeth into the pulpit and readeth to the people the Epistle in their vulgar; after, they peruse other things as our priests do. Then the priest readeth softly the Gospel in Latin. In the mean space the deacon goeth into the pulpit and readeth aloud the Gospel in the Almain tongue. Mr Cranmer saith it was showed to him that in the Epistles and Gospels they kept not the order that we do, but do peruse every day one chapter of the New Testament. After, the priest and the choir do sing the Creed as we do; the Secrets and Preface they omit, and the priest singeth with a high voice the Words of the Consecration; and after the elevation the deacon turneth to the people, telling to them in the Almain tongue a long process how they should prepare themselves to the communion of the flesh and blood of Christ; and then may every man come that listeth, without going to any confession. . . .

(*Original Letters*, ed. H. Ellis, 3rd Series, (1846), II, 191; spelling modernized.)

Church Order for Brandenburg–Nürnberg, 1533

ORDER FOR THE CELEBRATION OF THE MASS

First, when the priest comes to the altar, he may say the Confiteor, *or whatever arouses his devotion, and then read the Introit (so it be taken from holy Scripture), while the scholars (where there is a school) sing the Introit in Latin. But where, as in villages, there are not people for such Latin singing, they shall sing a Christian German hymn, according to the ability of the place. But where the people do not know such hymns, the pastors shall teach them to learn them. But in those towns and places where they have been, or are being, taught the Introit and other similar chants in German, let them continue.*

Then shall he read Kyrie eleison *and* Gloria in excelsis *in Latin, and the scholars or the people shall sing them in Latin or German as they are accustomed. Then the priest shall turn himself to the people, and say or sing* Dominus vobiscum *or 'The Lord be with you', followed by one or more collects, as the season requires, and for all kinds of Christian concern. And since these are spoken on behalf of the whole congregation, they shall be said in German, so that the people may hear and understand, and thus think and pray them meanwhile in their hearts. The preachers must exhort the people in their sermons to such earnest consideration and pondering in their hearts. And a good number of these are subjoined, that each man may make his own choice, provided that he always chooses one in the first place that relates to spiritual things. After that, if he wishes, or the condition and need of the time require, he may also pray for temporal goods, as for peace in*

*our time, or the fruits of the earth, etc., and other concerns common
to Christianity.*

Now follow the Collects, or Prayers.

(Twenty-five are printed at this point.)

*After the prayer shall be read a chapter from the Epistles of
the Apostles Paul, Peter, or John, etc., in German. The reader
shall begin thus:*

May your love receive with diligence the first chapter
of the Epistle of Saint Paul written to the Romans.

And at the end conclude thus:

That is the first chapter of the Epistle of Saint Paul to
the Romans.

*After the Epistle the priest may read an Alleluia with its verse
in Latin, or a Gradual taken from holy Scripture, and the
scholars may sing the same in Latin.*

*After that, he shall read a chapter from the Gospels or the
Acts of the Apostles; and then begin the Creed, which shall be
sung by the scholars in Latin, or by the people in German, as the
custom is.*

*Thereupon on feast-days shall follow the customary Sermon.
After the Sermon shall follow the Supper.*

ORDER FOR THE LORD'S SUPPER

*When the priest wishes to celebrate the Lord's Supper (if he
has others to communicate), he shall make the following
Exhortation to the people forthwith, and then the Words of the
Supper, where the Mass is sung, shall be said immediately, in the
manner following. Or if he reads the Mass, he shall read with
loud, intelligible words, so that those who stand around may hear
the same.*

The Exhortation[1] follows:

Beloved in God, since we now wish to remember and
celebrate the holy Supper of our Lord Jesus Christ,

---

[1] By Andreas Osiander, first included in Wolfgang Volprecht's Mass of 1524.

wherein he has given us his flesh for a food and his blood
for a drink, therewith to strengthen our faith, each of us
must examine himself most diligently, as Saint Paul
exhorts us. For this holy sacrament is given as a special
comfort and strength to poor, troubled consciences which
acknowledge their sins, fear the wrath of God and death,
and hunger and thirst after righteousness. If we examine
ourselves, and go each into his own conscience, as Saint
Paul teaches us, we shall certainly find nothing else than
all manner of horrible sins, and death which we have
incurred by our sins, and yet cannot in any way help
ourselves to escape.

Therefore our dear Lord Jesus Christ has had pity on
us, and was willing to become man because of our sins. In
this he fulfilled for us and our good the commandment
and the whole will of God, and took upon himself and
suffered, for us and for our redemption, death and all that
we had incurred by our sins. And, that we should firmly
believe this, and might live joyfully according to his will
through faith, after the supper he took bread, gave thanks,
brake it, and said : 'Take this and eat, this is my body,
which is given for you', that is, 'that I am become man,
and all that I do and suffer is all your own, happening for
you and your good ; as a sure sign and pledge of this,
I give you my body for food'. Likewise he also took the
cup and said : 'Take and drink ye all from this ; this is the
cup of the New Testament in my blood, which is shed for
you and for many for the forgiveness of sins. As often as
you do this, you shall thereby remember me', that is,
'since I have taken up your cause and taken your sins upon
me, I will offer myself for the sins in death, will shed my
blood, win grace and forgiveness of sins, and thus
establish a new testament, in which sins shall be forgiven
and not thought of any more for ever ; as a sure sign and
pledge of this I give you my blood to drink'.

Whoever now eats of this bread and drinks of this cup,

and hears these words of Christ, and assuredly believes this sign which he receives from Christ, he dwells in the Lord Christ, and Christ in him, and he will live for ever. Therefore we must now remember him and proclaim his death, namely that he died for our sins and rose again for our justification, and thank him for this. Everyone must take his cross upon him and follow Him, and love each other according to his commandment, as he loved us, for we are all one bread and one body, since we are all partakers of one bread, and drink from one cup.

Our Lord Jesus, in the night that he was betrayed, took bread, gave thanks, and brake it, and gave it to his disciples, and said : Take and eat, this is my body, which is given for you ; do this in remembrance of me. Likewise after supper he took also the cup, and gave thanks, and gave it to them, and said : Drink ye all from this, this is my blood of the new testament, which is shed for you and for many, for forgiveness of sins ; do this as often as ye drink in remembrance of me.

Then follows Sanctus *in Latin or German, and then immediately:*

Oremus.

Preceptis salutaribus moniti et divina institutione formati, audemus dicere : Pater noster, qui es in coelis, sanctificetur nomen tuum, adveniat regnum tuum, sicut in coelo, et in terra. Panem nostrum cotidianum da nobis hodie. Et dimitte nobis debita nostra, sicut et nos dimittimus debitoribus nostris. Et ne nos inducas in tentationem, sed libera nos a malo. Amen.

Then immediately:

Pax Domini sit semper vobiscum, etc.

Or in German, as follows:

Let us pray.

Our Father, who art in heaven, hallowed be thy name. Thy kingdom come, thy will be done, on earth as it is heaven. Give us this day our daily bread. And forgive us our trespasses, as we forgive them that trespass against us. And lead us not into temptation, but deliver us from evil. Amen.

The peace of the Lord be with you all. Amen.

After that shall all who had given notice beforehand go to the holy Sacrament or Supper of Christ, which shall be given to them with these words:

Take and eat, this is the body of Christ, which is given for thee.

And at the cup:

Take and drink, this is the blood of the new testament, which is shed for thy sins.

And where the pastor has no deacon, he shall give everyone the body of Christ before he gives anyone the cup; but where there are chaplains, one of them may give the cup to everyone that has received the body of Christ.

While this is taking place, the scholars shall sing Agnus Dei ; *but where no scholars are available, the congregation may sing that, or something else agreeable to the word of God and the requirement of the time, as the custom is. Where the number of people is so great that it drags on in length, there shall be sung, not only a Communion (also taken from holy Scripture), but also something else until the people have completed everything, such as the Respond* Discubuit Jesus,[1] *or something agreeable to Scripture. When the people have completed everything, there shall be said aloud a common prayer in German, which shall be a thanksgiving, thus:*

Let us pray.

O almighty, everlasting God, we give praise and thanks to thy divine kindness, that thou hast given us the saving

---

1 The text of this chant is as follows: 'Jesus sat down, and his disciples with him, and said, "With desire I have desired to eat this Passover with you before I suffer"; and he took bread, and gave thanks, and broke it, and gave to them, saying, "This is my body". And taking the cup, he gave thanks, and gave to them, and said, "This is my blood. Eat and drink from this, all of you, and do it, whenever you do it, in remembrance of me". Glory be to the Father . . .'

flesh and blood of thine only Son Jesus Christ our Lord to eat and drink; and we humbly beseech thee that thou wouldest work in us through thy holy Spirit, that, as we have received this holy sacrament with our mouth, so also we may with strong faith lay hold of, and ever retain, thy divine grace, forgiveness of sins, union with Christ, and eternal life, as is signified and promised therein; through our Lord Jesus Christ thy Son, who liveth and reigneth with thee in the unity of the Holy Spirit, true God, ever and eternally. Amen.

Benedicamus Domino. Deo gratias.

After that, he shall bless the people thus:

The Lord bless you and keep you. The Lord lighten his countenance upon you and be gracious unto you. The Lord lift up his countenance upon you and give you peace. Amen.

Or thus:

God be gracious and merciful unto us, and give us his divine blessing. May he lighten his countenance upon us and give us his peace. Amen.

Or thus:

God the Father, and the Son, and the Holy Spirit bless and preserve us. Amen.

Or thus:

The blessing of God the Father and of the Son and of the Holy Spirit be with you and remain with us all for ever. Amen.

(For references, see Bibliography.)

Church Order for Pfalz-Neuburg, 1543

The following prayer is inserted between the Exhortation from the Brandenburg-Nürnberg Order and the Words of Institution:

O Lord Jesu Christ, the only true Son of the living God, who hast given thy body for us all in the bitter pains of death, and hast shed thy blood for the forgiveness of our sins, and who, moreover, hast commanded all thy disciples to eat and to drink the same thy body and thy blood, and thereby to commemorate thy death; we bring before thy divine Majesty these thy gifts of bread and wine; and we pray thee by thy divine grace, goodness, and might, to hallow, bless, and create, that this bread may be thy body and this wine thy blood, and that all who eat and drink thereof may attain to everlasting life; who with the Father, in the unity of the Holy Spirit, livest and reignest for ever and ever. Amen.

(Translated by Bishop John Dowden, *Further Studies in the Prayer Book*, 67–8.)

Church Order for Cologne, 1545

(A Simple and Religious Consultation)

OF THE PREPARATION TO THE SUPPER
OF THE LORD

Seeing that the Lord's Supper, as we said before, ought not to be celebrated but with his disciples, and forasmuch as the ministers must be faithful disposers of the mysteries of God, and must take great heed that they cast not an holy thing before dogs and pearls before swine, we will that the pastors admit no man to the Lord's Supper which hath not first offered himself to them, and that, after that he hath first made a confession of his sins, being catechized, he receive absolution according to the Lord's word.

No man must be admitted to the holy Supper but he be first tried.

And that there may be a certain and appointed time for the doing hereof, I mean, that they which shall communicate be prepared and sanctified to the communion of Christ with an holy instruction and prayer, let the pastors procure that the people be called together in the temple at eventide the day before the celebration of the Lord's Supper, and let them make a preparation and sanctification unto the Lord's board, after this sort.

Where clerks shall be, or scholars, let them in the mean season, while the people come together, sing a psalm or two, with a dominical antiphon and[1] hymn, which yet we will have to be pure, that is to say, dissenting in no part from the holy Scripture. To this let them add the Song of the Lord's mother, Magnificat, and some convenient collect.

A lesson or sermon concerning the holy Supper.

Afterward, when the people be come together, they shall sing a psalm in the Douch[2] tongue. And then the pastor or minister to

[1] Latin: &; 1547 and 1548: or.
[2] i.e. German.

whom the office of this preparation is committed shall read some place of the Lord's Supper out of the Evangelists, or out of Paul, chapters x, xi of the first to the Corinthians, or out of the Lord's sermon, John vi. For though the Lord speak not in that place of the sacrament of the Supper, which he had not yet made, nevertheless he preacheth of the true eating of his body and drinking of his blood, for the exhibition whereof he afterward instituted the holy Supper. Out of such lessons the ministers shall diligently teach the people to what use the Lord ordained his Supper, and how we may receive it wholesomely, after this sort.

A SHORT INSTITUTION OR SERMON OF THE LORD'S SUPPER

Forasmuch as we intend to keep tomorrow the most holy Supper of our Saviour Christ, by his help, for the celebration of a blessed remembrance of him, and confirmation of our faith, first it is convenient to declare with few words and call to our minds the mystery of this right divine sacrament.

Before all things then, the Lord offereth unto us his flesh and his blood, and biddeth us to take the same, affirming that we shall not have life, but shall remain in everlasting death, except we eat his flesh and drink his blood. Let us remember and acknowledge that our flesh and blood, that is to say, our whole nature, is through wickedness so lost and adjudged to eternal death by the just wrath of God that of ourselves we can never obtain everlasting life and the inheritance of the heavenly kingdom.

How our nature (flesh and blood) be corrupt and lost.

This remembrance and acknowledging of our destruction ought utterly to humble and cast us down before the Lord, and to cut our hearts with such repentance of sins that we should be pricked forth and enflamed to seek and receive with sure faith and great[1] desire the grace of God

---

[1] Latin: *summo*; 1547 and 1548: greatly.

offered to us in the word and sacraments, and the restitution and renewing of ourselves through the communion of Christ and wholesome participation of his flesh and blood.

By the body and blood of Christ our body and blood are sanctified again and restored.

Furthermore, let us diligently consider that the eternal word of God, the Son of God almighty, to deliver us out of this misery, was made flesh, was made our brother, that there might be some holy flesh and holy blood, that is to say, a very heavenly and divine man, by whom the flesh and blood of all us might be restored and sanctified, which thing is then brought to pass when we truly eat his flesh and drink his blood, John vi. Here it is meet that we be moved the more to wonder at and to embrace with certain faith and greedier will in this only-begotten Son of God, our Saviour, the exceeding and unspeakable love of God towards us, who gave his Son unto us, that, believing in him, we should not perish, as we were born and as we deserved, but have everlasting life, which he deserved and giveth unto us.

After what sort Christ giveth us his flesh and blood in the holy Supper.

Thirdly, let us acknowledge and firmly believe that the Lord Jesus truly offereth unto us this his sanctifying flesh and blood in his holy Supper with visible signs of bread and wine, by the ministry of the congregation, and exhibiteth the same unto the remission of sins, to be meat of everlasting life, to confirm the covenant of God's adoption and of everlasting life, for so be his words. Wherefore they cannot deceive, and they shall remain when heaven and earth pass away ; and they truly exhibit and give unto us the things that they preach, so that we[1] apply true faith unto them. 'Take', saith he, 'eat, this is my body, that is given for you' ; item, 'drink of this all ; this is my blood of the new testament, which is shed forth for you and for many unto the remission of sins'. We must receive these words with true faith, and doubt nothing but that the Lord, when we celebrate the holy Supper after his

The fruits and benefits of the holy Supper.

[1] Latin: *accommodemus*; 1548: they. 'So that', i.e. provided that.

institution, is in the midst of us, and offereth himself unto us by the ministry of the congregation, which he instituted for the same purpose, and delivereth his body and blood and all his merits and satisfaction for our sins, which he performed, his body and blood being offered upon the cross; giveth us also[1] remission of sins, and the grace of the Father, and the right of the testament of the everlasting covenant, of adoption, and communion unto the life of God; so that the bread that we break in the holy Supper is truly even to us the communion of his body, and the cup at which we bless, the communion of his blood.

Therefore let us ever religiously consider why the Lord doth often exhibit unto us this holy and wholesome communion of himself in the sacrament, namely for this purpose, that he may bring us daily into the knowledge of our sins and more earnest repentance, that we may desire more fervently remission of the same by him, and receive it with perfecter faith and greedier minds, and so be more confirmed and set forward in a new life through the true communion of him, that so we may daily more and more abide and live in him, and he in us, and be more fully his body and members, and he our head; which thing we profess when we all receive the communion of him in his sacrament, so being partakers of his body and blood as we in common be partakers of one bread and cup.

Finally, we must pray and labour also to receive these heavenly gifts with true faith and great reverence, and that we celebrate the wholesome remembrance of the Lord with godly joy and pleasant thankfulness, and that we give up ⟨and consecrate⟩ ourselves and all ours to him, and testify the same with collations and alms for the use of the poor, liberally and according to every man's power; finally, that we ever praise and magnify Christ in all our words and works for these so great benefits: for his incarnation whereby he was made our head and brother;

How the memory of Christ must be thankfully used in the holy Supper.

---

[1] 1547 *omits* giveth us also.

for his most bitter death whereby he satisfied for our sins ;
for his resurrection, and ascension into heaven, and
heavenly kingdom which he administereth at the right
hand of the Father ; and maketh us perfect and absolute
in his life, being quickened with his Spirit and set in
heavenly things, which life he hath given in the life of
God, and it is an everlasting life ; for this wholesome
communion of his body and blood, whereby we are
continued in this same life of God, and are set forward and
ever finished up ; [for all which things] we must chiefly
give thanks in the communion of this Supper. And
forasmuch as our God is such one as alloweth not wickedness, neither can all they stand before him which work
iniquity, it is necessary that we know that those men must
not be admitted to the Supper of the Lord, that is to say,
to his communion, which live without true faith and love,
by whom the glory of God is manifestly blemished and his
congregation offended ; [I mean,] all unbelievers and
manifest idolaters which call upon ⟨and adore⟩ saints
departed, angels, or other creatures, which honour
[painted or] graven stocks. Item, all enchanters and sooth-
sayers, which will preserve cattle and other things against
perils with their consecrations, [yea, and I mean] those
too which believe such enchantments ; and the manifest
despisers and blasphemers of God, the mockers of God's
word and sacraments. [Item,] all those which at appointed
times wildly continue in neglecting sermons and other
open exercises of the congregation ; which obey not
according to God's commandment their parents, ordinary
officers, and masters, but speak evil of them and rail upon
them, do them despite, and resist them seditiously and
stubbornly ; which bring not up their children, family,
and such as they have charge of, nor instruct them in
godliness, honesty, and justice. [Furthermore I mean]
murderers and all those which willingly continue in hatred
of their brethren, in brawlings, and shedding of their

What
manner of
men they be
that ought
not to be
admitted to
the holy
Supper of the
Lord.

neighbours' blood. [Item,] all whoremongers, adulterers, and drunkards; all thieves, usurers, raveners, dicers, unlawful gainers, exercisers of false merchandises ;[1] all those likewise which live idly without a lawful excuse and burden others ; all ill-speakers, ⟨deceivers,⟩ liars, perjured men,[2] backbiters, and which[3] confess not the truth and righteousness, and confirm not the same with their testimonies, where they are bound to do it by reason of their vocation. All these fellows, as long as they live and continue in such sins, neither have a true purpose to amend their lives ⟨in the faith of Christ,⟩ may in no wise be admitted to the holy Supper of the Lord, seeing that they be restrained and excluded from thence by God, by his own word.

ANOTHER EXHORTATION

Forasmuch as, dearly beloved in the Lord, we shall celebrate tomorrow, by God's grace, the most holy Supper of the Lord Jesus Christ, wherein he hath given us his flesh for meat and his blood for drink, to confirm our faith and very Christian life : it is convenient that every man try himself with great diligence, as St Paul exhorteth us. For this sacrament was given of the Lord for singular consolation and comfort to wretched and afflicted consciences, which do earnestly feel and confess their sins, which be stricken with the fear of the wrath of God and of death, and hunger and thirst the righteousness of God. But if every one of us will examine ourselves, as St Paul teacheth, we shall find none other thing but all manner of horrible sins and everlasting death, which we have deserved through our sins. For the reward of sin is death, from which we can by no means deliver ourselves.

How we ought to prove ourselves.

---

[1] 1548: merchandise.   [2] 1547: perjurers.   [3] 1548 *om.* and.

Wherefore our Lord Jesus Christ, taking pity upon us, was made man for our sins, that he might fulfil the law and the whole will of God for us, and procure our salvation, and that he himself might suffer death and all that we had deserved through our sins, only for us and our redemption. Which thing that we might firmly believe, and that through faith we might joyfully live after his will, when supper was ended he took bread, gave thanks, and brake it, saying, 'Take, eat, this is my body that is given for you', that is to say that 'I am made man, and further, whatsoever I do and suffer, all that is yours, and it is given to you, and is done for your salvation. For the testification and confirmation whereof, and that you may daily abide and live more and more in me, and I in you, I give my body unto you to be meat, and meat of everlasting life.' After the same manner he took the cup also, saying, 'Take, drink of this all; this is the cup of the new testament in my blood, which is shed forth for you and for many, unto remission of sins. As often as ye shall do this, do it in the remembrance of me', that is to say, 'seeing that I have now taken the charge of you, and have translated your sins upon me, I will deliver myself unto death for them, I will shed my blood; I will deserve grace and remission of sins for you, and I will set up a new testament wherein sins shall be pardoned, and all remembrance of them shall be abolished. For a pledge and witness of all these things, and to confirm and further my life in you, I give you my blood to drink.' He then that eateth of this bread after this sort and drinketh of this cup, and firmly believeth these words which he heareth of the Lord and signs which he receiveth, eateth truly and wholesomely the flesh of Christ and drinketh his blood, and more fully receiveth into himself whole God and man, with all his merits and favour wherewith the Father embraceth him, with the right and participation of everlasting life; he abideth in Christ the Lord, and the Lord in him, and he shall live for

ever. Let us then godly reckon[1] these things with ourselves, and let us confirm and stir up our faith in him ; let
us celebrate the remembrance of him worthily ; let us
most studiously in all our words and deeds exalt his death,
resurrection, heavenly glory, and kingdom ; let us rejoice
in our own behalf that this Son of God died for our sins, The true
rose again for our justification, ascended into heaven, and remembrance
whereof
reigneth at the right hand of the Father ; furthermore, let Christ gave
us manfully, every one of us, take up our cross, and commandment.
valiantly follow this our captain, and love one another
according to his commandment, as he loved us. For all we
are one bread and one body because we be partakers of
one bread and one cup.

*After this sermon there shall a prayer be made for all the
necessities of the congregation, and chiefly for those men which
shall communicate the next day.*

*And when the people have ended their secret prayers, the
minister shall conclude the preparation with this collect.*

Almighty, everlasting God, heavenly Father, because
we can please thee only in thy dear Son, sanctify our
bodies and souls, and grant us that tomorrow we may
receive the wholesome communion of him in his holy
Supper with a godly and faithful desire, and all thankfulness ; that, being confirmed again concerning thy perpetual
mercy and love towards us, and ever going forward in a
new life, we may live unto thee and serve thee[2] through
our Lord Jesus Christ,[2] with more fear and study, to the
praise of thy name and profit of thy people. Amen.

*After this public institution of them that the next day shall come
to the Lord's table, let a private instruction follow of all, one by
one, that shall profess that they will be the Lord's guests. Let all
such be heard and instructed of the ministers, one by one, in order.*[3]

---

[1] Latin: *reputemus*; 1547: recompense; 1548: recount.
[2] This phrase should come at the end of the prayer.
[3] 1547 omits the whole paragraph.

HOW THE LORD'S SUPPER MUST
BE CELEBRATED

When the people be come together unto this ministration, forasmuch as it is agreeable to religion that, as often as we appear before the Lord, before all things we should acknowledge and confess our sins, and pray for remission of the same, the minister which shall administer the Lord's Supper, when he shall come to the altar, shall make a confession in the name of the whole congregation, and that in the Douch tongue, which all may understand, after this sort:

Almighty, everlasting God, the Father of our Lord Jesus Christ, the maker of all things, the judge of all men, we acknowledge and we lament that we were conceived and born in sins, and that therefore we be prone to all evils, and abhor from all good things; that we also have transgressed thy holy commandments without end and measure, in despising thee and thy word, in distrusting thy aid, in trusting ourselves and the world, in wicked studies and works, wherewith we have most grievously offended thy majesty and hurted our neighbours. Therefore we have more and more buried ⟨and lost⟩ ourselves into eternal death. And we are sorry for it with all our hearts, and we desire pardon of thee for all the things that we have committed against thee; we call for thy help against sin dwelling in us, and Satan the kindler thereof; keep us that we do nothing hereafter against thee, and cover the wickedness that remaineth in us with the righteousness of thy Son, and repress it in us with thy Spirit, and at length purge it clean out. Have mercy upon us, most ⟨good and⟩ gentle Father, through thy Son our Lord Jesus Christ. Give and increase thy holy Spirit in us, who may teach us to acknowledge our sins truly and thoroughly, and to be pricked with a lively repentance of

the same, and with true faith to apprehend and retain
remission of them in Christ our Lord ; that, dying to sin
daily more and more, we may serve and please thee in a
new life, to the glory of thy name and edifying of thy
congregation. For we acknowledge that thou justly
requirest these things of us, wherefore we desire to
perform the same. Vouchsafe thou, O Father of heaven,
which hast given us a will, to grant us also that we may
study to those things with all our hearts which pertain to
our health, through our Lord Jesus Christ.

Hear the Gospel. John iii.

God so loved the world that he gave his only-begotten
Son, that all which believe in him should ⟨not perish, but⟩
have life everlasting.

Or, 1 Timothy i.

This is a sure saying and worthy of all embracing, that
Jesus Christ came into this world to save sinners.

Or, John iii.

The Father loveth the Son and hath given all things
into his hands ; he that believeth in the Son hath everlasting life.

Or, Acts x.

All the prophets bear witness unto Christ, that all that
believe in him receive remission of their sins through him.

Or, 1 John ii.

My little children, if any have sinned, we have a just
advocate with the Father, Jesus Christ, and he is an
atonement for our sins.

*When the pastor hath showed to the people one of the said
Gospels, he shall say further:*

Because our blessed Lord hath left this power to his
congregation that it may absolve them from sins and
restore them into favour of the heavenly Father which,
being repentant for their sins, do truly believe in Christ
the Lord, I, the minister of Christ and the congregation,
[declare and] pronounce remission of ⟨all⟩ sins, the favour

of God, and life everlasting [1]through our Lord Jesus Christ[1] to all them which be sorry for their sins, which have true faith in Christ the Lord and desire to approve themselves unto him. Amen.

After this, where clerks or scholars shall be, they shall sing somewhat in Latin taken out of the holy Scriptures for an entrance [or beginning].

After that, [they shall sing] Kyrie eleison *and* Gloria in excelsis, *and because that* Kyrie eleison *is a common prayer of the congregation, and* Gloria in excelsis *is also a common thanksgiving, let the people sing both in Douch.*

After this song, he that shall execute the holy ministry shall recite a collect in Douch, singing or reading,[2] but so that all the people may well understand it. For therefore the minister speaketh this sentence to the people, 'The Lord be with you', and, 'Let us pray', and the people answereth, 'And with thy spirit', signifying thereby that they also pray together with the minister. For so Chrysostom interpreteth this saying. And because this must be a common prayer of the whole congregation, it is called a collect, for that, that a prayer gathered of the wishes of all that be present is offered to God by the minister, or because it is a prayer of the congregation gathered together and praying together unto the Lord. But the purer collects and more consonant to the holy Scriptures must be chosen out, of which sort we will cause some to be set forth.

After the collects there shall follow according to the custom a lesson of an Epistle, which shall be read in such a place (the reader turning his face to the people) that it may be heard and understanded of the whole congregation. Wherefore it shall be also read in Douch, because that lesson pertaineth to the instruction and admonition of the people. After the Epistle, where clerks be, let Alleluia *be sung in Latin, or a grail, or some[3] sequence, if they have any pure, and some Douch song. Then let the Gospel be read in Douch to the people, which reading an interpretation and*

---

[1] This phrase should come at the end of the Absolution.
[2] 1547 *omits* singing or reading.   [3] 1547 omits.

ordinary sermon shall follow forthwith; and after the sermon a prayer for all states of men and necessities of the congregation, after this sort.

Almighty, everlasting God and merciful Father, which by thy dear Son our Lord Jesus Christ and his Apostles commandest that we should come before thee in his name, and didst promise that thou wouldst mercifully give us whatsoever, agreeing together, we should ask in his name, we beseech thee by ⟨the same⟩ thy Son, our only Saviour, first that thou wilt mercifully forgive us all our sins and iniquities which we acknowledge and confess here in thy sight, and that thou wilt favourably turn away from us through the blood and satisfaction of thy Son, our mediator, thy[1] most just wrath which we have deserved through so manifold transgressions of thy commandments. And confirm thou in us thy holy Spirit, that we may wholly give over ourselves to the obedience of thee now and ever, that calling upon thee always for ourselves and for other ⟨in true faith⟩ we may obtain thy grace and help.

First we must desire remission of sins and the holy Ghost [to be given unto us].

We pray thee therefore chiefly for thy congregations: deliver them from all wolves, hired servants, which either spoil and devour thy sheep miserably, or traitorously forsake them and destroy them, and proudly rejoice and delight themselves in their destruction. Give them good and faithful ministers and pastors, and preserve the same. Increase thy holy Spirit in all persons which be at this holy ministry, that therein they may faithfully serve thee, and with the profit of thy flock, that thy scattered sheep may through thy Gospel be gathered to thy dear Son, the high and only true shepherd and bishop of our souls, Jesus Christ, from all straying either of errors or of sins; briefly, that they may be brought again to the true communion of him, that there may be one flock and one shepherd.

For the Church and ministers of the same.

So we pray thee also, holy Father, for thy servants the

[1] 1548: the.

ministers of civil governances, for our most gracious Emperor and King, for all other kings, princes, and magistrates. And specially we pray thee for our most reverend Archbishop and right excellent Prince, for his council and officers, for the council and magistrates of this city. Give ⟨and confirm to⟩ all these thy holy Spirit, that they may truly know and embrace Christ thy Son, to whom thou hast given all power and all judgment in heaven and in earth ; and that according to their strength they may so serve his kingdom, that they may so govern us ⟨and all men⟩ which are indeed subjects to them, but be the creatures of thy hand and the sheep of thy pastures, that, in this place and everywhere, we may live a peaceable and quiet life with all godliness and honesty, and, being delivered from all fear of our enemies, we may serve thee in all righteousness and holiness.

We pray also, heavenly Father, for all those which yet pertain not to thy kingdom : cause the light of thy Gospel to shine unto them also ; draw them to thy Son, our Saviour, that believing in him they may be saved with us. And as touching them whom thou hast somewhat drawn unto him, so that they grant him to be their Saviour and the Saviour of all men, but nevertheless have not yet bound themselves to all obedience of the Gospel, increase in these the faith and knowledge of thy Son which thou hast given them, that they may thoroughly give over themselves unto the obedience of him and of his congregation, and that they may magnify thee in the same manner throughout all their life with godly sayings and doings.

For the tempted and afflicted. Furthermore we pray thee, Father, merciful God, the great comforter of the afflicted, for all those whom thou chastisest with the cross and some affliction, and exercisest unto patience with poverty, exile, fetters, infamy, diseases, and other calamities and mischances. Grant to them that they may acknowledge thy fatherly and medicinable hand, under which they may humble themselves with all their hearts. Comfort ⟨and lift up⟩ their minds with faith and confidence of thy mercy, which moderateth all things, yea, even adversities, for the health of thine, and deliver them from all evils. Grant to us also that through their correction and punishment we may acknowledge that we have deserved things much more grievous, that we may amend our lives in time, before worse plagues happen unto us.

Last of all we pray thee, eternal God, heavenly Father, for us which here come together in thy sight, to thy word, prayer, and sacraments : lighten the eyes of our mind, grant us to ⟨ponder and⟩ consider with perfect faith that we have a nature corrupted from the beginning, that our flesh and blood cannot enjoy thy kingdom, but only commit sin and deserve eternal death, and increase the same destruction with daily sins ; and that thou, most merciful Father, of thy unmeasurable mercy didst look upon us, and sentest into this world thy eternal Word, thy Son, our flesh and brother ; and, that he might deliver us by his death from this our destruction, and restore us to thy image and praise of thy name, that thou deliveredst him to the cross and death ; and that he gladly offered himself unto thee in the cross for our sins, and satisfied for the same, through love and pity of us ; that he reconciled us unto thee ; and moreover that he offereth unto us his body and blood to be meat and drink, that we may live in him and he in us. Grant, heavenly Father, that we may consider and apprehend all these things with true and lively faith now and throughout all our lives, that, denying ourselves, we may utterly refuse the sottish and blind judgment of our reason, and repress naughty and noisome lusts, and wholly give over ⟨and consecrate⟩ ourselves to him, thy dear Son, our Lord and only Saviour and restorer ; that we seek and receive comfort in all things, all help, aid, and safeguard in him only, in his death,

For them that be present at the ministry.

cross, and resurrection. Now also let us receive his holy body and blood with sincere faith and all thankfulness, and let us ever magnify ⟨and praise⟩ him, and thee in him, for all thy exceeding benefits which thou hast given in making, governing, and restoring us ; for the incarnation, passion, and death of thy Son, whereby he purged our sins and reconciled us unto thee ; for his resurrection, ascension into heaven, and heavenly governance, whereby he restored us unto thee, and moveth and reneweth us unto all thy pleasure.

Finally, for this most ample benefit that he here delivereth himself unto us to be meat and drink unto eternal life, that so thy divine name may be daily more and more sanctified by us and in us, thy kingdom may be established and spread abroad by us unto other, that all things may be done among us in the earth according to thy will with such fervency and cheerfulness as they be done in heaven. And that these things may be done in us, give us also our daily bread, all necessary things for our bodies, prosperous health and peace, that we may enjoy these things unto the glory of thy name ; and forgive us our debts and sins which we daily commit, and mercifully pardon us of the punishments which we have deserved, as we also in the sight of thy majesty do gladly and heartily forgive all them which have offended us. And suffer not our tempter, our old enemy, which studieth ever to lead us from thee and thy word, to overthrow us at any time with his temptations. But deliver us from him and all evil, for thou only art our God and Father, thine is the kingdom, the power, and glory for ever. Amen.

Another and a short⟨er⟩ form of praying.

Merciful God, heavenly Father, which commandest us to come together in thy name, and in the name of thy Son, our Lord and Saviour Christ, and through the same our only mediator to pray thee for all things the which we desire for ourselves and for other, adding a more ample

promise that we should obtain whatsoever we would ask
of thee : trusting this thy commandment and promise, we
stand in the sight of thy divine majesty, we pray and
beseech thee, in the name of thy dear Son, our only
Saviour, that thou wilt forgive us all our iniquities and
sins, that thou wilt renew our hearts with thy holy Spirit,
and stir up and kindle the same to thy Son Christ, and
that for all the necessities of thy congregation and of all
men we may ⟨with true confidence⟩ call upon ⟨and pray
to⟩ thee, and whatsoever is good for us unto the glory of
thy[1] name.

We pray thee, then, chiefly for thy congregations : For the
deliver and preserve them from all those ministers whom congregation
and its
thou hast not sent; send them ⟨and preserve⟩ such ministers.
[ministers] as with all faithfulness and diligence will seek
thy scattered sheep, and bring them to Christ our Lord,
their only good shepherd, and will study to feed them
faithfully under him, that all ungodliness, heresies, sects,
all naughty doctrines and perverse service of God may be
taken away, and that in the unity of true faith and
knowledge of thy Son we may grow and go forward to all
things that please.

So we pray thee also for the Emperor, for our King, for For the
all kings, princes, and common powers and officers, and magistrates.
specially for our most reverend Archbishop, for his
councillors and officers, for the council and commonalty of
this city; grant that all these may execute their office
according to thy will, and they may turn away ⟨and repel⟩
all noisome things from their subjects, and procure and
maintain all good things, that, being delivered out of the
hands of our enemies, we may serve thee with a quiet
mind in all holiness and righteousness.

We pray furthermore, merciful Father, for all men : as
thou wilt be the Saviour of all men, draw them to thy Son
which yet pertain not to him, and grant that they whom

[1] 1548: his.

thou hast drawn to him already may grow and be confirmed daily more and more in the knowledge and love of him.

We pray also for them whom thou chastisest with sundry miseries and afflictions for an example unto us, that thou wilt comfort them and deliver them from all evils; and grant us that we may diligently regard thy fatherly nurture which thou settest before us in them, considering that we have deserved grievouser things, that in time we may judge and amend ourselves, that it be not needful that we be corrected and condemned of thee.

Grant also to us all which here in thy sight come together in thy word, prayer, alms, and divine sacraments, that we may truly come together only in thy name and in the name of thy dear Son; that we may take hold of thy divine law and holy gospel with true faith; that, dying daily more and more to ourselves, we may wholly give over ourselves to thy dear Son, our only Saviour, who only through his stripes and most bitter death hath redeemed us from sins and eternal damnation; hath restored us into thy favour through his resurrection and heavenly kingdom ⟨which he governs⟩; hath called us unto himself into his congregation, and hath planted us into himself unto everlasting life, and made us his own members; that we should live more and more in him and he in us, that thy [holy] name may be more largely sanctified by us in all our life and all our doings, that thy kingdom may be amplified ⟨in us and⟩ by us[1] in other, ⟨and may spread further,⟩ that at length all things may be done among us on earth with such promptness and cheerfulness as they be done in heaven. And for this purpose, that we may wholly live and serve unto thee, give us also our daily bread, etc. (as in the prayer before).[2]

Let the congregation sing the Creed. *After this solemn prayer let the whole congregation sing the Creed. For this confession of our faith when the Gospel is heard*

[1] 1547 and 1548: amplified by us and in other.   [2] *See p.* 348.

and declared ought to be done of right by all men communally, as all equally heard the Gospel and the declaration thereof.

And because no man can hear the Gospel with faith, and know At what time
and consider out of the same how great love and gentleness God the oblations must be
hath showed towards us in that, that he gave us his Son and all given.
things with him, which shall not out of this faith wholly give over and bind himself to our Lord Jesus Christ, this thing followeth also out of the nature of true faith, that the faithful study to declare this binding of themselves to the obedience of Christ, and thankfulness of their minds for so great goodness of God toward themselves, which at that time they more earnestly remember, with holy oblations for Christ, being needy in his little ones. Therefore, while the Creed is in singing, let the faithful offer their free oblations, every man according to the blessing which he hath received of the liberal and bounteous hand of God. To which office of faith and godliness the pastors and teachers shall diligently exhort the people, teaching them that these oblations ought to follow the confession of faith and prayer, even by the very nature of true religion, neither can be absent from the same, when we want not wherewith to declare this liberality. And, that this work of religion may be conveniently done and rightly commended to the faithful, we will The place
that there be some notable place appointed in every temple, not far where offerings must be
from the altar, which every man may comely go to, and where the laid up.
faithful may offer their oblations openly before the whole congregation. Which, after that the sacrament is ended, the officers of the holy treasury shall gather together and shall lay them up in the treasury, the congregation looking upon them.

It was the manner of the old Church, and that taken out of God's word, that, after the preaching of the gospel, before the ministration of the sacrament should begin, not only those should be commanded to go out of the temple which were not admitted into the congregation nor pertained thereunto, but they also which What
were not yet repentant and not reconciled to the congregation manner of men must be
with open absolution of sins. Therefore because this discipline was excluded from the ad-
taught of the Lord himself, and ought of right to be called again ministration
into the congregation, the pastors shall diligently and often ⟨warn of the sacraments.

and⟩ exhort those which live in such sins as be against their conscience, that they leave them and turn themselves with all their hearts unto the Lord. And, after that they be restored into the favour of God, and begin again to be the true disciples of the Lord, let them be present at the Lord's Supper and communicate ⟨from it in the sacraments of the Lord⟩.

But if any will not suffer themselves to be brought thereunto, and will continue in their sins with so great contempt of God and his Christ, let the preachers declare to such that they may not be present at the Lord's holy Supper; and, if they take upon them to be present, that they do despite unto Christ and provoke upon themselves the most grievous judgment of God. As for other which live not with an evil conscience, and yet receive not the sacrament with other, or seldom receive it, the pastors must often warn them that it pertaineth to the duty of a Christian man to be often partaker of the Lord's board, and so to feed and strengthen his faith, and to witness the same unto the congregation to the edification of many, seeing that God hath instituted ⟨and delivered⟩ this most holy exercise of religion for his, that they might thereby be established and enflamed in faith and study of godliness; wherefore we see that they which neglect so great a benefit of God become daily colder in all godliness and religion. For they grievously offend God through contempt of his bounteousness, and they hurt the congregation very sore with that evil example, and moreover they make themselves guilty of the Lord's body and blood, abhorring this meat and drink of everlasting life so irreligiously and so unthankfully.

But forasmuch as both the knowledge of this mystery, and moreover all the discipline of the congregation, is so much gone out of use, and thereof cometh so great weakness of the very[1] faithful, the pastors must restore to the people the knowledge and institution of so great mysteries with convenient and timely admonition, and not trouble any man with untimely rigorousness, as we admonished before. For first the sheep of Christ so miserably scattered and diseased must be fully brought to Christ and be healed, before that

How weak consciences must be gently handled.

[1] i.e. truly.

any rigorous discipline be restored and exercised among them. But howsoever the rest be handled in the congregation at this time, they nevertheless that shall be admitted to the communion, as soon as they have made their oblation, must go together to that place that shall be appointed unto them, nigh to the altar. For in every temple there must some place be appointed nigh the altar for them which shall communicate ⟨at the Lord's table⟩, according to the opportunity [and fitness] of every temple. They, then, which shall be admitted to the communion of the Lord's board shall stand in that place, the men in their proper place and the women in their place, and there they shall give thanks and pray religiously with the pastor. The giving of thanks shall be handled after the accustomed manner, but in Douch, that the people universally may give thanks ⟨to the Lord⟩, as both the example and the commandment of the Lord requireth, and also the old Church observed.

The priest. The Lord be with you.
The people. And with thy spirit.
The priest. Lift up your hearts.
The people. We have unto the Lord.
The priest. Let us give thanks unto the Lord our God.
The people. It is meet and right.
The priest.

It is verily a thing worthy, right, meet, and wholesome, that we give thanks unto thee always and everywhere, that we praise and magnify thee, Lord, holy Father, Almighty, everlasting God, through Jesus Christ our Lord, by whom thou madest us of nothing unto thine image, and hast appointed all other creatures to our uses ; and whereas we, through the sin of Adam sliding from thee, were made thine enemies, and therefore subject to death and eternal damnation, thou of thy infinite mercy and unspeakable love, didst send the same thy Son, the eternal Word, into this world ; who through the cross and death delivered us from sins and the power of the devil, and brought us again into thy favour by his holy Spirit whom he sent to us from

M

thee ; and gave his body and blood to be the food of a new and eternal life, that, being more confirmed through the trust of thy mercy and love, we should ever go forward to all that that is thy pleasure by renewing and sanctifying of ourselves ; and that we should glorify and exalt thee here and evermore in all our words and deeds, and sing unto thee without end with all thy holy angels and beloved children.

When there are special feasts and[1] commemorations of our Lord Jesus Christ, we must make mention of them also in the giving of thanks, examples whereof we shall hereafter set forth.

After these things, Sanctus *shall be sung; where clerks be, in Latin, but of the people in Douch, one side answering the other, thrice of both parts. As for that that is wont to be added, 'The Lord God of hosts'* and Benedictus, *it shall be sung communally of the whole congregation, and therefore in Douch.*

Straightway after this, let the priest sing the words of the Lord's Supper in Douch, 'Our Lord, the night in which he was delivered', etc. But these words must be sung of the priest with great reverence and plainly, that they may be well understanded of all men. And the people shall say to these words, Amen, *which all the old Churches observed, and the Greeks do yet observe the same. For the whole substance of this sacrament is contained in these words. And it consisteth altogether in the true understanding and faith of these words that the sacrament be wholesomely administered and received.*

After[2] *the people then have answered* ⟨*their*⟩ Amen, *the priest shall add:*

Let us pray.

Our Father, which art in heaven, etc.

To which prayer of the Lord the people shall say again ⟨*their*⟩ *Amen.*

The priest. The Lord's peace be ever with you.

The people. And with thy spirit.

After this, they which be admitted to the communion and do look for the same in their place shall come to the Lord's board

---

[1] Latin: *Quando festa sunt singularia et*; 1547 and 1548: When the feasts be singular.

[2] Latin: *Postquam*; 1547 and 1548: when.

religiously ⟨in order⟩ first men and then women; and the whole sacrament shall be given to them all, that they may be partakers of the body and blood of the Lord, receiving not only bread but also the cup, even as he instituted it.

At the exhibition of the body let the pastor say:

Take and eat to thy health the body of the Lord, which was delivered for thee.[1]

At the exhibition of the cup:

Take and drink to thy health the blood of the Lord, which was shed for thy sins.

After the communion, let Agnus Dei *be sung both in Douch and Latin, one side answering the other, where clerks be. And then let this Douch song be sung, 'Gott sei gelobet' ; item,'Jesus Christus unser Heiland', if the communion ⟨of the sacraments⟩ shall give so much time [and leisure].*

When the communion is ended, let the priest sing, turning to the people:

The Lord be with you.

The people. And with thy spirit.

The priest. Let us pray.

Almighty, everlasting God, we give thanks to thy exceeding goodness, because thou hast fed us with the body of thy only-begotten Son ⟨our Lord⟩ and given us his blood to drink. We humbly beseech thee, work in us with thy Spirit, that, as we have received this divine sacrament with our mouths, so we may also receive and ever hold fast with true faith thy grace, remission of sins, and communion with Christ thy Son. All which things thou hast exhibited unto us in these sacraments through our Lord Jesus Christ thy Son, which liveth and reigneth with thee in unity of the holy Ghost, very God and very man, for ever. Amen.

Another thanksgiving.

We give thee thanks, Father, Almighty God, which hast refreshed us with the singular gift of thy body and

---

[1] Latin: *pro te*; 1547 and 1548: for thy sins.

blood; we beseech thy goodness that the same may help to confirm our faith in thee, and to kindle mutual love among us, by the same our Lord Jesus Christ, etc.

Last of all, let the pastor bless the people with these words:

The Lord bless thee and keep thee; the Lord lighten his countenance upon thee and have mercy on thee; the Lord lift up his face upon thee and settle thee in peace. ⟨Amen.⟩

Or thus.

God have mercy on us and bless us, lighten his countenance upon us, and give us his peace. Amen.

Or thus.

God, the Father, the Son, and the holy Ghost, bless and keep us. Amen.

Or thus.

The blessing of God, the Father, the Son, and the holy Ghost, be with us and remain [with us] for ever. Amen.

But where clerks be not, as in villages, there let all be read and sung in Douch. But let the songs be so moderated as in every congregation shall make to the edification of godliness.

But forasmuch as our Lord instituted this his sacrament only for this purpose, that we should eat it and drink it for the remembrance of him, and not that we should set it forth or carry it about to be looked upon; and forasmuch as sundry abuses be brought in, the true use of this sacrament being overpassed, and so this sacrament hath been drawn to horrible superstition and ungodliness; for the taking away both of this superstition and ungodliness, and also sundry scruples of the weak,[1] and irreligious questions about these mysteries, the pastors and they that administer the sacrament shall endeavour themselves that, as often as the Supper shall be ministered, whether it be in the congregation or in private houses for sick folk, they count the number of them certainly which shall communicate, that according to the same they may receive pieces of bread and measure of wine. As for the remnants, after that the communion is ended, let the pastors

That the sacrament must neither be laid up to be kept, be set out as a thing to be showed, nor carried about.

---

[1] Latin: *imbecillium*; 1547: work.

themselves receive them forthwith, and let them not keep the same, nor lay them up in any place, nor carry them away, or set them forth to be beholded. For the word of God, which saveth us if we believe and obey it, and damneth perpetually if we do not believe nor obey it, hath this prescribed concerning his sacraments: 'Take and eat, this is my body; take and drink, this is my blood.' Therefore we must stand in this institution of Christ, and not institute a new usage without God's word about this most holy sacrament. And because also that here the Lord's death must be preached, and the communion of him confirmed in us, that through him we may be daily more crucified to the world, all worldly pomp must likewise be taken from this ministration, and all things must be so ordained and moderated that they may help forth and adorn the preaching of the cross and of the death of Christ.

(The translation is that published anonymously in 1548, with the spelling modernized and the variant readings of the first edition (1547) added in the notes. Mistranslations of the Latin are pointed out in the notes; words left untranslated are added in angle brackets 〈 〉; and words which have no counterpart in the Latin are enclosed in square brackets [ ].)

A Litany with Suffrages, 1544

As these holy prayers and suffrages following are set forth of most godly zeal for edifying and stirring of devotion of all true faithful Christian hearts; so it is thought convenient in this Common Prayer of procession to have it set forth and used in the vulgar tongue, for stirring the people to more devotion: and it shall be every Christian man's part reverently to use the same, to the honour and glory of Almighty God, and the profit of their own souls. And such among the people as have books and can read, may read them quietly and softly to themself; and such as cannot read, let them quietly and attentively give audience in time of the said prayers, having their minds erect to Almighty God, and devoutly praying in their hearts the same petitions which do enter in at their ears; so that with one sound of the heart and one accord God may be glorified in his Church.

And it is to be remembered that that which is printed in black letters, is to be said or sung of the priest with an audible voice; that is to say, so loud and so plainly that it may well be understood of the hearers: and that which is in the red is to be answered of the choir soberly and devoutly.

B.174, R.231.[1]

    O God the Father of heaven . . .

    O holy, blessed, and glorious Trinity, one God :[2] have mercy upon us miserable sinners.

---

[1] References to *The Book of Common Prayer*, 1549: B=F. E. Brightman, *The English Rite*, vol. 1; R=E. C. Ratcliff, *The First and Second Prayer Books of Edward VI*. Only those portions are printed which were omitted in 1549.

[2] Edition of 27 May; edition of 16 June adds 'three persons and'.

Holy Saint[1] Mary, mother of God our Saviour Jesus Christ:

Pray for us.

All holy Angels and Archangels, and all holy orders of blessed spirits:

Pray for us.

All holy Patriarchs and Prophets, Apostles, Martyrs, Confessors, and Virgins, and all the blessed company of heaven:

Pray for us.

Remember not . . .

B.176, R.232.

That it may please thee to be his defender and keeper . . .

We beseech thee to hear us, good Lord.

That it may please thee to keep our noble Queen Catherine in thy fear and love, giving her increase of all godliness, honour, and children.

We beseech thee to hear us, good Lord.

B.178, R.232.

That it may please thee to keep and defend our noble Prince Edward, and all the King's Majesty's children.

We beseech thee to hear us, good Lord.

That it may please thee to illuminate all Bishops . . .

B.180, R.233.

That it may please thee to give to our use the kindly fruits of the earth, so as in due time we may enjoy them, and to preserve them.

We beseech thee to hear us, good Lord.

B.180, R.234.

That it may please thee to give us true repentance. . . .

Our Father, which art in heaven. *With the residue of the Paternoster.*

And suffer us not to be led into temptation.

But deliver us from evil. Amen.

The versicle . . .

[1] Edition of 27 May; edition of 16 June reads 'Holy Virgin Mary'.

B.182, R.235.

O Lord, arise, help us, and deliver us for thy honour.[1]

Glory to the Father, the Son, and to the Holy Ghost, as it hath been from the beginning, is, and shall be ever, world without end. Amen . . .

Pitifully behold the dolour of our heart . . .

We humbly beseech thee, O Father . . . most righteously have deserved. Grant this, O Lord God, for our mediator and advocate Jesus Christ's sake.[2] Amen.

B.184.

O God, whose nature and property is ever to have mercy and to forgive, receive our humble petition ; and though we be tied and bound with the chain of our sins, yet let thy pitifulness of thy great mercy loose us ; for the honour of Jesu Christ's sake, our mediator and advocate.[3] Amen.

Almighty and everliving God, which only workest great marvels, send down upon our bishops and curates, and all congregations committed to their charge, the healthful spirit of thy grace ; and that they may truly please thee, pour upon them the continual dew of thy blessing ; grant this, O Lord, for the honour of our advocate and mediator Jesu Christ.[4] Amen.

We beseech thee, O Lord, to show upon us thine exceeding great mercy, which no tongue can worthily express ; and that it may please thee to deliver us from all our sins, and also for the pains that we have for them deserved ; grant this, O Lord, through our mediator and advocate Jesu Christ.[5] Amen.

Grant, we beseech thee, O Almighty God, that we in our trouble put our whole confidence upon thy mercy,

---

[1] Edition of 27 May has 'honour' first and 'name's sake' second.

[2] Enlarged in 1549 with a phrase from the fourth collect following.

[3] Omitted in 1549, restored in 1559, transferred to *Prayers* in 1662.

[4] Omitted in 1549, restored in 1559, transferred to *Morning* and *Evening Prayer* in 1662.

[5] Omitted in 1549 and never restored.

that we may against all adversity be defended under thy protection ; grant this, O Lord God, for our mediator and advocate Jesu Christ's sake.[1] Amen.

B.188, R.235.

Almighty God, which hast given us grace ... life everlasting. Amen.

[1] Omitted in 1549, except for one phrase transferred to the fourth collect above; the rest never restored.

Cranmer's Projected Processional

According to your highness commandment ... I have translated into the English tongue, so well as I could in so short a time, certain processions, to be used upon festival days, if after due correction and amendment of the same your highness shall think it so convenient. In which translation, forasmuch as many of the processions, in the Latin, were but barren, as meseemed, and little fruitful, I was constrained to use more than the liberty of a translator: for in some processions I have altered divers words; in some I have added part; in some taken part away; some I have left out whole, either for bycause the matter appeared to me to be little to purpose, or bycause the days be not with us festival days; and some processions I have added whole, because I thought I had better matter for the purpose, than was the procession in Latin: the judgment whereof I refer wholly unto your majesty; and after your highness hath corrected it, if your grace command some devout and solemn note to be made thereunto (as is the procession which your majesty hath already set forth in English), I trust it will much excitate and stir the hearts of all men unto devotion and godliness: but in mine opinion, the song that shall be made thereunto would not be full of notes, but, as near as may be, for every syllable a note; so that it may be sung distinctly and devoutly, as be in Mattins and Evensong *Venite*, the hymns *Te Deum, Benedictus, Magnificat, Nunc dimittis*, and all the Psalms and Versicles; and in the Mass *Gloria in excelsis, Gloria Patri*, the Creed, the Preface, the *Pater noster*, and some of the *Sanctus* and *Agnus*. As concerning the *Salve festa dies*, the Latin note, as I think, is sober and distinct enough ; wherefore I have travailed to make the verses in English, and have put the Latin note unto the same. Nevertheless they that be cunning in singing can make a much more solemn note thereto. I made them only for a proof, to see how English would do in song. But bycause mine English verses lack the grace and facility I would wish they had, your majesty may cause some other to make them again, that can do the same in more pleasant English and phrase. As for the sentence, I suppose [it] will serve well enough.

(*Miscellaneous Writings*, PS, 412.)

The Order of the Communion, 1548

First the Parson, Vicar, or Curate the next Sunday or holy day, or at the least one day, before he shall minister the Communion, shall give warning to his parishioners, or those which be present, that they prepare themselves thereto; saying to them openly and plainly as hereafter followeth or suchlike.
B.652–6, R.216–7.[1]

Dear friends, and you especially . . . as you would that God should forgive you.
B.656–8, R.217.

And if there be any of you . . . warrant of God's word to the same.

The time of the Communion shall be immediately after that the priest himself hath received the sacrament, without the varying of any other rite or ceremony in the Mass, until other order shall be provided; but as heretofore usually the priest hath done with the sacrament of the Body, to prepare, bless, and consecrate so much as will serve the people, so it shall continue still after the same manner and form, save that he shall bless and consecrate the biggest chalice, or some fair and convenient cup or cups, full of wine with some water put into it; and that day not drink it up all himself, but, taking one only sup or draught, leave the rest upon the altar covered, and turn to them that are disposed to be partakers of the Communion, and shall thus exhort them as followeth.
B.650–2, R.214–6.

Dearly beloved in the Lord . . . all the days of our life.

[1] References to *The Book of Common Prayer*, 1549: B = F. E. Brightman, *The English Rite*, vol. II; R = E. C. Ratcliff, *The First and Second Prayer Books of Edward VI*. Only those portions are printed which differ from 1549.

Then the priest shall say to them which be ready to take the sacrament.

B.650, R.215.

If any man here . . . destruction both of body and soul.

Here the priest shall pause awhile to see if any man will withdraw himself; and if he perceive any so to do, then let him commune with him privily at convenient leisure, and see whether he can with good exhortation bring him to grace; and after a little pause the priest shall say.

B.696, R.224.

You that do truly . . . meekly kneeling upon your knees.

B.696–8, R.224.

Then shall a general confession . . . humbly upon their knees.

Almighty God . . . through Jesus Christ our Lord.

Then shall the priest stand up and, turning him to the people, say thus.

Our blessed Lord, who hath left power to his Church to absolve penitent sinners from their sins, and to restore to the grace of the heavenly Father such as truly believe in Christ, have mercy upon you, pardon and deliver you from all sins, confirm and strengthen you in all goodness, and bring you to everlasting life.

Then shall the priest stand up and, turning him toward the people, say thus.

B.698, R.225.

Hear what comfortable words . . . to save sinners.

Hear also what Saint John saith.

If any man sin, we have an advocate with the Father, Jesus Christ the righteous ; he it is that obtained grace for our sins.

Then shall the priest kneel down and say, in the name of all them that shall receive the Communion, this prayer following.

B.698–700, R.225.

We do not presume . . . his most precious blood. Amen.

Then shall the priest rise, the people still reverently kneeling; and the priest shall deliver the Communion, first to the ministers, if any be there present, that they may be ready to help the priest, and after to the other. And when he doth deliver the sacrament of the Body of Christ, he shall say to everyone these words following.

The Body of our Lord Jesus Christ, which was given for thee, preserve thy body unto everlasting life.

And the priest delivering the sacrament of the Blood, and giving everyone to drink once and no more, shall say.

The Blood of our Lord Jesus Christ, which was shed for thee, preserve thy soul to everlasting life.

B.700, R.226.

If there be a deacon . . . in form before written.

Then shall the priest, turning him to the people, let the people depart with this blessing.

B.710, R.228.

The peace of God . . . and of his Son Jesus Christ our Lord.

To the which the people shall answer,

Amen.

Note, that the bread that shall be consecrated shall be such as heretofore hath been accustomed. And every of the said consecrated breads shall be broken in two pieces at the least, or more by the discretion of the minister, and so distributed. And men must not think less to be received in part than in the whole, but in each of them the whole Body of our Saviour Jesus Christ.

Note, that if it doth so chance that the wine hallowed and consecrated doth not suffice or be enough for them that do take the Communion, the priest, after the first cup or chalice be emptied, may go again to the altar, and reverently and devoutly prepare and consecrate another (and so the third, or more, likewise), beginning at these words, 'Simili modo postquam coenatum est', *and ending at these words,* 'qui pro vobis et pro multis effundetur in remissionem peccatorum', *and without any levation or lifting up.*

Liber Precum Publicarum, 1560

At Commendations of Benefactors

At the end of each term, let there be a commendation of the Founder, and of other famous men by whose beneficence the College is enriched. Let its form be this.

First let the Lord's Prayer be recited with a loud voice.

Our Father, which art in heaven, etc.

Then let three Psalms be recited:

I will magnify thee, O God. Psalm 145.

Praise the Lord, O my soul. Psalm 146.

Praise the Lord, for it is a good thing. Psalm 147.

Thereafter let chapter 44 of Ecclesiasticus be read.

This finished, let a sermon follow, in which the preacher shall proclaim the boundless generosity of the Founder; let him show how great is the value of learning; how greatly they are to be praised who promote learned studies by their beneficence; what an ornament to the Realm it is to have learned men who can give true judgment on matters of controversy; how the Scriptures are to be praised, and how greatly they exceed all human authority; how useful their teaching is for the common people, and how widespread it should be; how noble and royal it is for him to whom God has committed the care of all his people to labour for the increase of ministers of the word, and to see that they are honourable and well-educated; and other things of that kind, which pious and learned men can enhance with praise.

This sermon concluded, let there be sung,

Blessed be the Lord God of Israel.

At the end let there be added this:

Minister. The righteous shall be had in everlasting remembrance.

Answer. He will not be afraid of any evil tidings.

Minister. The souls of the righteous are in the hand of God.

Answer. And there shall no torment touch them.

Let us pray.

Lord God, the resurrection and the life of them that believe, who art always to be praised, both in the living and in the dead, we give thee thanks for our Founder *N.* and our other benefactors, by whose bounty we are here nurtured in religion and learned studies; beseeching thee that we, rightly using these gifts to thy glory, may together with them be brought to the immortal glory of the resurrection; through Christ our Lord. Amen.

Celebration of the Lord's Supper at funerals, if the friends and neighbours of the deceased wish to communicate.

COLLECT

O merciful God ... and rising again may reign with thee in everlasting life; through our Lord Jesus Christ. Amen.

EPISTLE. I THESS. IV (13–18).

I would not, brethren ... with these words.

GOSPEL. JOHN VI (37–40).

Jesus said ... at the last day.

OR THIS GOSPEL. JOHN V (24–29).

Jesus said to his disciples and to the Jews: Verily, verily, I say unto you, He that heareth my word, and believeth on him that sent me, hath everlasting life, and shall not come into condemnation, but is passed from death unto life. Verily, verily, I say unto you, The hour is coming and now is, when the dead shall hear the voice of the Son of God; and they that hear shall live. For as the Father hath life in himself, so hath he given to the Son to have life in himself; and hath given him authority to execute judgment also, because he is the Son of Man. Marvel not at this : for the hour is coming in the which all that are in the graves shall hear his voice, and shall come forth : they that have done good, unto the resurrection of life; and they that have done evil, unto the resurrection of evil.

(The text translated is printed by Procter and Frere, 123.)

An Admonition to the Parliament, 1572

... Now to the second point, which concerneth ministration of Sacraments. In the old time, the word was preached before they were ministered; now, it is supposed to be sufficient if it be read. Then, they were ministered in public assemblies; now, in private houses. Then, by ministers only; now, by midwives and deacons, equally. But because, in treating of both the sacraments together, we should deal confusedly, we will therefore speak of them severally. And first for the Lord's Supper, or Holy Communion.

They had no introit, for Celestinus a pope brought it in about the year 430; but we have borrowed a piece of one out of the mass-book. They read no fragments of the Epistle and Gospel; we use both. The Nicene Creed was not read in their Communion; we have it in ours. There was then accustomed to be an examination of the communicants, which is now neglected. Then, they ministered the sacrament with common and usual bread; now, with wafer cakes brought in by Pope Alexander, being in form, fashion, and substance like their god of the altar. They received it sitting; we kneeling, according to Honorius' decree. Then it was delivered generally and indefinitely, 'Take ye and eat ye'; we particularly and singularly, 'Take thou and eat thou'. They used no other words but such as Christ left; we borrow from papists, 'The body of our Lord Jesus Christ which was given for thee', etc. They had no *Gloria in excelsis* in the ministry of the sacrament then, for it was put to afterward; we have it now. They took it with conscience, we with custom. They shut men, by reason of their sins, from the Lord's Supper; we thrust them in sin to the Lord's Supper. They ministered the sacrament plainly; we pompously, with singing, piping, surplice- and cope-wearing. They simply as they received it from the Lord; we sinfully, mixed with man's inventions and devices. And as for Baptism, it was enough with them, if they had water, and the party to be baptized faith, and the minister to preach the word and minister the sacraments.

Now, we must have surplices devised by Pope Hadrian, interrogatories ministered to the infant, godfathers and godmothers brought in by Hyginus, holy fonts invented by Pope Pius, crossing and suchlike pieces of popery, which the Church of God in the Apostles' times never knew (and therefore not to be used), nay (which we are sure of), were and are man's devices, brought in long after the purity of the primitive Church.

To redress these, your wisdoms have to remove (as before) ignorant ministers, to take away private communions and baptisms, to enjoin deacons and midwives not to meddle in ministers' matters; if they do, to see them sharply punished. To join assistance of elders and other officers, that, seeing men will not examine themselves, they may be examined and brought to render a reason of their hope. That the Statute against wafer cakes may more prevail than an Injunction. That people be appointed to receive the sacrament rather sitting, for avoiding of superstition, than kneeling, having in it the outward show of evil, from which we must abstain. That excommunication be restored to its old, former force. That papists nor other, neither constrainedly nor customably, communicate in the mysteries of salvation. That both the sacrament of the Lord's Supper and Baptism also may be ministered according to the ancient purity and simplicity. That the parties to be baptized, if they be of the years of discretion, by themselves and in their own persons; or, if they be infants, by their parents (in whose room, if upon necessary occasions and businesses they be absent, some of the congregation, knowing the good behaviour and sound faith of the parents); may both make rehearsal of their faith, and also, if their faith be sound and agreeable to holy Scriptures, desire to be in the same baptized. And finally, that nothing be done in this or any other thing, but that which you have the express warrant of God's Word for.

(ed. Frere and Douglas, 13–15.)

... In all their order of service there is no edification, according to the rule of the Apostle, but confusion; they toss the Psalms in most places like tennis balls. The people, some standing, some walking, some talking, some praying by themselves, attend not to the minister. He again posteth it over as fast as he can gallop. For either he hath two places to serve, or else there are some games to be played in the afternoon, as lying for the whetstone, heathenish dancing for the ring, a bear or a bull to be baited, or else Jackanapes to ride on horseback, or an interlude to be played, and if no place else can be gotten, it must be done in the church, etc. Now the people sit and now they stand up. When the Old Testament is read, or the Lessons, they make no reverence, but when the Gospel cometh, then they all stand up. For why? They think that to be of greatest authority, and are ignorant that the Scriptures came from one Spirit. When Jesus is named, then off goeth the cap, and down goeth the knees, with such a scraping on the ground that they cannot hear a good while after, so that the word is hindered; but when any other names of God are mentioned, they make no curtsey at all, as though the names of God were not equal, or as though all reverence ought to be given to the syllables. We speak not of ringing when Mattins is done, and other abuses incident, because we shall be answered that by the Book they are not maintained; only we desire to have a book to reform it. As for organs and curious singing, though they be proper to popish dens, I mean to cathedral churches, yet some others also must have them. The Queen's chapel and these churches must be patterns and precedents to the people of all superstitions . . .

(ed. Frere and Douglas, 29–30.)

A Second Admonition to the Parliament, 1572

... The book is such a piece of work as it is strange we will use it. Besides, I cannot account it praying, as they use it commonly, but only reading or saying of prayers, even as a child that learneth to read, if his lesson be a prayer, he readeth a prayer, he doth not pray ; even so is it commonly a saying and reading prayers, and not praying ; the child putteth off his cap as well as the minister. For though they have many guises, now to kneel and now to stand, these be of course, and not of any prick of conscience or piercing of the heart most commonly. One, he kneeleth on his knees, and this way he looketh, and that way he looketh ; another, he kneeleth himself asleep ; another kneeleth with such devotion that he is so far in talk that he forgetteth to arise till his knee ache, or his talk endeth, or service is done. And why is all this, but that there is no such praying as should touch the heart ? And therefore another hath so little feeling of the Common Prayer that he bringeth a book of his own ; and though he sit when they sit, stand when they stand, kneel when they kneel, he may pause sometime also, but most of all he intendeth his own book, is this praying ? God grant us to feel our lacks better than this, and to take a better order than this for prayer ; it is and will be all naught, else ...

(ed. Frere and Douglas, 114–15.)

Proposals for Revision, 1689

(Specimen extracts)

(ADDITIONAL PETITIONS IN THE LITANY)

From all infidelity and error; from all impiety and profaneness; from all superstition and idolatry,

From pride, vainglory, and hypocrisy; from envy, hatred, and revenge; from all rash censure, contention, and uncharitableness,

From drunkenness and gluttony; from sloth and misspending of our time; from fornication, adultery, and all uncleanness,

From lying and slandering; from vain swearing, cursing, and perjury; from covetousness, oppression, and all injustice,

Good Lord, deliver us.

That it may please thee to endue us with the graces of humility and meekness, of contentedness and patience, of true justice, of temperance and purity, of peaceableness and charity,

We beseech thee to hear us, good Lord.

A preparatory Prayer for the receiving of the Communion, to be read on the Lord's day, or some weekday or days before.

O God, who hast ordained holy mysteries for a communication of our Saviour's wonderful love in laying down his life for us, and for the communication of the benefits of his death and Passion to us; we beseech thee to dispose all those who intend to receive the holy Sacrament to come to thy Table with such sincere repentance of all their sins, and unfeigned resolution of better obedience, with such an humble faith and ardent love unto thee and unto all men, that they may comfortably hope for thy gracious pardon, and for the power of thy Holy Spirit, to carry them by patient continuance in well doing unto eternal life, through Jesus Christ our Lord. Amen.

A prayer to be said in any time of Calamity (Sancroft).

Almighty God and most merciful Father, we miserable sinners do here humbly acknowledge before thee that we are unworthy of the least of all thy mercies; we confess, O Lord, in the bitterness of our souls, that we have grievously sinned against thee, that all orders of men amongst us have transgressed thy righteous laws, that we have hitherto rendered both thy mercies and thy judgments ineffectual to our amendment. It is of thy mere mercy, O Lord, that we are not consumed, for which our souls do magnify and bless thy name. O God, who hast hitherto spared us, to the end that thy goodness might lead us to repentance, let it be thy good pleasure to give unto us all that godly sorrow which worketh repentance to salvation, not to be repented of; that thou mayest turn from thy heavy displeasure against us, and mayest rejoice over us to do us good, through the merits and mediation of Jesus Christ our Lord and only Saviour. Amen.

(RUBRIC BEFORE THE EMBER PRAYERS)

Whereas the Apostles did use prayer and fasting before they ordained, and that it has been the practice of the Church to enjoin Fasts in the four weeks of the year commonly called Ember weeks before the Lord's days appointed for ordination, to implore the blessing of God upon them that are to ordain, and upon those that are to be ordained ; it is therefore earnestly recommended to all persons to spend some part of those days in prayer to God for his blessing on the Church and on all that are to be sent out to officiate in it. And it is most solemnly charged on all that are concerned in Ordinations, chiefly on the persons that are to be ordained, to spend those days in fervent prayer and fasting, for the due preparing of themselves to be initiated into holy Orders.

This rubric is to be read immediately after the Apostles' Creed on the Lord's day next before any of the Ember weeks.

(COLLECT FOR CHRISTMAS DAY: ADDITIONS IN ITALICS)

Almighty God, who hast given us thy only-begotten Son, *the brightness of thy glory and the express image of thy person,* to take our nature upon him and *to be born of a pure Virgin ; grant that we, being regenerate and made thy children by adoption and grace, may be daily renewed by thy Holy Spirit, *till Christ be perfectly formed in us, and we be made partakers of a divine nature,* through the same our Lord Jesus Christ, who liveth and reigneth with thee and the same Spirit, ever one God, world without end. Amen.

(PROPER PREFACE FOR GOOD FRIDAY)

Who hast not spared thine own Son, but delivered him up for us all, that by making himself a sacrifice for our sins, he might redeem us from all iniquity, and purify to himself a peculiar people zealous of good works. Therefore with Angels, &c.

* as at this time *omitted.*

(RUBRIC AFTER THE COMMUNION SERVICE)

If any, not being satisfied herewith shall, some day in the week before they intend to receive the Holy Communion, come to the Minister of their Parish, and declare that they are verily persuaded in conscience that they cannot receive it kneeling without sin, then the Minister shall endeavour to give them satisfaction in this matter, after which, if they still press it, then the Minister shall give them the sacramental bread and wine in some convenient place or pew without obliging them to kneel.

(RUBRIC AFTER BAPTISM OF INFANTS)

Whereas the sign of the Cross is, by this office, appointed to be used in Baptism, according to the ancient and laudable custom of the Church; it is not thereby intended to add any new rite to the sacrament as a part of it, or as necessary to it; or that the using that sign is of any virtue or efficacy of itself; but only to remember all Christians of the death and cross of Christ, which is their hope and glory; and to put them in mind of their obligation to bear the cross in such manner as God shall think fit to lay it upon them, and to become conformable to Christ in his sufferings.

If any minister at his institution shall declare to his Bishop that he cannot satisfy his conscience in baptizing any with the sign of the cross, then the Bishop shall dispense with him in that particular, and shall name a Curate, who shall baptize the children of those in that parish who desire it may be done with the sign of the Cross according to this office.

(PRAYER AFTER CONFIRMATION, TO FOLLOW THE SECOND COLLECT AFTER THE LORD'S PRAYER)

Accept, good Lord, of the dedication which these thy servants have made of themselves unto thee by the solemn renewal of their baptismal vow and covenant. And as they have now given up themselves unto thee and consented to be governed in all things by thy will, so do thou vouchsafe to receive them into thy special favour and grace to fulfil in them all the good pleasure of thy goodness, and the work of faith with power. Possess their minds perpetually with a serious and lively remembrance of what they have now promised. Confirm and settle the godly resolutions they have now made. Sanctify them throughout that they may become the temples of the Holy Ghost, and in the end be presented faultless before the presence of thy glory with exceeding joy, through Jesus Christ our Lord. Amen.

(For references, see Bibliography.)

A Form of Consecrating Churches, Chapels, and Churchyards, or Places of Burial, 1714

When the bishop and the clergy, of which there shall be two at least, have entered the church or chapel in their several habits, let them, as they walk up from the west to the east end, repeat alternately the 24th Psalm, the bishop beginning, 'The earth is the Lord's, etc., with 'Gloria Patri'.

When they are come to the Lord's Table, the bishop sitting in his chair shall have the instrument of dedication, donation, and endowment of the church or chapel, churchyard or burial place presented to him by the founder, or some proper person, which he shall cause to be read by his register, or other officer deputed for that purpose; and after that the bishop shall lay such instrument or instruments upon the Table, and standing on the north side thereof shall turn to the congregation and say:

Dearly beloved in the Lord. Forasmuch as devout and holy men as well under the law, as under the gospel, moved either by the secret inspiration of the blessed Spirit, or by express command of God, or by their own reason and sense of the natural decency of things, have erected houses for the public worship of God, and separated them from all profane and common uses, in order to fill men's minds with greater reverence for his glorious majesty, and affect their hearts with more devotion and humility in his service, which pious works have been approved and graciously accepted by our heavenly Father; let us not doubt, but he will also favourably approve this our godly purpose of setting apart this place in solemn manner to the performance of the several offices of our religious worship, and let us faithfully and devoutly beg his blessing on this our undertaking and say : (*The bishop kneeling shall say the prayer following*)

O eternal God, mighty in power, of majesty incomprehensible, whom the heaven of heavens cannot contain, much less the walls of temples made with hands, and who yet hast been graciously pleased to promise thy especial presence in whatsoever place, even where two or three of thy faithful servants shall assemble in thy name to offer up their supplications and their praises to thee ; vouchsafe, O Lord, to be now present with us, who are gathered here together to consecrate this place with all humility and readiness of heart to the honour of thy great name, separating it henceforth from all unhallowed, ordinary, and common uses, and dedicating it entirely to thy service, for reading therein thy most holy word, for celebrating thy holy sacraments, for offering to thy glorious majesty the sacrifices of prayer and thanksgivings, for blessing thy people in thy name, and performing of all other ordinances. Accept, O Lord, this service at our hands, and bless it with such success, as may tend most to thy glory, and the furtherance of our happiness, through Jesus Christ, our blessed Lord and Saviour. Amen.

After this let the bishop stand up, and turning his face toward the congregation, say the following prayers:

Regard, O Lord, the supplications of thy servants, and grant that whoever shall be dedicated to thee in this house by baptism, may be sanctified with the Holy Ghost, delivered from thy wrath, received into the ark of Christ's Church, and ever remain in the number of thy faithful and elected children. Amen.

Grant, O Lord, that they who at this place shall in their own persons undertake to renew the promises and vows made by their sureties for them at their baptism, may receive such a measure of thy Holy Spirit, that they may be enabled faithfully to fulfil the same, and grow in grace to their lives' end. Amen.

Grant, O Lord, that whosoever shall receive in this place the blessed sacrament of the body and blood of Christ thy Son, may come to that holy ordinance with faith, charity, and true repentance ; and being filled with thy grace and heavenly benediction, may to their great and endless comfort obtain remission of their sins, and all other benefits of his passion. Amen.

Grant, O Lord, that by thy holy word, which shall be read and preached within this place, the hearers thereof may both perceive and know what things they ought to do, and may have grace and power to fulfil the same. Amen.

Grant, O Lord, that whosoever shall be joined together in this place in the holy estate of matrimony, may faithfully perform and keep the vow and covenant betwixt them made, and may remain in perfect love together unto their lives' end. Amen.

Grant, we beseech thee, blessed Lord, that whosoever shall draw near unto thee in this place to give thee thanks for the great benefits they have received at thy hands, to set forth thy most worthy praise, to confess their sins unto thee, humbly to beg thy pardon for what they have done amiss, or to ask such other things as are requisite and necessary as well for the body as the soul, may do it with that steadfastness of faith, that seriousness, attention, and devout affection of mind, that thou mayest accept their bounden duty and service, and vouchsafe to them whatsoever else in thy infinite wisdom thou shalt see to be most expedient for them. And this we beg for Jesus Christ his sake, our blessed Lord and Saviour. Amen.

After this let one of the priests (the appointed curate of the place, if he be present) begin and read the service for the day, except where it is otherwise ordered.

Proper Psalms. xxxiv, cxxii, cxxxii.

The first lesson. 1 Kings VIII, *from verse 22 to verse 62.*

The second lesson. Hebrews x, *from verse 19 to verse 26.*

Then go on with the rest of the service, as upon Litany days: after which let the bishop proceed to the Communion Service, and after the Commandments, and one of the Collects for the King, instead of the Collect for the day shall be used this following:

O most gracious Lord God, we acknowledge that we are not worthy to offer unto thee any thing belonging to us, yet we beseech thee out of thine infinite goodness graciously to accept the dedication of this place to thy service, and to prosper this our undertaking; receive the prayer and intercessions of us and all other thy servants, who either now or hereafter entering into this house shall call upon thee, and give both them and us grace to prepare our hearts to serve thee with reverence and godly fear; affect us with an awful apprehension of thy heavenly majesty, and with a deep sense of our own unworthiness, that so approaching thy sanctuary with lowliness and devotion, and bringing with us clean thoughts, pure hearts, bodies undefiled, and minds sanctified, we may be an acceptable people in thy sight, through Jesus Christ our Lord. Amen.

Epistle. 1 Cor. II, *from verse 17 to verse 29.*

Gospel. St John II, *from verse 13 to verse 17.*

Then shall follow the Nicene Creed and sermon, after which the bishop is to proceed in the Service of the Communion. If the church or chapel was built or endowed by any private person or persons, then the bishop may add the following prayer immediately after the 'Gloria in excelsis':

Blessed be thy name, O Lord, that it hath pleased thee to put it into the heart of thy servant *N.* to erect this house for thy honour and worship. Bless, O Lord, him, his family, and substance, and accept this his pious charitable work; remember him concerning this, wipe not out this kindness that he hath shewed for thy house, and the offices thereof; and grant that all they who shall enjoy the benefit of this pious work, may shew forth their thankfulness by making a right use of it to the glory of thy blessed name, through Jesus Christ our Lord. Amen.

Prevent us, O Lord, etc.

The peace of God, etc.

When the service in church is finished, let the bishop and clergy with the people go into the churchyard, and standing in some convenient place, let the bishop say the following prayers:

O God, who hast taught us in thy holy word that there is a difference between the spirit of a beast, that goeth downward to the earth, and the spirit of a man, which ascendeth up to God, who gave it; and likewise hast taught that the bodies of thy saints are committed to the ground in sure and certain hope of the resurrection to eternal life; accept, we beseech thee, this charitable work of ours in separating this portion of ground, that they may rest in peace, and be preserved from all indignities; and give us all grace, that by the frequent instances of mortality we behold, we may learn and seriously consider how frail and uncertain our condition here on earth is, and so number our days, as to apply our hearts unto wisdom; that in the midst of life thinking upon death, and daily preparing ourselves for the judgment that is to follow, we may have our part in the resurrection with him who died for our sins, and rose again for our justification, and now liveth and reigneth with thee and the Holy Ghost, one God, world without end. Amen.

The grace of our Lord Jesus Christ, and the love of God, and the fellowship of the Holy Ghost be with you all evermore. Amen.

If there be only a churchyard to be consecrated adjoining to any church or chapel, let the common service of the day be read in the church or chapel, and at the end thereof let the instrument of donation be read before the bishop in the churchyard, and then let the bishop use the foregoing prayer.

But if the churchyard or burial place be remote from the church or chapel, it shall suffice to use only the prayer before appointed for that purpose, the instrument of donation being first read.

(Printed in T. Wilkins, *Concilia Magnae Britanniae et Hiberniae,* 4 vols (1737), IV 668–9.)

Thanksgiving for Harvest, 1862

Proper Psalms: 34, 65, 67, 81, 103, 104, 136, 144, 145, 147, 150.

Proper Lessons: Genesis 8 : 15–22 ; 9 : 8–16 ; Deuteronomy 8 : 7–20 ; 26 : 1–11 ; 28 : 1–14 ; 32 : 7–19 ; 33 : 7–29 ; Isaiah 28 : 23–29 ; Hosea 2 : 14–23.

COLLECTS

One or more of the three following Collects shall be used, instead of the Collect of the Day. But on Sundays and Holy Days, the Collect of the Day shall be first read.

O Almighty and everlasting God, Who hast given unto us the fruits of the earth in their season ; Grant us grace to use the same to Thy glory, the relief of those that need, and our own comfort, through Jesus Christ, Who is the living Bread which cometh down from Heaven and giveth life unto the world ; to Whom, with Thee and the Holy Ghost, be all honour and glory, world without end. Amen. *Or this.*

O Almighty God and Heavenly Father ; we glorify Thee, that Thou hast again fulfilled to us Thy gracious promise, that while the earth remaineth, seed-time and harvest shall not fail. We bless Thee for the kindly fruits of the earth. Teach us, we beseech Thee, to remember, that it is not by bread alone that man doth live ; and grant us evermore to feed on Him Who is the true Bread which cometh down from Heaven, Jesus Christ our Lord, to

Whom with Thee, O Father, and Thee, O Holy Ghost, be honour and glory for ever and ever. Amen.

Or the Collect of the Twenty-fifth Sunday after Trinity.

Stir up, we beseech Thee, O Lord, the wills of Thy faithful people; that they, plenteously bringing forth the fruit of good works, may of Thee be plenteously rewarded; through Jesus Christ our Lord. Amen.

A Prayer for Grace and Glory.

O Lord, we pray Thee, sow the seed of Thy Word in our hearts, and send down upon us Thy heavenly grace, that we may bring forth the fruits of the Spirit, and at the Great Day may be gathered by Thy holy Angels into Thy Garner; through Jesus Christ our Lord. Amen.

A Prayer for Christian Missions.

O Almighty God, Whose dearly beloved Son, after His resurrection from the dead, did send His Apostles into all the world to preach the Gospel to every creature; Hear us, we beseech Thee, O Lord, and look upon the fields now white unto harvest; bless those labouring for Thee in distant lands, and prosper Thou their handiwork; send forth more labourers into Thy harvest to gather fruit unto life eternal; and grant us grace to labour with them in prayers and offerings, that we, together with them, may rejoice before Thee; through Jesus Christ our Lord. Amen.

Then a Prayer may be said for a joyful Resurrection, as follows.

O Merciful God, the Father of our Lord Jesus Christ, Who is the Resurrection and the Life; we meekly beseech Thee to raise us from the death of sin unto the life of righteousness; that, when we shall depart this life, we may rest in Him; and that our mortal bodies, having been sown in weakness, may be raised in power, through the merits and mediation of Him Who is the First-fruits of them that slept, and Who died and was buried, and rose again for us, Jesus Christ, Thy Son our Lord. Amen.

After the General Thanksgiving, which shall always be used on this occasion, shall be said the following.

O most merciful Father, Who of thy gracious goodness hast heard the devout prayers of Thy Church, and hast granted us to gather in the kindly fruits of the earth in their season; we give Thee humble thanks for this Thy bounty, beseeching Thee to continue Thy lovingkindness towards us, that our land may yield her increase; through Jesus Christ our Lord. Amen.

Or this.

O Lord God of Hosts, Who dwellest in the high and holy place, and yet hast respect unto the lowly; Who makest Thy sun to rise on the evil and on the good, and sendest rain on the just and on the unjust; Who by Thy mighty power dost order all things in heaven and earth; we yield Thee hearty thanks that Thou hast safely brought us to the season of harvest, visiting the earth and blessing it, and crowning the year with Thy goodness: we praise Thee for the fruits of the ground which Thou hast bestowed upon us, filling our hearts with food and gladness. For these and all Thy mercies we laud and magnify Thy glorious Name; beseeching Thee to give unto us the increase of all spiritual gifts, the bright light of the Sun of Righteousness, and the dew of Thy heavenly blessing; and so plant us here in the house of the Lord, that we may flourish everlastingly in the courts of the house of our God; through Jesus Christ our Lord, to Whom with Thee and the Holy Ghost be all honour and glory, now and for evermore. Amen.

THE ORDER OF THE ADMINISTRATION OF THE LORD'S SUPPER, OR HOLY COMMUNION

Instead of the Collect of the Day, shall be used one of the Collects provided above for Morning and Evening Prayer.
The Epistle: 1 Thessalonians 5 : 14–24.
The Gospel: Matthew 13 : 36–44 *or* John 6 : 5–15.

The 'Shortened Services' Act, 1872

2. The shortened Order for Morning Prayer or for Evening Prayer, specified in the schedule to this Act, may, on any day except Sunday, Christmas Day, Ash Wednesday, Good Friday, and Ascension Day, be used, if in a cathedral, in addition to, and if in a church in lieu of, the Order for Morning Prayer or for Evening Prayer respectively prescribed by the Book of Common Prayer.

3. Upon any special occasion approved by the ordinary there may be used in any cathedral or church a special form of service approved by the ordinary, so that there be not introduced into such service anything, except anthems or hymns, which does not form part of the Holy Scriptures or Book of Common Prayer.

4. An additional form of service varying from any form prescribed by the Book of Common Prayer may be used at any hour on any Sunday or holy-day in any cathedral or church in which there are duly read, said, or sung as required by law on such Sunday or holy-day at some other hour or hours the Order for Morning Prayer, the Litany, such part of the Order for the Administration of the Lord's Supper or Holy Communion as is required to be read on Sundays and holy-days if there be no Communion, and the Order for Evening Prayer, so that there be not introduced into such additional service any portion of the Order for the Administration of the Lord's Supper or Holy Communion, or anything, except anthems or hymns, which does not form part of the Holy Scriptures or Book of Common Prayer . . .

5. Whereas doubts have arisen as to whether the following

forms of service, that is to say, the Order for Morning Prayer, the Litany, and the Order for the Administration of the Lord's Supper or Holy Communion, may be used as separate services, and it is expedient to remove such doubts : Be it therefore enacted and declared that any such forms of service may be used together or in varying order as separate services, or that the Litany may be said after the third collect in the Order for Evening Prayer, either in lieu of or in addition to the use of the Litany in the Order for Morning Prayer, without prejudice nevertheless to any legal powers vested in the ordinary ; and any of the said forms of service may be used with or without the preaching of a sermon or lecture, or the reading of a homily.

6. Whereas doubts have arisen as to whether a sermon or lecture may be preached without the common prayers and services appointed by the Book of Common Prayer for the time of day being previously read, and it is expedient to remove such doubts : Be it therefore enacted and declared, that a sermon or lecture may be preached without the common prayers or services appointed by the Book of Common Prayer being read before it is preached, so that such sermon or lecture be preceded by any service authorized by this Act, or by the Bidding Prayer, or by a Collect taken from the Book of Common Prayer, with or without the Lord's Prayer . . .

The Schedule authorizes the following omissions from Morning or Evening Prayer:
The Exhortation, 'Dearly beloved brethren . . .'
Venite
All the Psalms appointed but one
One of the Lessons
One of the Canticles
The Lesser Litany and the second Lord's Prayer
The Prayers for the Queen, the Royal Family, and the Clergy.

Rubrics on Reservation, 1911–28

1911   The bishops' proposals of 1911 (report no. 427).
1917   A memorandum drawn up by the bishops in July 1917 and made public in 1918; full text in Bell, *Randall Davidson*, II 813–14.
1923   *Revised Prayer Book (Alternative Services) Measure* (N.A. 84).
1924   The rubrics substituted by the House of Clergy (C.A. 158).
1927} The Book of Common Prayer with the additions and
1928} deviations proposed in those years.

1911

When the Holy Communion may not by reason of grave difficulty be celebrated at the sick person's house, the Priest may (with the consent of the sick person) on any day when there is a celebration of the Holy Communion in the church set apart at the open Communion so much of the consecrated Bread and Wine as shall serve for the sick person, and so many as shall communicate with him (if there be any), and, the open Communion being ended, he shall, on the same day and with as little delay as may be, go and minister the same....

If the consecrated Bread and Wine be from any urgent cause not taken immediately to the sick person, they shall be kept in such place and after such manner as the Ordinary shall direct, so that they be not used for any other purpose whatsoever....

1917

II. We decline to go beyond the limitations with respect to Reservation to which the two Convocations in their Upper Houses have respectively agreed, and cannot recognize permanent Reservation as covered by the terms of either resolution.

1923

But when the Holy Communion cannot reverently or without grave difficulty be celebrated in private, and also when there are several sick persons in the parish desirous to receive the Communion on the same day, it shall be lawful for the Priest (with the consent of the sick person or persons), on any day when there is a celebration of the Holy Communion in the church, to set apart at the open Communion so much of the consecrated Bread and Wine as shall serve the sick person (or persons), and so many as shall communicate with him (if there be any). And, the open Communion ended, he shall, on the same day and with as little delay as may be, go and minister the same. If the consecrated Bread and Wine be from any urgent cause not taken immediately to the sick person, they shall be kept in such place and after such manner as the Ordinary shall direct, so that they be not used for any other purpose whatsoever. . . .

When the aforesaid provision is not sufficient to secure that any communicant at his last hour should be able to receive the Holy Communion, the Curate, with the permission of the Ordinary, given in accordance with the Canon, or such rules as may be from time to time made by the Archbishops and Bishops in their Convocations, may make further provision to meet the needs of the sick and dying.

1924

According to long-existing custom in the Catholic Church, the priest may reserve so much of the Consecrated Gifts as may be required for the Communion of the sick and others who could not be present at the celebration in church, and for this purpose only.

The consecrated Bread and Wine so reserved shall be reserved, kept, and administered in all respects in accordance with such rules as shall be framed by the Archbishop and Bishops of the Province or with Canons lawfully passed by the Convocations of the Province and (subject to such Rules and Canons) with the directions of the Bishop ; nor shall any part of the consecrated Bread or Wine be reserved, kept, or administered otherwise than as may be prescribed by such Rules, Canons, and Directions.

1927

When the Holy Communion . . . (*as in 1923*) . . . minister the same.

If further provision be needed in order to secure that any sick person may not lack the benefit of the most comfortable Sacrament of the Body and Blood of Christ, the Priest, if licensed by the Bishop so to do, may, to that end, when the Holy Communion is celebrated in the church, reserve so much of the consecrated Bread and Wine as is needed for the purpose. And the Bishop shall grant such licence if satisfied of the need, unless in any particular case he see good reason to the contrary.

The consecrated Bread and Wine set apart under either of the two preceding rubrics shall be reserved only for the Communion of the Sick, shall be administered in both kinds, and shall be used for no other purpose whatever. There shall be no service or ceremony in connexion with the Sacrament

N2

so reserved, nor shall it be exposed or removed except in order to be received in Communion, or otherwise reverently consumed. All other questions that may arise concerning such Reservation shall be determined by rules, framed by the Archbishop and Bishops of the Province, or by Canons lawfully made by the Convocation of the Province, and subject to any such rules and Canons, by the directions of the Bishop.

RULES

1. The consecrated Bread and Wine set apart under the Rubricks of the Alternative Order of the Communion of the Sick shall be reserved in an Aumbry set in the North Wall of the Sanctuary or of the Chapel; or, if need be, shall be reserved in some other place approved by the Bishop.

2. The Aumbry shall consist of a safe firmly fixed into the wall and provided with an adequate lock, the key of which shall be deposited in a secure place accessible only to those who have the right to move the consecrated Bread and Wine.

3. The receptacle in which the consecrated Bread and Wine are reserved shall be kept locked, and the door shall only be opened when it is necessary to move or replace the consecrated Elements for the purpose of Communion or renewal.

4. The consecrated Bread and Wine shall be renewed at least once a week.

5. The manner in which the Reserved Sacrament is to be conveyed to the Sick is to be subject to the direction of the Bishop.

1928

When the Holy Communion . . . (*as in 1923 and 1927*) . . . minister the same.

If the Bishop is satisfied that in connexion with hospitals, or in time of common sickness, or in the special circumstances of any particular parish, the provisions of the preceding rubrick are not sufficient, and that there is need of further provision in order that sick and dying persons may not lack the benefit of the most comfortable Sacrament of the Body and Blood of Christ, he may to that end give his licence to the Priest, to reserve at the open Communion so much of the consecrated Bread and Wine as is needed for the purpose. Whenever such licence is granted or refused, the Minister, or the people as represented in the Parochial Church Council, may refer the question to the Archbishop and Bishops of the province.

The consecrated Bread and Wine ... (*as in 1927*) ... reverently consumed.

The consecrated Bread and Wine thus set apart shall be reserved in an aumbry or safe. The aumbry shall (according as the Bishop shall direct) be set in the North or South wall of the sanctuary or of any chapel thereof, or, if need be, in the wall of some other part of the church approved by the Bishop, provided that it shall not be immediately behind or above a Holy Table. The door of the aumbry shall be kept locked, and opened only when it is necessary to move or replace the consecrated Elements for the purposes of Communion or renewal. The consecrated Bread and Wine shall be renewed at least once a week. . . .

Proposals for an Alternative Canon, 1920–8

1920   The Frere-Drury Canon agreed upon at the Conference of November 1919 and accepted by Convocation in 1920 (Bell, *Randall Davidson*, II 1326 n 3 ; Frere, *Correspondence*, 75–80).

1923   Revised Prayer Book (Alternative Services) Measure (N.A. 84).

1924 A⎫ The two Canons put forward by a conference in
1924 B⎭ the Jerusalem Chamber, November 1923, and accepted by the Houses of Clergy and Laity (C.A. 158).

1926   The Canon agreed upon at the Farnham Conference in April 1926 (Frere, *Correspondence*, 104–5).

1927/8 The Book of Common Prayer with the additions and deviations proposed in those years.

1920	1923	1924A	1924B	1926	1927/8
Exordium	Exordium	Exordium[1]	Exordium[1,2]	Exordium[1,2]	Exordium[1]
'Hear us...'	'Hear us...'	'Hear us...'[3]	—	'Hear us...'[3]	—
Words of Institution	Words of Institution	Words of Institution	Words of Institution	Words of Institution	Words of Institution
Anamnesis	Anamnesis	Anamnesis[4]	Anamnesis	Anamnesis[4]	Anamnesis[4]
—	—	—	Prayer of Oblation	Prayer of Oblation[5]	Epiclesis[3]
Epiclesis	—	—	Epiclesis[6]	Epiclesis[7]	Prayer of Oblation
—	Prayer of Oblation	Prayer of Oblation	—	—	
Lord's Prayer	Lord's Prayer	Lord's Prayer	Lord's Prayer	Lord's Prayer	Lord's Prayer
Communion	Communion	Communion	Communion	Communion	Communion
Prayer of Oblation		—			
Prayer of Thanksgiving	Prayer of Thanksgiving	Prayer of Thanksgiving	Prayer of Thanksgiving	Prayer of Thanksgiving[8]	Prayer of Thanksgiving

1. Beginning: 'All glory [and thanksgiving] be to thee'.
2. Including: 'to take our nature upon him'.
3. Including: 'bless and sanctify [both us and, 1927/8] these thy [gifts and, 1924 A] creatures of bread and wine, that they may be unto us the Body and Blood...'
4. Including: 'celebrate and make [set forth, 1927/8] ... the memorial...'
5. Much abbreviated.
6. Including: 'bless and sanctify both us and these thy gifts...': that we ... may be partakers of his most blessed Body and Blood....
7. On the communicants.
8. Including: 'Here we offer and present unto thee...'

SUMMARY

There is agreement between all the proposals on including six elements in the same order :
Exordium
Words of Institution
Anamnesis
Lord's Prayer
Communion
Prayer of Thanksgiving
All agree on including some form of epiclesis, but disagree on what form and where to put it. The position of the Prayer of Oblation is also controversial.

Prayer Book (Alternative and Other Services) Measure, 1965

1. (1) In the case of any of the forms of Service prescribed by the Book of Common Prayer it shall be lawful to use ... such form or forms of Service alternative to the form of Service so prescribed, and deviating (whether by way of addition, omission, substitution or otherwise) from the form of Service so prescribed, as may be approved by the Convocations of Canterbury and York for experimental use, every such form of Service being in their opinion neither contrary to, nor indicative of any departure from, the doctrine of the Church of England. ...

(3) An alternative form of Service approved under this section may be used only during the period stated in the approval which period shall not exceed seven years from the date of the approval:

Provided that:

(*a*) ... the aforesaid period may from time to time be extended or renewed for further periods ... not exceeding ... seven years;

(*b*) no period ... shall continue beyond the expiry of fourteen years from the date of the coming into effect of the first approval ...

3. A form or draft of a form of Service approved ... under this Measure may not be used ... in any Church in a parish without the agreement of the Parochial Church Council of the parish ... or in the case of Services known as Occasional Offices if any of the persons concerned objects beforehand to its use.

4. (1) It shall be lawful to use in any Cathedral or Church or elsewhere forms of Service approved by the Convocations of Canterbury and York for use within their respective provinces on occasions for which no provision is made in the Book of Common Prayer . . .

(2) It shall be lawful to use in any Cathedral or Church or elsewhere forms of Service which, subject to any regulations made from time to time by the Convocation of the Province, may be approved by the Ordinary for use to meet circumstances for which no provision is made in the Book of Common Prayer . . .

5. Subject to the provisions of this Measure the Minister may in his discretion make and use variations which are not of substantial importance in any form of Service prescribed by the Book of Common Prayer or authorized for use under this Measure according to particular circumstances.

6. Subject to the provisions of this Measure and to any regulations made from time to time by the Convocation of the Province, the Minister may on occasions for which no provision is made in the Book of Common Prayer or under section four of this Measure use forms of Service considered suitable by him for those occasions. . . .

Bibliography

ABBREVIATIONS

ACC	Alcuin Club Collections
CA	Church Assembly (Reports of)
CQR	*Church Quarterly Review*
EETS	Early English Text Society
HBS	Henry Bradshaw Society
JEH	*Journal of Ecclesiastical History*
JTS	*Journal of Theological Studies*
LACT	Library of Anglo-Catholic Theology
NA	National Assembly (Reports of)
PS	Parker Society
SJT	*Scottish Journal of Theology*
SS	Surtees Society
STC	*Short Title Catalogue*

The figures ¹ and ² refer to 1st and 2nd editions respectively. Place of publication is not given for books published in London.

PART I—TEXTS

CHAPTER I

BREVIARIES

The Hereford Breviary (1505), ed. W. H. Frere and L. E. G. Brown (1904 & 1911: HBS XXVI, XL, XLVI).

Breviarium ad usum insignis Ecclesiae Sarum (1531), ed. F. Procter and C. Wordsworth, 3 vols (Cambridge 1879, 1882, 1886).

—— English translation of the Office for Advent Sunday in Documents, p. 292.

Breviarium ad usum insignis Ecclesiae Eboracensis (1493), ed. S. W. Lawley (Durham 1880 & 1883: SS LXXI, LXXV).

CONSUETUDINARIES

The Use of Sarum, ed. W. H. Frere (Cambridge 1898 & 1901). Vol. I, Consuetudinary; vol. II, Ordinal.

MANUALS

Manuale ad usum percelebris Ecclesiae Sarisburiensis (1543), ed. A. J. Collins (1960: HBS XCI).

—— ed. W. Maskell, in *Monumenta Ritualia Ecclesiae Anglicanae* ¹(1846) 1 3–160; ²(Oxford 1882) 1 3–227.

—— ed. W. G. Henderson, in *York Manual*, below, App. 1 (incomplete).

—— English translation of the Orders for Baptism and Confirmation in J. D. C. Fisher, *Christian Initiation* (1965: ACC XLVII) 158–181.

E. C. Whitaker, *The Baptismal Liturgy* (1965) 74–89.

Manuale et Processionale ad usum insignis Ecclesiae Eboracensis (1509 & 1516), ed. W. G. Henderson (Durham 1875: SS LXIII).

MISSALS

Missale ad usum percelebris Ecclesiae Herfordensis (1502), ed. W. G. Henderson (Leeds 1874).

Missale ad usum insignis et praeclarae Ecclesiae Sarum, ed. F. H. Dickinson (Burntisland 1883). Collation of many printed editions.

—— ed. J. W. Legg (Oxford 1916). From MS of *c.* 1250.

—— English translation by F. E. Warren, 2 vols (1913: ACC XI).

—— English translation of Mass for Advent Sunday in Documents, p. 269.

Missale ad usum insignis Ecclesiae Eboracensis, ed. W. H. Henderson (Durham 1874: SS, LIX, LX). Collation of all MSS and the five printed editions.

W. Maskell, *The Ancient Liturgy of the Church of England* (¹1846; ²Oxford 1882). The Missals of Sarum, Hereford, York, 'Bangor', and Rome in parallel columns.

ORDINALS

Ordinale Exon, ed. J. N. Dalton (1909, 1925, 1940: HBS XXXVII, XXXVIII, LXIII, LXXIX).

Ordinale Sarum sive Directorium Sacerdotum, ed. W. Cooke and C. Wordsworth (1901, 1902: HBS XX, XXII).

See also Consuetudinaries, above.

The Tracts of Clement Maydestone, ed. C. Wordsworth (1894: HBS VII). *Crede michi* and *Defensorium Directorii*.

—— *Defensorium Directorii*, ed. W. Maskell, in *Monumenta Ritualia Ecclesiae Anglicanae*, ¹(1846) II 337–51; ²(Oxford 1882) III 345–365.

PONTIFICALS

The Pontifical of Egbert, Archbishop of York, A.D. 732–766, ed. W. Greenwell (Durham 1853: SS XXVII).
Liber Pontificalis Christopheri Bainbridge, Archiepiscopi Eboracensis, ed. W. G. Henderson (Durham 1875: SS LXI).
The Canterbury Benedictional, ed R. M. Woolley (1917: HBS LI).
The Pontifical of Magdalen College, ed. H. A. Wilson (1910: HBS XXXIX). A Canterbury book containing the archiepiscopal Use.

PRIMERS, ETC.

W. Maskell (ed.), in *Monumenta Ritualia Ecclesiae Anglicanae* ¹(1846) II 1–178; ²(Oxford 1882) III 1–183. From MS in English, *c.* 1410.
H. Littlehales (ed.), *The Prymer or Prayer Book of the Lay People in the Middle Ages* (1891). Vol. I from MS in English, *c.* 1400; vol. II, collation of thirteen MSS, 1350–1450.
H. Littlehales (ed.), *The Prymer or Lay Folks' Prayer Book* (1895 & 1897: EETS CV, CIX). Vol. I, from MS in English, *c.* 1425; vol. II includes essay by E. Bishop, 'On the Origin of the Prymer'.
C. Wordsworth (ed.), *Horae Eboracenses* (1536) (Durham 1920: SS CXXXII).
E. Hoskins, *Horae beatae Mariae Virginis, or Sarum and York Primers* (1901). Summarizes the contents of all printed Primers.

PROCESSIONALS

Processionale ad usum insignis ac praeclarae Ecclesiae Sarum (1508), ed. W. G. Henderson (Leeds 1882).
—— ed. C. Wordsworth, in *Ceremonies and Processions of the Cathedral Church of Salisbury* (Cambridge 1901). From MS of fifteenth century.
York Processional, see *Manuale* ... (above).

OTHER TEXTS REFERRED TO

T. F. Simmons (ed.), *The Lay-Folk's Mass-Book* (1879: EETS LXXI). Thirteenth-century English devotional texts.

J. W. Legg (ed.), *Tracts on the Mass* (1904: HBS xxvII). Includes B. Langforde, *Meditations in the time of Mass.*

J. Mirk, *Festial*, ed. T. Erbe (1905: EETS, Extra Series xcvI). Sermons for the Church year.

F. Clark, *Eucharistic Sacrifice and the Reformation* ([1]1960; [2]1967) 543–60. Generous selection of popular expositions of the theology of the Mass.

The Greater Excommunication, in T. Cranmer, *Works*, ed. J. E. Cox (Cambridge 1846: PS) II 281–2.

—— Other forms in W. Maskell, *Monumenta Ritualia Ecclesiae Anglicanae*, [1](1846) II 286–305; [2](Oxford 1882) III 309–30.

The following books and articles are relevant; the numbers refer to Parts II and III of this Bibliography.

Books: 3, 13, 14 (pp. 78–93), 33 (pp. 1–21), 34 (pp. 594–608), 38 (pp. 59–80), 46, 50, 51 (pp. 140–232), 55, 81 (pp. 68–89), 92, 93, 94, 104 (pp. 91–203), 110, 112, 113, 117.
Articles: 135, 151.

CHAPTER 2

COLLECTIONS

Æ. L. Richter, *Die evangelischen Kirchenordnungen des sechszehnten Jahrhunderts*, 2 vols (Leipzig [1]1846, [2]1871).

E. Sehling, *Die evangelischen Kirchenordnungen des xvi. Jahrhunderts*, 13 vols so far, still in publication (Leipzig 1902–13; Tübingen, 1955–).

J. Beckmann, *Quellen zur Geschichte des Christlichen Gottesdienstes* (Gütersloh 1956).

B. J. Kidd, *Documents illustrative of the Continental Reformation* (Oxford [1]1911, [2]1967).

LUTHER

Richter (above) 1 12–10, 35–40.
Sehling (above) 1 3–24.
ed. O. Dietz (Munich 1940). Offprint from Weimar Edition of *Works*.
ed. H. Lietzmann (Bonn 1909). *Liturgische Texte*, IV.
—— English translation in *Works*, ed. U. S. Leopold, LIII (Philadelphia 1965).
—— *Formula Missae* and *Deutsche Messe* in Beckmann (above) 122–133.
—— English translation in Kidd (above) 193–202.
—— English translation of Baptism and Matrimony in Documents, pp. 318–23.

ZWINGLI

De Canone Missae Epicheiresis, in *Werke* (Corpus Reformatorum, LXXXIX: Leipzig 1908) II 552–608.
Aktion oder Brauch des Nachtmahls in Beckmann, 142–8; *Werke* (Corpus Reformatorum, XCI: Leipzig 1915) IV 1–24.
—— Latin version in Kidd, 444–8.
Baptism Service: English translation in Kidd, 423–4.

BUCER

F. Hubert, *Die Strassburger liturgischen Ordnungen* (Göttingen 1900). Collation of forms from 1524 to 1561.
—— English translations in W. D. Maxwell, *An Outline of Christian Worship* (Oxford 1936) 91–7 (1525 form; Hubert, C²), 102–10 (1539 form; Hubert, K).
M. Bucer, *Grund und Ursach . . . der Neuerungen an dem Nachtmahl des Herren* (1524), in *Deutsche Schriften*, ed. R. Stupperich (Gütersloh 1960) 1 185–278.
—— English translation of description of service in Documents, p. 324; Maxwell, 100–1.

KIRCHENORDNUNGEN

Brandenburg and Nürnberg
Richter, 1 176–211.

Sehling, XI 140–205.
—— Communion Service in Beckmann, 137–41.
—— English translation in Documents, pp. 327–32.

Albertine Saxony
Richter, I 307–15 (1539 only).
Sehling, I 264–81 (1539 and 1540).

Electoral Brandenburg
Richter, I 323–34.
Sehling, III 39–90.

Pfalz-Neuburg
Richter, I 362–7.
Sehling, XIII 46–99.
—— English translation of the 'Canon' prayer in Documents, p. 333.

Calenberg and Göttingen
Richter, II 26–30.
Sehling, VI 788–843.

Hesse-Cassel
Richter, I 295–306.
Sehling, VIII 113–44.

CALVIN

La Forme des Prières in *Joannis Calvini Opera Selecta*, ed. P. Barth and D. Scheuner (Munich 1952) II 1–58 (1542 edition).
—— Latin version in Kidd, 615–28.
—— Communion Service in Beckmann, 149–65.

COLOGNE

Hermann von Wied, *Einfaltigs Bedencken* (Bonn 1543).
Richter, II 30–54.
—— Latin version, *Simplex ac Pia Deliberatio* (Bonn 1545). No modern edition.

—— English translation of *Deliberatio, A Simple and Religious Consultation* ([1]1547, [21]1548: STC 13213, 13214).
—— Baptism Service in T. M. Fallow, *The Order of Baptism* (1838), 29–54.
—— Communion Service, in Documents, pp. 334–57.

QUIÑONES

Breviarium Romanum a Francisco Cardinali Quignonio editum, ed. J. W. Legg (Cambridge 1888). Text of 1535 edition, without introduction or notes.
The Second Recension of the Quignon Breviary, ed. J. W. Legg (1908 & 1912: HBS XXXV, XLII). Vol. I, text of 1536 edition; Vol. II, introduction and notes, dealing with 1535 edition as well.

Books: 13, 14 (pp. 94–179), 23, 34 (pp. 625–39), 39, 72, 75, 76, 98 (pp. 69–110).
Articles: 121, 158, 160.

CHAPTER 3

[G. Joye], *Hortulus Animae* (Strasbourg 1530; no reprint).
Three Primers put forth in the Reign of Henry VIII, ed. E. Burton, (Oxford 1834) 1–103, Marshall's (1535); 305–436, Hilsey's (1539); 437–527, The King's (1545); incomplete.
Formularies of Faith put forth by authority during the Reign of Henry VIII, ed. C. Lloyd (Oxford 1825) 1–20, *Ten Articles* (1536); 21–211, *The Bishops' Book* (1537); 213–377, *The King's Book* (1543).
—— *The King's Book,* ed. T. A. Lacey (1932).
Injunctions (1538), ed. W. H. Frere, *Visitation Articles and Injunctions of the Period of the Reformation* (1910: ACC XIV, XV, XVI) II 34–43.
—— ed. H. Gee and W. J. Hardy, in *Documents illustrative of English Church History* (1896) 275–81.
The Rationale of Ceremonial 1540–1543, ed. C. S. Cobb (1910: ACC XVIII).
—— in J. Collier, *Ecclesiastical History,* part II, book III, ed. T. Lathbury (1852) V 104–22.

Cranmer's Liturgical Projects, ed. J. W. Legg (1915: HBS L). First scheme, 3–22; second scheme, 115–53; valuable introduction.

—— ed. F. A. Gasquet and E. Bishop, in *Edward VI and the Book of Common Prayer* ([1]1891) 312–94 (appendixes I–IV; incomplete).

The 1544 Litany, ed. J. E. Hunt, *Cranmer's First Litany, 1544, and Merbecke's Book of Common Prayer Noted, 1550* (1939). Facsimile of the first edition, including the Exhortation.

—— ed. W. K. Clay, in *Private Prayers put forth by authority during the Reign of Queen Elizabeth* (Cambridge 1851: PS) 563–76. See also Documents, pp. 358–61.

Injunctions (1547) ed. W. H. Frere, *Visitation Articles* (above) II 114–30.

—— ed. E. Cardwell, in *Documentary Annals of the Reformed Church of England* (Oxford 1839) I 4–24.

—— also in T. Cranmer, *Works*, ed. J. E. Cox (Cambridge 1846: PS) II 498–504.

The Order of the Communion (1548), ed. H. A. Wilson (1908: HBS XXXIV). Facsimile; includes translations into Latin, by A. Aless, and German, by M. Coverdale, of 1548.

—— ed. J. Ketley, in *The Two Liturgies, A.D. 1549, and A.D. 1552* (Cambridge 1844: PS) 1–8.

—— ed. W. Maskell, in *The Ancient Liturgy of the Church of England* ([1]1846, [2]Oxford 1882) 294–302.

See also Documents, pp. 364–6.

Books: 13, 17, 19, 33, 35, 36, 47, 52, 62, 63, 72, 86, 93, 94, 100 (pp. 89–154), 103, 105, 112, 113.
Articles: 122, 150, 156, 157, 169.

CHAPTER 4

The Book of the Common Prayer and Administration of the Sacraments, and other Rites and Ceremonies of the Church: after the Use of the Church of England (1549), ed. F. E. Brightman, *The English Rite*, 2 vols ([1]1915, [2]1921). Reproduces 'verbatim, litteratim, and punctatim' the Whitchurche issue of June 1549.

—— ed. E. C. Ratcliff, in *The First and Second Prayer Books of Edward VI* (1949: Everyman Library). The Whitchurche issue of March 1549.

—— ed. J. Ketley, in *The Two Liturgies, A.D. 1549 and A.D. 1552* (Cambridge 1844 : PS). The Whitchurche issue of May 1549, with modernized spelling, collated with five other issues.

—— ed. J. Parker, in *The First Prayer-Book of Edward VI* (Oxford 1877).

—— ed. W. B., in *The First Prayer Book of King Edward VI, 1549* (1887).

The Clerk's Book of 1549, ed. J. W. Legg (1903: HBS xxv).

J. Merbecke, *The Book of Common Prayer Noted* (1550), ed. J. E. Hunt, *Cranmer's First Litany, 1544, and Merbecke's Book of Common Prayer Noted, 1550* (1939) facsimile. Editions in modern notation are usually adapted for use with the 1662 or 1928 services.

The Form and Manner of Making and Consecrating of Archbishops, Bishops, Priests, and Deacons (1550). Included in all modern editions of the 1549 Book listed above.

T. Cranmer, *Works*, ed. J. E. Cox, 2 vols (Cambridge 1844 & 1846: PS).

—— ed. T. Jenkyns, 4 vols (Oxford 1833).

—— *A Defence of the True and Catholic Doctrine* . . . (1549), in *The Work of Thomas Cranmer*, ed. G. Duffield (Appleford 1964), 45–231, with interesting introduction by J. I. Packer, x–xli.

Missale mixtum . . . dictum Mozarabes (1500), ed. A. Leslie (1755), in J. P. Migne, *Patrologia Latina*, LXXXV.

M. Bucer, 'De Ordinatione Legitime Ministrorum Ecclesiae revocanda', in *Scripta Anglicana*, ed. C. Hubert (1577) 238–59.

The Debate in the House of Lords, December 1548, is in F. A. Gasquet and E. Bishop, *Edward VI and the Book of Common Prayer* ([1]1891) 395–443 (appendix v).

Books: 13, 15, 16, 17, 20, 33, 35, 36, 38, 41, 52, 62, 63, 69, 72, 77, 78, 80, 85, 86, 94, 95, 99, 105.
Articles: 121, 131, 138, 147, 148, 166, 169, 170, 174, 179, 180.

CHAPTER 5

The Book of Common Prayer and Administration of the Sacraments and other Rites and Ceremonies in the Church of England, 1552. Included with all modern editions of the 1549 Book listed above, all of which print Whitchurche's second issue of 1552; Ketley collates it with three other issues.

A Primer, or Book of Private Prayer (1553), ed. J. Ketley, in *The Two Liturgies* (Cambridge 1844: PS) 357–484.

A Short Catechism (1553); *Forty-two Articles* (1552), in ibid. 485–582.

Chronicle of the Gray Friars of London (1189–1556), ed. J. G. Nichols (1852: Camden Society, LIII).

C. Wriothesley, *A Chronicle of England during the reigns of the Tudors from 1485 to 1559*, ed. W. D. Hamilton, 2 vols (1875 & 1877: Camden Society, New Series XI, XX).

H. Robinson (ed.), *Original Letters relative to the English Reformation*, 2 vols (Cambridge 1846 & 1847: PS).

N. Pocock (ed.), *Troubles connected with the Prayer Book of 1549* (1884: Camden Society, NS XXXVII).

M. Bucer, 'Censura super Libro Sacrorum', in *Scripta Anglicana*, ed. C. Hubert (1577) 456–503.

—— Useful summaries in Brightman, I cxliii, cxliv; Proctor and Frere, 73–6; Smyth, *Cranmer and the Reformation under Edward VI*, 237–43.

J. Hooper, *Early Writings*, ed. S. Carr (Cambridge 1853: PS). Includes the sermons on Jonah (1550).

J. Hooper, *Later Writings*, ed. C. Nevinson (Cambridge 1852: PS).

J. à Lasco, *Forma ac Ratio tota ecclesiastici Ministerii* (1551), ed. A. Kuyper, *Johannis à Lasco Opera* (Amsterdam 1866) II 1–277.

V. Poullain, *Liturgia Sacra* (1551). No modern edition.

—— Excerpts in Procter and Frere, 86–8.

—— 1554 edition, Richter (see Chapter 2) II 149–60.

Books: 13, 15, 17, 20, 33, 35, 36, 38, 41, 62, 69, 72, 75, 85, 86, 94, 95, 105.

Articles: 123, 128, 134, 139, 147, 148, 150, 169, 170, 174, 179, 180.

CHAPTER 6

A Brieff Discours off the Troubles begonne at Franckford in Germany Anno Domini 1554, abowte the Booke off Common Prayer and Ceremonies (1575), ed. E. Arber (1908).

—— ed. J. Petheram (1846).

The Liturgy of Compromise used in the English Congregation at Frank-fort, ed. G. W. Sprott (Edinburgh 1905) 203–60. Bound with *The Book of Common Prayer*, *1552*, ed. H. Wotherspoon.

J. Calvin (translated by W. Huycke), *The Form of Common Prayers used in the Churches of Geneva* (1550: *STC* 16560).

J. Knox, *The Form of Prayers and Ministration of the Sacraments*, *etc.*, *used in the English Congregation at Geneva* (1556) ed. W. D. Maxwell, *The Liturgical Portions of the Genevan Service Book* ([1]Edinburgh 1931, [2]London 1965).

W. K. Clay (ed.), *Liturgical Services of the Reign of Queen Elizabeth* (Cambridge 1847: PS). Litanies of 1558 and 1559; Prayer Book of 1559; Godly Prayers; *Liber Precum Publicarum*, 1560; Calendar of 1561; Occasional Forms of Prayer, 1560–1601.

—— English translation of 'Commendation of Benefactors' in Documents, pp. 367–9.

E. Benham (ed.), *The Prayer Book of Queen Elizabeth* (Edinburgh 1909). Also includes Calendar of 1561 and a selection of Occasional Forms.

H. Gee, *The Elizabethan Prayer-Book and Ornaments* (1902). Includes the *Device for Alteration of Religion*, 'Guest's Letter', and numerous other documents relating to the year 1559.

W. K. Clay (ed.), *Private Prayers put forth by authority during the Reign of Queen Elizabeth* (Cambridge 1851: PS). Primer, 1559; *Orarium*, 1560; *Preces Privatae*, 1564; Christian Prayers, 1578; Litany, 1544.

Injunctions given by the Queen's Majesty (1559), ed. W. H. Frere, *Visitation Articles* (see Chapter 3) III 8–29.

—— ed. E. Cardwell, in *Documentary Annals* (see Chapter 3) I 178–209.

—— ed. H. Gee and W. J. Hardy, in *Documents* (see Chapter 3) 417–42.

Interpretations and further Considerations, ed. W. M. Kennedy, in *The 'Interpretations' of the Bishops* (1908: Alcuin Club Tracts, VIII).

—— ed. W. H. Frere, in *Visitation Articles*, III 59–73.

—— ed. E. Cardwell, in *Documentary Annals*, I 204–9 (footnotes).

Advertisements partly for due order . . . , ed. W. H. Frere, in *Visitation Articles*, III 171–80.

—— ed. E. Cardwell, in *Documentary Annals*, I 287–97.

—— ed. H. Gee and W. J. Hardy, in *Documents*, 467–75.

A. Nowell, *A Catechism written in Latin*, ed. G. E. Corrie (Cambridge 1853: PS).

H. Robinson (ed.), *The Zurich Letters*, 2 vols (Cambridge 1842 & 1845: PS).

W. H. Frere and C. E. Douglas (ed.), *Puritan Manifestoes* ([1]1907, [2]1954). The two *Admonitions to the Parliament* (1572).

—— Extracts in Documents, pp. 370–4.

The Waldegrave Prayer Book (c. 1584), ed. P. Hall, in *Fragmenta Liturgica* (Bath 1848) 1.

The Middelburgh Prayer Book (1586), ed. P. Hall, in *Reliquiae Liturgicae* (Bath 1847) 1.

R. Hooker, *Of the Laws of Ecclesiastical Polity* (1594, 1597 & 1600). Several modern reprints.

Books: 3, 13, 20, 25, 26, 31, 35, 36, 38, 41, 47, 53, 59, 69, 72, 75, 82, 83, 84, 89, 94, 95, 107, 108.

Articles: 137, 165, 167, 170.

CHAPTER 7

W. Barlow, *The Sun and Substance of the Conference . . . at Hampton Court* (1604), ed. E. Cardwell, *A History of Conferences* (Oxford 1841) 167–212 (with related documents).

Other related documents, ed. R. G. Usher, in *The Reconstruction of the Church of England* (New York and London 1910) II 331–54.

An Abridgment of that book which the Ministers of Lincoln Diocese delivered to His Majesty upon the first of December 1605 (1605: STC 15646).

A Survey of the Book of Common Prayer ([1]1608, [2]1610: STC 16450 & 16451).

L. Andrewes, *Minor Works*, ed. J. Bliss, in *Works*, VI (Oxford 1854: LACT). Includes *Notes on the Book of Common Prayer*, 141–58, and *Preces Privatae*, 223–338.

J. Cosin, *Notes on the Book of Common Prayer*, ed. J. Barrow, in *Works*, V (Oxford 1855: LACT). Contains the three *Series of Notes* and the *Particulars*.

J. Cosin, *A Collection of Private Devotions* (1627), ed. P. G. Stanwood (Oxford 1967).

—— ed. (?), in *Works*, II (Oxford 1845: LACT) 83–334.

G. W. Sprott (ed.), *Scottish Liturgies of the Reign of James VI* (Edinburgh 1901). Contains the draft of 1618, the first draft for the 1637 book, and the second edition of the 1620 Ordinal.

G. Donaldson (ed.), 'A Scottish Liturgy of the Reign of James VI', in *Scottish Historical Society Miscellany*, x (1965) 87–117. Draft of 1616–17.

The Scottish Liturgy of 1637, ed. G. Donaldson, in *The Making of the Scottish Prayer Book of 1637* (Edinburgh 1954) 95–247.

—— ed. P. Hall, in *Reliquiae Liturgicae* (Bath 1847) ii.

—— ed. J. Cooper, in *The Book of Common Prayer . . . for the use of the Church of Scotland* (Edinburgh 1904).

—— Communion Service only, ed. W. J. Grisbrooke, in *Anglican Liturgies of the Seventeenth and Eighteenth Centuries* (1958) 163–182.

—— ed. J. Dowden, in *The Scottish Communion Office of 1764* (²Oxford 1922) 177–85.

W. Laud, *History of the Troubles and Trial*, ed. J. Bliss, in *Works*, iii (Oxford 1853: LACT) 273–463. Laud's account of the Scottish Liturgy and his eucharistic theology.

A Copy of the Proceedings of some worthy and learned Divines (1641), ed. E. Cardwell, in *A History of Conferences* (Oxford 1841) 270–7. The Lords' Committee.

A Directory for the Public Worship of God (1645), ed. T. Leishman, in *The Westminster Directory* (Edinburgh 1901).

—— ed. P. Hall, in *Reliquiae Liturgicae* (Bath 1847), iii.

—— Communion Service only, ed. B. J. Wigan, in *The Liturgy in English* (²Oxford 1964) 185–7.

R. Sanderson, *A Liturgy in Times of Rebellion*, ed. W. K. Jacobson, in *Fragmentary Illustrations of the History of the Book of Common Prayer* (1874) 1–40.

J. Taylor, *An Apology for Authorized and Set Forms of Liturgy* (1649), ed. R. Heber, in *Works* (1828) vii 277–90.

J. Taylor, *A Collection of Offices* (1658), ed. R. Heber, in *Works*, xv 237–389.

—— Communion Service only, ed. W. J. Grisbrooke, in *Anglican Liturgies of the Seventeenth and Eighteenth Centuries* (1958) 183–199.

A. Sparrow, *A Rationale upon the Book of Common Prayer* (1655), ed. J. H. Newman (Oxford 1839).

H. L'Estrange, *The Alliance of Divine Offices* (1659), ed. (?) (Oxford 1846: LACT).

M. Wren, *'Advices'* (1660), ed. W. K. Jacobson, in *Fragmentary Illustrations of the History of the Book of Common Prayer* (1874), 43–109; and see below.

J. Cosin, *Particulars to be considered, explained, and corrected in the Book of Common Prayer* (1660), ed. J. Barrow, in *Works*, v (Oxford 1855: LACT) 502–25; and see below.

The Durham Book, ed. G. J. Cuming (1961). Includes Wren's *'Advices'*, Cosin's *Particulars*, and the *'Fair Copy'*.

The Exceptions against the Book of Common Prayer; The Answer of the Bishops to the Exceptions of the Ministers (1661), ed. G. Gould, in *Documents relating to the Settlement of the Church of England by the Act of Uniformity of 1662* (1862) 111–76 (with several other relevant documents).

—— ed. E. Cardwell, in *A History of Conferences* (Oxford 1841) 303–363.

R. Baxter, *The Reformation of the Liturgy*, ed. P. Hall, in *Reliquiae Liturgicae* (Bath 1847) IV.

'The Fair Copy', ed. G. J. Cuming, in *The Durham Book* (1961) 8–260 (footnotes) and 264–84, 290–2 (text).

—— Communion Service only, ed. W. J. Grisbrooke, in *Anglican Liturgies of the Seventeenth and Eighteenth Centuries* (1958) 353–374.

'The Annexed Book': *Facsimile of the Original Manuscript of the Book of Common Prayer . . .* (1891).

—— ed. F. E. Brightman, in *The English Rite*, 2 vols ([1]1915, [2]1922).

'The Convocation Book': *Facsimile of the Black-letter Prayer-book containing Manuscript Alterations and Additions made in the year 1661 . . .* (1871).

'The State Services', ed. A. P. Perceval, in *The Original Services for the State Holidays* (1838).

I. Walton, *The Life of Dr Robert Sanderson* (1678). Many modern reprints.

'The Sealed Books' (1662), ed. A. J. Stephens, in *The Book of Common Prayer* (1849–54). The definitive printed copies.

P. E. More and F. L. Cross (ed.), *Anglicanism* (1935). Anthology of the 'Caroline Divines'.

V. Staley (ed.), *Hierurgia Anglicana*, 3 vols (1902). Sixteenth- and seventeenth-century evidence for ceremonial.

Books: 2, 3, 11, 13, 20, 21, 25, 26, 35, 36, 37, 41, 42, 59, 69, 72, 84, 85, 94, 95, 108.
Articles: 126, 141, 142, 143, 144, 145, 146, 168, 170, 172, 173.

CHAPTER 8

J. W. Legg (ed.), *English Orders for Consecrating Churches in the Seventeenth Century* (1911: HBS XLI). Numerous forms, including those of Andrewes and Cosin.

The Form of Consecrating of Churches, Chapels, and Churchyards, or Places of Burial (1714), in Documents, pp. 380-5.

A. P. Perceval (ed.), *The Original Services for the State Holidays* (1838). Original and later versions of the 5 November, 30 January, 29 May, and Accession Services.

T. Comber, *A Companion to the Temple* (1672), 7 vols (Oxford 1841).

W. Nicholls, *A Comment on the Book of Common Prayer* (1710).

C. Wheatly, *A Rational Illustration of the Book of Common Prayer of the Church of England* (1710; Oxford 1810, 1819; London 1845, 1848).

The Proposals for Revision of 1689, ed. W. H. Black (1854). Includes the diary of John Williams.

——— ed. J. Taylor (1855). Incomplete, omitting Calendar and Collects.

——— Calamy's summary and other related documents in E. Cardwell, *A History of Conferences* (Oxford 1841) 426–58.

Extracts in Documents, pp. 375-9.

T. Lindsey, *The Book of Common Prayer reformed according to the plan of the late Dr Samuel Clarke* (1774).

——— ed. P. Hall, in *Fragmenta Liturgica* (Bath 1848) VII. Edition of 1791, 'compiled for the use of the English Church at Dunkirk'.

[J. Jones], *Free and Candid Disquisitions relating to the Church of England, and the Means of advancing Religion therein* (1749).

J. Wesley, *The Sunday Service of the Methodists, with other Occasional Services* (1786).

Anon., *An Essay for a Review of the Book of Common Prayer, to which is added a Specimen thereof . . . attempted by an Impartial Hand* (1734).

COLLECTIONS

W. J. GRISBROOKE, *Anglican Liturgies of the Seventeenth and Eighteenth Centuries* (1958: ACC XL). Texts with full commentary, Communion Services only; details below.

P. Hall, *Fragmenta Liturgica*, 7 vols (Bath 1848). Details below.

E. Stephens, *The Liturgy of the Ancients* (1696); *A Complete Form of Liturgy* (n.d.), Grisbrooke, 201–45; Hall, II 1–91.

W. Whiston, *The Liturgy of the Church of England, reduced nearer to the Primitive Standard* (1713), Grisbrooke, 247–61; Hall, III.

J. Henley, *The Primitive Liturgy and the Eucharist* (1727), Grisbrooke, 263–71; Hall, IV 85–119, 149–66.

The Nonjurors' Forms:

A Communion Office taken partly from Primitive Liturgies, and partly from the First English Reformed Common-Prayer-Book, together with Offices for Confirmation and Visitation of the Sick (1718), Grisbrooke, 273–96; Hall, V 1–78.

——— ed. J. Dowden, in *The Scottish Communion Office of 1764* (²Oxford 1922) 210–22.

——— Confirmation only, in *Confirmation, or the Laying-on of Hands*, (1926) I 232–5.

[T. Deacon], *A Complete Collection of Devotions* (1734), Grisbrooke, 297–316; Hall, VI.

——— Confirmation only, in *Confirmation . . .* (above) I 240–3.

The Communion Service of the Scottish Prayer Book of 1637

n.d.   Hall, V 81–119

1724   Hall, V 121–43

1743   Hall, V 145–68 (= 1735, 'in the natural order')

1755   Hall, V 169–91 (ed. W. Falconar)

1735 and 1755 in P. A. Lemprière, *The Scottish Communion Offices* (Edinburgh 1909). In parallel columns with 1637, 1764, and 1889.

T. Rattray, *An Office for the Sacrifice of the Holy Eucharist* (1744), Grisbrooke, 317–32; Hall, I 151–88.

The Scottish Communion Office of 1764, Grisbrooke 333–48; Hall, V 193–224.

—— ed. J. Dowden, in *The Scottish Communion Office of 1764* (²Oxford 1922) 115–32.

—— ed. P. A. Lemprière (above).

The Proposed American Prayer Book (1786), ed. P. Hall, in *Reliquiae Liturgicae* (Bath 1847) v. Summary in Procter and Frere, 239.

Bishop Seabury's Communion Office, ed. S. Hart (New York, ¹1874), ²1883). Facsimile.

The Book of Common Prayer . . . according to the use of the Protestant Episcopal Church in the United States of America (Philadelphia 1790).

—— Communion Service only, in B. J. Wigan, *The Liturgy in English* (²1964) 52–61 (notes).

W. McGarvey, *Liturgiae Americanae* (Philadelphia 1895). Proposed Prayer Book of 1786 and Prayer Books of 1790 and 1892 in parallel columns.

Books: 1, 3, 10, 12, 21, 27, 37, 40, 41, 67, 68, 87, 89, 111.
Articles: 154, 159, 176, 182.

CHAPTER 9

Thanksgiving for Harvest (1862); Shortened Services Act, 1872, see Documents, pp. 386–90.

Reports of the Royal Commission on Ritual, 4 vols (1867, 1868, 1870, 1870).

The Convocation Prayer Book (¹1880, ²1907).

The Book of Common Prayer according to the use of the Church of Ireland (Dublin 1878).

The Book of Common Prayer . . . according to the use of the Protestant Episcopal Church in the United States of America (Philadelphia 1892).

—— ed. W. McGarvey, in *Liturgiae Americanae* (Philadelphia 1895).

—— Communion Service only, ed. J. Dowden, in *The Scottish Communion Office of 1764* (²Oxford 1922) 133–42; ed. B. J. Wigan, in *The Liturgy in English* (²1964) 52–61 (notes).

The Book of Public Prayers and Services for the use of the people called Methodists (1883).

o

Report and Minutes of Evidence of the Royal Commission on Ecclesiastical Discipline, 5 vols (1906). Includes Archbishop Davidson's masterly historical survey of the growth of 'Ritualism', II 340–74.

The 1871 Lectionary and the Accession Service of 1901 may be found in any standard edition of the Prayer Book of more recent date.

J. Wordsworth, *The Form of Prayer and Order of Ceremonies in use in the diocese of Salisbury* (1899). Consecration of Churches.

Books: 3, 9, 27, 28, 41, 64, 71, 74, 88, 89.
Articles: 124, 125, 127, 177, 178.

CHAPTER 10

COLLECTIONS

B. J. Wigan, *The Liturgy in English* ([1]1962, [2]1964: ACC XLIII). Communion Services of 1549, 1662, and thirteen later revisions up to 1959, and four non-Anglican services.

C. O. Buchanan, *Modern Anglican Liturgies* (1968). Published too late for inclusion in detail.

The Revised Prayer Book (Permissive Use) Measure (1923). N.A. 84; the proposals of the Church Assembly Committee.

Report of the Committee on Prayer Book Revision (1922). 'The Green Book', sponsored by the English Church Union.

A New Prayer Book, 3 parts (1923). 'The Grey Book'.

A Survey of the Proposals for the Alternative Prayer Book, 3 parts (1923–4: Alcuin Club Prayer Book Revision Pamphlets, 12, 13, 14). 'The Orange Book', also known as 'The Yellow Book'.

The Book of Common Prayer with additions and deviations approved in 1927 (1927).

The Book of Common Prayer with additions and deviations approved in 1928 (1928).

—— Communion Service only, in Wigan (above), 62–72.

Rubrics on Reservation and Alternative Canons, in Documents, pp. 391–8.

The Communion Office of the Church of Scotland (1889), draft, ed. J. Dowden, in *The Scottish Communion Office of 1764*, ([2]Oxford 1922) 235–49.

— in P. A. Lemprière, *The Scottish Communion Office* (Edinburgh 1909).

The Communion Office of the Church of Scotland (1911), draft, in Dowden (above), 249–67.

The Book of Common Prayer ... and the permissible additions to and deviations from the service books of the Scottish Church (Edinburgh 1912).

The Scottish Book of Common Prayer (Edinburgh 1929).

—— Communion Service only, in Wigan (above), 38–51.

The Book of Common Prayer ... according to the use of the Protestant Episcopal Church in the United States of America (New York 1928).

—— Communion Service only, in Wigan, 52–61.

The Book of Common Prayer according to the use of the Church of England in the Dominion of Canada (Cambridge 1922).

—— Communion Service only, in Wigan, 26–37 (notes).

A Book of Common Prayer ... for use in the Church of the Province of South Africa (1954).

—— Communion Service only, in Wigan, 73–81.

The Chronicle of Convocation, 25 vols (1906–30). Debates on Revision indexed under 'Royal Letters of Business'.

Proceedings of the Church Assembly, 10 vols (1921–30).

Books: 4, 5, 6, 7, 8, 9, 24, 29, 43, 44, 45, 57, 58, 60, 61, 65, 69, 70, 72, 73, 79, 89, 90, 101, 116.
Articles: 129, 132, 149, 155, 163, 164, 175, 181.

CHAPTER 11

The Book of Offices, being the Orders of Service authorized for use in the Methodist Church (1936).

The Book of Common Worship, as authorized by the Synod 1962 (1963) (i.e. of the Church of South India).

—— Communion Service only, in Wigan (above, Chapter 10), 205–218.

Baptism and Confirmation (1958). Report of the Church of England Liturgical Commission, with proposed forms of service.

The Revised Catechism (1962).

The Revised Psalter ([1]1963; [2]with pointing, 1966).

The Lambeth Conference 1958 (1958).

The Book of Common Prayer according to the use of the Anglican Church of Canada (Cambridge 1959).

—— Communion Service only, in Wigan, 136–44.
The Bombay Liturgy, in Wigan, 94–113.
The Colombo Liturgy, in Wigan, 82–93.
The Book of Common Prayer of the Church of India, Pakistan, Burma and Ceylon (1960).
—— Communion Service only, in Wigan, 114–26.
The Japanese Liturgy, in Wigan, 127–35.
The Liturgy of the Church of the Province of the West Indies, in Wigan, 175–82.
A Liturgy for Africa (1964). Also in L. W. Brown, *Relevant Liturgy* (1965) 65–87.
Alternative Services: First Series (1965). Proposed by the archbishops of Canterbury and York.
The Prayer Book (Alternative and Other Services) Measure (1965), in Documents, pp. 399-400.

Books: 4, 5, 7, 18, 29, 32, 34, 49, 56, 66, 102, 106, 114, 115.
Articles: 130, 133, 152, 153, 161, 162, 171, 183.

PART II—BOOKS

1. C. J. Abbey and J. H. Overton, *The English Church in the Eighteenth Century* (1878) II 409–520 (especially ch. 5).

2. G. W. O. Addleshaw, *The High Church Tradition* (1941).

3. G. W. O. Addleshaw and F. Etchells, *The Architectural Setting of Anglican Worship* (1948).

4. Anon., *Prayer Book Revision in the Church of England* (1957). Memorandum of the Church of England Liturgical Commission; useful discussion of 1928.

5. Anon., *Principles of Prayer Book Revision* (1957). Report of a Select Committee of the Church of India, Pakistan, Burma and Ceylon; detailed analysis of the 1928 group of revisions and full treatment of Indian forms.

6. W. J. Armitage, *The Story of the Canadian Revision of the Prayer Book* (Cambridge 1922). 422 pages on a conservative revision; useful for identifying sources.

7. R. T. Beckwith, *Prayer Book Revision and Anglican Unity* (1967). An Evangelical critique.

8. G. K. A. Bell, *Randall Davidson, Archbishop of Canterbury*, 2 vols (1935). Chapters 6, 17, 25, 39, 50, and 82 form a history of the 1928 Book.

9. J. Bishop, *Methodist Worship in relation to Free Church Worship* (1950). Much useful detail.

10. F. R. Bolton, *The Caroline Tradition of the Church of Ireland* (1959). Text and discussion of Irish Consecration Order.

11. R. S. Bosher, *The Making of the Restoration Settlement* (1951).

12. J. C. Bowmer, *The Sacrament of the Lord's Supper in Early Methodism* (1951).

13. F. E. Brightman, *The English Rite*, 2 vols ([1]1915, [2]1922). Indispensable.

14. Y. Brilioth, trs. A. G. Hebert, *Eucharistic Faith and Practice, Evangelical and Catholic* (1930). Good on Luther.

15. G. W. Bromiley, *Baptism and the Anglican Reformers* (1953).

16. S. Brook, *The Language of the Book of Common Prayer* (1965).

17. P. N. Brooks, *Thomas Cranmer's Doctrine of the Eucharist* (1964).

18. L. W. Brown, *Relevant Liturgy* (1965). Commentary on *A Liturgy for Africa*, by one of the compilers, 50–63; text, 65–87.

19. C. C. Butterworth, *The English Primers (1529–1545)* (Philadelphia 1963). Analysis of contents to show relationship.

20. E. Cardwell, *Documentary Annals of the Reformed Church of England*, 2 vols (Oxford 1839).

21. E. Cardwell, *A History of Conferences and other Proceedings* (Oxford 1841).

22. E. Cardwell, *Synodalia*, 2 vols (Oxford 1842). Useful, though not 100 per cent accurate, collections of documents.

23. W. O. Chadwick, *The Reformation* (1964). Pelican History of the Church, III.

24. E. C. Chorley, *The new American Prayer Book, its history and contents* (New York 1929). Brief but useful.

25. P. Collinson, *The Elizabethan Puritan Movement* (1967). N.B. part VII, ch. 3, puritan worship; part VIII, ch. 5, the Hampton Court Conference.

26. H. Davies, *The Worship of the English Puritans* (1948).

27. H. Davies, *Worship and Theology in England*: IV, 'From Watts and Wesley to Maurice, 1690–1850' (Princeton 1961).

28. —— v, 'From Newman to Martineau, 1850–1900' (Princeton 1962).

29. —— vi, 'The Ecumenical Century, 1900–1965' (Princeton 1966). Immensely readable background material.

30. J. G. Davies, *A Select Liturgical Lexicon* (1965).

31. P. M. Dawley, *John Whitgift and the Reformation* (1955). Elizabethan church furnishing and devotional practice, 112–20.

32. P. M. Dawley (ed.), *The Anglican Congress 1954* (1955). Topic ii, 'Our Worship', 68–100, valuable papers by M. H. Shepherd and D. C. Dunlop.

33. A. G. Dickens, *The English Reformation* (1964). Latest and best general survey.

34. G. Dix, *The Shape of the Liturgy* (1945). Must be read, but with caution.

35. J. Dowden, *The Workmanship of the Prayer Book* (1902).

36. J. Dowden, *Further Studies in the Prayer Book* (1908). The first to make many points now generally accepted.

37. C. W. Dugmore, *Eucharistic Doctrine from Hooker to Waterland* (1942).

38. C. W. Dugmore, *The Mass and the English Reformers* (1958). See also review by T. M. Parker, in *JTS* ns xii (1961) 134–46; and reply by Dugmore, in *JTS* ns xiv (1963) 231–3.

39. G. R. Elton, *Reformation Europe 1517–1559* (1963).

40. G. Every, *The High-Church Party 1688–1718* (1956). Ch. 3, 43–60, is the best treatment of the 1689 proposals.

41. E. H. Fellowes, *English Cathedral Music from Edward VI to Edward VII* (1941).

42. W. K. Firminger, *The Alterations in the Ordinal of 1662: why were they made?* (1898).

43. W. H. Frere, *Correspondence on Liturgical Revision and Construction*, ed. R. C. D. Jasper (1954: ACC xxxix). Essential for 1928 and South Africa.

44. W. H. Frere, *Some Principles of Liturgical Reform* (1911).

45. W. H. Frere, *The Anaphora* (1938). 'A weighty defence of the 1928 Canon'.

46. W. H. Frere, *The Principles of Religious Ceremonial* (1907).

47. W. H. Frere, *Visitation Articles and Injunctions of the Period of the Reformation*, 3 vols (1910: ACC xiv, xv, xvi). Vol. i, Introduction and Index; ii, 1536–1558; iii, 1559–1575.

48. M. Frost, *Historical Companion to Hymns Ancient and Modern* (1962).

49. T. S. Garrett, *The Liturgy of the Church of South India* (Madras ¹1952, ²1954). Informative comment by one of the compilers; fuller than the same author's *Worship in the Church of South India* (1958).

50. F. A. Gasquet, *The Eve of the Reformation* (1906). Abundant quotations from contemporary writers.

51. F. A. Gasquet, *Parish Life in Mediaeval England* (1906).

52. F. A. Gasquet and E. Bishop, *Edward VI and the Book of Common Prayer* (¹1890; the 3rd edition, 1928, lacks the appendixes).

53. H. Gee, *The Elizabethan Prayer Book and Ornaments* (1902). Main thesis improbable, but several useful documents.

54. G. Harford, M. Stevenson, and J. W. Tyrer (edd.), *The Prayer Book Dictionary* (¹n.d., ²1925). Many articles can still be read with profit.

55. F. Ll. Harrison, *Music in Medieval Britain* (1963). Ch. 2 describes the sung portions of the rite in great detail.

56. A. G. Hebert (ed.), *The Parish Communion* (1937).

57. H. H. Henson, *Disestablishment* (1929). Important Introduction.

58. H. H. Henson, *Retrospect of an Unimportant Life*, II, '1920–1929' (1943). Ch. 15, 'Prayer Book Revision' is essential reading.

59. F. Higham, *Catholic and Reformed: A Study of the Anglican Church, 1559–1662* (1962). A pleasant introduction to the period.

60. P. B. Hinchliff, *The South African Liturgy* (Cape Town 1959). The definitive history.

61. P. B. Hinchliff, *The South African Rite and the 1928 Prayer Book* (1960) (pamphlet).

62. C. Hopf, *Martin Bucer and the English Reformation* (Oxford 1946). Review by E. G. Rupp, in *JTS* XLVIII (1947) 114–9.

63. H. E. Jacobs, *The Lutheran Movement in England during the Reigns of Henry VIII and Edward VI, and its Literary Monuments* (Philadelphia 1892). Not now recommendable.

64. R. C. D. Jasper, *Prayer Book Revision in England 1800–1900* (1954). Definitive summary of voluminous material.

65. *Lambeth Conference, 1908, Report of the* (1908).

66. *Lambeth Conference 1958, The* (1958). Part II 78–98, 'The Book of Common Prayer'.

67. A. B. Lawson, *John Wesley and the Christian Ministry* (1963). Comparison of the two Ordinals.

68. J. W. Legg, *English Church Life from the Restoration to the Tractarian Movement* (1914). Fascinating background material.

69. P. le Huray, *Music and the Reformation in England 1549–1660* (1967).

70. E. O. T. Lewis, *Till death us do part* (Penarth 1961). Modern revisions of the Marriage Service.

71. R. F. Littledale, *Catholic Revision* (1867).

72. W. K. Lowther Clarke (ed.), *Liturgy and Worship* (1932). 'A companion to the 1928 Prayer Book'; articles by F. E. Brightman and E. C. Ratcliff repay reading.

73. W. K. Lowther Clarke, *The Prayer Book of 1928 Reconsidered* (1943). Detailed and balanced criticism.

74. F. D. Maurice, *The Prayer Book* (1852, reprinted 1966).

75. W. D. Maxwell, *The Liturgical Portions of the Genevan Service Book* (¹Edinburgh 1931; ²London 1965). Indispensable.

76. W. D. Maxwell, *An Outline of Christian Worship* (Oxford 1936). From a Reformed standpoint, with good documentation.

77. E. C. Messenger, *The Lutheran Origin of the Anglican Ordinal* (1934).

78. G. A. Michell, *Landmarks in Liturgy* (1961).

79. E. Milner-White, *The Occasional Prayers in the 1928 Book Reconsidered* (1930).

80. L. L. Mitchell, *Baptismal Anointing* (1966: ACC XLVIII). Appendix 1, 177–87, on Anglican use.

81. J. R. H. Moorman, *Church Life in England in the Thirteenth Century* (Cambridge 1945).

82. J. E. Neale, *Elizabeth I and her Parliaments 1559–1581* (1953). Cited as Neale, I.

83. J. E. Neale, *Elizabeth I and her Parliaments 1584–1601* (1957). Cited as Neale, II.

84. J. F. H. New, *Anglican and Puritan* (1964).

85. J. Parker, *An Introduction to the History of the successive Revisions of The Book of Common Prayer* (Oxford 1877). Badly arranged, but still useful.

86. T. M. Parker, *The English Reformation to 1558* (Oxford 1950).

87. A. E. Peaston, *The Prayer Book Reform Movement in the Eighteenth Century* (Oxford 1940). Pioneer work in a neglected field.

88. A. E. Peaston, *The Prayer Book Revisions of the Victorian Evangelicals* (Dublin 1963). Supplements Jasper's monograph, no. 64.

89. A. E. Peaston, *The Prayer Book Tradition in the Free Churches* (1964). Authoritative.

90. W. Perry, *The Scottish Prayer Book, its value and history* (Cambridge 1929). Useful account of the preparation of the 1929 book by a participant.

91. C. S. Phillips, *Hymnody Past and Present* (1938).

92. C. E. Pocknee, *Liturgical Vesture: its Origins and Development* (1960: Alcuin Club Tracts, xxx). Illustrated.

93. F. M. Powicke, *The Reformation in England* (Oxford 1941).

94. F. Procter and W. H. Frere, *A New History of the Book of Common Prayer* (1901). Meticulously documented.

95. E. C. Ratcliff, *The Booke of Common Prayer of the Churche of England: its Making and Revisions 1549–1661* (1949: ACC xxxvii). Eighty facsimile illustrations.

96. E. C. Ratcliff, *The English Coronation Service* (1936). Traces service from A.D. 856 onwards; text of 1911.

97. E. C. Ratcliff, *The Coronation Service of Her Majesty Queen Elizabeth II* (1953). Text with introduction and notes; the two books are complementary, and essential for study of this rite.

98. L. D. Reed, *The Lutheran Liturgy* (²Philadelphia 1960). The fullest study in English.

99. C. C. Richardson, *Zwingli and Cranmer on the Eucharist* (*Cranmer Dixit et Contradixit*) (Illinois 1949). An intervention in the Dix-Timms debate, see part iii.

100. E. G. Rupp, *Studies in the Making of the English Protestant Tradition* (Cambridge ¹1947, ²1966). Ch. 6, 'Henry VIII and the German Protestants; ch. 7, 'Confessional Literature, 1537–47'.

101. M. H. Shepherd, Jr, *The Oxford American Prayer Book Commentary* (New York 1950). A mine of information.

102. M. H. Shepherd, *The Reform of Liturgical Worship* (Oxford 1961).

103. H. M. Smith, *Henry VIII and the Reformation* (1948).

104. H. M. Smith, *Pre-Reformation England* (1938).

105. C. H. Smyth, *Cranmer and the Reformation under Edward VI* (Cambridge 1926). Especially good on the refugee divines.

106. J. H. Srawley, *The Liturgical Movement* (1954).

107. D. Stevens, *Tudor Church Music* (1961). Ch. 4, 'Music for the English Rite', 50–63.

108. F. Streatfeild, *Latin Versions of the Book of Common Prayer* (1964).

109. F. Streatfeild, *The State Prayers and other Variations in the Book of Common Prayer* (1950).

110. H. B. Swete, *Church Services and Service-books before the Reformation* ([1]1896; [2]rev. A. J. Maclean, 1930).

111. N. Sykes, *Church and State in England in the XVIIIth Century* (Cambridge 1934). Ch. 6, 'The Whole Duty of Man'; ch. 9, 'Years of Plenty'.

112. N. Sykes, *The Crisis of the Reformation* (1938).

113. H. B. Walters, *London Churches at the Reformation* (1939).

114. E. C. Whitaker, *The Proposed Services of Baptism and Confirmation Reconsidered* (1960).

115. J. Winslow, E. C. Ratcliff, and others, *The Eucharist in India* (1920). Rationale, sources, and text of *Bombay Liturgy*.

116. F. T. Woods, *The Prayer Book Revised* (1927). Light on the bishops' intentions.

117. C. Wordsworth and H. Littlehales, *The Old Service Books of the English Church* ([1]1904, [2]1910). Authoritative treatment, pleasantly illustrated.

PART III — ARTICLES
(and chapters in composite works)

121. Anon., 'Capitulum Coloniense: an Episode in the Reformation', in *CQR* xxxi (1891) 419–36. On Cranmer's use of the *Antididagma*; attributed by Procter and Frere (2nd impression, ix) to F. E. Brightman.

122. Anon., 'Preparations for the First Prayer Book of Edward VI', in *CQR* xxxv (1892) 33–68. Survey of doctrinal pamphlets.

123. Anon., 'Preparations for the Second Prayer Book of Edward VI', in *CQR* xxxvi (1892) 137–66.

124. Anon., 'Liturgical Revision', in *CQR* iii (1876) 34–63. Summarized in Jasper, 85–9.

125. Anon., 'Revision of the Rubrics by the Ritual Commission

and the Convocations', in *CQR 18* (1880) 269–305. Adds nothing to Jasper's book.

126. Anon., 'The Original Manuscript of the Prayer Book', in *CQR* xxxii (1891) 465–92.

127. Anon., 'The Royal Commission on Ecclesiastical Discipline', in *CQR* lxiii (1906) 1–39.

128. A. Beesley, 'An Unpublished Source of the Book of Common Prayer: Peter Martyr Vermigli's *Adhortatio ad Coenam Domini Mysticam*', in *JEH* xix (1968) 83–8.

129. C. R. D. Biggs and W. C. Bishop, 'The Prospects and Principles of Prayer Book Revision', in *CQR* lxxi (1910) 82–119.

130. J. C. Bowmer, 'The Methodist Book of Offices', *London Quarterly & Holborn Review*, October 1966, 268–76. Mainly lists of names.

131. F. E. Brightman, '"Common Prayer"', in *JTS* x (1909) 497–528.

132. F. E. Brightman, 'The New Prayer Book Examiued', in *CQR* civ (1927) 219–52.

133. L. W. Brown, 'The Making of a Liturgy', in *SJT* iv (1951) 55–63. The C.S.I. Liturgy analysed by one of the compilers.

134. E. C. E. Bourne, 'Cranmer and the Liturgy of 1552', in *CQR* clv (1954) 382–90.

135. H. de Candole, 'Devotion at Communion in Christian Antiquity and in the Middle Ages', in *Theology* xxxvi (1938) 6–14.

136. H. de Candole, '"We receive this Child"', in *Theology*, lxiv (1961) 237–41.

137. P. Collinson, 'The Authorship of *A Brieff Discours off the Troubles Begonne at Franckford*', in *JEH* ix (1958) 188–208.

138. A. H. Couratin, 'The Holy Communion 1549', in *CQR* clxiv (1963) 148–59.

139. A. H. Couratin, 'The Service of Holy Communion, 1552–1662', in *CQR* clxiii (1962) 431–42.

Nos. 138 and 139 were reprinted as *The Service of Holy Communion, 1549–1662* (1963).

140. G. J. Cuming, 'Advent and the Prayer Book', in *Theology*, liv (1951) 449–55.

141. G. J. Cuming, 'The Grand Debate', in *CQR* clviii (1962) 29–39.

142. G. J. Cuming, 'The Making of the Durham Book', in *JEH* VI (1955) 60–72.

143. G. J. Cuming, 'The Prayer Book in Convocation, November 1661', in *JEH* VIII (1957) 182–92.

144. G. J. Cuming, 'The Making of the Prayer Book of 1662', in *The English Prayer Book 1549–1662* (1963) 82–114.

145. G. J. Cuming, 'Two Fragments of a Lost Liturgy?', in *Studies in Church History*, III (Leiden 1966) 247–53.

146. M. H. Curtis, 'The Hampton Court Conference and its Aftermath', in *History*, XLVI (1961) 1–16.

147. G. Dix, 'Dixit Cranmer et non Timuit', in *CQR* CXLV (1947/8) 145–76; CXLVI (1948) 44–60 (a reply to no. 180). Also reprinted with fresh pagination.

148. C. W. Dugmore, 'The First Ten Years, 1549–59', in *The English Prayer Book 1549–1662* (1963) 6–30.

149. E. Evans, 'Occasional Prayers in the Deposited Book', in *CQR* CXLI (1946) 155–75.

150. W. H. Frere, 'Edwardine Vernacular Services before the First Prayer Book', in *JTS* I (1900); reprinted in *Walter Howard Frere: A Collection of his Papers in Liturgical and Historical Subjects*, ed. J. H. Arnold and E. G. P. Wyatt (Oxford 1940: ACC XXXV) 5–21.

151. W. H. Frere, 'York Service Books', in *A Collection . . .* (see no. 150) 159–69.

152. T. S. Garrett, 'Baptism in the Church of South India', in *SJT* VIII (1955) 385–91.

153. T. S. Garrett, 'The Ordinal of the Church of South India', in *SJT* XII (1959) 400–13.

154. R. George, 'The Means of Grace', ch. 8 in R. E. Davies and E. G. Rupp (edd.), *A History of the Methodist Church in Great Britain* (1965) I 259–73. Summarizes recent work on Wesley's *Abridgment*.

155. A. C. Headlam, 'In Defence of the New Prayer Book', in *CQR* CIV (1927) 199–218. With list of contemporary publications.

156. C. Hopf, 'A Sermon of Martin Luther in the English Primer', in *JTS* XLIII (1942) 194–200.

157. C. Hopf, 'The Story of the Passion and Resurrection in the English Primer', in *JTS* NS II (1951) 68–82.

158. C. Hopf, 'An English Version of parts of Bucer's Reply to the Cologne *Antididagma* of 1544', in *JTS* NS XI (1960) 94–110.

159. F. Hunter, 'Sources of Wesley's Revision of the Prayer Book in 1784–8', in *Proceedings of the Wesley Historical Society*, XXIII (1942) 123–33. Important.

160. J. A. Jungmann, 'Why was Cardinal Quiñonez' Reformed Breviary a Failure?', in *Pastoral Liturgy* (1962) 200–14.

161. J. R. Macphail, 'Doing over a Liturgy', in *SJT* VII (1954) 376–92.

162. J. R. Macphail, 'Worship in the Church of South India', in *SJT* XVII (1964) 25–42.

163. E. Milner-White, 'The 1928 Revision of the Prayer Book', in *Theology*, XXXV (1937) 72–7. Confined to the Introduction to Morning and Evening Prayer.

164. A. Mitchell, 'A Liturgical Essay', in *The Churchman*, XLIII (1929) 51–62. Constructive and forward-looking proposals by an Evangelical.

165. J. E. Neale, 'The Elizabethan Acts of Supremacy and Uniformity', in *English Historical Review*, LXV (1950) 304–32. Should be read as well as Neale's books.

166. W. Page, 'The First Book of Common Prayer and the Windsor Commission', in *CQR* XCVIII (1924) 51–64.

167. T. M. Parker, 'The Problem of Uniformity, 1559–1604', in *The English Prayer Book 1549–1662* (1963) 31–55.

168. B. Porter, 'Cosin's *Hours of Prayer*: A Liturgical Review', in *Theology*, LVI (1953) 54–8.

169. E. C. Ratcliff, 'The Liturgical Work of Archbishop Cranmer', in *JEH* VII (1956) 189–203. Reprinted in *Thomas Cranmer 1489–1556* (1956) 25–44. A masterly summary.

170. E. C. Ratcliff, 'The English Usage of Eucharistic Consecration, 1548–1662', in *Theology*, LX (1957) 229–36, 273–80.

171. E. C. Ratcliff, 'The Ordinal of the Church of South India', in *Theology*, LXIII (1960) 7–15.

172. E. C. Ratcliff, 'Puritan Alternatives to the Prayer Book', in *The English Prayer Book 1549–1662* (1963) 56–74. The *Directory* and Baxter's Liturgy.

173. E. C. Ratcliff, 'The Savoy Conference and the Revision of the Book of Common Prayer', in G. F. Nuttall and W. O. Chadwick (edd.), *From Uniformity to Unity 1662–1962* (1962) 89–148.

174. C. C. Richardson, 'Cranmer and the Analysis of Eucharistic Doctrine', in *JTS* NS XVI (1965) 421–37.

175. C. K. Sansbury, 'Recent Anglican Revisions of the Eucharistic Prayer', in *Theology*, LIX (1956) 281–8.

176. W. F. Swift, 'Methodism and the Book of Common Prayer', in *Proceedings of the Wesley Historical Society*, XXVII (1949) 33–41.

177. W. F. Swift, " 'The Sunday Service of the Methodists' ", in ibid. XXIX (1954) 12–20.

178. W. F. Swift, " 'The Sunday Service of the Methodists", a Study of Nineteenth-century Liturgy', in ibid. XXI (1958) 112–18, 133–43.

179. H. E. Symonds, 'Cranmer and the Edwardine Prayer Books', in *Theology* XLIX (1946) 171–6, 200–4.

180. G. B. Timms, 'Dixit Cranmer', in *CQR* CXLIII (1946/7) 217–34; CXLIV (1947) 33–51. A reply to Dix's book; see no. 147. Also reprinted with fresh pagination.

181. E. C. Trenholme, 'The Revision of the Prayer Book', in *CQR* XCVII (1923) 34–48. With list of contemporary publications.

182. E. Vincent, 'An Eighteenth-Century Attempt at Revision', in *Theology*, XIV (1927) 353–7 – i.e. *The Book of Common Prayer revis'd, corrected, and enlarged* (1734).

183. G. G. Willis, 'The Historical Background of the English Lectionary of 1955', in *JEH* IX (1958) 73–86.

Notes

CHAPTER 1

1. (1847: Camden Society, 1st Series, XXXVII) 23; my translation. The author is thought to be Andrea Trevisano, who was in England in 1498.

2. e.g. *Venetian Calendar*, II 91; Cranmer, *Works on the Supper* (PS) 229.

3. See, e.g., Srawley, *The Early History of the Liturgy* (²Cambridge 1949) 31; Jungmann, *The Early Liturgy* (1960) 42.

4. Psalms are quoted throughout with the numbering of the Book of Common Prayer.

5. Op. cit. 46.

6. *The Shape of the Liturgy*, 605–8.

7. Mirk, *Festial*, 168–9.

8. Cranmer, *Works on the Supper* (PS) 229.

9. Addleshaw and Etchells, *The Architectural Setting of Anglican Worship*, 15–18.

10. A full description in Frere, *The Principles of Religious Ceremonial*, 97–102.

11. Detailed analysis in Brightman, *The English Rite*, I ccxvi.

12. Maynard Smith, *Pre-Reformation England*, 133–41; Frere, *Visitation Articles and Injunctions*, II 185–7 n.

13. Figures from Pollard and Redgrave, *Short Title Catalogue*.

CHAPTER 2

1. Urbanus Rhegius, *Novae Doctrinae ad Veterem Collatio* (1526), English translation by William Turner, *A Comparison between the Old Learning and the New* (1537); quoted from Gasquet, *The Eve of the Reformation*, 17–18.

2. Brilioth, *Eucharistic Faith and Practice*, 95–103.

3. Brilioth, 111–14; Maxwell, *Outline of Christian Worship*, 76.

4. Brightman, *The English Rite*, I xxx–xxxvii; Brilioth, 110–25; Maxwell, *Outline*, 73–80; *Liturgy and Worship*, 139–41.

5. Brilioth, 153–64; Maxwell, *Outline*, 81–7; *Liturgy and Worship*, 143–4.

6. Maxwell, *Outline*, 87–111; Maxwell, *Genevan Service Book*, passim; *Liturgy and Worship*, 141–2. See also Documents, p. 324.

7. Brightman, I, xxxviii–xxxix.

8. See Documents, p. 326.

9. Sehling, XI 48 n 20. The former attribution to Volprecht appears to be mistaken.

10. Brightman, I xxxix–xli.

11. Brightman, I xli–xliii.

12. Brightman, I xliv–xlv.

13. Brightman, I xliii–xliv.

14. *Original Letters* (PS) 266.

15. Sehling, VIII I 30.

16. Brilioth, 164–79; Maxwell, *Outline*, 112–19; Maxwell, *Genevan Service Book*, passim.

17. Brightman, I xxviii–xxx.

18. Brightman, I xlv–xlix; *Liturgy and Worship*, 144–5.

19. Brightman, I xxvi–xxviii; *Liturgy and Worship*, 137–8.

CHAPTER 3

1. Butterworth, *The English Primers*, passim; also C. Hopf, *Martin Bucer*, and his articles listed in the Bibliography (nos. 156–7).

2. Brightman, I li, lii.

3. Brightman, I l, li.

4. Frere, *Visitation Articles*, II 46.

5. Brightman, I lii, liii.

6. Smyth, *Cranmer and the Reformation under Edward VI*, 76–7.

7. Sehling, IV 349–50 (N.B. note 1); Richter, I 248–60 (the original German version); Smyth, *Cranmer*, 74–7.

8. Brightman, I lxxvii, lxxviii (this is the scheme called by Brightman 'the second').

9. Brightman, I liii–lv.

10. Brightman, I lv.

11. Brightman, I lv, lvi.

12. Brightman, I lvii, lviii.

13. Wilkins, *Concilia*, III 861–3, quoted in Procter & Frere, 30 n 3, and 31 n 1.

14. Brightman, I lxxvi, lxxvii (this is the scheme called by Brightman 'the first', *Horarum canonicarum series*).

15. Brightman, I lviii–lxviii, 174–90; II 934–44. Dowden, *Workmanship of the Prayer Book*, xv, xvi, 140–58, 253–9.

16. Texts in *Processionale ... Sarum*, 107–112; *Breviarium*, II 249–55; *Manuale*, 115–17. *Commendatio*: Maskell, I 97–102. Luther: *Works* (Eng, trans.) LIII 153–70. See also Documents, p. 358.

17. Brightman, I lxi; Documents, p. 362.

18. Brightman, I liii, where the reading '*adversity*' is an error taken over from Burton, *Three Primers*.

19. Cranmer, *Works* (PS) II 415–16.

20. Cardwell, *Documentary Annals*, I 4–24. Cranmer, *Works* (PS) II 498–504. Frere, *Visitation Articles*, II 114–30.

21. Wriothesley, *Chronicle*, II 2.

22. Ibid. I 187. Frere, 'Edwardine Vernacular Services' (see Bibliography, no. 150).

23. Brightman, I lxxi–lxxvi; II 650–8, 696–700. Documents, p. 364.

24. I lxxiv. Add: 'reusque constituitur corporis et sanguinis Domini' (fo. 86); 'non possint ad mensam Domini accedere' (fo. 88).

25. Dowden, *Further Studies*, 317–343.

26. *Orignal Letters* (PS) 17.

CHAPTER 4

1. Proclamation before *The Order of the Communion*.

2. Burnet, *History of the Reformation*, part II, book I, record 25.

3. Procter and Frere, 37; cf. n 2.

4. 1549 Act of Uniformity: Gee and Hardy, 358–66.

5. Article by W. Page (see Bibliography, no. 166).

6. Proctor and Frere, 47 n 2.

7. 1549 Act of Uniformity: Gee and Hardy, 358–66.

8. Gasquet and Bishop, 395–443 (appendix V).

9. *Original Letters* (PS) 470.

10. Wriothesley, *Chronicle*, II 9.

11. Dowden, *Further Studies*, 79–81.

12. *Processionale Sarum*, 91–2.

13. Dowden, *Further Studies*, 67–8; Documents, p. 333.

14. Procter and Frere, 450–8; the similarities of language indicated by italics should be treated with caution.

15. I cvi; for '91b' read '92b', and add: 'per eundem unicum Mediatorem ... in unitate verae fidei ... in tuo nomine vere conveniamus' (fo. 94 a & b).

16. I cvi.

17. *Original Letters* (PS) 266.

18. Cranmer, *Works* (PS) II 217–18; II 342–4.

19. *Original Letters* (PS) 351.

20. *Eucharistic Faith and Practice*, 95.

21. Brightman, II 662; (1921 edition only) I ccxxx.

22. *Private Prayers of the Reign of Queen Elizabeth* (PS) 274–97.

23. Brightman, II 726.

24. Brightman, II 726, 732, 734.

25. Dowden, *Further Studies*, 46–53.

26. Brightman, I cxix; II 726, 728, 732, 734, 744.

27. Frere, *Visitation Articles*, II 21 n.

28. Brightman, I cxxiii.

29. Dowden, *Workmanship*, 259–60.

30. Ibid. 159–64.

31. *Processionale Sarum*, 26–30; *Breviary*, II 249–55.

32. Frere, *Visitation Articles*, II 55.

33. Procter and Frere, 61.

CHAPTER 5

1. *Original Letters* (PS) 350–1.

2. Ibid. 79.

3. *Gray Friars Chronicle*, 62.

4. *Original Letters*, 72; Bucer, *Censura*, 493–4.

5. Cranmer, *Works* (PS) I 92.

6. Pocock, *Troubles*, passim, including the Articles of the rebels, and Udall's answer; Cranmer's answer is in *Works* (PS) II 163–87.

7. *Original Letters* (PS) 79.

8. Pocock, 128.

9. *Early Writings* (PS) 479.

10. *Original Letters*, 426, 566.

11. Cardwell, *Documentary Annals*, I 81–4, 89–90; Frere, *Visitation Articles*, II 241–5.

12. *Gray Friars*, 67, 69; Wriothesley, *Chronicle*, II 47.

13. Procter and Frere, 68 n 2.

14. Strype, *Memorials of Archbishop Cranmer*, II 662–3.

15. 1583 edition, 1067. Original Latin text in article by A. Beesley (see Bibliography, no. 128).

16. Procter and Frere, 68 n 2.

17. *Original Letters*, 82, 568.

18. *Censura*, 465, 477, 493.

19. Collected in Brightman, I cxlv.

20. Gee and Hardy, 369–72.

21. *Early Writings*, 492.

22. I clix, 130.

23. e.g. G. G. Willis, review in *JEH* xv (1964) 118.

24. *Opera*, I 188b.

25. Frere, 'Edwardine Vernacular Services' (Bibliography, no. 150).

26. *Early Writings*, 144; *Later Writings*, 133.

27. *Censura*, 473.

28. *Gray Friars*, 75.

29. *Early Writings*, 534.

30. *Gray Friars*, 66.

31. *Dixit Cranmer et non Timuit*, 15.

32. *Zwingli and Cranmer on the Eucharist*, 30, 21, 34.

33. *Cranmer and the Reformation under Edward VI*, 66.

34. *Dixit Cranmer*, 25.

35. *The Mass and the English Reformers*, 198–200, 126, 160.

36. *Thomas Cranmer's Doctrine of the Eucharist*, 90–1.

37. *Censura*, 477–81.

38. *Early Writings*, 479.

39. Ibid. 536.

40. Brightman, I cl, cli.

41. I clvi.

CHAPTER 6

1. *Zurich Letters* (PS) I 349.

2. Ibid. I 248.

3. See further, Sprott, *The Liturgy of Compromise*, Introduction, and *The Troubles . . . at Frankfurt*, passim.

4. Procter and Frere, 129–31.

5. *Original Letters* (PS) II 754 (Cox and others to Calvin).

6. See further Maxwell, *John Knox's Genevan Service Book*.

7. Gee and Hardy, 416–17.

8. Brightman, I clxvi–clxviii.

9. T. M. Parker, in *The English Prayer Book 1549–1662*, 43.

10. Gee, *Elizabethan Prayer-Book*, 195–202.

11. Article and book (1) in Bibliography (nos. 165 and 82).

12. *The Seconde Parte of a Register* (1586), ed. A. Peel, II 84 (quoted in Neale's article).

13. Gee, *Elizabethan Prayer-Book*, 215–24.

14. See further the full note by F. E. Warren in *Hierurgia Anglicana*, III 245–59.

15. Title-page of the first edition.

16. Frere, *Visitation Articles*, II 204–12.

17. Brightman, I clxxiii, clxxiv.

18. *Liturgical Services of the Reign of Queen Elizabeth* (PS) 548–561.

19. Frere, *Visitation Articles*, III 33, 36, 41.

20. Book II, no. 17.

21. Frere, *Visitation Articles*, III 108–10; Gee, *Elizabethan Prayer-Book*, 273–6.

22. Addleshaw and Etchells, 30–6.

23. *Zurich Letters* (PS) I 63, 73–4.

24. Cardwell, *Documentary Annals*, I 334–8.

25. Stevens, *Tudor Church Music*, 50–63.

26. Brightman, I clxxvii, clxxviii.

27. Cardwell, *Synodalia*, 111–46.

28. *Zurich Letters*, I 164, 281; II 361.

29. H. Davies, *Worship of the English Puritans*, 33–4.

30. *Zurich Letters*, I 345–55.

31. A phrase which recurs in Whitgift's writings.

32. Neale, I 198.

33. ed. Frere and Douglas, 20–30.

34. Ibid. 114–17; see also Documents, p. 370; and Hooker, *Ecclesiastical Polity*, book v, ch. 27, section 1.

35. Peaston, *Prayer Book Tradition*, 16–34; Clay, *Liturgical Services*, xv–xix; Procter and Frere, 133–5.

36. Neale, II 62; Procter and Frere, 131–3.

37. Neale, II 148, 159.

CHAPTER 7

1. Cardwell, *Conferences*, 131.

2. Ibid. 214–15.

3. Cosin, *Works* (LACT) v 455–6; Cosin later became Overall's chaplain.

4. i.e., one of the six parts of the *Homily against Wilful Rebellion* (book II, no. 21).

5. A. Cade, *A Sermon of the Nature of Conscience* (Cambridge 1636), Epistle Dedicatorie.

6. Cardwell, *Conferences*, 273.

7. Cosin, *Works* (LACT) v 114.

8. Andrewes, *Minor Works* (LACT) 153, 158; Staley, *Hierurgia Anglicana*, II 99–104.

9. Cardwell, *Conferences*, 234.

10. John Evelyn, *Diary*, 12 October 1651.

11. Donaldson, *The Making of the Scottish Prayer Book of 1637*, 31–40.

12. Ibid. 45.

13. Quoted ibid. 52.

14. Laud, *Works* (LACT) III 343, 353.

15. Cardwell, *Conferences*, 273.

16. E. C. Ratcliff, in *The English Prayer Book 1549–1662*, 64. See further, H. Davies, *The Worship of the English Puritans*, 127–42.

17. Title-page.

18. Cuming, *The Durham Book*, 287–8.

19. Cosin, *Works* (LACT) v 516–17, 336.

20. Clarendon, quoted in Gould, *Documents relating to . . . the Act of Uniformity of 1662*, 5.

21. M. Sylvester, *Reliquiae Baxterianae* (1696), 234, 232.

22. Cuming, *The Durham Book*, 158, 192, 196, 218, 38.

23. Staley, *Hierurgia Anglicana*, III 335–9.

24. Sylvester, *Reliquiae Baxterianae*, 234.

25. Laud, *Works* (LACT) III 343.

26. Quoted from B. H. G. Wormald, *Clarendon* (Cambridge 1951) 240 ff.

27. Gould, *Documents*, 109.

28. See further H. Davies, *The Worship of the English Puritans*, 155–61.

29. Gould, *Documents*, 412.
30. Cosin, *Correspondence* (SS LV) II 31.
31. Cuming, *The Durham Book*, 180.
32. Parker, *Introduction to the History*, cccix, cccx.
33. E. Pearse, *The Conformists Plea for the Nonconformists* (1682) 32.
34. Brightman, I cc, cci.
35. Brightman, I cciii.
36. E. Calamy, *Abridgment of Mr Baxter's History* (1713) 159.
37. Brightman, II 720.
38. Cuming, article (see Bibliography, no. 143).
39. Brightman, I ccxxiv.
40. H. A. Ll. Jukes, 'A Tribute to Bishop Skinner', in *Studies in Church History*, III (Leiden 1966) 242–6.
41. Cuming, articles (see Bibliography, nos. 143 and 145).
42. Walton, *Life of Dr Robert Sanderson* (1678) fo. 15.

CHAPTER 8

1. Sermon IV, 168.
2. *Letters*, III 152.
3. Quoted from Grisbrooke, *Anglican Liturgies*.
4. Bolton, *Caroline Tradition of the Church of Ireland*, 251.
5. Documents, p. 380.
6. Bolton, *Caroline Tradition*, 47–8, 251–2.
7. Bisse, *Beauty of Holiness*, 95 n, 130 n.
8. *Directions given by Edmund Lord Bishop of London to the Clergy of his Diocese* (1724).
9. See further Addleshaw and Etchells, especially chapters 5 and 6, and appendix II.
10. J. W. Legg, *English Church Life*, 184–5.
11. Ibid. 117 (1683).
12. G. Every, *The High Church Party*, to which these paragraphs are greatly indebted, 23–4.
13. Ibid. 45.
14. Cuming, *The Durham Book*, 222–4.
15. Every, *High Church Party*, 47.
16. Cuming, *The Durham Book*, 140–2. See Documents, p. 375.

17. N. Sykes, *Church and State*, 270.
18. Wilkins, *Concilia*, IV 660–6.
19. So F. Hunter, quoted in Peaston, *Prayer Book Tradition*, ch. 3.
20. Bowmer, *The Sacrament of the Lord's Supper*, 87.
21. Grisbrooke, *Anglican Liturgies*, 39.
22. Hall, *Fragmenta Liturgica*, I 101–48.
23. Grisbrooke, *Anglican Liturgies*, 95.
24. Hall, *Fragmenta Liturgica*, V 4–5.
25. Forms by Falconar and Rattray in *Confirmation, or the Laying-on of Hands*, I 235–40.
26. Summary in Procter and Frere, 239.

CHAPTER 9

1. Bell, *Randall Davidson*, I 459.
2. R. Laurence, *An Attempt to illustrate those Articles of the Church of England, which the Calvinists improperly consider as Calvinistical* (Oxford 1805); see Sermon I, n 7; III, n 18; VIII, n 11.
3. Jasper, *Prayer Book Revision*, ch. 2.
4. Ibid. ch. 3.
5. Addleshaw and Etchells, ch. 7.
6. *Report on Ecclesiastical Discipline*, 8.
7. Frere, *Hymns Ancient and Modern, Historical Edition*, xcviii, xcix.
8. *Ecclesiastical Discipline*, 55.
9. *Report on Ritual*, I 120.
10. Jasper, ch. 5.
11. *Sermons on the Prayer Book* (1848–9) XI.
12. Documents, p. 386.
13. Jasper, 132–3, 50, 63–7.
14. Quoted from Peaston, *Prayer Book Revisions of the Victorian Evangelicals*, 8.
15. *Report on Ritual*, I 132–57.
16. Ibid. I 158–62.
17. Ibid. II 31–398.
18. Jasper, 97–8.
19. Anon., 'Liturgical Revision', in *CQR* (October 1876) 44–5.

20. *Report on Ritual*, IV ix, xviii, 122.
21. Documents, p. 389.
22. *Ecclesiastical Discipline*, 59.
23. Bell, *Randall Davidson*, I 465.
24. *Ecclesiastical Discipline*, 59–61.
25. Jasper, ch. 9.
26. *Ecclesiastical Discipline*, 62.
27. *Prayer Book Dictionary*, 243; *Liturgy and Worship*, 711–12.
28. *Prayer Book Dictionary*, 2; *Liturgy and Worship*, 787.
29. Procter and Frere, 244 n 3.
30. Ibid. 230–4.
31. Ibid. 250–2; Jasper, 79.
32. Swift, article (Bibliography, no. 176) 40.
33. Peaston, *Prayer Book Tradition*, 57–8.
34. *Ecclesiastical Discipline*, 1.
35. Ibid. 12–15.
36. Ibid. 53.
37. Ibid. 18–48.
38. Ibid. 52.
39. Ibid. 75–6.
40. Ibid. 77.

CHAPTER 10

1. II 152–3.
2. Bell, *Randall Davidson*, I 653.
3. Op. cit. 190–2.
4. Frere, *Correspondence*, ed. Jasper, 26.
5. Ibid. 75, 80; Bell, II 1326.
6. Frere, *Correspondence*, 94.
7. Ibid. 98.
8. Bell, II 1330.
9. Ibid.
10. A useful list in Bell, II 1385–9.
11. Bell, II 1329–31.
12. Frere, *Correspondence*, 106–7.
13. Ibid. 124.
14. Bell, II 1347.
15. Frere, *Correspondence*, 144–6.

16. Bell, II 1348.

17. Ibid. I 351; Frere, *Correspondence*, 177–8.

18. Bell, II 1358.

19. Ibid. I 359.

20. Henson, *Retrospect*, II 152.

21. Henson, *Disestablishment*, 20.

22. Bell, II 1337; Lowther Clarke, *Prayer Book of 1928 Reconsidered*, 75 n 2.

23. Lowther Clarke, 4.

24. Op. cit. 82.

25. Lowther Clarke, 5.

26. Op. cit. 95–7.

27. Ibid. 100.

28. Summary in *Liturgy and Worship*, 298–300.

29. Convocation Report no. 475.

30. Op. cit. 22–69.

31. Frere, *Correspondence*, 55.

32. Frere, *Some Principles*, 138.

33. Ibid. 164.

34. Frere, *Correspondence*, 55.

35. Woods, *The Prayer Book Revised*, 57.

36. Frere, *Some Principles*, 168–9.

37. Ibid.

38. Lowther Clarke, 22–6.

39. Frere, *Some Principles*, 195.

40. Ibid.

41. Frere, *Correspondence*, 55.

42. *Proceedings of the Church Assembly*, 14 & 15.11.23. Documents, p. 397.

43. Frere, *Correspondence*, 124.

44. Ibid. 106.

45. Article in *CQR*, xc 371.

46. Frere, *Correspondence*, 220.

47. Ibid. 114.

48. Bell, II 805–6.

49. Ibid. 811.

50. Ibid. 813.

51. C. H. Smyth, *Cyril Forster Garbett, Archbishop of York* (1959) 195.

52. Bell, II 1348. See Documents, p. 391.
53. Frere, *Some Principles*, 208.
54. Frere, *Correspondence*, 92–4.
55. Orange Book, II 16.
56. Lowther Clarke, 66.
57. Report of Lambeth Conference, 1908.
58. *Principles of Prayer Book Revision*, 1–10; *Prayer Book Revision in the Church of England*, 48–50.
59. Perry, *Scottish Prayer Book*, 37.
60. Armitage, *Story of the Canadian Revision*, ad loc.
61. Ibid.
62. Frere, *Correspondence*, 203–9.
63. Ibid. 210.
64. Hinchliff, *South African Liturgy*, 113–15.

CHAPTER II

1. Summary in *Liturgy and Worship* (later impressions), 540 n.
2. Lowther Clarke, 49 n 1.
3. Dix, *Shape of the Liturgy*, 713.
4. Bishop, *Methodist Worship*, 134.
5. Dix, 48.
6. Garrett, *Liturgy of the Church of South India*, passim.
7. L. W. Brown, in article (Bibliography, no. 133).
8. *Report*, 2.80–1.
9. Ibid. 1.47.
10. Ibid. 2.81–5.
11. Ibid. 2.86–7.
12. *Principles of Prayer Book Revision*, 68–70.
13. Ibid. 69–73.
14. Ibid. 79.
15. *Report*, 2.81.
16. Documents, p. 399.

Index

Accession Service, 125, 140, 168, 169, 206, 240
Addleshaw, G. W. O., 249
Admonitions, *133*, 134, 138, *370* ff.
Advertisements, 126, 152, 196, 215
'*Advices*', *149* ff., 160
Agenda, 30
Aless, A., *124*
Alternative Services (1966), *263* ff., 399 ff.
Althamer, A., 40
American Prayer Book, *189* ff., *208*, 238, *239* ff., 260
Anamnesis, 17, 79, 144, 152, 217, 228–30, 251, 258, 260–3, 284, 396 ff.
Andrewes, L., 140, 141, 144, 152, 168, 184, 189, 208
Anne, Queen, 169, 183
Annexed Book, 160
Anointing, *see* Unction
Answer of Bishops, *155* ff., 165
Ante-Communion, 82, 105, 129, 142, 156, 201, 205, 207, 211, 256
Anthem, 125, 129
Antididagma, 45, 79
Antiphon, 23, 27, 28, 31, 47, 70, 73, 88, 89, 114, 129, 225, *269* ff., 334
Apocrypha, 70, 115, 137, 138, 143, 146, 155, 161, 179, 199, 207, 223
Apostolic Constitutions, 182–7
Aquinas, T., 18, 64
Articles, 52, 92, 109, 115, 130
Athanasian Creed, 23, 47, 52, 56, 72–4, 103, 176–80, 190, 192, *200* ff., 207, 215, 217, 225
Authorized Version, 137, 138, 143, 146, 155, 161, 179, 199, 207, 223
Azariah, Bishop, 261

Bacon, F., 178
Baptism, 25, 34, 36, 39, 41, 43, 46, *83* ff., *110* ff., *231*, 254, 318 ff;

of adults, 166; private, *84* ff., *111* ff., 119, 126, 131 ff., 136 ff., 164, 177, 179–81, 231
Barry, F. R., 218
Baxter, R., 153, 154, 157, 167, 173, 179, 206, 231
Becket, T., 53
Bells, 101, 126
Benedictional, 30, 291
Benefactors, Commemoration of, 124, *367* ff.
Benson, E. W., 204
Benson, R. M., 225
Bernard of Clairvaux, 57
Beveridge, W., 173
Bible, Great, 50, 54, 68–70, 72, 74, 161
Bidding of Bedes, 16, 54, 72, *281* ff., 291 n
Bishops' Book, 53
Bisse, T., 168
'Black Rubric', 114, 122, 161, 162, 190
Blessing of Ashes, 27, 60, 91
Blessing of Font, 25, 86, 110, 144, 146, 153, 164, 231
Blessing of Light, 27, 60
Blow, J., 170
Bombay Liturgy, 252, *259* ff., 260
Bond, W., 77
Bonner, E., 96, 97
Book of Common Order, 132, 250, 252
Book of Common Prayer (1549), 52, 54, 59, ch. 4 passim, 98, 106, 119, 124, 141–5, 149–52, 168, 181–7, 224, 227 ff., 242 ff., 250, 256, 262; (1552) ch. 5 passim, 118, 127, 149, 228, 250; (1662) ch. 7 passim; (1928) ch. 10 passim
Brandenburg, Electoral, *42*, 46, 62, 77, 89
Brandenburg-Nürnberg, 40, 42, 44–7, 52, 62, 72, 77, 82, 84, 86, 87, *327* ff., 333
Brenz, J., 40, 47
Brett, T., 168, 184

Breviary, 29, 47, 51 ff., 53, 54, 66, 69, 70, 72
Bridges, R., 247
Brightman, F. E., 10, 63, 78, 79, 104, 115, 214, 216
Brilioth, Y., 81
Brooks, P. N., 109
Browne, G. F., 215, 236
Brunfels, O., 49
Bucer, M., 33, 34, 36 ff., 43 ff., 48, 49, 62, 65, 93–5, ch. 5 passim, 125, 132, 135, 146, 150, 324 ff., 334 ff.
Budd, H., 258
Bugenhagen, J., 52
Bullinger, H., 96, 98, 109, 117, 132
Burial, 27, 41, 42, 47, 89 ff, 113, 119, 124, 130, 148, 234 ff; Communion after, 27, 69, 90, 113, 124, 234, 368 ff
Burnet, G., 173, 176
Burrows, W. O., 229
Burton, E., 192

Calamy, E., 173, 178, 179
Calenberg-Göttingen, 42, 70
Calvin, J., 43 ff., 48, 99, 102, 106, 109, 118, 120, 123, 146
Canadian Prayer Book, 225, 241 ff., 257–9
Canon, 16, 18, 32, 33, 36–8, 42, 68, 77 ff., 105 ff., 144, 152, 159, 162, 183, 217–19, 228–31, 235, 281, 396 ff.
Canons, 131, 139, 142, 145, 152, 162
Capito, W., 59
Cardwell, E., 192
Carlstadt, A., 33
Cartwright, T., 134, 138
Cassel, 43–5, 62
Catechism, 35, 40, 50, 86, 88, 113, 115, 126, 130, 131, 137 ff., 140, 255
Cecil, W., 121
Ceremonies, Of, 92, 113
Chants, Anglican, 170
Charles I, 142, 143, 165, 168
Charles II, 151, 153, 165, 168

Charles V, Emperor, 59, 65
Chase, F. H., 219, 236
Cheke, J., 99
Chrism, 25. See also Unction
Chrisom, 25, 84, 99, 110, 114, 231, 243, 320
Churching, 90 ff., 113, 117, 127, 234
Clarendon, Earl of, 151, 153, 154, 159
Clarke, S., 176, 178
Clarke, W. K. L., 223
Clerk's Book, 69, 102
Clement VII, 47
Clementine Liturgy, see Apostolic Constitutions
Close, Dean, 197
Cole, W., 118
Collection of Offices, 136, 147, 173, 189
Collects, 16, 40, 52, 74, 82, 155, 161, 164, 176, 272, 327 ff., 344, 377
Collier, J., 184
Cologne, 41, 44 ff., 62 ff., 334 ff.
Colombo Liturgy, 257, 259 ff.
Comber, T., 172, 192
Commandments, Ten, 35, 38, 43, 50, 54, 60, 86, 106, 113, 120, 126, 127, 139, 173, 177, 184, 190, 211, 227
Commendations, 24, 27, 49, 130
Commination, 83, 91, 104, 114, 235, 240, 259, 261
Common Prayer, 41, 43
Communion of Sick, 26, 42, 88, 89, 99 ff., 113, 356. See also Reservation
Compline, 23, 33, 52, 60, 70 ff., 142, 235, 265, 315 ff.
Compton, H., 173
Confession, private, 21, 26, 33, 61, 63, 108, 158, 161, 186, 261, 341
Confirmation, 25, 39, 42, 46, 86 ff., 113, 119, 132, 136 ff., 164, 165, 180, 186, 208, 232, 241 ff., 261, 264, 379
Confiteor, see Priest's preparation
Consecration of churches, 30, 141, 168, 170, 206, 207, 241, 380 ff.
Consuetudinary, 30
Convocation Book (1661), 160
Convocation Prayer Book (1880), 204 ff.

Cope, A., 139
Cosin, J., ch. 7 passim, 168, 192, 206, 437
Cotton, G., 225
Coverdale, M., 50, 51, 65, 89, 255, 291 n
Cox, R., 67, 119, 121
Cranmer, T., chs. 3, 4, 5 passim, 181, 258, 362 ff.
Creed, Dr, 160
Croft, W., 169
Cross in baptism, sign of, 25, 35, 46, 83, 110 ff., 119, 131 ff., 136 ff., 139, 141, 156, 161, 174, 177, 181, 183, 190, 207, 378
Crumwell, T., 51, 53

Davidson, R. T., ch. 10 passim
Day, G., 66, 67, 97
Day, J., 128
Deacon, T., 184, 186, 188
Deaconesses, 210, 220
Dead, Prayers for the, 17, 21, 50, 79, 90, 105, 106, 121, 124, 133, 142, 144, 152, 162, 163, 183, 222, 227, 239, 284, 368
Dearmer, P., 212, 216, 218, 247
Deutsche Messe, 34, 40, 41
Devotions (Cosin), 142, 152, 165
Dibdin, L., 210
Directorium, 30
Directory (1645), 146, 157, 179
Dirige, 24, 48, 50, 51, 59, 68, 89, 130
Disquisitions (Jones), 177 ff., 179, 192
Dix, G., 19, 109, 249 ff.
Döber, A., 39
Dowden, J., 225, 236, 237, 333 n
Drury, T. W., 217, 236, 326
Dryander, F., 65, 81, 96
Dugmore, C. W., 101, 109
Dunlop, D. C., 256
Durham Book, 151 ff., 154, 156–9, 160, 162, 174

Ebury, Lord, 197 ff.
Edward VI, 59, 116
Einfältiges Bedenken, 44, 79

Elevation, 20, 33, 34, 82, 98, 198, 211, 326
Eliot, T. S., 13, 245
Elizabeth I, 120, ch. 6 passim, 168
Elyot, Sir T., 40, 61, 326
Encheiridion (Cologne), 44, 45, 53, 87
Epiclesis, 79, 82, 108, 144–6, 150, 152, 157, 181, 183, 184, 189, 190, 217, 220, 228–30, 243, 251, 396 ff.
Erasmus, 59
Etchells, F., 249
Evensong, 24, 52, 60, 68, 72 ff., 101, 103 ff., 115, 129, 142, 144, 253
Exceptions, 136, 155 ff., 161, 168, 174, 179 ff.
Excommunication, Greater, 28, 91
Exorcism, 25, 28, 34, 46, 77, 83, 84, 86, 110
'Experts, Committee of', 216, 224, 228

Fair Copy, 158, 160
Falconar, W., 187 ff., 439
Falkland, Lord, 153
Farel, G., 44, 109
'Farnham' Canon, 230, 397
Fawkes, G., 139
Festial, 19 ff.
Field, J., 132, 370 ff.
Fisher, G. F., 246
Fisher, J., 115
Form of Prayers, 118, 120, 121, 123, 131, 134, 151
Formula Missae, 33, 35, 61, 64
Forbes, R., 188
Foxe, J., 118, 132
Fraction, 17, 82, 109, 146, 157, 179, 229, 251, 264, 366
Francis I, 59
Francis Xavier, 225
Frere, W. H., 9, 78, ch. 10 passim

Gadderar, J., 187
Gararde, Brother, 19
Garbett, C. F., 234, 246
Gardiner, S., 80, 96, 97, 100, 101, 105, 108
Gauden, J., 161

Gibson, E., *171*
Gibson, E. C. S., 216, 219, 236
Gilby, A., 118
Godparents, 25, 39, 46, 84, 86, 110, 111, 131 ff., 155, 164, 175, 181, 201, 206, 231 ff., 253, 319–20, 371
Goodrich, T., 66, 99, 100
Gore, C., 247
Gowrie Conspiracy, 140
Gradual (book), 29; (psalm) 16, 34, 75, 273, 328, 344
Grindal, E., *128*
Gropper, J., 44
Guest, E., 121
Gunning, P., 160, 162, 163
Gunpowder Treason, 139, 166, 169

Haddon, W., 124
Hales, J., 136
Hall, Bishop of Vermont, 236
Hampton Court Conference, *137* ff.
Hardenberg, A., 45
Harvest Thanksgiving, 169, 189, 196 ff., 207, 240, *386* ff.
Hatton, C., 134
Haynes, S., 67
Heath, N., 97
Heber, R., 194, 205
Hebert, A. G., 248
Henchman, H., 159
Henley, J., 183
Henry VIII, ch. 3 passim, 83
Henson, H. H., 212
Herbert, G., 258
Hereford, Use of, 31, 52, 64
Hermann von Wied, *44* ff., 53, 62 ff., ch. 4 passim, 104, 108, 111, 113, 191, *334* ff.
Herschel, W., 223
Hilles, R., 43
Hilsey, J., 51. *See also* Primers
Holbeach, H., 66
Homilies, Books of, 60, 75, 88, 125, 126, 139, 169
Hooker, R., 92, 134, 135

Hooper, J., 65, 96, 100, 106, 108–10, 113, 114
Horden, J., 258
Horne, G., 11
Horne, R., 117
Hortulus Animae, 49, 50
Hours, Little, 23, 24, 33, 52, 70, 130
Huycke, W., 44, 118, 120
Hymns, 22, 23, 33, 48, 52, 73, 94, 128, 177, 182, 189, 194, 247, 293 ff., 334, 355

Indian Prayer Book, 260 ff., 264
Inglis, C., 258
Injunctions, 50, 56–8, 60, 91, 98, 125, 126, 128, 152
Institution of a Christian Man, 53
Interpretations, 125, 126
Introit Psalms, 16, 34, 74, 75, 89–94, 108, 269, 328
Invitatories, 22, 70, 73, 224, 258, 263, 292
Irish Prayer Book, 169 ff., 189, *207* ff., 224, *240* ff., 263

Jagow, Matthias von, 42
James I, 136, 143, 168
James II, 168
Japanese Communion Service, *261* ff.
'Jerusalem Chamber' Canons, 230, *397*
Joachim II, 42
Jonas, J., 41, 84, 86
Jones, J., 177–9
Joye, G., *49*
Justin Martyr, 15

Kalendar, 41, *73* ff., 123, 175, 223, 258
Kantz, K., 33
Katherine, Queen, 115
Keble, J., 194, 258
Keeling, W., 192
Ken, T., 225, 258
Kidder, R., 193
King, E., 204
King's Book, 53, 79, 86, 87, 104
King's Primer, *see* Primer

Kirchenordnungen, *39* ff.
Kiss of Peace, 15, 17, 33, 41, 46, 87
Kneeling at communion, 114, 119, 121,
    122, 131 ff., 141, 143, 156, 378
Knox, J., 114, 118, 120, 131, 140

Lambeth Conference, 198, *236* ff.,
    241, *255–7*, 262
Lang, C. G., *230*, 245
Langforde, B., 19
Lasco, J. à, 65, 98, 100, 102, 104, 114
Latin Prayer Book, *123* ff., 130, 149,
    367
Laud, W., 141, 143, 144, 146, 258
Lauds, *22* ff., *70* ff., *301* ff.
Laurence, R., 191
Lay-Folk's Mass-Book, 18
Learning, New, 32, 60, 67
Lessons, 17, ch. 2 passim, 50, 52, 54,
    60, 69 ff., 115, 122, *199* ff., 217,
    223, 235, 246
L'Estrange, H., 149, 150, 153, 182, 192
Letters of Business, Royal, *212*
Lever, T., 118
Liddon, H. P., 202
Lincolnshire Ministers, 140
Lindsey, T., *178* ff., 180 ff., 192
Litany, 24, 28, 35, 40, 47, 50, 51,
    55–8, 59–61, 64, 78 ff., 82, 83, 86,
    92, 93, 102, 104, 117, 120, 122,
    123, 125, 162, 205, *358* ff.
Liturgical Commission, *254* ff., 257, 263,
    265
Liturgy for Africa, *262* ff.
Liturgy in times of Rebellion, *147*
'Liturgy of Compromise', *119*
Liturgy of St Basil, 64, 184, 259
Liturgy of St John Chrysostom, 58,
    123, 259
Liturgy of St James, 64, 148, 184, 187,
    238, 250, 252, 259, 260
Lloyd, C., 191–3
Lloyd, G., 166
Lords' Committee, *145*, 150
Luther, M., *32* ff., 39, 40, 42, 46–50, 55,
    57, 58, 61, 64, 75, 81, 82, 87, 89,
    106, 111, 181, *318* ff.

McDonald, R., 258
Mackonochie Judgment, 199
Maclean, A. J., *236*, 238
Maldonatus, 150
Manual, 30, 39, 55, 68
Manual acts, 109, 144, 163, 209
Marshall, W., 50, 51. *See also* Primer
Martyr, Peter, 65, 67, 98–100, 104,
    106, 113, 114, 132
Mary, Queen, 96, 116, 117, 119
Maskell, W., 24
Mass (Sarum), *15* ff.
Matrimony, 25, 35, 39, 41, 42, 43,
    47, 87, 113, *232*, *321* ff.
Mattins, *22* ff., 24, 33, 43, 47, 50, 52,
    54, 60, 68, 69 ff., 101, *103* ff., 115,
    125, 129, 142, 144, 147, 253, *292* ff.
Maurice, F. D., 13, 196
Maxwell, J., 143
May, W., 166
Megander, 109
Melanchthon, 42, 44, 52
Merbecke, J., 69, 78, 83, 89, 90, 102,
    170
Methodist books, *179* ff., *208* ff., *245* ff.,
    250
Millenary Petition, *136*
Milman, H., 196
Milner-White, E., 255, 260
Mirk, J., 19, 63
Missal, 28, 54, 68
Moore, J., 172
Morin, J., 176
Morley, G., 153, 154, 159, 161
Morning Prayer, *see* Mattins
Mozarabic Rite, 72, 86, 147, 209, 252
Müntzer, T., 33

Neale, J. E., 121
Neale, J. M., 193 ff., 208
Necessary Doctrine, 53
Nelson, R., 172
Newman, J. H., 192 ff., 225
Nicholls, W., 172
Nicholson, W., 159
Nightingale, F., 258
Nocturns, 22, *294* ff.

None, 23, 142, *312*
Nonjurors, 173, *183* ff., 187, 190, 192, 238, 256
Norton, T., 132
Notes, Certain, 83, 92, 102, 114, 130
Nowell, A., 131, 137, 138
Nuremberg, *39* ff., 61, 62, *326*

Oecolampadius, J., 33, 80
Oes of St Bridget, 24, 51
Offering, 17, 18, 32, 33, 42, 67, 79 ff., 145, 162, 183, 187 ff., 242, 260, 262 ff.
Offertory, 15, 16, 32, 33, 36, 37, 75, 82, 105, 129, 141, 144, 152, 184, 243, 275 ff.
Office, Daily, *22* ff., 33, 34, 49, 103
Office of the Dead, *see Dirige*
Orarium, *129* ff., 142
Order of the Communion, *61* ff., 75, 88, 100, 103, 105, 106, 124, 149, 228, *364* ff.
Ordinal (Sarum), 30; (1662) 158, *163* ff., 165
Ordination, 35, *92* ff., 97, 102, 114, 142, 143, 147
Ornaments Rubric, 122, 146, 164, 174, 190, *195* ff., 200, 201, 203 ff., 214, 215, 224, 263
Osiander, A., 40–2, 77, 328 n
Overall, J., 138, 141, 150, 437

Paget, F., 210, 225
Palm Sunday, 28, 59, 60
Palmer, W., 192
Parish Communion, *248* ff.
Parker, J., 160
Parker, M., 126, 129
Parsons, F. R., 218
Particulars (Cosin), *150* ff.
Patrick, S., 169, 172, 173, 176
Pax Domini, see Kiss of Peace
Pearson, J., 163
Penitential Psalms, 24, 26, 27, 49, 55, 88, 91, 113
Pfalz-Neuburg, 42, 77, *333*
Philip of Hesse, 44

Pickering, W., 192
Pie, 30
Placebo, 24
Playford, J., 171
Pollock, B., 219
Pontifical, 30, 68, 93, 97, 145
Portiforium (Portuis), 29
Poullain, V., 65, 100, 102, 104, 106, 117, 119, 120, 191
Prayer for the Church, 16, 45, 78, 105, 106, 142, 175, 178, 182, 187, 189, 190, 194, 201, 227, 256, 264, *345* ff.
Prayer of Humble Access, 64, 103, 105, 119, 144, 174, 214, 217, 228 ff., 239, 242, 257, 260, 262–4
Prayer of Oblation, 78 ff., 105, 111, 141, 144, 145, 150, 151, 183, 184, 189, 205, 217, 228, 258, 264
Prayer of Thanksgiving, 34, 36, 38, 41 ff., 75, 77, 88, 103, 105, 106, 111, 141, 147, 181, 205, 258, 264, 331 ff., 355
Preces Privatae (1564), 83, *130*
Preface(s), 16, 37, 42, 46, 74, 75, 174, 263, 281, 353 ff., 377; to 1549 Book, 69; to 1662 Book, *166* ff.
Priest's preparation, 15 ff., 33, 211, 235, 261, 269
Prime, *23*, 52, 70 ff., *304* ff.
Primer, 24, 49; Marshall's, *50*, 51, 53, 55, 57; Hilsey's, *51*, 72, 79, 90; the King's, *58* ff., 60, 61, 72, 73, 89, 90, 97, 129; (1553), 115, 117, 123
Privy Council, 195, 199, 202–4
Procession, Easter, 74, 83, 103
Processional, 30, 55, 58, 68, 83, *362* ff.
Proposals of *1689*, *172–6*, 177–9, 192, 207, *375* ff.
Psalms, 22–4, 69, 129, 170, 181, 247 ff., 255
Psalms, Metrical, 118, 120, 125, 129, 147, 156, 170, 171, 175
Psalter, 24, 38 ff., 43, 45, 49
Public Worship Regulation Act, 203
Purcell, H., 170
Purchas Judgment, 203

Pusey, E. B., 192, 202

Quicunque vult, see Athanasian Creed
Quiñones, F. de, 47 ff., 52, 54, 69, 72, 73, 103

Rabe, A., 43
Ratcliff, E. C., 10, 259
Rationale of Ceremonies, 53
Rattray, T., 187, 188, 439
Ravenscroft, T., 170
Reconsecration, 65, 100, 139, 144, 152, 163, 181, 209, 230, 366
Redman, J., 67
Reformatio Legum Ecclesiasticarum, 116, 132
Reformed Liturgy, 154, 157, 179
Reservation, 211, 215, 218 ff., 220, 233 ff., 356 ff., 391 ff.
Responsory, 22, 27, 28, 31, 34, 47, 60, 70, 73, 89, 295 ff., 331
Reynolds, E., 154, 165
Reynolds, J., 138
Revised Version, 236
Rhegius, U., 431
Richardson, C. C., 109
Riddell, R., 195
Ridley, N., 66, 80, 97, 98, 109, 114
Ridsdale Judgment, 203
Rigg, J. H., 209
Ring, Wedding, 26, 87, 119, 131 ff., 136, 156, 175, 209, 321
Ritual, 30
Ritualism, 194, 197, 202–4
Robertson, T., 67
Robinson, J. A., 225
Rogation Procession, 28, 55, 126
Royal Commission on Ecclesiastical Discipline, 210 ff., ch. 10 passim
Royal Commission on Ritual, 198 ff.
Rugg, W., 97

Sacerdotal, 30
Sacrifice, 18, 32, 105, 141, 145, 151 ff., 162, 174, 184, 186, 256
Sancroft, W., 157–9, 166, 172–4, 376
Sanctorale, 28, 73, 74, 123

Sanderson, R., 145, 147 ff., 153, 154, 159–61, 163, 165–7, 188
Savonarola, 50
Savoy Conference, 153 ff., 168, 174
Saxony, Albertine, 41, 44, 46, 47, 84, 191
Schwartz, T., 37
Scott, Sir W., 193
Scottish Communion Office (1764), 187 ff., 190, 238
Scottish Liturgy (1637), 143 ff., 149, 150, 152, 153, 158, 164, 165, 182, 187, 190, 238
Scottish Prayer Book, 224 ff., 232, 237 ff., 242, 252, 260, 262
'Sea Service', 166
Seabury, S., 189, 190, 207
Sequence, 16, 31, 35, 40, 75, 89, 273, 344
Series I, see *Alternative Services*
Service-books, Medieval, 28 ff.
Sext, 23, 27, 91, 142, 310 ff.
Shaftesbury, Lord, 198, 201, 202
Sharp, J., 172 ff.
Shaxton, N., 91
Sheldon, G., 153, 154, 158, 159, 161, 167, 168
Shortened Services Act, 202, 205, 389 ff.
Shorter Prayer Book, 246 ff.
Simple and Religious Consultation, 45, 68, 105
Simplex ac Pia Deliberatio, 45, 62, 84
Skinner, R., 159, 164
Skip, J., 66, 67
Smith, W., 189
Smyth, C. H., 109
Somerset, Duke of, 60, 67, 97, 98
South African Prayer Book, 242 ff., 251, 260, 261
South India, Church of, 250 ff., 259, 260, 262
Southampton, Earl of, 161
Sparrow, A., 149, 152, 182, 192
Staley, V., 223
State Services, 139, 165, 166, 168, 169, 196

Stephens, A. J., 192
Stephens, E., *181* ff.
Sternhold and Hopkins, 120, 129, 170, 171, 177
Stillingfleet, E., 173, 176
Strasbourg, *36* ff., 43–6, 48, 59, 63, 77, 102, 104, 106, *324* ff.
Strickland, W., 132
Surplice, 21, 41, 92, 95, 114, 119, 127, 131, 132 ff., 136, 139, 156, 174, 194, 371
Survey of the Book of Common Prayer, 140, 150

Tait, A. C., 201
Tallis, T., 129, 170
Tate and Brady, 171
Taverner, R., 59
Taylor, Jeremy, 136, 147, 150, 153, 170, 173, 182, 186, 189
Taylor, John, 67
Temple, W., 218 ff.
Temporale, 28, 73, 74
Tenison, T., 173
Terce, 23, 142, *309* ff.
Thanksgivings, 138
Thirlby, T., 66, 67, 79
Tillotson, J., 173, 178
Timms, G. B., 109
Tracts for the Times, 193
Trevisano, A., 431
Turner, W., 431

Unction, 25, 26, 83, 84, 86, 88, 94, 95, 99, 110, 113, 183, 186, 233, 239, 245
Unity, Prayer for, 169, 206
Usages, 183
Ussher, W., 145, 163

Vadianus, J., 80
Vaughan Williams, R., 247
Veneration of the Cross, 28, 59, 60

Vespers, *22* ff., 33, 34, 41, 45, 47, 54, 70 ff., 142, *313* ff.
Vestments, 21, 33, 34, 35, 41, 48, 92, 94, 95, 97, 98, 108, 122, 127, 198, 203, 211, 219, 226, 263
Visitation of the Sick, 26, 41, 47, 55, *88*, 113, 119, 139, 141, 165, 176, 180, 186, *232*
Vives, L., 59
Volprecht, W., 328 n, 432

Wafers, 65, 82, 127, 131, 152, 163, 198, 201, 203, 207, 211, 226, 366, 370 ff.
Walton, I., 166
Warner, J., 159
Watts, I., 171
Webb, B., 193
Wedderburn, J., 143, 144, 146, 150, 152
Wesley, C., 171, 181 ff., 258
Wesley, J., 168, *179* ff., 182, 208, 258
West Indian Liturgy, *262*
Wheatly, C., 172, 192
Whiston, W., *182* ff., 186
Whitgift, J., 134, 135, 436
Whittingham, W., 118
Wilberforce, S., 200
Wilcox, T., 133, *370* ff.
William III, 169, 172, 183
Williams, Bishop of Huron, 241
Williams, J., 141, 145
Winnington-Ingram, A. F., 216
Winslow, J. C., 259
Winton, Earl of, 187
Witzel, G., 42
Wordsworth, J., 206, 214, 225, 241
Woods, F. T., 219
Wren, Sir C., 171
Wren, M., ch. 7 passim, 174

York, Use of, 31, 52

Zwingli, H., 33, *35* ff., 39, 46, 48, 64, 77, 80, 97, 103, 105, 109, 135, 144